EXISTENCE AND FAITH

Rudolf (Karl) Bultmann was born on 20th August, 1884 in Wiefelstede, Germany. After studying at Marburg, Tübingen and Berlin he became a lecturer at Marburg, and was Professor of New Testament studies there from 1921-1951. Professor Bultmann has also taught at Breslau and Giessen, and was Gifford Lecturer in 1955. Among his best known works in English are *Theology of the New Testament, Essays: Philosophical and Theological, Jesus Christ and Mythology, Jesus and the Word* and *Primitive Christianity in its Contemporary Setting.*

EXISTENCE AND FAITH

SHORTER WRITINGS OF
RUDOLF BULTMANN

*Selected, translated and
introduced by
Schubert M. Ogden*

COLLINS

THE FONTANA LIBRARY
THEOLOGY AND PHILOSOPHY

First published in Great Britain by
Hodder & Stoughton Ltd., 1961
First issued in the Fontana Library, 1964

CONTENTS

PREFACE

The purpose of this book, as is more fully explained in the Introduction, is to give a representative selection of Rudolf Bultmann's shorter writings. The volume includes at least one work from each of the five decades of his scholarly career; and the variety of the writings presented, in both type and content, is virtually as great as that of his own authorship. Thus it is to be hoped that the book as a whole will contribute significantly to the more adequate understanding and critical appropriation of his achievement on the part of English-speaking readers.

As regards the translation, the reader will note that I have followed the precedent set by John Macquarrie's *An Existentialist Theology* (1955) in not translating the German word *"existentiell"* in either its adjectival or adverbial employments. Since this word, like its related but carefully distinguished counterpart *"existential,"* is used by Bultmann as a *terminus technicus* and, moreover, can be translated only by either obscuring its distinction from *"existential"* or entailing the use of awkward English equivalents for the latter, this has seemed to be the best course. The general sense of the term, as is usually made clear by the context, is "that which has to do with the individual's own unique situation and responsibility," though the reader will doubtless also want to refer to Bultmann's own clarifications in *Jesus Christ and Mythology* (1958), pp. 66 and 74. I have likewise accepted the suggestion of Kendrick Grobel (cf. *Theology of the New Testament*, I [1951], 253 n.) and made use of the obsolete Middle English verb "rightwise" to translate the German verb *"rechtfertigen"* in the few instances in which it occurs. It will also be noted that I have for the most part followed the Revised Standard Version of the Bible in translating citations from Scripture.

7

However, where Bultmann's own German translation of the Greek text significantly differs from the RSV, I have always followed the former. And the same also holds true of my use of Kirsopp Lake's translation of *The Apostolic Fathers* in the Loeb Classical Library for citations from those sources.

It is a pleasant duty to acknowledge my gratitude to those who have been of particular help in realizing this project. To Professor Bultmann himself I am indebted not only for unfailing assistance whenever I requested it, but also for kindly granting permission to include in the volume the autobiographical statement that he originally sent me in 1956. I am also grateful to three of my esteemed colleagues at Perkins School of Theology in Southern Methodist University: to Professors Fred D. Gealy and Van A. Harvey for many helpful suggestions regarding the translation; and to Professor Decherd H. Turner, Jr., Librarian of Bridwell Library, who completely relieved me of the responsibility of securing the necessary sources. In the matter of identifying quotations from German literature I have been greatly helped by Mrs. Margareta Neovius Deschner. And I have special reason to be thankful for the judicious copy editing of Mr. Aaron Asher. Professor Paul Schubert of Yale University, through his student and now also my colleague, Mr. Victor Furnish, was likewise of material assistance in determining the final contents of the volume. Finally, I must record the inimitable support of my wife, Joyce, who fully shared with me in all the stages of the volume's preparation.

November 1959   S. M. O.

INTRODUCTION *by Schubert M. Ogden*

I

Rudolf Bultmann is one of the most significant figures on the contemporary theological scene. By whatever criteria one judges such significance—whether quantitative or qualitative, whether with reference to specific areas of concern (i.e., "historical," "systematic," or "practical" theology) or to theological inquiry as a whole—his contribution is unchallengeably among the most important of our time. In the course of a long and productive scholarly career, which already spans half a century and still continues with unabated power, he has come to be one of the most decisive influences on the direction of Protestant theology in the twentieth century. The basic reason for this, undoubtedly, is that to an extent that seems to distinguish him among his contemporaries he has become a part of all that he has met theologically, and thus embodies in his own achievement virtually all of the important motives in the long tradition of German theology in which he stands. Of his work, as perhaps of no other, it can be said that it represents an integral and creative restatement of the cumulative wisdom of classical Protestant theology in its several decisive phases.[1]

It is not surprising, then, that English-speaking theologians have become increasingly interested in Bultmann's achievement and that the prediction has been ventured that he " will have a growing influence, especially on the theology and the church of America."[2] British and American theology hardly seems subject to the sharp changes of front and decisive new developments that have been so striking a feature of the theology of the Continent; and in America particularly the continuing influence of so-called " liberal " theology is so great

that there is little likelihood of any lasting restoration of
" orthodoxy " under whatever name it may appear. Indeed, the
safest generalization about contemporary American theology
in its most significant Protestant forms is that it still remains
firmly committed to the two great concerns of theological liberalism. However much American theologians have attempted
to learn from the " new Reformation theology " and its definitive criticisms of liberal theology's constructive formulations,
they have neither rejected liberalism's historical-critical method
nor questioned its basic claim that the modern cultural situation requires a radical reformulation of the church's proclamation. Thus it is not at all accidental that the theologian
who currently enjoys the highest eminence among us is Paul
Tillich; for in Tillich's work, just as in Bultmann's, there has
been the consistent effort to do full justice to the legitimate
motives of liberal theology, even while moving " beyond " it
at many crucial points. It is with good reason, then, that
Markus Barth has seen in Tillich's widespread influence an
indication that Bultmann's work also will play an increasingly
important role in our American theological conversation.[3]
With several of his most important writings already available
in English translations, and with the growing discussion among
us especially of his more recent work, his effect on the future
of American theology promises to be profound.

It is all the more essential, therefore, that the full scope of
his contribution be clearly recognized. That it has rather generally *not* been recognized may seem strange in view of the
widespread discussion of his theology which has been so
marked a feature of our most recent theological history. Nevertheless, the fact remains that important aspects of his work are
still largely unknown to English-speaking readers and that
even those aspects of it that are known to them are frequently
misunderstood because they are not seen in their proper context. The very fact, for example, that all but one of the full-
scale studies of his theology by English-speaking theologians are
based almost entirely on writings published since the Second

World War is an indication that we do not have an adequate impression of his total achievement.[4] This is not to imply, of course, that there are differences between an " early " and a " later " Bultmann that are as decisive as those between the " early " Barth of *The Epistle to the Romans* and the " later " Barth of the *Church Dogmatics*. Indeed, the truth of the matter is that Bultmann has been expressing essentially the same position for over thirty years. However, because so little of his work has been generally known to English-speaking readers the impression it has created among them has been at best limited and at worst incorrect. Two examples may serve to make this clear.

It is widely supposed that the basic method and results that Bultmann has referred to since 1941 by the words " demythologization " and " existential interpretation " represent a relatively " late " stage in his theological development. Thus even John Macquarrie, for instance, writes that " after the Second World War there took place a further development in theological thought, and of this we have taken Rudolf Bultmann as representative "; and the context makes clear that the " further development " to which Macquarrie refers is Bultmann's " existentialist theology " with its call for " radical demythologizing."[5] The truth, of course, as several of the writings included in the present volume make clear, is that " demythologization " and " existential interpretation " have been the substantial meaning of Bultmann's thought since the formative period of the so-called " dialectical theology." Indeed, any careful reader of Bultmann's *Jesus* (first published in 1926 and available in English translation since 1934) should be able to confirm immediately the complete agreement between the essential argument of that early book and Bultmann's most recent discussion in the opening chapters of *Jesus Christ and Mythology* (1958). Be this as it may, however, the main point is that Bultmann's work will hardly be correctly understood until its more recent phase is seen in its strict and unbroken continuity with the phase that went before. In fact, one may venture to suggest that the " final clarification " of Bultmann's relationship with Karl Barth, which, as Bultmann himself points out, " has not yet been reached," waits upon seeing this continuity.[6]

The second example concerns the prevailing understanding of Bultmann's views regarding the " historical Jesus " and, specifically, the latter's relation to the " Christ of the kerygma." It is commonly held among English-speaking theologians that Bultmann (1) presents the historical Jesus as " little more than a teacher of practical philosophy ";[7] and therefore (2) denies any basic continuity between the Jesus of history and the Christ of faith by " stripping " the former of his " numinous characteristics."[8] That such a complete misunderstanding of Bultmann's position should have so generally prevailed in the English-speaking world may seem all but inexcusable to the careful student of even those of his writings that have long been available in translation.[9] Nevertheless, it is probably only in the light of works hitherto available solely in German that a conclusive refutation of this misunderstanding is possible. In any case, it is difficult to see how any one who takes seriously what Bultmann says in the essay " Jesus and Paul," which is included below, can still persist in such a view. " If Paul, like the earliest community, saw in Jesus the Messiah, he did nothing other than affirm Jesus' own claim that man's destiny is decided with reference to his person." Surely the Jesus who is spoken of here, as in many other parallel places in Bultmann's writings,[10] is understood to be something radically " more " than " simply a teacher of practical philosophy "; and while Bultmann might understandably be reluctant to attribute this " more " to Jesus' " numinous personality," there can be no question whatever that he has consistently affirmed an essential continuity between the Jesus of history and the Christ proclaimed by the Christian church.[11]

We may also note that the relevance of this point to some of the most recent developments in Protestant theology is profound indeed. For if what has just been said is correct, then it must inevitably be asked just how " new " the so-called " new quest of the historical Jesus " really is.[12] That there may indeed be such " new " tendencies in the " post-Bultmannian " developments both on the Continent and elsewhere seems evident enough. But it still remains a fair question whether the extent of the alleged " newness " may not depend entirely too much upon seeing it against the background of a highly oversimplified and even false impression of Bultmann's own position.[13]

The general situation of which these examples are merely illustrative (and other examples could also be given) should be sufficiently clear. And by the same token the justification for the present volume of a select number of Bultmann's shorter writings should also have become evident. There is hardly a better or more direct way to fill out and also to correct the prevailing understanding of his theological achievement than by permitting himself to speak more fully to us. And it is to this end that the several writings comprised in this volume have been selected. An effort has been made not only to present a fair sample, both as to type and as to content of his shorter works, but also to select writings that will significantly illumine facets of his contribution which are presently either little known or quite likely inadequately appreciated by English-speaking readers. Thus the volume not only includes two sermons, a meditation, and an address, but also a long review, a letter to an editor, and a polemical article occasioned by reactionary developments in the postwar German Evangelical Church. Also, it comprises several representative essays on specific problems in exegetical and systematic theology, including lengthy monographs on " The New Approach to the Synoptic Problem," " Paul," and " The Concept of Revelation in the New Testament," as well as the most extended discussion of Bultmann's relation to the philosophy of Martin Heidegger which he has ever given us. Finally, the volume also includes the first autobiographical statement ever to be published; and one of the sermons to which reference

has just been made even antedates the one decisive shift in
Bultmann's thought that took place as a consequence of Karl
Barth's *Epistle to the Romans.* In the obvious sense, of course,
this early sermon is only indirectly relevant to an understanding of Bultmann's characteristic position. Yet in a more
profound sense, even it can contribute importantly to the one
controlling purpose of promoting a more adequate understanding and appreciation of his *total* theological achievement; and as the careful reader will be quick to see, its basic
differences in form of expression and even in conception cannot obscure a continuity with all that has come after it that
is almost equally striking.

In a word, this volume is offered to the reader in the hope
that it will open up to him more fully one of the most
significant theological contributions of our time. And if the
tenor of these remarks has given the impression that, for one
student at least, this significance is an overwhelmingly *positive*
significance, this is a correct impression.

II

Having attempted to introduce Bultmann's work in a somewhat general way and with reference to our current theological
situation, I propose now to take up a much more difficult
task. I want to try to state as simply and directly as possible
what seems to me to define the inner unity or underlying
structure and movement of his thought. In other words, I
want to essay the kind of critical interpretation of his theology which—as he himself has succinctly defined it—" distinguishes what is said from what is meant and measures the
former by the latter."[14]

It will be obvious, of course, that such an effort is a risky
business at best and is particularly hazardous when undertaken within the limitations of a brief introduction. Nevertheless, of the various possible alternatives, this procedure seems

to me to afford the most promise of achieving the aim that this Introduction is concerned to achieve. At the very least it will provide the reader with a hypothesis as to what Bultmann basically wants to say to him, which can focus his own reading and reflection and which he himself can then confirm or deny as seems to him best. And so far as the details of Bultmann's view are concerned, there is hardly the need or the possibility of improving upon his writings themselves.

Therefore, I proceed at once to state what seems to me to constitute the underlying unity of Bultmann's theology. And I begin by quoting at length a well-known passage from the Preface to the second edition of Karl Barth's *Epistle to the Romans*.

> If I have a " system " it consists in the fact that I keep in mind as persistently as possible what Kierkegaard called the " infinite qualitative difference " between time and eternity in both its negative and its positive meaning. " God is in heaven and you are on earth." The relation of *this* God to *this* man, the relation of *this* man to *this* God, is for me at once the theme of the Bible and the essence of philosophy. The philosophers speak of this crisis of human knowing as the primal source, while the Bible sees at this parting of the ways Jesus Christ.[15]

I know of no better way to characterize Bultmann's own " system " than by saying of it the principal thing that the " early " Barth here says of his. For in Bultmann's case also, what constitutes the inner integrity of all that he really intends to say is his affirmation of the " infinite qualitative difference " between time and eternity in its several negative and positive implications. Indeed, we may lay it down as a rule that *one ought never to suppose he has correctly understood anything that Bultmann says, as regards either the method or the content of his theology, until he is able to see it as permitted or required by this basic dialectic.*[16]

But now what exactly does this mean? What is this " dialectic " that defines the inner structure and movement of Bultmann's theology? Undoubtedly the most direct way to answer these questions is simply to present the understanding of God in his relation to the world which is everywhere expressed or implied in Bultmann's writings. However, in making this presentation we must take into account a certain peculiarity of his thought. It is characteristic of his theology that the explication of *God* and the world takes place in terms of "analogies" drawn from the relation of *man* to the world. This whole notion of "analogy," which Bultmann takes pains to distinguish from "myth,"[17] is one of the most unillumined facets of his thought; and I do not want to presume upon his answers to certain questions (e.g., *Analogia entis* or *analogia fidei?*) by what I say here. Nevertheless, there can be no doubt that the relation of God to the world, as he conceives it, is significantly illumined by the analogous relation that exists between the self and its world. Thus it is quite proper if we first attempt to make clear this latter relationship.

According to Bultmann, the essential thing that must be said about man is that he is an "existing" self or person in the general sense clarified by existentialist philosophy. This means, fundamentally, that man's inmost reality—his being a self or an "I"—completely transcends not only the external world with which he is always inextricably involved, but also the inner world that is defined by his own subjective feelings and experiences. As "existence," he is something radically other and more than the reality disclosed within the basic subject-object correlation of rational consciousness. Whatever falls within this correlation, or, in other words, every "object" or "content," is finally transcended by the inmost kernel of his selfhood, which is never an "object" or a "what," but always only a "how"—i.e., a certain way of being related to the various "whats" or "contents" that constitute the self's inner and outer world. More specifically, there are in the last analysis two such ways in which man can be related to his world. Either he can "lose" himself in it by identifying himself with its "contents" and thus shutting himself against the future self that it is always being given him to become, or he can remain open to this future self by preserving an inner distance or freedom from his world and all that falls within it. In a word, man is a uniquely " historical " being whose " historicity " (*Geschichtlichkeit*), as Heidegger puts it, is either " inauthentic " or " authentic." To be a man is to be continually confronted with the decision, which is posed by one's present encounters with other persons and with destiny, whether to " lose " oneself in the past constituted by one's inner and outer world or rather to become the new future self that it is always being offered one to become.

Clearly the main idea in this understanding of man is that the self in its deepest centre is something " qualitatively " other than rational mind or " spirit " (*nous; Geist*) and its correlative world.[18] Although the self is always related to a world— and, to be sure, either authentically or inauthentically—it itself is radically " beyond " the world and can never be simply identified with it. Indeed, even in the mode of inauthentic existence, the self cannot be entirely " lost "; for it itself in its authentic freedom and responsibility is the only ultimate cause or explanation of its own inauthenticity.

Now it is precisely this idea of the self's " qualitative " transcendence of its world that holds, *mutatis mutandis,* of the relation of *God* to his world, i.e., to the world in general or simply as such. And Bultmann is quite explicit in pointing out that this connection is by no means accidental.[19] Even as man in his inmost selfhood is something radically other and more than the inner and outer world with which he is always related, so also is God as sovereign grace and judgment, or as *supreme* " I," " infinitely " and " qualitatively " transcendent of the entire created order with which he stands in relation. Thus, according to Bultmann, God is not only not to be identified with any of the specific contingent occurrences that make up the actual course of nature and history, but also stands infinitely beyond the eternal principles of things as these may be hypostatized in a cosmic " Spirit " or eternal " Idea of the

Good." To be sure, Bultmann does say that the eternal norms of the true, the good, and the beautiful, as conceived by classical idealism, are "nothing other than the law of God" and that therefore the general relation between "humanism and Christianity" may be appropriately construed in terms of the relation of "law and Gospel."[20] Nevertheless, as is made clear precisely by this statement, God as sovereign Creator and Redeemer is "wholly other" than the realm of eternal Spirit and Idea. Just as man in his finite "historicity" transcends the whole sphere of the subject-object correlation, so also does God as infinite Thou or "Existent" transcend all that falls within the macrocosmic counterpart of this same sphere.

But now, as the above statement of Barth's suggests, this basic understanding of God in relation to the world has both "negative" and "positive" implications that are of fundamental importance. In the first place, it means *negatively* that there is *nothing* that man is or has or does (and the same thing is also true, of course, of the created order generally) that is directly divine or can be assigned a divine function or significance. God infinitely transcends the world, and everything human and creaturely is only indirectly or "paradoxically" identical with him.[21] In this sense, it must be said that his judgment of the world is total and indiscriminate. However, it is clear that we would completely misunderstand Bultmann if we were to conclude that this is the only sense in which the negative meaning of God's relation to the world is to be construed. For precisely because this relation is not quantitative but qualitative, there is another sense in which God's judgment of the world is also always a discriminating judgment. This will become clear if we but recall Bultmann's statement, cited above, that the basic norms of truth, goodness, and beauty, which are implicit in man's nature as rational mind or "spirit," are "nothing other than the law of God"—the same law, namely, that is "holy, just, and good" (Rom. 7:12). Because in positing the world, God also posits the norms that are regulative of its appropriate penultimate fulfilments, his judgment of the world is never merely an indiscriminate judgment, but rather sharply discriminates between what does and what does not conform to these essential creaturely norms. His will stands unalterably opposed to anything that frustrates his creation's highest possible fulfilment.

In saying this, of course, we have already spoken of the *positive* meaning of God's relation to man and the world. For it is just because God affirms the world and its own immanent norms that his negative relation to the world is also always a discriminating relation. Nevertheless here, too, we would be badly misled if we supposed that this exhausted God's positive significance for the world. For while God does indeed will all that is agreeable to his law and is unalterably opposed to anything that violates it, there is another and deeper sense in which he also affirms *everything*—even that which opposes his will. In other words, because God's positive relation to the world is likewise completely qualitative, the world's *non*-identity with him is also something "paradoxical." And in this sense it is necessary to say that his redemption of the world is as total and indiscriminate as his judgment of it.

The basic point that we are concerned to make is that it is this underlying conception, together with its other implications, that defines the inner structure and movement of Bultmann's theological achievement. It remains now to justify this claim. Although anything like an exhaustive justification of it is naturally out of the question, we can at least give some idea as to how the principal things that Bultmann "says" are significantly illumined by this hypothesis as to what he "means." Specifically, we can try to indicate how his characteristic statements regarding both the method and the content of theology are either permitted or required by this one underlying conception.

As regards his theological *method,* there are three main considerations. First, it is clear that it is only in the light of the underlying conception we have sought to explicate that what he means by "demythologization" is finally either possible or necessary. This statement must be made with particular emphasis because of the all but complete failure of English-speaking theologians to grasp its significance.[22] It is widely supposed that Bultmann's real reason for proposing to demythologize the church's traditional proclamation is the exigency of the present apologetic situation, in which Christians are required to witness to a " scientific " world. From his own repeated statements on the matter, however, it is evident that this exigency is not at all the *cause* of his proposal, but simply its *occasion*.[23] For him, the only final reason why demythologization is either possible or necessary is " faith itself " or, in other words, the understanding of God and man that has been developed above. We *can* critically set aside any previous theological formulation of faith, including even those of the canonical theologians themselves, because every theology is an entirely human affair and thus as such has no directly divine significance or function.[24] On the other hand, we *must* set aside all specifically " mythological " formulations because they completely obscure the fact that God's difference from the world is not merely " quantitative " but " qualitative."[25] Therefore, I repeat, the only way in which one can possibly do justice to Bultmann's own understanding of " demythologization " is to see it as a direct implication of his fundamental view of God and the world.

And a precisely similar statement must be made, secondly, about his positive attitude toward existentialist philosophy. The familiar assumption that this attitude also is apologetically grounded and springs primarily from his concern to speak relevantly to the " aggravatedly modern man " must contend with his own unequivocal statements, which specify a different basic cause.[26] Whenever he himself undertakes to explain why existentialist philosophy is so important to his work, the reason he most often gives is that the former " offers the most adequate perspective and conceptions for understanding human existence " and therewith also helps theology " to find the right concepts for speaking of God non-mythologically."[27] In other words, the ultimate explanation of Bultmann's extensive use of existentialist philosophy is that it enables him to express more adequately than any other conceptuality he knows the underlying conception of God and man which he is primarily concerned to convey.

Finally, I would suggest, it is also only with reference to this same underlying conception that Bultmann's well-known practice of a thoroughgoing kind of historical-critical research can be fully appreciated. However exaggerated may be the familiar claim that he is a " radical sceptic " in basic matters of historical judgment,[28] it can hardly be doubted that he is indeed singularly free of the defensiveness and special pleading that so frequently blight the historical work of other theologians. My point is that this freedom becomes completely understandable in the light of his basic theological position. It is precisely because he recognizes that God's relation to the world is not quantitative but qualitative and, further, that faith and history also are only related " paradoxically," that he is free to pursue his critical investigations in a free and thoroughgoing way. Thus even his work as a " radical " historical-critic (although not, of course, its particular results!) is an indirect expression of his one fundamental thought.

So far, then, as concerns the *content* of his theology, it must suffice to point out quite briefly that in this respect also his statements again and again presuppose the one basic insight to which we have tried to point. Thus whether one considers his approach to the meaning of revelation or his restatement of the doctrines of creation and the " last things,"[29] it is perfectly plain that the fundamental meaning intended is the one of which we have spoken. And the same is true of his interpretation of sin and forgiveness, his " forensic " doctrine of " righteousness by faith," and his characteristic way of explicating the nature of the Christian life as a life of radical freedom and responsibility.[30] Moreover, the reader can hardly fail to notice the frequency with which one and the same passage —namely, I Cor. 7:29-31—is either quoted or alluded to throughout the writings included in this volume. What he may not know, however, is that this is equally characteristic of Bultmann's other writings and that it constitutes one of the most incontrovertible evidences of the correctness of what we have been saying. What is clearly presupposed by the notion that the Christian's participation in the world is subject to the reservation " as though not " is the dialectical relation of God and world which is the inmost meaning of Bultmann's theology. And so we might go on to show that the same is also true of his many statements regarding the relation of indicative and imperative and the way in which he typically elaborates the basic dialectic of " love " and " justice."

But now the question is bound to arise whether we have not entirely neglected to mention what seems to be the principal " content " of Bultmann's theology. Is not the vast bulk of his statements directed toward explicating the decisive occurrence of salvation and revelation in Jesus Christ and in developing the doctrines of church, word, and sacraments which are cognate with that occurrence? And is not the crucial test of the validity of our hypothesis whether it can also illumine *these* statements?

Indeed it is; for there can be no question that by far the larger proportion of Bultmann's work has the sole purpose of making clear the significance of the event Jesus Christ and all that it implies. However, as the reader of the present volume can readily confirm for himself, many—if not, indeed, most— of the things that Bultmann says in this connection also can be adequately explained only by reference to the same determinative conception. In fact, the whole import of his " demythologized " or " existentially interpreted " christology only becomes apparent against the background of the qualitative character of God's relation to man. Thus whether one considers his characteristic way of interpreting the resurrection of Christ[31] or his repeated insistence that the present is the *only* locus of revelation,[32] it is evident that what is presupposed is this one basic understanding.

Nevertheless, it must be frankly acknowledged that not everything Bultmann says about Jesus Christ is consistent with what we have taken to be his " real intention." Specifically, his characteristic claim that it is *only* in this event that God's final judgment and redemption are so revealed as to make an authentic human existence factually possible manifestly stands in tension with what otherwise seems to be his intended meaning.[33] For if this claim is taken in its most natural sense, it obviously entails a "quantitative" construction of God's significance for man and the world and thus not only threatens Bultmann's entire theological method, but is inconsistent with most of the content of his theology as well.[34] That such a structural inconsistency does indeed characterize his theology as it actually stands is one of the most assured results of the discussion of his work which has been carried on for the last decade and a half.[35] What we have tried to do here is simply to identify the general background against which this inconsistency may be most clearly viewed. It is true, of course, that if the general point we have been making is correct, then the lines have also been clearly indicated along which a christology that is more in keeping with Bultmann's own intention must be sought. The task plainly posed by an immanent criticism of his theology is to develop a christology that in *all* its points will give full expression to " the infinite qualitative difference of time and eternity."[36]

This Introduction, however, is not the place to pursue this task. Our purpose here has been simply to lead the reader as deeply as possible into the inner structure and movement of Bultmann's own achievement. And if in doing this we have also found it necessary to point to the fundamental problem that his theology poses, this, too, has been for the sake of making his work more fully understandable. Thus we may hope to convey to the reader by example as well as by precept that his first responsibility is not to criticize Bultmann's work, but to understand it. And to the fulfilment of that responsibility we sincerely invite him.

CONCERNING THE HIDDEN
AND THE REVEALED GOD*

"What no eye has seen, nor ear heard, nor the heart of man conceived, what God has prepared for those who love him," God has revealed to us through the Spirit. For the Spirit searches everything, even the depths of God. For what person knows a man's thoughts except the spirit of the man that is in him? So also no one comprehends the thoughts of God except the Spirit of God. But we have not received the spirit of the world but rather the Spirit that comes from God, that we might know what God has given us in grace. (I Cor. 2:9 ff.)

If I am to celebrate Pentecost this year, then there are two pictures that hover before my eyes and refuse to be suppressed. What the one presents is something that now lies many years in the past—the Pentecost that I once celebrated as a child in my home in the country. Spring-green birch boughs bedecked the house and filled it with their sweet, sharp fragrance, while yet others adorned the door, there to be played upon by the light of the sun. Both household and village were clothed in bright festal garments and marched to the church when the bells exultantly sounded across the countryside. Over the whole day lay the brilliant light of the sun and the happy sound of the bells; and Pentecost was a festival of joy.

The other picture is of Pentecost just a year ago. On that day I stood in a military hospital in the midst of the wounded and could hardly bring myself to say that Pentecost should be a festival of joy. Pain and misery stared at me out of large, questioning eyes, and the spirits of strife and alarm, of blood and terror, hovered oppressively through the room. And my thoughts went out to those who still stood outside in the peril

* "*Vom geheimnisvollen und offenbaren Gott*," *Die Christliche Welt*, xxxi (1917), 572-9. (The subtitle reads " Sermon for Pentecost, 1917.")

of battle and to those others for whom the boughs of spring have no fragrance and the rays of the sun cast no light.

These are the two pictures, the two inimical pictures, that refuse to be suppressed, though each would deny the other and suppress it. They are antagonistic pictures that both demand their rights and fill one's heart with pain.

I

And yet, this antagonism is really none other than the one that all of us now experience—and indeed fearfully experience, insofar as we have lived through the peacetime that is past with vigour and longing, excitement and joy, and now likewise experience wartime with the whole might of our heart —the heart that would let itself be permeated, filled, and sated by all the powers of ringing, roaring life. It is just then that we suddenly stop because we are filled with awe. We sense the frightful contrast of forces and powers that we call " life " and no longer know whether we should receive them into ourselves or whether we must rather close ourselves against them. Indeed, we become strangers to ourselves when we sense what inimical forces and currents we can receive into our lives. What is it that is still our self, our nature, when once it could enjoy itself gladly and unabashedly in the feeling that it was sustained by a power of serenity and goodness that controls the world? When we could and wanted to let ourselves be moved by a current that seemed to flow in harmony and life-emitting rhythm? Whereas now we look into powers of life which are cruel and harsh, which sometimes command and make demands on us with brassy voices, only at other times to stand dumb in pitiless silence, full of riddles and mystery! If this that we see now is the nature of life, then was what went before an illusion? Or is it that we at least did not understand it so then and must now pass judgment against ourselves, must stifle whatever of the past is still alive in us and still constitutes a part of our self?

Yes, how many shadows have fallen over our past! How unreal so many of its hours now seem! Were there such hours once, hours of carefree joy with our friends who, having died the deaths of heroes, now rest in their graves? Those hours of pure, unalloyed joy in work and creation, of devotion to the precious powers of spiritual life, of pure enjoyment in the ripe fruits of human creativity? Hours the worth and certainty of which now threaten to disappear? I do not speak of the hours of which we must be ashamed, though there were those hours also—hours of thoughtlessness and wasted time, hours that were petty and deplorable. They, too, lie behind us and ought to be behind us. With respect to them, we rightly sense that they have become strange to us, that we ought to have become more mature and serious. However, what now fills us with pain is that we have received into our inner lives powers of life that now belong to our present existence, that have rights in us that we cannot deny but must affirm—but that we still have not found the way to bring them into harmony, to view them in unity with the newer powers of life which have entered our lives with brutal force and have also demanded their rights, which we likewise must affirm. For here also I do not mean the powers of illusion, delusion, and falsehood. These are powers whose rights we deny, which we disavow by inwardly overcoming them in ourselves and working for their outward overcoming as well. Rather I mean the painfully great powers, the woefully oppressive and dreadfully humiliating powers, that demand recognition—like the thought of sacrificing everything precious and worthy of love, of tearing oneself away from a world full of light and warmth, which was our world, the steeling and stretching of oneself beyond the limits of human powers, the facing of a silent world in which pain and sorrow demand their due.

This split is not really a split between the past and the

present, but rather runs through our lives here and now. For, as I have said, the old powers of life are still present in us— indeed, are alive in us not only as the background of our self, which has become second nature, or simply because they are present in memory, but also—and the longer the war lasts the more so—as actually making themselves felt in our present thinking and working. In fact, we have hours in which they alone rule and we can forget the others. But then come the hours of awakening in which this all once again becomes strange to us. We no longer understand ourselves, and become strangers to ourselves. For we gaze into the abyss of our nature, and our self appears as a play of strange powers. We gaze into the abyss of life, and its opposing powers are incomprehensible to us. We look down into a depth of which we never dreamed.

And at this point we hear the strange word of Paul concerning the depths of God. The depths of God! We too gaze into a depth and are seized with horror. Do we want to say then that we gaze into the depths of God? Indeed, what is God, if not the infinite fullness of all the powers of life that rage around us and take our breath away, filling us with awe and wonder? What are these powers of life that sustain us and carry us away, that blend us together and separate us, that tear us apart and weld us together, if not the powers of the infinite God, who is full of creative might and joy, of endless forms and riddles? But do we dare to say this? There is also a word in the New Testament about those who say they have known the depths of Satan. And what about us? What kind of a depth are we looking into? Is it really the depth of the forces of *life*, of the forces of *God*? Or is it rather an abyss of *death*, a grappling of devilish powers that we see? Is it really the play of satanic forces that envelops our little, vain, fanciful self and mocks at it? Or is it the sway and movement of the great and infinitely creative power of God?

This is the question that gives us pain. And we will have

neither rest nor security till we know that the powers really are forces of life and of God—till we not only see a confused and senseless strife of powers, but also hear in all of the enigmatic and abysmal darkness the sound of one great and deep tone, which hovers everywhere, giving to everything rest and security, and blending it all into one mighty harmony.

It frequently happens that in listening to a piece of music we at first do not hear the deep, fundamental tone, the sure stride of the melody, on which everything else is built, because we are deafened by the fullness of detail, the veritable sea of sounds and impressions which overwhelms us. It is only after we have accustomed our ear that we find law and order, and as with *one* magical stroke, a single unified world emerges from the confused welter of sounds. And when this happens, we suddenly realize with delight and amazement that the fundamental tone was also resounding before, that all along the melody had been giving order and unity. Could it be, then, that here, too, we need only accustom our eye and ear in order to see the harmony and to hear the great and mighty note of unity—to see *God* in this confusion of forces?

II

If we want to see God, then the first thing we should say to ourselves is that we may not see him as we have conceived him. We must remind ourselves that he may appear to be wholly other than the picture we have made of him; and we must be prepared to accept his visage even if it terrifies us. Can we not see him in the present? Has our old picture of him fallen to pieces? If so, then we must first of all be grateful that we have lost our false conception; for the only way we can see him is as he actually is.

But were we not certain before that we had him and were experiencing him? Did he not so lay hold upon our heart that it trembled and rejoiced? None of us, of course, may dispute this. But what we nevertheless do see now is that we pictured him too small. He is greater; he is infinite. And if he at one time showed himself to us, i.e., allowed us to see a part of his infinite nature, he has also provided that we can never become complacent about this and imagine that we have known him completely. New sides of his infinity constantly emerge, strange and enigmatic; and as he himself is infinite, so also must our knowledge of him be infinite—never static and at rest, but constantly ready to yield anew, to allow itself to be raised anew.

And should it seem strange to us when we look into the depths, when we stand before riddle and mystery, as though God could not be found there? No! God *must* be a hidden and mysterious God, full of contradictions and riddles. Otherwise our inner life would become static, and we would lose the power to obtain experience from life's fullness. For what does "experience" mean? It means constantly to enrich oneself anew, to allow oneself to be given something anew. It means to perceive that miraculous forces hold sway in the world, which we cannot reckon with, cannot enlist as mere factors in our work. It means to know that over and above our knowledge, our work, yes, and even our moral duty, there is something else—a fullness of life that streams in upon us completely as a gift, completely as grace. Experience means to receive a destiny into oneself. Not simply to endure a destiny, like the grain of sand with which the wind and the waves play, or like the coin that wanders from hand to hand—both of which, to be sure, endure a destiny, but always without being influenced in their inmost being by any of the forces that drive them. Experience means to make your destiny truly your own. And this means always to be open for what is given to us, always to be ready to experience miracles. Not the miracles in which an earlier age had its joy—miracles opposed to nature and to understanding—but rather the miracles of life, the miracles of destiny. To want to have experience means to be ready to take miracle and mystery into oneself—or, to express it somewhat differently, *it means to have reverence and humility in the presence of life.* For only when we approach life reverently and humbly can we hear God's voice in all its roar.

God has to be hidden and mysterious if we are to approach him in humility and reverence. Indeed, this is so even among men. We often feel with pain that we are mysteries to one another. " For there is no bridge that leads from man to man." And yet, when we rightly reflect on it, there is something precious in our being mysteries to ourselves, in our never being completely known to one another, in our being unable ever to see through even the person who is closest to our heart and to reckon with him as though he were a logical proposition or a problem in accounting. For if we were thus able to reckon with him, he would seem flat and empty to us and we would no longer be able to lavish our heart on him. Indeed, we want precisely from the person we love most that his riches be inexhaustible and that they bring forth every day some new miracle. We rejoice in hiddenness and mystery because it is a promise to us of the wonderful and undreamed-of powers that slumber in the heart of the other, awaiting only our readiness for their revelation. And this it is that throws across the bridge from one man to another—the acknowledgment of hiddenness and mystery, humility and reverence in the presence of the other's uniqueness, divine trust in the miracles that richly and ever more richly well up out of his inmost being, blessing and overwhelming us with grace.

And so God also has to be hidden and mysterious so that we may approach him in humility and reverence. But then he is also infinitely filled with contradictions and terrors. Scarcely is he known than he again disappears; and we once more stand in the presence of the unknown God, with whom we must wrestle anew till he gives himself to be known and speaks his name.

> *I would know thee, thou Unknown One,*
> *Who dost lay hold of my soul in its depths,*
> *Moving through my life like a storm,*
> *Incomprehensible, and yet kin to me!*
> *I would know thee, and even serve thee!**

God has to be hidden and mysterious, a God filled with contradictions; for what unfolds itself within such contradictions is the riches of an infinite creativity. And if we gaze down into undreamed-of depths and the contradictions of life threaten to break our hearts, we will still give thanks in humility and reverence that nothing has been spared us; and this we will do even now in this time of terror.

> *Thou art a thicket of contradictions.*
> *I may rock thee like a child,*
> *And yet thy curses are accomplished,*
> *Which are frightful among the peoples.**

To be sure, it is wanton and shameful to proceed from some fixed concept of God and hastily locate the war and its suffering in the divine plan for the world, looking upon it as judgment and punishment and on this basis erecting sermons calling men to repentance. But it is just as wanton and undignified to say that God is not present in this war and its horrors. No, there is yet a far more profound view than the standpoint of the preacher of repentance who so quickly sees through God's intentions in ruling the world. This view has its beginning in humility and reverence. It knows that we will always see God as wholly other than we thought him to be. It expects

---

* *Ich will dich kennen, Unbekannter,*
　Du tief in meine Seele Greifender,
　Mein Leben wie ein Sturm Durchschweifender,
　Du Unfassbarer, mir Verwandter!
　Ich will dich kennen, selbst dir dienen!
　　　　(Friedrich Nietzsche, " *Dem unbekannten Gott* ")
* *Du bist der Wald der Widersprüche.*
　Ich darf dich wiegen wie ein Kind,
　Und doch vollziehn sich deine Flüche,
　Die über Völkern furchtbar sind.
　　　　(Rainer Maria Rilke, " *Studenbuch* ")

of man the faith that, even with the most frightful destiny, God believes man capable of something grand and wants to make him completely free and noble. To be sure, it is our duty, the duty of mankind, to see to it that nothing as horrible as this war ever again falls over the earth. And yet, if the age of perpetual peace would come, would we not have to give thanks to God that our generation, that we, were permitted to experience this violence, which laid upon humanity such a burden as was never laid on it before? And would we not desire that no future generation ever forget what has been possible on earth? For never before has God expected something so grand from the race of men; never before have we experienced that everything became so strange to us and we stood in God's presence naked and alone; never before have we been so permitted to gaze into the depths of God!

III

But always we speak of the depths of *God*! May we do this? Is it *only* the depths, *only* hiddenness and mystery that constitute his being? Is there not always the temptation, then, that these depths are an abyss of death, that this riddle is the cunning of Satan? Indeed, mystery is *not* all there is to God; nor do we call that voice the voice of piety that is intoxicated with the terrible and the mysterious, that revels in the twilight zone of contradictions and in the motley of the enigmatic. That would be mere playing—indeed, would be sin. It would be the exact opposite of the humility and reverence that are the substance of piety. No, riddle and mystery lose their meaning if they are not loved for the sake of what lies behind them, if they do not awaken in us the presentiment of a rich and inexhaustible solution, if we are not brought to want a revelation and indeed to long for it with all our hearts. What makes riddle and mystery divine to us is precisely that we want an infinite *revelation* of God. And it is only because this revelation is *God's* revelation, is infinite, that it has to lead through riddle and mystery.

God the mysterious and hidden must at the same time be the God who is revealed. Not, of course, in a revelation that one can know, that could be grasped in words and propositions, that would be limited to formula and book and to space and time; but rather in a revelation that continually opens up new heights and depths and thus leads through darkness, from clarity to clarity.

The God who is revealed! One thing we must know, that through all the riddle and mystery there is a way, a sure direction. And how do we attain this certainty? "The Spirit searches everything, even the depths of God." What kind of a being is this Spirit? Paul also tells us that we men are mysteries to one another and that only a man's own inmost being, his spirit, knows his thoughts; to the other person they remain hidden. And yet, we know that we have the power to reveal ourselves to one another. If we approach a man with humility and reverence for what lies within him, then his hidden being is unveiled and he gives to us of his inmost self; he permits us to gaze into his being. It is not that we see through him and compute him, but rather that he gives us a part of himself that opens up to us a view into his depths. And so it is also with God. It is not that we compute him and puzzle him out, but only that he gives us a part of his being, his Spirit, that opens our eyes. And this is the bridge that leads from man to God: reverence and humility, the readiness to yield oneself, to let oneself be given a gift. The heart that in the darkness humbles itself most deeply and implores the most vehemently, "O that thou wouldst rend the heavens and come down!" is the first to hear, "I will pour water upon him that is thirsty, and floods upon the dry ground."

If the split in our heart frightens us, we do not want to stifle it. If the contradiction between the powers of life frightens us, we ought not to close ourselves against them. And if we keep our heart from becoming closed and embittered and remain open in humble longing and reverent trust, then we will sense the power of the Spirit at work in our hearts. Paul tells us: " We have received the Spirit that comes from God, that we might know what God has given us in grace." Can we also say, when we pause to reflect on ourselves, that something in this confusion that has been given us is grace? That would be the test whether God's Spirit has begun his work in our hearts, to open our eyes.

Yes, I think we can say this. And even if it were only that the veil that hid the reality of life from us has been lifted, that an old and illusory concept of God has fallen to pieces, the whole process would not appear so senseless to us because there would still be something in it that brought us inner gain. We have learned to pose questions to destiny in a completely new and more profound sense. And do not answers also here and there flash before us? Have we not learned that there are forces in the heart of man of which we never dreamed? Have we not learned that there are duties that raise man high above everything commonplace, even, indeed, above everything that we once thought to be high and noble? Has not a reverence arisen in us for a greatness in mankind such as we never dreamed of, a greatness that reveals to us the forces of God in man? We have seen men and still see them on whose shoulders rests a superhuman responsibility, but who bear it without going to pieces. We see a sense of sacrifice and a heroism that wreathe even the humblest brow with a crown of glory. And one mystery has been revealed to us for which we had lost our sense; I mean the greatness of what we call " tragic." We have learned once again that even harshness and cruelty may be expected of a man for the sake of something higher without his thereby being defiled—and, indeed, in such a way that he may even be ennobled. We have learned that he, like God, can accept death and destruction into his work so that life may grow out of them. If we were to eliminate the tragic from human life, then we would eliminate the supreme test to which man's dignity can be put—namely, to make his destiny, even

the most frightful destiny, entirely his own and to become lord
of it. To be sure, in peacetime our poets found gripping
words in which to express the melancholy in life, the pain and
sorrow that encounter men in their struggle with nature and
fate. But the power to understand the tragic was lost to us.
What the war has once again given us is the crowning glory of
the tragic.

But has the war not also revealed all of the dark, demonic
forces of the human heart—all the passions of self-seeking and
falsehood, of brutality and hate? Do we dare say here also that
we gaze into the depths of God? Yes, we dare to say it even
here! For this sight is a powerful reflection on ourselves and a
perception of the miraculous riches of all the opposed forces
and passions, all the heights and depths, that dwell in the soul
of man—and in our souls also : for the human soul is still *one*
great unity. And if in seeing this sight we are at first seized
with horror, it still is a sight of indescribable grandeur :

> *Yes, everything is in thee that only the cosmos offers,*
> *Heaven and hell, judgment and eternity.**

This is not to say that we want to leave men, to leave us ourselves, as we are. But precisely this sight with all its heights
and depths, with all the fullness of the violent and the demonic, of the passionate and the uncanny, teaches us to put the
goal of that which can and should become here all the higher.
What creative possibilities for God's plans! But even more,
what a mysterious wisdom of God is revealed here—a wisdom
that compels even the demonic forces of sin and falsehood to
merge in the harmony of the whole, so that even satanic power
can only be a power that constantly wills evil, only constantly
to create good. What a hidden wisdom of God that uses all
the wild, unleashed passions only in order to put man's dignity
to the supreme test, to give him the highest nobility of his
being!

And do we not have a picture that concretely embodies all

---

* *Ja, alles ist in dir, was nur das Weltall beut,*
Der Himmel und die Höll, Gericht und Ewigkeit.

this and places before our very eyes all that we have been struggling so hard to say? Do we not have a picture in which God's hidden and revealed wisdom is embodied—the wisdom that is able to bring all of the demonic powers of darkness into its plan of salvation; that is able to create a noble life out of the agony of death and forsakenness; that swallows death up in victory and transforms a crown of thorns into the crown of a king? Indeed we do have such a picture of promise and redemption in the picture of the crucified Christ. And the picture of the crucified one as the embodiment of the hidden and revealed wisdom of God may help us also to understand the mysteries with which we are presently struggling.

"The Spirit of God searches everything, even the depths of God." Because it is knowledge of the Spirit, it is not a knowledge that rests on conclusions and proofs and that every man can understand. Each of us must learn to see for himself, i.e., each of us must be ready to bow before the hidden God in reverence and humility, so that his heart will be open for God's Spirit and his eyes will learn to see the God who is revealed—the God who endlessly reveals himself. To be sure, opposing powers abide in us and keep us in tension. But thus will it be and thus should it be as long as we are mortal men; for only so can we remain alive and become richer and more mature. We will never find the formula that solves all the riddles and enables us to see all the contradictions harmonized. We succeed in this only from level to level. The conflict in us will remain, but it will have lost its pain. We receive the good conscience to bear the contradictions in ourselves and to affirm the conflicting powers of life that lay claim to our heart. For we know that the depths into which we gaze are really the depths of God; that mysteries and riddles constantly emerge anew, that God is a God of contradictions because he always wants to reveal himself more powerfully in his infinity as the Creator. Clarity will be given to us from level to level, and as the riddles increase, so also will God's graces. As he is infinite as the source of terror, so also is he infinite as the source of grace;

and the way must lead from every height through new depths to new heights. Thus there is law and order in God's working. If we have once acquired an ear for the divine melody, then it is always the same old theme endlessly proceeding in ever new ways, always blending itself into new harmonies, always more tempestuous, always more powerful. And if we kneel at first humbly and reverently before the hidden God of the riddle, then we kneel humbly and reverently before the revealed God of grace. And thus we may be permitted to see " What no eye has seen, nor ear heard, nor the heart of man conceived, what God has prepared for those who love him."

THE NEW APPROACH
TO THE SYNOPTIC PROBLEM*

The phrase "the synoptic problem" has usually denoted the question concerning the mutual relationships of the gospels of Matthew, Mark, and Luke. Ever since the end of the eighteenth century critical research has been engaged in examining the various hypotheses that might explain these relationships. By the end of the nineteenth century there was general agreement that the correct solution of the problem had been found. This solution went by the name of the two-document hypothesis. According to this theory the general content of the synoptic tradition can be traced essentially to two sources. One of these is the Gospel of Mark, which the authors of Matthew and Luke used as a source. The other is a collection of sayings of Jesus, which both Matthew and Luke used and which each combined with the text of Mark in his own way. It is true that Matthew and Luke used some other sources, but nearly all of the material in these gospels can be traced to Mark and to the collections of sayings (often called the *Logia*). In tracing these relationships it should be noted that both Mark and the collection of sayings were subjected to editorial redaction. It is quite possible that Matthew and Luke possessed Mark and the *Logia* in different recensions, and it is quite probable that the form of the Gospel of Mark used by them was earlier than the one with which we are familiar. However, the differences between these forms cannot have been very great. The *Urmarkus* (as this supposed earlier form was called) must have been essentially identical with Mark as it lies before us, minus a few slight later additions.

Two difficult questions, however, remained to be considered.

* "The New Approach to the Synoptic Problem," *The Journal of Religion,* vi (1926), 337-62.

First : How was the relationship between Mark and the *Logia* to be defined? Which was older, Mark or the *Logia*? Did Mark use the *Logia* at all? The second related question concerned the sources that the writer of Mark used in the composition of his gospel. Did he employ oral tradition simply, or did he have written sources as well? These two questions were considered important because of the goal toward which all this critical work was believed to lead, viz., the attainment of the most accurate possible picture of the life and the teaching of the historical Jesus.

At first those who attempted to write the life of Jesus simply used the oldest accessible sources, taking the outline of the Gospel of Mark as an accurate historical record of events and describing in this framework the course of the outer and inner development of Jesus. Even when it was suspected that there were legendary elements in many of Mark's narratives, such as those concerning the baptism and the transfiguration of Jesus and the miracle stories, it was nevertheless assumed that even in these there was a historical kernel. Most of the sayings of Jesus and the events of his life as recorded by Mark (particularly the controversial discourses) were considered genuinely historical, as was Mark's general outline of the life of Jesus. The portrait of Jesus sketched on the basis of these presuppositions had the following general traits : The inner development of Jesus was conditioned by his messianic consciousness. Probably his baptism was the occasion of the birth of this consciousness. Possibly in the beginning it was not yet clear and definite, but in the course of his career it came to be an assured conscious possession. In any case, at the beginning of his public ministry he did not announce himself as Messiah, but whenever the people suggested the idea he discountenanced it, for he desired that the recognition of his messiahship should gradually ripen in his hearers. Even to his disciples he did not at once acknowledge himself as Messiah. Instead, he permitted their belief in him as the Messiah to grow gradually until he felt that the hour had come when he might ask them,

"Who do you believe that I am?" When Peter, by his answer to this question, acknowledged his messiahship, he commanded the disciples to keep it secret. Not until the end of his ministry, at the triumphal entry into Jerusalem and before the Sanhedrin, did he publicly acknowledge himself as Messiah. So far as his outer career was concerned, it was held that at first the people welcomed him, but later gradually deserted him because he had disappointed the popular messianic expectations; that he incurred the hostility of the Scribes and Pharisees because of his utterances concerning the law, and this hostility finally brought him to the cross. Thus in general ran the interpretation based on the assumption of the essential historicity of Mark.

This conception was completely discredited by the researches of Wilhelm Wrede and Julius Wellhausen. In his work entitled *Das Messiasgeheimnis in den Evangelien* (1901) Wrede made a detailed examination of those utterances in Mark in which Jesus either concealed his messiahship or forbade the disciples to make it public. Wrede came to the conclusion that these utterances could not be accurate historical tradition, but must be theological interpretations of Mark. Wrede held that in the Christian community it was at first believed that Jesus would speedily return to earth as Messiah, but not that he had performed messianic deeds during his lifetime. Later, however, the necessity was felt for regarding his earthly life also as the life of the Messiah. Wrede argued that the author of Mark attempted to combine two views : first, the earlier tradition that had not indicated messianic traits in the work of Jesus, and second, the prevailing conviction that his work was nevertheless actually messianic. He held that Mark accomplished this by indicating repeatedly that Jesus was really the Messiah, but that this must not be publicly acknowledged. Wrede also made it clear that the outline of Mark's gospel is unhistorical; that Mark worked over genuine historical tradition, but grouped and interpreted this in accordance with his own dogmatic ideas. This investigation by

Wrede opened a further problem for research, namely, through a critical analysis of both Mark and the other synoptic gospels to distinguish between the oldest tradition and the additions or modifications that the evangelists introduced in their work of redaction—in short, the discrimination between tradition and redaction.

To the solution of this question Wellhausen made a significant contribution in his commentaries on the synoptic gospels which appeared between 1905 and 1911. One of the most important of his conclusions was as follows : The oldest tradition consisted almost entirely of small fragments (sayings or words of Jesus), and did not present a continuous story of the deeds of Jesus or any complete collection of sayings. When these fragments were collected, they were connected so as to form a continuous narrative. Wellhausen was of the opinion that Mark was older than the *Logia,* and was based on a better tradition. He showed not only that the evangelist's narratives connecting the fragments were secondary, but also that oral tradition was already steadily producing more and more new sayings of Jesus. Such secondary traditions Wellhausen believed to be especially characteristic of the *Logia.* This conclusion followed from the recognition of the important part played by the Christian community in the history of the synoptic tradition. In the primitive community at Jerusalem the spirit of Jesus continued to be active, and his ethical teaching was progressively elaborated and expressed in utterances which were then transmitted as the sayings of Jesus himself. Thus tradition shaped and handed down, in the form of words of Jesus, conceptions actually arising from the faith of the community, and portrayed these as regulations for church discipline and for missionary activity.

Notwithstanding his tendency to exaggerate in many particulars, Wellhausen brought clearly to light a principle which must govern research. We must recognize that a literary work or a fragment of tradition is a primary source for the historical situation out of which it arose, and is only a secondary source for the historical details concerning which it gives information.

So far as the *Logia* are concerned, this means that they are a primary source from which we can reconstruct a picture of the primitive community in which the *Logia* arose. Only after we have obtained such a historical picture of the community are we in a position to attempt to reconstruct the picture of Jesus and of his preaching. Wellhausen said : " The spirit of Jesus undoubtedly breathes in the utterances derived from the community at Jerusalem; but we do not derive a historical picture of Jesus himself from the conception of Jesus which prevailed in the community." This utterance should not be regarded simply as an expression of scepticism; it is, indeed, a positive achievement to be certain that we possess a source in which the spirit of Jesus is still active. When once we have learned to make the distinction in the *Logia* between those utterances that express specific interests of the Christian community or that are shaped in terms of Jewish piety, and those utterances that transcend these interests and express great original ideas, it becomes possible to employ the *Logia* with critical intelligence, so as to derive from them a definite conception of the preaching of Jesus.

Further research must proceed along the pathway indicated by Wrede and Wellhausen. If we define the total undertaking as that of distinguishing the different stages of the synoptic tradition from one another in order to identify the oldest, the very first task is to make a critical distinction between tradition and editorial redaction in the synoptic gospels. Now it is easy to discover the method of redaction employed in Matthew and Luke, since here we can compare the gospels with Mark and can note the way in which Matthew and Luke combined this gospel with the material of the *Logia*. When the process of gospel-making has been observed in this case, it becomes possible with considerable certainty to distinguish between tradition and redaction in the Gospel of Mark. This undertaking was systematically carried out by K. L. Schmidt, in his

book entitled *Der Rahmen der Geschichte Jesu* (1919). By
means of such an analysis it becomes clear that the original
tradition underlying Mark (with perhaps the exception of
the story of the passion) consisted almost entirely of small
isolated fragments; and that virtually all the descriptions of
place or time which connect the individual fragments into a
larger whole are due to redaction. In the case of Mark, this
editorial redaction is still quite primitive; but in Matthew, and
especially in Luke, it is already considerably developed. All
three evangelists have typical forms of transition from one
incident to another. They ring the changes on a rather limited
amount of material in order thus to construct the background
of individual scenes and to construct a framework for the
entire life of Jesus. They mention such items as the house, the
road, the mountain, the seashore; situations such as Jesus in a
ship, on a journey, as a guest at a meal, in the synagogue at a
religious service. As conventional accompaniments appear the
popular crowd, the foes of Jesus, and the ever-present disciples. In my own book, *Die Geschichte der synoptischen
Tradition* (1921), I presented in full these conclusions of K. L.
Schmidt and carried the study somewhat further.

As a result of this investigation it appears that the outline
of the life of Jesus, as it is given by Mark and taken over by
Matthew and Luke, is an editorial creation, and that as a
consequence our actual knowledge of the course of Jesus' life
is restricted to what little can be discovered in the individual
scenes constituting the older tradition. This conclusion, however, is not simply a negative one. It has also its positive
significance, since critical analysis has brought out portions
that can be regarded as original traditions.

Now a new problem arises. In the first place, we must ask
whether all the traditional bits are equally original or whether
we are not obliged to distinguish here also between earlier and
later tradition. In the second place, it must be asked whether
these traditions have been preserved intact or whether through
redaction by the evangelists or in the course of previous trans-

mission, they have not been altered, abridged, or expanded. What means do we possess for answering these questions?

The method of investigation called *Formgeschichte* is believed to furnish such means. This method starts from the observed fact that all literary presentations, particularly in primitive culture and in the ancient world, follow relatively fixed forms. This is true not only of written narratives, but also of oral tradition. It is to be noticed, for example, that folk tales, or proverbs, or folk songs transmitted orally, have their definite styles. Two factors must be noted in a study of form : first, the stylistic pattern that prevails in a particular kind of utterance, such as folk tales or riddles; and secondly, the laws conditioning the transmission of a literary fragment in either oral or written tradition. Certain examples of this will be given later. In the field of Old Testament literature the *formgeschichtliche* method was applied several years ago by H. Gunkel and his disciples. It was recognized that in the Old Testament the various types of literary style must be distinguished and the peculiar characteristics of each type must be examined, e.g., psalms, prayer forms, utterances expressing threats or rebukes, the oracles of the prophets, etc. The study of the history of this literature enabled scholars to determine where literary types were to be found in their original form and how these became altered in the course of their transmission.

In the New Testament this task of literary analysis is admittedly much more difficult, because the material is of much smaller compass and the period of its development is much shorter. Nevertheless, it is possible to distinguish in the material of the synoptic tradition certain specific literary types that have their own laws of style. If, now, the content of the tradition is expressed in the form of such special types, it is possible to place great reliance on this tradition, for these forms always offer definite resistance to any radical alteration. This resistance, of course, is only relative; for it is undeniable that the material actually underwent changes. If, however, we can succeed in identifying a particular literary type and its law of style, we can then frequently distinguish an original tradition from secondary additions. We thus obtain a test for determining the age of a literary utterance by noting whether it appears in the original pure form belonging to this type of literature or whether it shows marks of further stylistic development. It is easily understood that such investigation is very difficult and must be carried on with great caution. Conclusions, however, are reinforced when we not only note the laws of style belonging to a given type, but also discover the general laws that govern the transmission of material.

This last task, viz., the study of the laws that govern literary transmission, can be approached by observing the manner in which the Marcan material was altered by Matthew and Luke; and also how Matthew and Luke worked over what they took from the *Logia*. Here we observe a certain regular procedure that becomes still more evident when we carry the investigation to a later tradition, particularly to the apocryphal gospels, and see how in these the gospel material received further literary development. When once the laws governing such transmission of tradition are established we may assume that these laws prevailed also in the case of Mark and in the collection of the *Logia*. Then, it is frequently possible to attempt provisionally to reconstruct a literary form older than the one lying before us. The ability to make the necessary distinctions can be developed by studying the general laws that govern popular transmission of stories and traditions in other instances, for example, in the case of folk tales, anecdotes, and folk songs.

The primary task of identifying the specific types of the synoptic material and the laws of style governing each is made simpler through the fact that we are acquainted with similar species in contemporary rabbinical and Hellenistic literature. Just what types can be identified and more accurately described with the help of this material will be made clear in the following discussion.

In the first place, it must be shown how precisely the same

laws governing transmission of tradition observed elsewhere in popular literature were also operative in the synoptic tradition. Whenever narratives pass from mouth to mouth the central point of the narrative and general structure are well preserved; but in the incidental details changes take place, for imagination paints such details with increasing distinctness. In the later legends it is to be observed, for example, that names are sought for many people whom the gospels mention without naming them. What was the name of the woman with the issue of blood whom Jesus healed? Who were the thieves crucified with Jesus? What was the name of the captain of the guard over the grave of Jesus? Later legends undertake to tell us. Such legendary creations of the imagination are also to be observed in the gospels. Who were the two disciples mentioned in Mark 14 :13 whom Jesus sent on before to prepare the Passover meal? In Luke 22 :8 we have their names : Peter and John. Imagination always portrays in more precise and vivid form what it receives. Where Mark 9 :17 narrates that a father brought to Jesus his deranged son, we read in Luke 9 :38 that it was his only son. Mark says simply that the thieves crucified with Jesus reviled him (15 :32). Luke tells us that only one of them did this, while the other acknowledged Jesus and received from him a generous answer (23 :39-43). The scene in which Judas betrayed Jesus with a kiss is narrated in Mark without any accompanying words (14 :45). It is easy to understand that people later should ask : " What did Jesus say to him?" Matthew puts into the mouth of Jesus the words, " Friend, why hast thou come?" (26 :50). According to Luke, Jesus said, " Judas, betrayest thou the Son of Man with a kiss?" (22 :48). According to Mark 15 :37, Jesus died uttering a loud cry. What did he say? What were his last words? Luke 23 :46 puts in the mouth of Jesus the quotation from one of the Psalms, " Father, into thy hands I commend my spirit "; while the Gospel of John later represents Jesus as saying, " It is finished " (19 :30).

One further observation is important in this critical investi-

gation. The tendency of imagination to identify anonymous
persons more definitely led to the habit of describing the opponents with whom Jesus entered into controversy as scribes
or Pharisees. A careful comparison of the pertinent passages
shows that frequently an accusation against Jesus arose from
unnamed persons (for example, Luke 11 :15 and 16). Later,
however, under the dominance of the schematic representation
that the scribes and Pharisees were the persistent foes of Jesus,
it became impossible to imagine any other possibility than that
all the attacks upon Jesus came from them. It even became
inconceivable that a scribe should have put an honest question
to Jesus and should have been praised by him in such a fashion
as is narrated in Mark 12 :28-34. When Matthew tells this
story (22 :34-40) he represents the scribe as asking the question
in order to trap Jesus.

Let us now ask what literary types the *formgeschichtliche*
investigation can identify in the material of the synoptic tradition.

We can easily identify the type of miracle stories. Among
these we do not reckon the account of Jesus' controversy over
healing on a Sabbath day, for in this the miracle is a subordin-
ate incident, the principal theme being the violation of the
Sabbath and the controversy occasioned thereby. Characteristic
miracle stories are those in which the miracle constitutes the
main theme and is described with considerable detail, such as
the healing of the Gerasene demoniac, the cure of the woman
with the issue of blood, the raising of the daugher of Jairus
from death, the stories of the stilling of the storm, of walking
on the sea, of the feeding of the five thousand, and others.
These miracle stories, particularly the accounts of miraculous
healing, reveal one and the same style with definite characteristics. Since we know a great many miracle stories of Jewish and
Hellenistic origin, we can make a careful comparative study of
the miracle stories found in the gospels. We thus discover that
the gospel stories have exactly the same style as the Hellenistic
miracle stories. Accounts of miraculous healing run as fol-

lows : First, the condition of the sick person is depicted in such fashion as to enhance the magnitude of the miracle. In this connection it is frequently said that the sickness had lasted a long time. Occasionally it is stated that many physicians had attempted in vain to cure the sick person. Sometimes the terrible and dangerous character of the sickness is emphasized. All these traits are found in the synoptic narratives, just as they also appear in the stories that are told concerning the pagan miracle-worker Apollonius of Tyana. After this introductory description of the illness comes the account of the healing itself. The Hellenistic miracle stories often tell of unusual manipulations by the miracle-worker; the gospel accounts, however, seldom mention this trait (Mark 7:33 and 8:23). The gospels do, however, retain other typical items. They narrate that the Saviour came near to the sick person— perhaps close to his bed—that he laid his hand upon the patient or took him by the hand and then uttered a wonder-working word. Following a custom also characteristic of pagan miracle stories, the narratives of healing in the gospels occasionally reproduce this wonder-working word in a foreign tongue, as, for example, *Talitha Kumi* (Mark 5:41) and *Ephphatha* (Mark 7:34). Another typical trait appears when it is sometimes said that no one was permitted to see the actual working of the miracle (Mark 7:33 and 8.23). The close of the miracle story depicts the consequence of the miracle, frequently describing the astonishment or the terror or the approval of those who witnessed the miraculous event. In other cases the close of the narrative shows the one who is healed demonstrating by some appropriate action that he is entirely cured. Thus, in Mark 2:11 ff., the lame man who was healed carried away the bed on which he had been brought. Precisely the same thing is narrated in a Hellenistic miracle story told by Lucian of Samosata. In the Hellenistic stories of the exorcism of demons, the process was often described in drastic fashion by representing the demon on his expulsion as indulging in some destructive action, such as shattering a pillar or overturning a vessel containing water. In similar fashion, in the account in the fifth chapter of Mark, the demon who was expelled entered into a herd of swine and drove them into the sea. Many of the foregoing traits are also found in the rabbinical miracle tales. All of them appear in Hellenistic accounts. On the basis, then, of the similarity between the miracle stories in the synoptic gospels and those in Hellenistic literature we are forced to conclude that these miracle stories do not belong to the oldest strata of tradition, but, at least in their present form, were elaborated in Hellenistic Christianity.

It is true that the older Palestinian tradition also narrates miracles of Jesus, but, as we have already indicated, only those miracles that gave occasion for a controversy between Jesus and his opponents. One of the oldest types of the synoptic tradition consists of controversial utterances. This type is common to both the rabbinical and the synoptic tradition, and precisely the same characteristics of style may be observed in both. An act or attitude of someone (in the case of the Christian tradition, Jesus or a disciple of his) gives the occasion for an attack by an opponent. Familiar instances are the violation of the Sabbath requirements or a failure to observe some ritual of purification. The attack is answered by a defence, which appears in a specific form, very frequently an *ad hominem* query, or an illustration, or perhaps both together. To the charge that Jesus was healing on the Sabbath day came the answer in the form of the question, " Is it lawful to do good on the Sabbath day or to do evil?" (Mark 3 :4). In answer to the inquiry why his disciples did not fast, Jesus replies : " Can the children of the bridegroom fast when the bridegroom is with them?" Another way of replying is to give a Scripture citation.

It is characteristic of the style of these controversial discourses, as may be observed in similar rabbinical material, that the dialogue proceeds in crisp and trenchant form. The question asked or the illustration given in rejoinder contains the complete refutation of the opponent. We therefore conclude that, in the synoptic gospels, where the answer receives further elaboration, the elaborating words are a secondary contribution. This is undoubtedly the case in Mark 2:19, 2:20, where the question cited above is elaborated as follows: " So long as they have the bridegroom with them they cannot fast; but the days will come when the bridegroom shall be taken from them, and then will they fast in that day." The content of these words reinforces this conclusion, for they contain an allegorical prophecy of the death of Jesus and a justification of the later custom of fasting in the Christian community. Careful investigation shows that similar elaborations of an original tradition are found in other places.

The form of these controversial dialogues shows that this part of the tradition originated in the primitive Palestinian community, and the general content, along with many incidental observations, confirms this hypothesis. Accordingly, we must picture the life of this community moving within the limits of Judaism, engaged in disputes with the Jewish schools, and seeking to justify the correctness of its point of view by appeal to words of Jesus and by citations from Scripture. These controversial passages, then, precisely as in the case of rabbinical utterances, were transmitted not as historical narratives, but as polemic and apologetic material. It is therefore incorrect to regard these controversial utterances as accounts of actual historical scenes in the life of Jesus. It is true that the spirit of Jesus breathes in them; for his activity called the community into life and from him the community received the peculiar views with which the controversies are concerned. There is no reason to doubt that many genuine utterances attributed to Jesus in these discourses rest upon accurate historical recollection; but it must be admitted that the scenes depicted in them are not to be taken as narratives of actual events.

In confirmation of this conclusion, a further observation may be made. In many of the controversial discourses we find that it is not an objectionable attitude of Jesus, but rather the behaviour of his disciples, that furnishes the occasion for opposition. Thus we read that the disciples did not fast, that they plucked the heads of wheat on the Sabbath, that they did not practise ritual purification before eating. Why now were the disciples rebuked? Clearly Jesus could not have maintained a correct attitude in all these matters. The disciples must have learned their independent attitude only from him. When, now, we trace the origin of such a narrative to the apologetic necessities of the Christian community, the whole matter becomes clear. The " disciples " are nothing other than the community. This community, under the influence of Jesus, had broken with the old customs, and was defending its position against its opponents by appealing to an utterance of Jesus. This appeal, following the method of rabbinical literature, expresses itself in terms of a controversial discourse.

The form of controversial narrative, however, belongs to a more comprehensive species, to which I have given the name *apophthegmata,* taking the word from Greek literary history. The distinguishing character of an *apophthegma* is the fact that it portrays a minor scene that furnishes the framework for an important utterance of a hero, a philosopher, a religious preacher, or some other such person. The important thing is the utterance itself; the narrative framework serves only to portray a situation giving occasion to the utterance. Such *apophthegmata* are found very frequently in literature from many sources. In Greek literature, for example, Plutarch made a collection of many *apophthegmata.* Rabbinical literature also contains a large number, among which controversial discourses constitute only one class. We find also scholastic discussions—that is to say, discussions closely allied to controversial discourses—only here a zealous questioner requests an opinion from a celebrated rabbi. The evangelical tradition also contains such discourses. For example, Jesus was asked by a rich man, " What must I do to inherit eternal life?" A scribe asks him, " Which is the first commandment?" There are also biographical *apophthegmata,* i.e., accounts of an important scene in which the hero makes some utterance especially revealing his character. Thus Jesus says to a wavering follower, "Follow thou me and let the dead bury their dead." Again, when his relatives sought to take him home with them, he said, "Who is my mother and my brethren? Whosoever doeth the will of God the same is my brother and my sister and my mother." Here also careful examination shows that most of the synoptic *apophthegmata* must have originated in the primitive Palestinian community, and that they therefore represent a relatively ancient tradition, for the peculiar stylistic traits of the Greek *apophthegmata* are almost entirely lacking. At the same time it is sometimes possible to distinguish between more ancient and more recent *apophthegmata* in the synoptic gospels for many of them are unskilful imitations of an older pattern. There was a strong tendency to take utterances of Jesus which were originally transmitted without any setting and to put these into some appropriate setting, using in this process older *apophthegmata* as a pattern. As a criterion for such distinctions the following principle may be laid down; the most ancient *apophthegmata* are obviously those in which the setting and the utterance of Jesus have an intimate relation to each other, so that the one cannot be adequately understood without the other. On the other hand, those *apophthegmata* are more recent in which the setting and the utterances are only loosely related, the setting having been obviously an afterthought.

We have seen that the controversial utterances cannot be regarded as actual historical scenes. The same is true of the biographical *apophthegmata.* These are pictorial creations of the Christian community in which is brought to clear expression what the community held to be the character of their Master, what they experienced in relation to him, or how he fared in popular estimation. Thus, for example, the stories of the calling of the first disciples from their occupation as fishermen are not actual historical events. They lack entirely any portrayal of adequate motives or historical verisimilitude. These scenes simply give symbolic expression, such as one might find in a picture, to the general experience of the disciples when, through the wonderful power of Jesus, they were diverted from their previous manner of life. Thus the well-known story of Jesus preaching in Nazareth and his rejection there (Mark 6:1-6) is not a definite historical occurrence, but is a symbolic picture that vividly represents the attitude of the people as a whole to the preaching of Jesus.

When we undertake a critical investigation of the recorded words of Jesus we face a very difficult task. Is it possible here also to distinguish between a more ancient content and a later reworking? The first step in this investigation is to detach the utterances themselves from the setting given to them in the gospels, for this setting is due to the editorial work of the evangelists or of earlier collectors of the discourses. It is only when the utterances are thus disentangled from their setting that the real meaning of the words can be obtained; for in the editorial setting an artificial meaning is often given. Take, for example, the statement, " Agree with thine adversary quickly while thou art with him in the way, etc." In Matt. 5:25-6 these words urge a reconciliation. But in Luke 12:57-9 they take the form of a parable of warning, saying in effect: Exactly as in his earthly life a person, up to the very last, tries to settle a dispute out of court by some mutual agreement because it is impossible to be sure what judgment the court will make, so ought one, while it is still possible to do so, to take pains that he shall not appear as a defendant before the court of the heavenly judge. It is probable that in this case Luke has preserved the original meaning of the utterance. Frequently, however, it is no longer possible for us to determine just what the original meaning of a statement was. Even the evangelists did not know, but sought each in his own way to apply a traditional word of the Master in some practical fashion to the circumstances that he faced.

We can see with especial clearness in the parables the way

in which the content of tradition was influenced by the interpretation given to it by the evangelists. Adolf Jülicher discussed this in his study of the parabolic utterances of Jesus (see especially the second edition, 1910). The evangelists no longer understand the style of the ancient parables—a style common to both the synoptic and the rabbinical literature—but they regard the parables as allegories that in obscure fashion prophesied the fate of Jesus or of his community. As a matter of fact the parables were originally intended not to conceal ideas, but to make them clear and effective. The evangelists, however, frequently add secondary utterances to the original parables. These additions can occasionally be identified by a comparative study of the gospels themselves. In the parable of the royal feast (Matt. 22:6-7) some of those who were invited attacked and slew the king's servants who invited them to the feast; the king consequently sent his army against them, slew them, and burned their city. This is a very improbable item in the original parable, and the fact that Luke says nothing about it shows that it is an addition of Matthew's. Matthew intends this incident to refer allegorically to the destruction of Jerusalem as a punishment for the death of the prophets and messengers of God. It is only when we free ourselves completely from the interpretation that the evangelists have given to the parable and when we free the parables from secondary additions that we can hope to discover their original meaning. It is true that we are compelled to admit that in many cases we cannot determine the original meaning with any certainty. But in the process of analysis we receive much help by a comparison with the rabbinical parables, which reveal clearly the general method and style of parabolic utterances.

I have taken the parables of Jesus as an example. It is possible, however, in the transmission of other utterances of Jesus to observe similar processes, although in this article I have not space to develop the matter further. I can only call attention to a few instances where the current theological valuation of the person of Jesus influenced the transmission of his utterances. According to Luke 11 : 29-30, when doubters asked a sign from him, Jesus replied that no sign should be given to them but the sign of the prophet Jonah. This means that Jesus, like Jonah, was vindicated by his preaching of repentance. In Matt. 12 : 38-40, however, the utterance has been altered under the influence of the Christian belief in Jesus' death and resurrection, and the sign of the prophet Jonah is interpreted as follows : " As Jonah was three days and three nights in the belly of the whale so shall the Son of Man be three days and three nights in the heart of the earth." Again in Mark 8 : 38 we have an ancient utterance, " Whosoever shall be ashamed of me and of my word in this adulterous and sinful generation, the Son of Man also shall be ashamed of him when he cometh in the glory of his Father with the holy angels." In similar fashion, and perhaps in even earlier form, if we may judge by the parallelism of the phrases, Luke 12 :8-9 (following the *Logia*) reads : " Everyone who shall confess me before men, him shall the Son of Man also confess before the angels of God, but he that denieth me in the presence of men shall be denied in the presence of the angels of God." In both Mark and Luke, Jesus distinguishes himself from the Son of Man who is to come. In the Christian community, however, it was taken for granted that Jesus himself was the Son of Man. Accordingly, in Matt. 10 :32-3 the statement is altered to read : " Everyone, therefore, who shall confess me before men, him will *I* also confess before my Father who is in heaven. But whosoever shall deny me before men, him will I also deny before my Father who is in heaven."

The investigation of the changes that occurred in the transmission of the words of Jesus must be completed by an investigation of the style in which a tradition appears. Here it is possible to distinguish three typical literary forms in the utterances of Jesus, each one of which shows its peculiar characteristics of style. The first form includes the utterances that are usually known as the *Logia*. They might just as correctly be called "wisdom utterances," for they are forms of expression which have their parallels in Oriental wisdom literature. Unlike the Greeks, the Orient expressed its world-view and its appreciation of the significance of human life, not in systematic philosophy, but in the form of short proverbs often marked by crisp expression, pictorial vividness, and poetic beauty. Such "wisdom" is well known in the literature of ancient Egypt as well as in the Old Testament (the Wisdom of Solomon, or the Proverbs); it was also current in Judaism and was much used by the rabbis (Jesus, Sirach, and Sayings of the Fathers or Pirqe Aboth). Among the Arabs also this type of proverbial utterance was well developed. Many of the reported sayings of Jesus belong to this type of "wisdom" —for example, the words concerning laying up treasure (Matt. 6:19-21), or the words concerning anxious care (Matt. 6:25-34), or the utterance: "No man can serve two masters" (Matt. 6:24). Most of these sayings have direct parallels in the rabbinic literature. It is quite possible that Jesus actually uttered this or that proverb in precisely the form in which the synoptic gospels report it. It is also possible that he may have quoted certain proverbial utterances that were current among the people. But we must also reckon with the possibility that the Christian community put into his mouth many impressive statements that really came from the treasure house of Jewish "wisdom." In any case we have in these proverbial utterances no guarantee that they were original sayings of Jesus. They furnish very little information as to the characteristic historical significance of Jesus, since we can discover no essential differences between them and Jewish "wisdom."

Much more important are the precepts of Jesus. These are utterances that are contained in controversial discourses and other *apophthegmata*, but which lack the setting of these. Here belong, for example, the precepts concerning purity and divorce, alms-giving, prayer and fasting, and especially the great antitheses in the fifth chapter of Matthew: "Ye have heard that it was said by them of old . . . but I say unto you." These utterances are largely controversial utterances that arose out of opposition to the prevailing type of Jewish piety. They cannot, then, have been taken over from Judaism. Neither are they creations of the Christian community, at least not in their essential features; for the fact that the Palestinian community failed to understand the critical import of these utterances and to make practical application of them (as is seen in their attitude toward Paul) makes it reasonably certain that here the spirit of Jesus is alive. It is true that we find associated with these utterances others that can be regarded only as regulations for the community, disciplinary rules, and regulations for missionary activity. These last can have originated only in the Christian community itself. This can be made clear in part by a comparative study of the synoptic gospels. For example, it is obvious that the words found in Luke 17:3-4 concerning forgiveness are preserved in a more original form, while in Matt. 18:15-22 they have been transformed into rules for the life of the community.

A third type of sayings of Jesus is found in the prophetic and apocalyptic utterances. The prophetic sayings are those in which Jesus announces the coming of the Kingdom of God. Here belong such varied sayings as the Beatitudes, which stand at the beginning of the Sermon on the Mount, and the words of warning to the unrepentant; the woes addressed to the scribes, and the prophecy of the destruction of the temple. In these utterances also it is possible to detect with some probability genuine words of Jesus, for there can be no doubt that Jesus appeared as prophet and announcer of the coming Kingdom of God. This appears in the picture of the early community, for it lived in the conviction that it was the holy remnant of Israel, the community of the last days divinely called through Jesus. It is true that since there were prophets among the early Christians, some prophetic utterances that we, read in the synoptic gospels may have originated in the Christian community; but these are predominantly apocalyptic utterances, quite in the style of Jewish apocalyptic, furnishing details concerning the future, especially events connected with the " last days." Such apocalyptic utterances were simply taken over bodily from the Jewish apocalyptic tradition and worked over so as to suit Christian ideas. Wellhausen has clearly shown that a little Jewish apocalypse that has been enlarged by Christian tradition forms the basis of Mark 13 :5-27.

In addition to the literary types already discussed we find in the synoptic tradition still others, such as legends and narratives coloured with legendary material. Limitations of space prevent us from considering these here. I may simply call attention to the discussion in my book entitled *Die Geschichte der synoptischen Tradition* (1921), in which all the problems that have been indicated here are discussed at length, and to my little pamphlet, *Die Erforschung der synoptischen Evangelien* (1925), which furnishes an introduction to these problems.[1]

In conclusion we may note briefly the relationship between *formgeschichtliche* investigation and the *religionsgeschichtliche* interpretation of primitive Christianity. We showed earlier in this article how the traditional picture of Jesus has been dissolved, principally by the investigations of Wrede and Wellhausen. *Formgeschichtliche* analysis continues further this process of criticism and comes at first to the negative conclusion that the outline of the gospels does not enable us to know either the outer course of the life of Jesus or his inner development. We must frankly confess that the character of Jesus as a human personality cannot be recovered by us. We can neither write a " life of Jesus " nor present an accurate picture of his personality. Even in regard to the question of his messianic consciousness we seem compelled to admit ignorance. Since the words of Jesus in the oldest tradition mention the " Son of Man " only in the third person, it seems to me probable that Jesus distinguished himself from the Son of Man, and therefore did not regard himself as the Messiah. This complicated question, however, should receive much more detailed treatment than can be given in this article.

The outcome of *formgeschichtliche* investigation, however, is not merely negative. When critical analysis has been carried through and the different strata of tradition have been isolated; when, further, we keep in mind the fundamental principle that the first undertaking is to obtain a clear picture of the primitive community, then we may inquire concerning the more important matter, viz., the preaching of Jesus. On the basis of the three typical forms in which utterances of Jesus appear we can form three pictures of the preaching of Jesus : Jesus as a teacher of wisdom, Jesus as a lawgiver, and Jesus as a prophet. If we leave out of account the first picture as being the least probable, the fundamental problem as to the nature of the preaching of Jesus may be formulated as follows : How are the ethical and the eschatological utterances related to each other? Do they belong to one single picture or, as many investigators think, do they stand in such contrast that we must choose between them when we seek to know what the historical Jesus taught? Was Jesus a lawgiver, or was he a prophet? It is my conviction that these questions must be asked seriously; but I also believe that the answer must be : He was both; the ethical and eschatological utterances belong in a larger unity. I cannot here give the reasons for my conviction. I can only indicate the complicated nature of the *religionsgeschichtliche* questions by citing a particular instance. I have several times alluded to the fact that when we have isolated the various strata of tradition the question arises whether a given narrative originated in the Palestinian community or in the Hellenistic. The importance of this distinction was made clear by W. Bousset in his *Kyrios Christos* (second edition, 1921). He showed that primitive Palestinian Christianity was very different from Hellenistic Christianity. The former remained within the limits of Judaism and regarded itself as the true Israel; its piety was eschatological and it awaited Jesus as the coming Son of Man. Primitive Hellenistic Christianity, on the other hand, was a religion of cult, in the centre of which stood Jesus Christ as the " Lord " who communicated his heavenly powers in the worship and the sacraments of the community. It goes without saying that the recognition of this difference is of great importance in the analysis of the synoptic tradition. It means that the elements of cult-religion contained in the synoptic gospels are secondary, coming from Hellenistic sources.

Recent investigations and discoveries, however, have made it questionable whether primitive Palestinian Christianity can be regarded as a definite unity. It has been suggested that we must distinguish here two developments or two historical motives. The researches of the philologist Richard Reitzenstein have led to the probable conclusion that already in certain circles of Judaism there were stronger influences than had hitherto been supposed of Oriental, Iranian-Babylonian redemptionist religion and speculation, such as we find later in Gnosticism. This type of religion spread among groups of apocalyptists and in small sects that practised various rituals, particularly baptism. Such a sect within Judaism seem to have been the Essenes, about whom, unfortunately, we know very little. It is quite probable that John the Baptist and the sects bearing his name should be classed here. On this point new material of a surprising nature has recently come to light, although there is as yet no agreement as to the exact significance of the discovery. The Orientalist Mark Lidzbarski, who edited and translated the writings of the Gnostic sect of the Mandaeans, has given weighty reasons for the conjecture that these Mandaeans, who were formerly believed to have had their rise in Babylonia, really originated by the Jordan River, and that they were nothing other than the sect of John the Baptist. The sect, of course, later underwent a development in doctrine and practice. Characteristics of this sect were the ritual of baptism and certain remarkable cosmological and eschatological speculations. The Mandaeans also called themselves Nasoreans, meaning probably " Observers." It is to be noted that in Christian tradition Jesus also was frequently described by the title " the Nasorean," a word that cannot be etymologically derived from Nazareth, his actual or alleged home. Probably he was called Nasorean because he originally belonged to the sect of John the Baptist. The evangelical tradition preserves the memory of this in the statement that Jesus permitted himself to be baptized by John. In addition to this the earliest Christian tradition reveals a peculiar relationship to John the Baptist. The followers of Jesus and those of John the Baptist stood together in opposition to orthodox Judaism, but in relation to each other they were rivals. This is especially clear in the Fourth Gospel, but traces of it are retained also in the synoptic tradition. It seems probable, then, that Jesus and his community must be regarded as an offshoot from the community of John the Baptist. If this is true we must reckon with the possibility that the preaching of Jesus and of his first followers was perhaps more strongly influenced by Oriental-syncretistic conceptions than would be indicated by the later tradition, and that possibly eschatology played a much greater part in that early preaching than in later tradition. Here, however, most of the details are still quite uncertain. What has here been said is primarily to indicate some of the important problems that lie as yet unsolved before us.

FAITH AS VENTURE*

With considerable justice, it seems to me, the editor of this journal[1] has recently warned against misuse of the expression "venture of faith," insofar as what is meant by it is that one "risks" and if possible "drudges" to believe.[2] Such a venture of faith would clearly be a blind and risky groping in the dark. And even if faith can in some sense be spoken of as a "leap in the dark," still it is impossible to understand it as when, say, I stand at a crossroads and, lacking a signpost, venture to strike out in a certain direction and thus risk arriving at my goal or missing it.

Such talk of the venture of faith, Rade rightly thinks, contradicts Christian faith's peculiar certainty. Therefore, talk of faith as venture is legitimate only when what is meant by it is that faith "ventures *something.*" "Not to venture *faith itself,* but to venture *in* faith."

It seems to me that there is something very right being said here. But it also seems to me that underlying this particular formulation is the same misunderstanding that underlies the other way of talking. For if I venture something in faith, do I not at the same time venture faith itself? Do I not at the same time and for the first time venture to believe? Do I not place faith itself at stake? If I really venture in faith "to say to the mountain, 'Move hence to yonder place,'" what happens when the venture fails? Does not faith then also fail? Perhaps not—but note, *perhaps* not! For in any case, when I venture *in* faith I also venture *faith itself.*

For this reason, this antithesis seems to me to be false. To

* "*Der Glaube als Wagnis,*" *Die Christliche Welt,* xlii (1928), 1008-10.

be sure, it rightly wants to remind us that one cannot have an abstract faith in general and that the illusion that one has to "take the risk of faith" does not even know what faith means. For faith does not mean to accept the proclamation of God's forgiving love and to be convinced of its truth in general, but rather to regulate one's life by it. However, this does not mean to possess this conviction alongside of others as the most valuable and most important and occasionally or even frequently to reflect on it and to take comfort from it; rather it means to let my concrete now be determined by the proclamation and faith in it. If the proclamation of God's forgiving love is really valid for *me,* i.e., for me in my concrete life situation, then it is not at all understandable apart from that situation. And I am not to believe *in general*—*also* to believe *alongside of* or *behind* my other relationships—but rather am to believe *here and now* as one who has something to do (or to endure) and who is to do this thing in faith—who is *to venture what he does in faith and venture his faith in what he does.*

It is possible for me to hear the word of proclamation in a service of worship and in that situation to have nothing to do or to endure except to hear. It is perhaps possible that the word so strikes me that I submit to it in faith, that I venture to believe it. However, this faith would not be genuine if the everyday affairs in which I once again shortly find myself and for which the word is spoken do not appear in its light. If I do not allow my concrete present to be qualified by the word that is spoken to me, then I have not really believed it for all of my hearing. Only when I now actually understand myself and my situation in terms of the word, only when I now see or venture to see my neighbour in the other person who encounters me, only then have I believed and do I believe now.

Therefore, it is certainly right to contend against the view that one might venture faith itself without venturing something in faith, that there might be a venture *of* faith that was not at the same time a venture *in* faith.

But it must be said just as definitely that there is no venture *in* faith that is not simultaneously a venture *of* faith. For otherwise one would come out with exactly as abstract and general a faith as before. What would it mean to say that I might venture something in faith if I did not in so doing venture to believe? It would mean that here, too, faith was understood as a conviction or a state of feeling that lies *behind* my actual life instead of being at work *in* it. It would mean that faith was thought of as a possession of my " inner life " at which I could look and from which I could then look away to my " tasks and duties, exigencies and temptations." No, I " have " faith only when I have it ever anew *in* my duties and exigencies.

"Fear not, simply believe!"—this should not be taken to mean, " At last, venture to begin believing," but rather, " Venture to continue believing." Fine! But how is a " continuation " in faith possible, except that faith is laid hold of ever anew?—" Put the faith *that you have* to the test!" Fine! But how is this " having " of faith constituted? Can one " have " faith and then over and above this put it to the test? Or is it rather that one only " has " it insofar as he constantly puts it to the test—or, better, insofar as it is constantly tested? One does not " have " a friendship or a love except as something that is daily new. This " having " is quite a different thing from having money and goods or having convictions and feelings.

To be sure, there is an alternation in my looking. But this does not take place between my faith and my duties and exigencies, but rather between these duties and exigencies and that *in which* I have faith, namely, God and his word. Faith is certain of itself only in looking to its *object,* which is also its *source*; in looking at itself it is always uncertain. Thus faith is a " leap in the dark " because man would fain find security by looking at himself and yet must precisely let himself go in order to see the object of faith; and just this is a

E.F.   C "leap in the dark" for the natural man. But this does not mean any blind risk, any game of chance, any mere random groping, but rather a knowing venture. For man is not asked whether he will accept a theory about God that may possibly be false, but whether he is willing to obey God's will.

THE CONCEPT OF REVELATION
IN THE NEW TESTAMENT*

I. CLARIFICATION OF THE QUESTION THROUGH AN INQUIRY
INTO THE GUIDING PREUNDERSTANDING OF REVELATION

1. Provisional Definition of the Concept of Revelation and Its Differentiations. The question we are concerned to ask is what the New Testament understands by revelation. This question, however, is not the linguistic or philological question how a certain word that is not understood—ἀποκάλυψις, say—is to be translated (as though this word were simply an *x*). On the contrary, we stand in a tradition in which the translation of ἀποκάλυψις by " revelation " is already taken for granted. Therefore, we have already presupposed that the New Testament speaks of something such as we ourselves mean when we speak of " revelation." But because this is so, our question is evidently guided by a certain understanding of the concept of revelation. Therefore, it is necessary, first, to clarify this understanding that is already presupposed so that it will become completely clear what we are really asking; for only a clear question will hear a clear answer. If one were to ask, for example, what the New Testament understands by marriage or the state, then some understanding of marriage and the state also would thereby be presupposed—i.e., an understanding that would guide the question and apart from which it could not be asked. Thus what the New Testament understands by revelation can only be asked if we ourselves have some idea of what we understand by it—if we already have a concept of revelation.

And we actually have such a concept. In general, we under-

* *Der Begriff der Offenbarung im Neuen Testament* (Tübingen: J. C. B. Mohr, 1929).

stand by revelation *the disclosure of what is veiled, the opening up of what is hidden*—and, to be sure, in a sense that is differentiated in two ways: (1) Revelation is the *communication of knowledge by the word,* i.e., it is information through which we become acquainted with something that we were previously unacquainted with so that henceforth it is known. In this sense, instruction, for example, can mediate revelation; and we say that a book or a lecture or a conversation was a "revelation" to us, that it has "opened our eyes," etc. (2) Revelation is *an occurrence that puts me in a new situation as a self,* in which, to be sure, there is also given the possibility of knowledge (namely, about myself in my new situation), but without regard for whether or not this knowledge becomes explicit. In a crime, for example, there is "revealed" to me the abyss of man's nature; and in the death of a friend there is "revealed" to me something of what dying means. Through an experience my "eyes are opened" about myself— say, about my weakness or my unscrupulousness. One person "reveals" himself to another through an act of friendship or love and also through an act of hate or meanness. And, indeed, if in such cases the revelation is given by a word, this word has the character of an occurrence and is not merely a mediating and informing communication about some state of affairs. Rather the revealing word is itself the state of affairs or at least belongs indissolubly to it.

In the area of life that we designate (unclearly, to be sure, but in the present context adequately enough) with the title "religion," we speak of "revelation" in a more specific sense, but also with this same twofold differentiation. Here revelation means *that opening up of what is hidden which is absolutely necessary and decisive for man if he is to achieve "salvation" or authenticity*; i.e., revelation here is the disclosure of *God* to man—whether this disclosure is thought to take place through the communication of knowledge, through a mediating doctrine about God, or whether it is an occurrence that puts man in a new situation. All religions speak of re

velation in either the former or the latter sense.[1] And, to be
sure, what they thereby presuppose is that man cannot achieve
his authenticity by his own resources, that what is disclosed
in revelation is inaccessible to him simply as man. Therefore,
wherever " revelation " is spoken of in this sense there is
betrayed an understanding of human existence that knows of
man's limitation and wants to break through it. The question
to be put to the New Testament, then, is which of these two
views—that revelation is the communication of knowledge or
that it is an occurrence that puts man in a new situation—
determines its idea of revelation and wherein it sees man's
limitation and the overcoming of this limitation which takes
place through revelation.

2. The Motive of the Question and the Character of the
Answer That May Be Expected. Before we proceed to raise
this question, however, there is yet another preliminary question that must be asked for the sake of further clarification :
Why do we want to know what the New Testament understands by revelation? Our question concerning the New Testament's understanding is only meaningful if, in spite of our
preknowledge of revelation's meaning, we still do not know it
really and definitely. If we had a definitive knowledge of it,
then the question what idea the New Testament has about it
would be a mere hobby, and the inquiry itself, an interesting
article for an illustrated weekly or a Sunday supplement. In
fact, the question what other people once thought about revelation, asked in the consciousness that one himself already
knows what revelation is, is like the interest with which one
visits an exhibition of old locomotives; and the New Testament then becomes a room in the museum which people who
are interested call " history." Just as the visit to an exhibition
of locomotives can instruct us concerning progress in loco-
motive construction and can make understandable how the
trains in which we travel today have come to be, so can the
consideration of different concepts of revelation in " history "

exhibit the progress in ideas of revelation and explain why we today have precisely this or that idea of what revelation means. In this case, however, we are spectators—spectators even of ourselves, for whom our own concept of revelation also is an interesting historical phenomenon.

Why, then, do we ask if we already know what the concept of revelation means and if the only thing that can encounter us in the New Testament is one of the possible differentiations of this concept expressed with somewhat greater clarity? And yet, as we have seen, we cannot ask at all without having such a concept, any more than Meno could ask concerning the concept of virtue without already knowing in a certain sense what virtue is.

But perhaps we are also like Meno in that our preliminary knowledge of revelation is only a very vague knowledge, that it is a peculiarly not-knowing knowledge. That this is in fact the case is evident, first of all, because the two possibilities for understanding revelation—either as a communication of knowledge or as an occurrence that happens to us—cannot possibly be options that we can choose between as we please. If revelation is to bring us to our authenticity, then it must be one or the other of the two possibilities; and one of the two understandings must be false, must be a misunderstanding. Therefore, we clearly make inquiry of the New Testament (provided, of course, that we do not do it simply in order to classify its opinions in a scheme of concepts that we have already prepared) in the expectation that this question concerning the correct understanding of revelation may possibly be clarified.

But how is this to be done? In what sense can an answer be expected that says more than that, in the New Testament, revelation is not understood as the communication of knowledge, but rather as an occurrence that happens to me—or vice versa? Will the New Testament tell us simply and unambiguously what revelation is? In any case, any answer that may possibly be given in the New Testament must radicalize the preunderstanding of revelation that guides the question and, in so doing, lead one nearer to the decision as to which understanding is correct. How any answer of the New Testament is able to do this must be clarified further by elucidating the character of this preunderstanding.

We have said that I already know about revelation, yet without really knowing what it is. This is not to be interpreted, of course, as meaning that I know a *concept* of revelation, but do not know what revelation *itself* is. To divorce in this way knowledge of a concept of revelation and knowledge of revelation itself would be just as false as to separate knowledge of a concept of friendship and knowledge of friendship. If I do not know friendship *itself,* then I also can never understand the *concept* of friendship. For the origin of concepts is not isolated thinking in and by itself, but rather the actual life to which thinking belongs. To have a concept of revelation means nothing other than to know about revelation itself; just as one can only have a concept of light and life if he knows what light and life actually are.

But, to be sure, I can know what light and life are even when it is dark and I do not see anything. Even the blind man knows what light is.[2] And I can know what love and friendship are even if I have not found love and have not met any friend. Thus I know what revelation is without having found revelation—and yet I do not *really* know it. For the blind man also only really knows what light is when he sees, and the person who is friendless and unloved only really knows what friendship and love are when he finds a friend and is given love.

The reason, however, that we know about light and seeing and about friendship and love even when we do not have them is that they belong to our life and that we have a knowledge of our life—whether explicitly or not. We know about them because we know about what we have and what we are lacking, i.e., what we are dependent upon. *We know about revelation because it belongs to our life.* You cannot communicate a concept of revelation to someone in the way in which you can communicate to him that there are species of fish that bear their young alive or that there are carnivorous plants. There is no revelation in this sense. Rather if you speak to someone of revelation, you speak to him about his authentic life, in the conviction that revelation belongs to this life, just as do light and darkness and love and friendship.[3] Thus it is in this sense alone that a question addressed to the New Testament can be a genuine question, i.e., if it expects that from this source the questioner will hear something about himself—or, better, something that is said *to* himself.

This will become still clearer, however, if the other question that is to be directed to the New Testament is also considered somewhat more exactly—the question, namely, wherein it sees man's limitation. We have said that revelation and therefore the knowledge of revelation belongs to man's life. But how does revelation belong to his life? To know about revelation means to know ourselves as those who are dependent on revelation. For, as we have seen, the meaning of revelation consists in its being the means whereby we achieve our authenticity, which we cannot achieve by our own resources. Therefore, to know about revelation means to know about our own authenticity—and, at the same time, thereby to know of our limitation.

But to know about limitation means something different from knowing, say, about the boundaries of Persia and Afghanistan. It is not a mere perceptual knowledge about something that we just happen to light upon; rather our limitation is something that can only be experienced and laid hold of by actually living. And the knowledge of our limitation is not a certain knowledge that can be preserved in a proposition, but rather is a thoroughly uncertain knowledge against which we constantly rebel, which we constantly ignore and dismiss from our minds. It must always be brought to consciousness anew, always acquired anew, and always preserved only by resolve. Since our life is not something that we light upon and behold, but rather is something that we are ourselves, to know about our limitation is not to have perceived and established that such and such is the case. Rather such knowledge always has the character of affirmation or denial. Therefore, this knowledge is also never indifferent to us in the way in which the knowledge about the coiffure of Greek women of the Periclean Age generally can be indifferent; rather it is a knowledge that we must have even when we do not want it and, indeed, even when we conceal it from ourselves. For our life is motivated by the fact of its limitation; we carry our death around with us. But just because this is so, the question concerning revelation also qualifies our life; for it arises in connection with our limitation. And as we can affirm or deny or conceal the latter, so also can we affirm or deny or conceal the question concerning revelation.

Thus every man knows what is at issue when we speak of revelation; and yet he does not know it either, because he can only know of it as he knows of himself and his limitation and thus always only anew and differently. Therefore, if we are able to ask concerning the concept of revelation in the New Testament only on the basis of a knowledge of our own limitation, we do not ask on the basis of a certain knowledge that we possess, but on the basis of a peculiarly not-knowing knowledge.

Therefore, one also cannot expect the *answer* of the New Testament to be an opinion that one merely lights upon and can then proceed to classify in a previously prepared scheme of all the possible ideas about man's limitation. Rather, as we have seen, the question is only genuine when the questioner is willing to let the understanding of his limitation that, so to speak, hovers before him be radicalized. But the answer also cannot consist simply in a statement of where man's limits lie, so that one henceforth knows the right information; rather what is said about limitation—directly or indirectly—can only be understood if one is himself motivated by the question of his limitation and can only be affirmed or denied in resolve.

Accordingly, therefore, also the answer to the question how revelation is understood in the New Testament cannot be understood as a simple communication, but only as a _personal address_. The question concerning revelation is simultaneously the question concerning man's limitation; and an answer to the question, What is revelation? can only be perceived if the questioner is prepared to let his limitation be disclosed.

Now this does not mean, naturally, that there could not also be in the New Testament simple, direct statements about man's limitation and revelation that could be reproduced in a descriptive presentation. What must be kept in mind, however, is that an actual understanding of such statements is not possible if they are taken as simple communications and an original understanding of them on the basis of the self-understanding that they express is not carried out. For unless such an original understanding is realized, the interpretation remains bound to be the preunderstanding that the reader brings with him; the reader uncritically holds fast to his preunderstanding and characteristically supposes that he has to make a " value judgment " about what he is able to establish as the New Testament's understanding. Without a preunderstanding no one can ever understand what is said anywhere in literature about love or friendship, or life and death—or, in short, about man generally. The only difference is whether one naïvely and uncritically holds fast to his preunderstanding and its particular expression—in which case the interpretation remains entirely subjective—or rather explicitly and implicitly puts his preunderstanding in question, either out of instinct or out of the clear knowledge that man's understanding of himself is never closed, but rather must always be laid hold of anew in resolve. Only in this latter case does the interpretation achieve objectivity.

If the question is raised whether an interpretation of historical documents in which _resolve_ finally provides the basis for understanding is " scientific," then it must be replied that since such an understanding is the only appropriate one, it alone is scientific. For the science of history does not have to do with nature, which simply lies before us and whose objects can be grasped merely by looking at them, but rather has to do precisely with history, which can only be understood as such by one who participates in it and who also knows that interpretation itself must be a historical occurrence. And even as historical documents themselves cannot be understood from some unmotivated " superhistorical " standpoint, but only by a man who exists in history and is motivated by the question concerning his existence (i.e., who knows with that not-knowing knowledge of which we have been speaking), so also is it impossible for a historical presentation such as this simply to exhibit historical phenomena in an unambiguous way. Such a presentation can only help clarify the preunderstanding that is necessary for grasping the phenomena themselves. Therefore, in our case, it can show whoever asks about the concept of revelation in the New Testament what he is really asking about and thus guide him to hear the New Testament itself.

II CLARIFICATION OF THE QUESTION THROUGH A SURVEY OF THE UNDERSTANDINGS OF REVELATION IN THE TRADITION

Our question concerning the concept of revelation is guided by a not-knowing knowledge. That this knowledge really is a not-knowing knowledge, however, is obscured because it is always present in a specific expression or interpretation and actually reaches the individual in such a conceptually interpreted form. Thus it is necessary for him to break through this traditional interpretation to an original understanding of himself, i.e., of his question; and the discussion with the tradition, which ultimately can only have its bases in an original understanding of the subject matter itself, will be explicitly carried out in various ways. This criticism of the traditional conceptuality is the task both of philosophy and of the science of history. It is the task of history, insofar as the latter shows that we are dependent upon some specific understanding of human existence for our understanding of the concepts that we use every day. If we ask concerning the concept of revelation in the New Testament, then we are guided not only by a preunderstanding of revelation which belongs to our life, but also by a tradition that presents us with some specific interpretation of this preunderstanding, as well as of our existence generally. Therefore, the criticism of this tradition is the second route that we must travel in order to arrive at clarity in raising our question. And, to be sure, this route really ought to proceed from the present to the past; and it is only for the sake of brevity if we here reverse this order and, in what follows, attempt to give a concise survey of the ideas of revelation from medieval Catholicism to the present.

In the main ecclesiastical tradition, the concept of revelation is determined by the question of the relation of revelation and reason. The knowledge that in one way or another is given in revelation is thought of as analogous to rational knowledge. This is shown in *Catholicism,* where the relation is so defined that the knowledge of reason is supplemented and surpassed by the knowledge of revelation. Up to a certain level—in the *præambula fidei* of Thomas—both kinds of knowledge coincide. Indeed, this same understanding is also evident in the doctrine of twofold truth, where the knowledge of reason and the knowledge of revelation are set over against one another. In either case, the generic concept is the concept of knowledge; and reason and revelation are thought of as two different levels or ways of communicating knowledge. The supernaturalness of revelation (or its character as something that comes from the " beyond ") consists in the supernatural arrangement through which the communication of revealed knowledge takes place. What is revealed is for natural reason a mystery that is not yet known. Once it becomes known, however, the " not yet " is ended, and the knowledge of revelation is like any other kind of knowledge; it is possessed and preserved and can be passed on. Its supernaturalness is entirely limited to its origin, which, as soon as one has the knowledge, belongs to the past. Thus it is clear that, while in this view revelation is indeed understood to mean something that goes beyond the limits of the human, man's limitation itself is seen to lie in the limitation of what he can know. And this is so, to be sure, because, under the influence of the tradition of Greek antiquity, the being of man itself is so understood that he is thought to achieve his highest possibility in contemplative knowledge, in θεωρία. Blessedness consists in the *visio Dei*. Hence, revelation is understood as the communication of knowledge or of doctrine, wherewith God himself is assumed to be a particular being that can be the object of knowing. This is clearly shown by the proofs for his existence.

Much the same situation also obtains in *Protestant orthodoxy*. To be sure, the tendency to see man's highest possibility in knowing is here broken; and faith does not mean the acceptance of doctrines, but rather *fiducia* in the word of the forgiveness of sins. Nevertheless, the concept of revelation is not developed theologically in terms of this basic understanding, but rather remains under the domination of the tradition in being determined by the concept of knowledge; and revelation continues to be thought of as a supernatural arrangement for communicating doctrine. Therefore, here also the revelatory character of revealed knowledge is given, on the one hand, by its difference from the knowledge of reason and, on the other hand, by its supernatural origin.

In the age, then, in which reason became self-conscious— namely, in *the period of rationalism*—it no longer acknowledged the limit that was placed on it by such a view; i.e., it saw that man's real limitation does not lie in what he can know. And it is understandable that, after this had formerly been asserted to be his real limit and was now denied to be so, one at first no longer knew of *any* human limitation. Thus the concept of revelation either had to become superfluous or else lost its real meaning. If one spoke of revelation from the point of view of a consistent rationalism, he spoke of " natural revelation "—or, in other words, of a self-contradiction; for revelation can only be spoken of as supernatural.

The situation was not basically different, however, in the ensuing speculations of *idealism and romanticism.* According to such positions, "revelation" is not to be viewed, as in vulgar rationalism, as objectively present in the world and perceptible to rational knowledge, but rather means "the emergence into consciousness of the omnipresent and eternal basis of all phenomena, the recognition of something that was always true, the perception of a divine presence that could have been perceived before, since it was always there"; or "the becoming visible through phenomena of their omnipresent divine source."[4] One can say that here the character of revelation as something that comes from the "beyond" is maintained, inasmuch as it is recognized that man as he actually is is not authentic and that empirical facts as such cannot be revelation, but only the "Spirit" that attests itself in them. But man becomes aware of this Spirit when he reflects on *himself* as spirit and thereby finds the *"deus in nobis,"* i.e., when he flees from his concrete existence in time to his supertemporal essence. Thus man remains within himself; and he speculates about the identity of being and consciousness in order again to find himself even when he tries to get beyond himself.

Then, when man once again recognized that his life does not rest on reason, even if reason is understood as "spirit," and when he again understood his life as a riddle and thus became aware of his limitation, he once more appeared to acquire a real concept of revelation. And it is understandable if, in opposition to rationalism, revelation was defined as "the irrational." For this much, as least, is clearly correct in such a definition : *ratio* by itself cannot say anything about man's limits and what lies beyond them. Nevertheless, it is also false to identify the irrational with revelation and to imagine that when one speaks of the former he is speaking about God. Insofar as the "irrational" is not a purely formal, and thus also rational concept, but rather is intended to denote the actual riddle of human existence, it designates nothing more than precisely this characteristic riddle. Therefore, to hold that knowledge of this riddle is knowledge of God is to confuse God with the devil. But, of course, precisely in speaking of man's limitation, the possibility is once again given of speaking of revelation. However, it is just the knowledge of limitation, of the negative, of what man does *not* have that must remain determinative for the concept of the irrational; and " not having " may not suddenly (say, through the courtesy of the psychology of religion) be interpreted as " having." If I recognize that I stand in the midst of the irrational, then I can indeed once again meaningfully ask for revelation; but I ruin everything if I imagine that I have revelation in the irrational itself.

Nor is it otherwise if one attempts to supplement the thought of the irrational by " feelings " that, in face of the riddle of existence, can lay hold of man and convulse him: the feelings of creatureliness, of the numinous, etc. Even in the numinous, man does not become aware of God, but only of himself. And he is deceived if he interprets the numinous as the divine, even when his frightful shuddering is a blessed experience. For then he always asks only about himself and not really about something that lies beyond him. Indeed, what is finally behind such a view is nothing other than the romanticism that identifies the irrational with creativity, and whose concept of creativity is patterned after artistic creation. In the creative work of the artist, which appears to be distinguished from conscious shaping by reason and will, man imagines that he is lifted above the limits within which he moves in knowing and willing. The feeling of creativity seems to be revelation.

This concept of revelation is trivialized in the *liberalism* that combines rationalistic, idealistic, and romantic motives and thereby abolishes the idea that was decisive for romanticism, viz., that revelation is experienced in the moment of creative activity. It imagines rather that it can discover and observe creativity as something simply given in the world and in history. Thus man and humanity simply as such are taken to be creative; and what one can perceive in moral achievements and the phenomena of culture has the value of revelation. The movement of history from " darkness " to " light " is revelation; and the " personality " with its irrational powers is also revelation. Indeed, *everything* is revelation! Of course, in the long run, the genuine motive of the question of revelation will not let itself be silenced. There remains the dim awareness that revelation must be something that breaks through the limits of the human and cannot be commonly evident. And so—to be sure, with great diffidence—it is " experience " that presently comes to be named revelation—experience " understood as the perception of everything good, true, and beautiful, the experience in which one is extricated from the commonplace and, so it seems, also from his own limits, and senses himself in the stream of a larger, divine life.

In all of these attempts to say what revelation is, the thought is maintained—even where it is distorted into meaninglessness—that it is by means of revelation that man comes to his authenticity, in which he does not simply find himself and on which he must at least reflect if it is to be achieved. It is affirmed that man understands his existence as limited, i.e., as qualified by limitation, and that being limited is something that terrifies him and makes him anxious and places his existence in question. And what is everywhere said, in one way or another, in speaking of revelation is that this limitation is provisional, that the limits can be broken through.

For the rest, the various views of revelation are distinguished from one another according to the way man understands himself, i.e., wherein he sees the highest possibility of his being, through the realization of which he achieves his authenticity. Is man's real limitation that what he can know is always limited, that his knowledge needs to be supplemented? Perhaps so. But are not the limits of knowledge always being pushed farther back by man himself? Or is the real limitation of man his individuality, the being caught in his own wishes and plans and being bound to the horizon of his own ego? Perhaps so. But are not these limits also always being pushed back by man himself? Can he not devote himself to the good, the true, and the beautiful? Does not his will, his sense of duty, grow and develop in the communities in which he stands? And does he not learn to despise himself and others who do not acknowledge the claim of *humanitas*? Is he not here his own judge? Or is his limitation rather that of experience, that his life generally passes in a commonplace way without any great " experiences "? Perhaps so. But are not these limits also expanded by man? And, on the other hand, do not all experiences take place *within* man's limits? Is it not *he* who shudders and shouts for joy, who laughs and cries? And does not one who radically asks about his limitation and about what breaks through it want to be free precisely from himself?

In a corresponding way, there is also a difference between the various views in what they see as the content of revelation. Is revelation knowledge and doctrine? Perhaps so, perhaps one also receives something to know in revelation. But such knowledge must surely be a different knowledge than consists in doctrines, which one can accept and preserve, and which only acquire the character of revelation because of the remarkable way in which they have come into one's possession. Indeed, must it not be a knowledge that, just *when* I know it, *is* revelation and puts an end to my limitation and makes God present to me? Or is the content of revelation in moral achievement and the creation of culture? Perhaps so, perhaps this, too, has its basis in revelation. But in contemplating moral action and culture, we really only discover ourselves or, at best, an image of what we ought to be and can be. Or is the content of revelation to be found in " experiences "? Perhaps so, perhaps there *is* an experience in revelation. But if we look at our experiences, what really is revealed in them? Is it only the moment of ecstasy or of shuddering, so that in

the next moment we are the old persons that we were before—
so that revelation, once it is past, belongs to the inventory of
human existence, which shortly has no more interest for us?
Or is the content of revelation not the experience itself, but
rather what is revealed in the experience? But what then is
this? Is it the "numinous"? Indeed, there *is* something revealed in our experience here, but it is nothing other than the
riddle of our own existence, the uncanny fact of our limitation. And do we not conceal precisely what is revealed here
when we interpret this fascinating uncanniness as God?

III. THE CONCEPT OF REVELATION IN THE NEW TESTAMENT

1. *The "What" of Revelation: Life and Christ.* If we ask
now about the concept of revelation in the New Testament,
then we must ask, first of all, how man's limitation is understood there. And the answer is simple : *man is limited by
death,* the last and the real enemy (I Cor. 15 :26). And, by
the same token, the further answer is also simple : *revelation
gives life.* " For what does it profit a man to gain the whole
world and forfeit his life? For what can a man give in return
for his life?" (Mark 8 :36 f.). "Wretched man that I am!
Who will deliver me from this body of death?" (Rom. 7 :24).

To reach salvation means " to enter life " (Mark 9 :43, 9 :
45, etc.) or " to inherit life " (Mark 10 :17, etc.) The right way
is the way that " leads to life " (Matt. 7 :14). And that life
has been revealed is just what the Christian message proclaims : " And the life was made manifest, and we saw it, and
testify to it, and proclaim to you the eternal life that was with
the Father and was made manifest to us " (I John 1 :2). The
preaching of the Christian community is " the word of life "
(Phil. 2 :16) or " the word of this life " (Acts 5 :20); it goes
forth " in hope of eternal life" (Titus 1 :2, cf. 3 :7). One
does repentance unto life (Acts 11 :18), one believes " for
eternal life " (I Tim. 1 :16), and one is called to life (I Tim.

6 :12). For God is the One who raises the dead (II Cor. 1 :9; Rom. 4 :17), and Christ Jesus, the one " who abolished death and brought life and immortality to light " (II Tim. 1.10); he is the one who leads to life (Acts 3 :15). He is the bread of life, the light of life, the resurrection and the life; whoever believes in him and follows him has life (John 6 :48, 8 :12, 11 :25, 14 :6, 3 :15 f., etc.). As through Adam death came into the world, so through Christ life has come (Rom. 5 :12-21). Once the end of all our working was death, now it is life (Rom. 6 :21-3, cf. 7 :7-8 :2; Gal. 6 :8). If in this life only we have hoped in Christ, we are of all men most to be pitied (I Cor. 15 :19); but thanks be to God, who gives us the victory through our Lord Jesus Christ, so that we can say : " Death is swallowed up in victory! O death, where is thy victory? O death, where is thy sting?" (I Cor. 15 :55, 15 :57). The either/or that preaching poses is death or life (II Cor. 2 :16, 3 :6).

Death, therefore, is plainly looked upon as constituting the limit of man's existence and, to be sure, not simply in the sense that with it life comes to an end, but rather in the sense that it constitutes a disturbance of the whole of life. If it really is final, then life as a whole is meaningless (I Cor. 15 :32). Man rebels against death and knows that as one who is fallen under it he is not in his authenticity. But he does not have the possibility through his own resources of becoming lord over it. Thus death is not a problem in the sense that—as in Stoicism, say—it might be shown that it really does not concern us and that we, therefore, can become lord over it through an inner attitude and acquire an ideal immortality in tranquillity of soul. On the contrary, death *does* concern us, and we *cannot* become lord of it. Therefore, it also is not the case that what is revealed is an *idea* of life to which one can relate himself through knowledge; nor is such a knowing relation to dominate the whole of one's life. Rather what can be called revelation can only be what actually abolishes death. For what else could it be? Could it be a remarkable knowledge about God and the world? Of what help to me is all that I know in face of death? Could it be moral achievement and the creation of culture? All this is subject to death, just as I am myself, first of all. Could it be "experiences"? They do not save me from death. The "numinous," then? Indeed, what is that but death itself? No, revelation can only be the gift of life through which death is overcome.

It is this meaning of revelation which must indeed be understood. But the New Testament not only says *what* revelation is, it also says *that* it is. Revelation is an *occurrence* that abolishes death, not a doctrine that death does not exist.[5] But it is not an occurrence *within* human life, but rather one that *breaks in upon it from outside* and therefore cannot be demonstrated within life itself. "Eternal life" is not a phenomenon of this life; it consists neither in immortality—Christians die like everyone else—nor in spirituality or inwardness. It is to be perceived neither with the eyes nor with the mind or feelings. One can only believe in it. It will be attested in the resurrection of the dead; therefore, it is future and one only has it in hope. But is it thought of as a future phenomenon within the world, so that it would be the fulfilment of man's natural longing to hold on to himself as he already is? Is it simply the prolongation of what is called "life" now? Manifestly not; for in a certain sense it is already present. It is already a reality through the resurrection of Christ by which death is vanquished. In a certain sense the faithful have already died and have thereby been made alive. "For you have died, and your life is hid with Christ in God" (Col. 3:2). "If anyone is in Christ, he is a new creation; the old has passed away, behold, the new has come" (II Cor. 5:17). And the Johannine Jesus can say: "I am the resurrection and the life; he who believes in me, though he die, yet shall he live, and whoever lives and believes in me shall never die" (John 11:25 f.).

But is what has been said correct? Is not the new life

actually revealed in a specific way? Do we not have the first
fruits or the guarantee of the Spirit (Rom. 8 :23; II Cor.
1 :22, 5 :5)? Does he not teach us to cry " Father " (Rom.
8 :16) and to pray (Rom. 8 :26 f.)? And are not the gifts of
the Spirit at work in the congregation (I Cor. 12)? Is there
not a new knowledge that searches the depths of God (I Cor.
2 :10-16) and that can judge what is good and evil (Rom.
12 :2; Phil. 1 :9 f.)? And is there not the fruit of the Spirit
in moral action (Gal. 5 :22 f.)?

Certainly; but all such signs and miracles, such strange
workings of the Spirit, are just as ambiguous as were Jesus'
own miracles, which drew down on him the charge of being in
league with the devil (Mark 3 :22). For the anti-Christ also
works with deceptive demonstrations of power and with signs
and wonders (II Thess. 2 :9); and Satan can disguise himself
as an angel of light (II Cor. 11 :14). Therefore, it is madness
to boast of proofs of the Spirit (II Cor. 11 :12). And the
knowledge and judgment of the man of faith are not a secure
possession with which he is equipped, but rather are only
given to one who actually leads a new life in humility and
love (I Cor. 3 :1-3, 8 :1-3; Rom. 12 :2; Phil. 1 :9). Moreover,
this Christian life itself is not a fact that lies before one's eyes,
to which he can appeal and with which he can reassure himself. Rather it constantly stands under the imperative (Rom.
6) and is only actual as a possibility that is always endangered
and must constantly be laid hold of anew in the immediate
situation. The man of faith cannot appeal to his " good conscience " (I Cor. 4 :4); he is engaged in a constant struggle
with the flesh (Rom. 8 :13; Gal. 5 :16-25). Nor can he appeal
to the fact that this struggle is going on as though this were
some kind of a guarantee of the new life. For then he would
not be taking this struggle seriously. The man of faith stands
within the struggle, not outside of it, so that he could already
count it as a victory. But if he is actually engaged *in* the
struggle, then the outcome is always uncertain so long as he

looks to himself (I Cor. 10:12); Satan constantly lies in wait (I Cor. 7:5; II Cor. 2:11; I Thess. 3:5; Eph. 6:11; I Pet. 5:8).

The victory is certain only as the victory of Christ.

Who shall bring any charge against God's elect? Will God, who makes us righteous? Who is it that condemns us? Is it Christ Jesus, who died, yes, who was raised from the dead, who is at the right hand of God, who also intercedes for us? . . . No, in all these things we are more than conquerors through him who loved us. (Rom. 8:33-7).

This means, however, that all this holds good only on the presupposition of faith—faith not in the sense of a human attitude or frame of mind, but rather as faith *in* an occurrence, *in* Jesus Christ, who died and was raised for us.

Faith is not only able to work miracles and signs, but it alone is also able to see them as signs of life and as first fruits of the Spirit. Faith is not only the power of the new way of life, but it alone is also able to see that in the struggle between Spirit and flesh it is the Spirit who remains victor in spite of man's defeat. Faith is able to endure the paradox that the new life does not appear as life now, but, on the contrary, appears as ever-mounting death:

But we have this treasure in earthen vessels, to show that the transcendent power belongs to God and not to us. We are afflicted in every way, but not crushed; perplexed, but not driven to despair; persecuted, but not forsaken; struck down but not destroyed; always carrying in the body the death of Jesus, so that the life of Jesus may also be manifested in our bodies. For while we live we are always being given up to death for Jesus' sake, so that the life of Jesus may be manifested in our mortal flesh. (II Cor. 4:7-11)

We are treated as impostors, and yet are true; as unknown, and yet well known; as dying, and behold we live; as punished and yet not killed; as sorrowful, yet always rejoicing; as poor, yet making many rich; as having nothing, and yet possessing everything. (II Cor. 6:8-10)

I will all the more gladly boast of my weaknesses, that the power of Christ may rest upon me. For the sake of Christ, then, I am content with weaknesses, insults, hardships, persecutions, and calamities; for when I am weak, then I am strong (II Cor. 12:9 f.)

Otherwise, however, it is madness to boast of his own achievements, experiences, and marvellous deeds (II Cor. 11-12). Paul speaks of them not as though he could base his existence upon them, but refers to them only for the sake of his readers and for a specific reason, namely, to help his readers understand him.

The peace that Jesus gives is a different peace from that of the world (John 14:27); within the world it consists of anxiety and affliction and is peace only in him (John 16:33). The world will rejoice, but the disciples will be sorrowful (John 16:20).

Thus revelation consists in nothing other than the fact of Jesus Christ. His coming as such is designated as the revelation. Because he was sent, life was revealed (I John 1:2); he "appeared" (I John 3:5, 3:8, cf. 4:9; I Pet. 1:20; Heb. 9:26); he "was manifested in the flesh" (I Tim. 3:16). But, on the other hand, his revelation is yet to take place (I John 2:28; I Pet. 5:4; Luke 17:30), and one looks forward to it (I Cor. 1:7; I Pet. 1:13). Thus it is now a *veiled revelation*. "No man works in secret if he seeks to be known openly. If you do these things, reveal yourself to the world!"—thus do Jesus' brothers, who are without understanding, reproach him (John 7:4 f.). The "world" does not know that for it the revelation is hidden; thus it seeks a demonstration. The world cannot receive the Spirit because it does not see and know him (John 14:17); it cannot see the risen Lord (John 14:22 f.).

Therefore, life also is veiled, even though it has been revealed through Christ. The treasure is had in earthen vessels; the apostle bears in his body the life of Jesus in that he bears his death (II Cor. 4:7-11, see above). We ourselves also have yet to be revealed; for our life is still hidden with Christ in God (Col. 3:3). "We are God's children now, but it does not yet appear what we shall be. We know that when he appears we shall be like him; for we shall see him as he is" (I John 3:2). "I consider that the sufferings of this present time are not worth comparing with the glory that is to be revealed to us. For the creation waits with eager longing for the revealing of the sons of God" (Rom. 8:18 f.).

2. *The "How" of Revelation: the Word and Faith.* But what, then, is really revealed? Is the answer that the revelation has occurred in the sending of Jesus, in his incarnation, death, and resurrection, anything other than a myth? If life is still veiled, to what extent does the whole salvation-occurrence have anything to do with *me*? Does it speak at all of *my* reality? Is this life actually *my* life? And to what extent is something really revealed? How is the salvation-occurrence visible?

It is visible just as little as a cosmic event as it is as an inner experience. For it is revealed as *proclamation,* in the word.[6] In fact, we must note that precisely the proclamation is also designated as the revelation. Thus, for example, to what extent is the life of Jesus manifested when Paul carries in his body Jesus' dying (II Cor. 4:10 f.; see above)? It is manifested to the extent that he preaches and that his preaching is responded to in faith. Paul's ministry rests on his faith; because he believes, he speaks (II Cor. 4:13); and death (viz., the dying of Christ) is at work in him insofar as he gives himself up to his ministry, while life is at work in his hearers insofar as they believe (II Cor. 4:12). Thus Paul has be-

come Christ himself for his hearers—not because he is deified
and is gazed upon by them as a pneumatic, but because he
preaches to them. " So we are at work for Christ (perhaps
we must even translate, " in Christ's stead ") in such a way
that God makes his appeal through us. We beseech you on
behalf of Christ (or " in Christ's stead "), be reconciled to
God!" (II Cor. 5 :20). Consequently, Paul can designate
the now in which the preaching encounters the hearer as the
eschatological now in which salvation is revealed : " Behold,
now is the acceptable time; behold, now is the day of salvation!" (II Cor. 6 :2). As God has let his light shine on the
apostle, so the apostle sheds forth the light of the knowledge
of God's glory in the face of Christ (II Cor. 4 :6).

This is the theme of the whole first part of II Corinthians.
When Paul spreads the word of the gospel he spreads life (II
Cor. 2 :14-6 :10). Through the apostle, God reveals the fragrance of his knowledge in every place; the apostle is the
aroma of Christ for those who are being saved as well as for
those who are perishing : to the one a fragrance from death
to death, to the other a fragrance from life to life (II Cor.
2 :14-16). Therefore, the character of his ministry is precisely
that of openness or unveiledness; thus it corresponds to the
new covenant as a covenant of life, whereas the old covenant
as a covenant of death was characterized precisely by veiledness
(2 :17-3 :18). Thus even as God's act of salvation is precisely
a revealing, so also is the meaning of the apostolic ministry
that it reveals (4 :1-6). But this revelation that takes place in
preaching is insofar paradoxical as what is evident to the eye
of the natural man is not life, but only death. Life is veiled in
the death of Christ; it is never a phenomenon within the
world that can be proved, and one never " has " it as a thing
that is seen, but only as the object of faith (4 :7-5 :10). In the
eyes of God, the revelation that takes place in preaching is
unambiguous; but in the eyes of man it is always ambiguous
because it addresses itself to the consciences of its hearers,
demanding of them decision, and thus remains veiled to the

eyes of unfaith (5:11-15, cf. 4:2, 2:15 f.). This characteristic, however, completely corresponds to the character of
Christ, who also is not to be understood as he presents himself
to our eyes (" according to the flesh "). Thus, like Christ, the
preaching apostle himself must be understood as one who
reveals life precisely in death (5:16-6:10).

The post-Pauline literature holds fast to this basic thought.
The Gospel of John simply identifies Jesus with the word.
And, according to the spurious doxology in Romans, the
mystery that was kept secret for long ages is revealed in the
kerygma (Rom. 16:25 f.); and the author of Colossians identifies the *proclaimed word of God* with the mystery hidden for
ages and generations, but now revealed to the saints (Col.
1:25 f.). That Christ has abolished death and brought life
and immortality to light has occurred through the *gospel,* for
which the apostle has been appointed herald, preacher, and
teacher (II Tim. 1:10 f.). As one can speak of the revelation
of *life,* so one can also say that at the proper time God has
revealed his word through the *preaching* with which the
apostle has been entrusted (Titus 1:3). This all corresponds
to the Pauline thought that God's act of salvation consists in
his having instituted the " *ministry of reconciliation* " or the
" *word* of reconciliation" (II Cor. 5:18 f.) and that the
gospel is the " power of God for salvation to everyone who
has faith " (Rom. 1:16).

" To everyone who has faith ! " For the peculiar thing about
this revelation of life is that it neither " reveals " an idea of
life nor—as the occurrence that it is—produces " life " as a
phenomenon that can be found in the world. Rather it is an
occurrence that has the possibility of spreading *death* as well
as life (II Cor. 2:15 f., 4:2 f.). It reveals life wherever it
evokes the response of *faith* (II Cor. 2:14-6:10). Therefore,
it can also be said that faith is revealed : " Now before faith
came, we were confined under the law, kept under restraint
until faith should be revealed " (Gal. 3:23). In the same
sense, Hebrews can say that at one time " the way into the

sanctuary" was not yet "revealed" (Heb. 9 :8); and as the Johannine Jesus can say that *he* has overcome the world (John 16 : 33), so the community can confess that their *faith* is what has overcome it (I John 5 : 4).

Thus what the New Testament understands by revelation can only become clear when these two series of statements are both maintained and related to each other : (1) life is revealed, Christ is revealed; (2) the word of proclamation and faith are revealed.

The first series makes clear that revelation is not illumination or the communication of knowledge, but rather an occurrence, while the second series makes just as clear that this revelation-occurrence cannot be a cosmic process which takes place outside of us and of which the word would merely bring a report (so that it would be nothing other than a myth). Thus revelation must be an occurrence that directly concerns *us,* that takes place in us ourselves; and the word, the fact of its being proclaimed must itself belong to the occurrence. The preaching is itself revelation and does not merely speak about it, so that it mediates a content that one can understand or to which he can relate himself through knowledge and thereby " have " the revelation. If preaching communicates a content, it at the same time addresses us; it speaks to our consciences, and whoever refuses to let himself be addressed likewise does not understand what is communicated. He is blind (II Cor. 4 : 4), and for him the revelation is veiled (II Cor. 4 : 3).

If the primary meaning of revelation in any case is that God *does* something, then the meaning of this deed or occurrence as something wrought by *God* is strictly maintained, in that it is asserted not that this occurrence is a fact within the world—even one of the greatest possible cosmic dimensions—but rather that it is precisely an " eschatological " fact, i.e., the kind of fact in which the world comes to an end. Therefore, it can never become merely an event in the past that one simply perceives; rather even as it remains ambiguous and

therefore can be understood merely as such a past event—
even as one can inquire about the " historical Jesus" or
" Christ according to the flesh " (II Cor. 5 :16) and can also
establish his natural origin (John 6 :42, 7 :27 f.)—even so it
is understood in its true character only when it is understood
as something that takes place in the present, in my particular
present.[7] The way in which it is made present, however, is
through preaching, which does not make it present by communicating something about the past, by reminiscing, but
rather by presenting it in the form of an address.[8] And just
as preaching, if thought of merely as a mediating communication about the past, would be completely misunderstood, so
also, on the other hand, would the fact of salvation be misunderstood if it were thought of as an isolated fact that happened in some place and at some time and that requires to be
mediated to the present through a communication. As the
preaching itself belongs to the fact of salvation, so also is this
fact not what it is without the preaching. Thus there also is
no way whereby the hearer of the preaching can get behind it,
whether in order to find a " historical Jesus " or to find some
cosmic process that has occurred in a certain place and at a
certain time. Rather everything that is decisive for him takes
place in his present; " *now* is the day of salvation." Revelation encounters man in the word—in the word that sounds
forth in his present; and it thereby actually happens to him
whether he understands that it does or not. Faithful and unfaithful alike are qualified by the revelatory occurrence; for
them the decision has been made, either to live or to die.

John expresses it in this way : Jesus is the *krisis*; whoever
believes in him has passed from death to life; whoever does
not believe in him is already judged (3 :18, 5 :24). John also
expresses the basic paradox in the sharpest possible way.
Jesus is sent as the revealer. But what does he reveal? *That*
he is sent as the revealer. It is this that one is to believe and
thereby have life. Thus Jesus reveals life; but not in the sense
that he gives us insight into it and opens the way to it, but in

the sense that he himself *is* it, the way and the life at the same time (14:9).[9] How is this riddle to be understood? It is *not* to be understood so long as one observes from the outside; for from that perspective these statements must look like a complete circle. Outside of faith revelation is not visible; there is nothing revealed on the basis of which one believes. It is only *in* faith that the object of faith is disclosed; therefore, faith itself belongs to revelation.

3. *Revelation as Occurrence under the Headings of the Righteousness of God, the Forgiveness of Sins, Freedom, and Love.* If, by means of revelation as an occurrence wrought by God, death is abolished and life is revealed, then " life " is not thought of as an objective condition in which we find ourselves, but rather as a mode of being that we lay hold of in faith. This must be made still clearer, however, by showing how various other things can be designated as the content of revelation. Paul refers to the gospel as the power of God for salvation because it is in it that " *the righteousness of God* is revealed through faith for faith " (Rom. 1:16 f.). " The righteousness of God," to which the law and the prophets bear witness, has now been revealed apart from law (Rom. 3:21). Actually, this can mean nothing other than that *life* has been revealed; for " righteousness " and " life " are parallels. Man has to choose whether he will be a " slave of sin," which " leads to death," or a " slave of obedience " (i.e., faith), which " leads to righteousness." The end of one's erstwhile slavery to sin is death, whereas becoming a slave of God has as its end eternal life (Rom. 6:16 and 21 f.). Similarly, Paul also says nothing other by this than that *Christ* has been revealed; for Christ is our " righteousness " (I Cor. 1:30) and, in the same way as the gospel, is the " power of God " (I Cor. 1:24).

The righteousness of God means the righteousness that God imparts by his word, the acquittal that frees man of his sin. Thus substantially the same thing is said when, in Johannine terminology, Jesus is said to have "appeared to take away sin" or "to destroy the works of the devil" (I John 3:5, 3:8). In order really to understand this, however, it is necessary to explain what is meant by "sin."

If, according to Paul, the new mode of being is characterized by "faith," then the old way of existing was characterized by the "law" (Gal. 3:23). But the "law" led to "sin" (Rom. 5:20, 7:14 ff.; Gal. 3:19, 3:22). How so?

Paul does not understand sin primarily as immorality. On the contrary, he develops the thought that it is immorality only in a secondary sense, viz., as the consequence of the primal sin that man does not honour God as God (Rom. 1:21). If this is so, however, it is easy to understand that it is precisely the law that characterizes the old aeon of sin: the law that demands obedience is misused by the Jews as a means of self-glorification and boasting. They turn obedience into an accomplishment and imagine that they themselves can secure their existence, that they are able to establish their own righteousness by what they themselves accomplish. "For, misconstruing the righteousness that comes from God, and seeking to establish their own, they did not submit to the righteousness of God" (Rom. 10:3). The primal sin is not an inferior morality, but rather the understanding of oneself in terms of oneself and the attempt to secure one's existence by means of what one himself establishes, by means of one's own accomplishments. It is the boasting and self-confidence of the natural man. Paul speaks of it as putting confidence in the flesh (Phil. 3:2-11).

For just this is the essence of "flesh": the essence of the man who understands himself in terms of himself, who wants to secure his own existence. Thus for any believer who still wants to subject himself to the law, Christ has died in vain; for he attests thereby that he is a sinner; he has begun "in the Spirit" only to end "in the flesh" (Gal. 2:17-21, 3:3). Boasting according to the flesh is precisely putting confidence in one's own accomplishments (II Cor. 11:18). Those whom

Paul struggles against at Corinth, who carry on their struggle with weapons of flesh (II Cor. 10:4), are those who boast of themselves, who compare their own accomplishments with those of others, who recommend themselves, who demand a legitimation and thus imagine that a man is proved by some visible accomplishment (II Cor. 10-13). The sin of the Jews is repeated in the pneumatic who has forgotten: "What have you that you did not receive? If then you received it, why do you boast as if it were not a gift" (I Cor. 4:7). The real man of faith counts everything that he can point to as refuse (Phil. 3:7 f.); he puts his confidence solely in God, who raises the dead (II Cor. 1:9); he boasts of nothing save the cross of Christ (Gal. 6:14), and therefore with respect to himself, only of his weakness (II Cor. 12:9).

This, then, is sin: rebellion against God, forgetting that man is a creature, misunderstanding oneself and putting oneself in God's place. And it is exactly in this way that John also understands it. For him, the decisive concept that corresponds to the Pauline concept of "flesh" is "world." By "world" he understands humanity as it constitutes itself and takes pride in what it has and does; it is the world of sound common sense with its ideals and norms, its traditions and its knowledge; it is the world of possibilities that can be disposed of, which does not reckon with any other possibilities and looks upon what it does not understand as absurd and ridiculous. The "world" does not know that it is limited by God, and therefore it does not know him even if it imagines that it does. This is its sin.[10]

This humanity that lives "according to the flesh" or this "world," is subject to "death." For death and sin are connected in a remarkable way: sin is the sting of death (I Cor. 15:56); and through sin death has come into the world. (Rom. 5:12 ff.). For sin takes for secure what is really insecure, for definitive what is provisional. Because man understands himself in terms of what he accomplishes and produces, because he thus takes his god*less* being to be his authentic, his ultimate being, he is punished by death's—i.e., the death to which the whole of his present existence is subject—also acquiring for him the character of being authentic and ultimate. Because he tries to cling to his provisional being he slips away from himself. If, however, he could once again understand himself as provisional and could surrender his provisional being, then death also could once again become something provisional for him. But if, instead, he clings to the provisional, he is always already past. The unfaithful are dead in their sins (Col. 2:13; Eph. 2:1, 2:5).

What, then, is the meaning of the righteousness of God or the forgiveness of sin? Naturally, it cannot consist in the remission of moral failures, so that the problem of "sins committed after baptism" could seriously arise. Rather it consists in the original relation of creation's being reproduced, i.e., in the breaking of the sinful continuum in which I always already stand, the continuum of existence "according to the flesh" or "of the world," and in the old revelation's once again being made visible.

For the revelation in Christ is not the first. Man could already have known God earlier. From the beginning, the "word" was the "light" of men (John 1:4). How so? Well, because the word was the Creator, because it is only in the word that the creation had its life. And this life was the light of men, i.e., in knowing about its own creatureliness the world would have known about God. Naturally, this light, this knowledge about God is not a cosmological or theological theory, but rather is an understanding of oneself through acknowledging the Creator. But the world has displaced this knowledge by the knowledge of what it itself does and has. Its not knowing has the character of having forgotten. Man has forgotten whence he comes; he understands himself in terms of what he makes, whereas he always has his existence from the reality from which he comes. In a similar way, Paul teaches (in Stoic terminology) that man should have recognized the world as creation and honoured God as God, although, in fact, he has done exactly the opposite.

Thus there is a " natural revelation," or, at least, there *was* one. But it is not something that simply lies before one's eyes, nor is the knowledge of it a knowledge of the world, a theistic view of God. Rather it is a knowledge by man of himself, an understanding of himself as a creature and thus an honouring of God. This possibility has especially been given to the Jew through the law, in which he daily encounters God's claim and by which he is daily led to see that he does not exist by and for himself, but that his being is limited by the claim under which he stands.

But man misunderstands himself and puts himself in the place of God. And every man comes out of a history that is governed by this misunderstanding. He comes out of a lie; he is determined by the flesh whose power he cannot break. Were he to imagine that he could break it, he would assume that he does not have himself in his own power after all and would thereby merely repeat the primal sin. There is another possibility only if it is given to him to come into his present from somewhere other than from a lie and from sin. And that this possibility *is* given is what is proclaimed in the message of Christ.

According to Paul, Christ is the "second man" or the "last Adam" (I Cor. 15:21 f., 15:45-9; Rom. 5:12-19), "the first-born among many brethren" (Rom. 8:29); he is the one who establishes a new humanity with which the new aeon begins. "To be in Christ" means "to be a new creation" (II Cor. 5:17); "to be in the Spirit" means to stand in this new mode of being, this new history that has been established by Christ, i.e., by the reconciliation, the forgiveness of sins that God has carried out in him. Or expressed in Johannine terminology, Jesus is the *krisis*; his coming is the turn of the aeon; the prince of this world is judged. Whoever believes in Jesus as the one sent by God no longer belongs to the "world," but has passed from death to life.

E.F.   D

But to belong to the new aeon, to have life, is not a new status of nature in which dying has ceased to occur. Life is always given only in hope. "For we are saved in hope. But hope in what is seen is not hope; for who hopes for what he sees? But if we hope for what we do not see, we wait for it with patience" (Rom. 8:24 f.). "For we walk by faith, not by sight" (II Cor. 5:7). Thus the Johannine Jesus prays for his own: "I do not ask that thou shouldst take them out of the world, but that shouldst keep them (in the world) free from evil" (John 17:15). Therefore, the new life stands under the imperative (Rom. 6; Gal. 5:13-25). The "law" is not simply done away with by the "gospel"; it *is* done away with as the law that demands accomplishments, i.e., as it was understood by the Jews who misunderstood their existence. But as the authentic will of God is now brought precisely to its fulfilment: God demands man's obedience. And the difference from the earlier situation is that now the possibility of obedience is actually given, that now the "flesh" can be overcome in the "Spirit."

Thus the life of the man of faith is not removed from its historical conditions; it continues in its historicity, i.e., it always has the possibility of losing itself. Life is a possibility that *can* be laid hold of, but it is also a possibility that always *must* be laid hold of. *That* it can be laid hold of constitutes the "freedom" of the faithful man. This freedom, however, is not caprice or "doing what one wants." For since man is a historical being, "doing what one wants" is always only a relinquishing of oneself, i.e., a relinquishing of oneself to the past. Authentic freedom can only be freedom from oneself and thus the freedom to do what one ought. But this freedom is authentic freedom because in it man does what he *really* wants to do, namely, to achieve his authenticity (cf. Rom. 6:15-22, 8:2; Gal. 5:1, 5:13, etc.; John 8:32-6). Through forgiveness, the past out of which one comes is blotted out; he comes into his now precisely out of forgiveness and therefore is free for the future.

This means negatively that, for the man of faith, everything worldly or provisional once again acquires the character of being provisional; he knows that "the form of this world is passing away" (I Cor. 7 :31; cf. I John 2 :17), and his having is a "having as though he did not have" (I Cor. 7 :29-31). Therefore, dying also has become for him a "dying as though he did not die." To be sure, his life must be understood in terms of the resurrection of the dead and not as the immortality of the soul; i.e., it must not be understood as a clinging to what one has and is, to the provisional, but rather as the surrender of all this. The man of faith stands under the sentence of death (II Cor. 1 :9), and he must take this death upon himself. Thus he enters into utter darkness. But the Christian hopes precisely where there is no hope (Rom. 4 :18), namely, in God who raises the dead and calls into existence the things that are not (Rom. 4 :17; cf. II Cor. 1 :9).

Positively, however, freedom means freedom to obey, i.e., to love. For "love is the fulfilling of the law" and "he who loves his neighbour has fulfilled the law"; for all of the law's commandments with their "Thou shalt not" are summed up in this sentence, "You shall love your neighbour as yourself" (Rom. 13 :8-10; Gal. 5 :14). To be sure, this was already known earlier; the proclamation of the prophets, including that of Jesus himself, had in this sense proclaimed the law as the real will of God, and in itself the commandment of love is nothing "new." It *is* new, however, insofar as it has now become a possibility for man—thereby, namely, that God has loved us in Christ and that we therefore come into our now as those who are loved and thus are free to love in return. "But God shows his love for us in that while we were yet sinners Christ died for us" (Rom. 5 :8). Our love has its basis in his love; "we love because he first loved us" (I John 4 :19). And one can only receive his love by loving in return (John 13 :34 f., 15 :9-13). For God's love is not an observable fact within the world that one might perceive, but rather is his revelation. Thus love also is designated precisely as the content of revelation:

> In this the love of God was revealed among us, that God sent his only Son into the world, so that we might live through him. In this is love, not that we loved God, but that he loved us and sent his Son to be the expiation for our sins. (I John 4:9 f.)

4. *The Knowledge Based in Revelation.* What, then, has been revealed? Nothing at all, so far as the question concerning revelation asks for doctrines—doctrines, say, that no man could have discovered for himself—or for mysteries that become known once and for all as soon as they are communicated. On the other hand, however, *everything has been revealed, insofar as man's eyes are opened concerning his own existence and he is once again able to understand himself.* It is as Luther says: " Thus, in going out of himself, God brings it about that we go into ourselves; and through knowledge of him he brings us to knowledge of ourselves.[11] There is no other light shining in Jesus than has always already shined in the creation. Man learns to understand himself in the light of the revelation of redemption not a bit differently than he always already should understand himself in face of the revelation in creation and the law—namely, as God's creature who is limited by God and stands under God's claim, which opens up to him the way to death or to life. If the revelation in Jesus means salvation as an understanding of oneself in him, then the revelation in creation meant nothing other than this understanding of oneself in God in the knowledge of one's own creatureliness.

Therefore, the Johannine Jesus, at the conclusion of the farewell discourses, can say that the fulfilment of revelation is that no one needs any longer to ask questions (John 16:23 f.). Man always asks questions because he does not understand himself; if he does understand himself, however, all questioning ceases. He then is transparent to himself; he has become " light." For if Jesus is the " light " that enlightens every man, this does not mean that he gives them a capacity for knowledge (or strengthens such a capacity), by means of which the things of the world may be illumined, but rather that he gives them the light through which they may understand themselves. " Awake, O sleeper, and arise from the dead and Christ shall give you light " (Eph. 5 :14). " For once you were darkness, but now you are light in the Lord " (Eph. 5 :8; cf. II Cor. 3 :18, 4 :6). This is the condition of " fullness of joy " in which all questioning ceases and everything is understood (John 15 :11, 16 :24, 17 :13).

Revelation does not provide this self-understanding, however, as a world-view that one grasps, possesses, and applies. Indeed, it is precisely in such views that man *fails* to understand himself, because he looks upon himself as something simply given and tries to understand himself as a part of the world that lies before him. Revelation does not mediate a world-view, but rather addresses the individual as an existing self. That he thereby learns to understand himself means that he learns to understand his now, the moment, as a now that is qualified by the proclamation. For existence in the moment is his authentic being. And just as little as the proclamation communicates something that happened in a certain place and at a certain time, but rather says what has occurred to the person being addressed, so little is faith the knowledge of some fact within the world or the willingness to hold some remarkable dogma to be true. Rather it is the obedience that obeys God not in general or *in abstracto,* but in the concrete now. The man of faith understands his now as one who comes out of a sinful past and therefore stands under God's judgment, but also as one who is freed from this past by the grace that encounters him in the word. Thus he for the first time sees the other person as his neighbour and in understanding the neighbour understands himself. Such faith is something that man does, but it is never something that has been done, never a work that he produces or accomplishes. Rather it is the momentary act in which he lays hold of him-

self in his God-given freedom. And the man of faith understands himself only in such an act.

Thus it becomes completely clear that revelation is an act
of God, an *occurrence,* and not a communication of supernatural knowledge. Further, it is clear that revelation reveals
life, for it frees man from what is provisional and past and
gives him the future. Even so, it is clear that *Christ* is revelation and that revelation is the *word*; for these two are one and
the same. Christ is not the act of God's love as a fact within
the world that one can find some place and demonstrate to be
an " act of love." All possible demonstrations that the historical Jesus loved this man or that, many men or all men,
do not say what has to be said, i.e., what is said by the proclamation of Christ—that God has loved us in Christ and
reconciled us to himself (II Cor. 5:18; John 3:18). For the
love directed to *me*—and this alone can make me a new creature—cannot be demonstrated by historical observation. It
can only be promised to me directly; and this is what is done
by the proclamation. To go behind the Christ who is preached
is to misunderstand the preaching; it is only in the word, as
the one who is preached, that he encounters us, that the love of
God encounters us in him. But once again, it must be emphasized that the word is what it is—namely, revelation—not
because of its timeless content, but rather as an address that is
brought to us here and now by common ordinary men. Therefore, *faith* also, like the word, is revelation because it is only
real in this occurrence and otherwise is nothing. It is no disposition of the human soul, no being convinced, but rather the
answer to an address.

It is also completely clear how *the righteousness of God* is
revealed; namely, neither as an idea nor as a condition that is
brought about in us, a quality that is produced in us. Rather
it is awarded to us and will be awarded to us in the address
that encounters us. As we should obey the word, so also
should we " obey " the righteousness of God (Rom. 6:18,
10:3). Thus the interpretation of the Reformers is correct:

righteousness is "imputed" to us as *justitia aliena*. And so it also becomes clear that and how *love* is revealed. For it would be a misunderstanding of *justitia aliena* to suppose that the rightwised sinner is only looked at "as if" he were righteous. No! he *is* righteous, even if he really is so only when righteousness is awarded to him. But if he *is* righteous, then he understands himself and sees his neighbour and knows what he owes him (Rom. 13:8).

Then there is indeed a *knowledge* that is also given in revelation, however little the latter is a supernatural arrangement for communicating remarkable doctrines. I am given a knowledge, namely, of myself, of my immediate now, in which and for which the word of proclamation is spoken to me. Thus it is not an observer's knowledge, not a world-view in which man is interpreted as a phenomenon within the world on the basis of certain general principles of explanation, but rather a knowledge that is only opened up to me in laying hold of the possibility for understanding myself that is disclosed in the proclamation; it is a knowledge that is only real in the act of faith and love. And if such knowledge can also be explicated theologically, still theological knowledge always has a "dialectical" character, in the sense, namely, that as a knowledge that is preserved it is always spurious, however "correct" it may be, and that it is only genuine when the act of faith is realized in it, when the resolve to exist in faith is carried through to the end. For "whatever does not proceed from faith is sin" (Rom. 14:23).

5. *Revelation as the Revelation of God.* Thus Jesus Christ has revealed God: "I have revealed thy name to the men whom thou gavest me out of the world" (John 17:6). "I made known to them thy name, and I will make it known, that the love with which thou hast loved me may be in them, and I in them" (John 17:26).

God is thus revealed as the One who limits man and who brings him to his authenticity in his limitation—namely, whenever this limitation is understood as *God's* limitation. Thus the preunderstanding of revelation that man already has is radicalized and thereby corrected : it is not for him to break through his limits, but rather to understand himself in them. However, he cannot set to work to carry through such a self-understanding as his own undertaking; he can only hear that and where his limit is set, for this limit is God : " No one has ever seen God; the only Son who is in the bosom of the Father, he has made him known " (John 1 :18). " All things have been delivered to me by my Father; and no one knows the Son except the Father, and no one knows the Father except the Son and any one to whom the Son chooses to reveal him " (Matt. 11 :27).

As little as the knowledge that revelation gives is a knowledge that can be discovered once for all and then mediated to others by a " shortened way,"[12] but rather is a knowledge that must always be acquired anew and by going the long way around, so little will one who understands this be able to speak of a " development " of revelation (or even of faith in revelation) in the history of religion. Only phenomena within the world are subject to development, not revelation or the faith that belongs to it. Since each person has to begin at the beginning in Christianity, there also is no history of Christianity within the general history of human culture, in the sense, say, of a history of problems that progresses from level to level, solution to solution. On the contrary, every generation has the same original relation to revelation.[13] What develops is only (1) the conceptual explication of our preunderstanding of revelation; and (2) the theological or conceptual explication of faith's knowledge of itself which has its basis in revelation. In other words, all that develops is simply our way of talking about revelation.

Furthermore, the question concerning the " absoluteness " of the Christian revelation or of the Christian faith can also no longer arise. If the question means that an attempt is made outside of faith to rank the various religions—including the

Christian one—as phenomena within the world, then it is meaningless from the very outset; for all that falls within the range of such a question is relative, not absolute. The question can be raised meaningfully only from the standpoint of faith, insofar as doubt is not meaningless. However, if it *is* raised in faith, it is still a meaningless question; for then it has already been decided, since faith is the answer to revelation. Nevertheless, the history of religion does have meaning for Christian faith; for because faith understands itself, it understands the various " religions "—including the " Christian " religion—as the question for God or for revelation[14] and sees at work in them the same preunderstanding that it alone radically understands.

6 : *The New Testament as Revelation.* So far, all that has been said is an explication of what is said in the New Testament or, at least, this is what it has attempted to be. If we were clear that such an explication can only be undertaken on the basis of a preunderstanding and in the readiness to let this preunderstanding be radicalized, it must be admitted now at the conclusion that all explication must remain in the realm of preunderstanding and that the radicalizing only really takes place when what is said in the New Testament is truly heard. When that happens, however, the question concerning the concept of revelation in the New Testament meets with the latter's claim to *be* revelation; i.e., the New Testament is able to tell us what it understands by revelation only by at the same time asserting that it itself is revelation. It has been shown, however, that no complex of timeless truths can be named that could be designated as revelation; rather it is the proclaimed word of Christ that is revelation. Therefore, the New Testament itself is revelation only insofar as it is kerygma or insofar as it " preaches Christ " (Luther); and this means that there is a criterion for determining the extent to which the New Testament's statements speak as revelation. But this criterion can in no case be applied by a disinterested investigation in

order to exclude this or that section of the New Testament as falling below the standard of genuine revelatory statements; for this criterion can always be effective only in faithfully hearing what the New Testament says. If one here and there fails to be addressed by the word of Christ, he of course does not have the right to say that it must be there or even to suppose that it could be. But he will ask himself whether his not hearing may not possibly have its basis in a not wanting to hear. If it cannot be denied in principle that there can be statements in the New Testament that are not revelatory, it nevertheless is not a meaningful task to name them.

To be sure, certain New Testament statements can be named that speak of revelation in the form of a theological explication; and with respect to them the critical question to what extent the knowledge based in revelation is expressed in them in a conceptually adequate way is appropriate and necessary. However, the demand to say once for all and unambiguously what the word of God is must be rejected because it rests on the idea that it is possible to designate a complex of statements that can be found and understood with respect to their " content."

To be sure, what is meant by " word of God" can be clarified in a formal way; but precisely this formal clarification tells us that no " content " of the word of God can be conclusively exhibited, but rather can only be heard in the immediate moment. Thus, in response to the question what the New Testament understands by revelation, it asks the counterquestion whether it itself is heard as revelation.

THE HISTORICITY OF MAN
AND FAITH*

I

Regretfully, I have not previously had time to go into the pertinent and penetrating questions that have been addressed to me by Gerhardt Kuhlmann.[1] I want now to try to reply to him.

If Kuhlmann agrees with me that the concept "existence" must be the methodical starting-point of theology, since the latter's theme is existence in faith, then his misgivings about my work grow out of my dependence on Heidegger's existential analysis of man in my effort to explicate existence in faith in a theological or conceptual way. Kuhlmann rightly stresses that Heidegger's method may not be understood as a formal technical proceeding that can be transferred as one pleases to some other object than the natural man—thus, in this particular case, to the man of faith. Rather the method is determined by its object; and therefore when I take over the concepts of Heidegger's existential analysis, I also in fact take over the object of this analysis. Thus the object of my theological research is in truth not *existence in faith,* but rather *the natural man.* The central theme of theological research, i.e., the revelation through which existence in faith receives its determination, is thereby profaned and falsified; I simply "repeat" the philosophical analysis of man and authorize it *post festum* in that I mythologize its concepts.

Indeed, a method is not separable from its object. However, the object of an existential analysis of man is man; and it

* "Die Geschichtlichkeit des Daseins und der Glaube: Antwort an Gerhardt Kuhlmann," Zeitschrift für Theologie und Kirche, N.F., xi (1930), 339-64.

is likewise man that is the object of theology. Therefore, the relation of philosophy and theology is not immediately transparent. The first thing that may be said is that the theme of philosophy (at any rate, so far as man falls within its realm) is *the natural man,* while the theme of theology is *the man of faith.*

In this instance, however, "natural" does not have the theological meaning of antidivine, but is a purely formal ontological designation; i.e., the philosopher completely disregards whether something like faith or unfaith can take place.[2] Were he to reflect on such phenomena, all he could say is that his analysis exhibits the condition of the possibility that a man can comport himself faithfully or unfaithfully.[3] The "atheism" of philosophy is not identical with the theological concept of unfaith. (How such atheism is to be judged from the standpoint of faith is not to be discussed here.) Since faith and unfaith are answers to a concrete and contingent proclamation, which addresses itself to a concrete human being, an explicit consideration of them by philosophy would be just as absurd as its considering whether in a concrete case a proposal of marriage is to be accepted or rejected. Nevertheless, the philosophical analysis of man will have to exhibit the conditions of the possibility that something like a proposal of love and its acceptance or rejection can take place—however little it has any particular proposal in view. And in a similar way, philosophy does not consider the Christian proclamation (i.e., the *positum* that makes theology a positive science in contradistinction to philosophy, whose object is not a particular being, but being as such[4]); and yet philosophy alone provides the possibility of understanding conceptually what is meant by such things as "proclamation," "word," "address," "hearing"—although, to repeat, it does not teach one to understand some concrete proclamation in particular.

For our purpose here, we may express the difference between philosophy and theology in some such way as this : philosophy shows that my being a man uniquely belongs to me, but it does not speak of my unique existence; this, however, is exactly what theology does. And in this sense, theology shares in a peculiar way in the character of address that belongs to the sermon (i.e., it speaks only for those who hear this sermon —which, of course, is intended for everyone and is addressed to everyone—whereas philosophy speaks for every man). Philosophy, on the other hand, can show that to speak of or from my concrete existence can only mean to address others or to answer an address from them. If theology presupposes the actualization of a particular address, philosophy can only say what address means in general. Philosophy sees *that* man is only a particular concrete man who is determined by some specific " how "; it speaks of the " that " of this " how," but not of the " how " itself. Theology, however, speaks of a specific " how "—yet not by jumping into a hole that has been left open by philosophy in the totality of what is knowable or in the system of the sciences. Rather it can have its own original motive only because the man who is determined by that specific " how " has need of theology for his own realization. Philosophy, however, points out that the " that " of a particular concrete " how " is essential to man, without ever actually speaking of a concrete " how." Its real thémè is not existence, but existentiality, not the factual, but factuality; it inquires concerning existence with respect to existentiality, but it does not speak to concrete existence.[5]

What has been said should have made clear in a provisional way that philosophy and theology have the same object, namely, man, but that they make it their theme in different ways : philosophy by making the being of man its theme, i.e., by inquiring ontologically into the formal structures of human existence; and theology by speaking of the concrete man insofar as he is faithful (or is unfaithful—which is also something positive and not negative), i.e., insofar as his " how " is characterized by the fact that he has been or is to be encountered by a specific proclamation. Thus we can also say that theology as a positive science (in contradistinction to

philosophy) is in principal a historical science in that it speaks
of a specific occurrence in human existence.

At the same time, however, what has been said has inti-
mated something further—namely, that theology as a science
can make fruitful use of the philosophical analysis of human
existence. For the *man of faith* is in any case a *man*, just as
the proclamation out of which faith arises encounters him as a
human word. His sin and the forgiveness of his sin, which are
revealed to him in the proclamation, are phenomena within
human existence—or, better, are *also* that[6]—when they are
declared by him as a man of faith. If they are such phenomena, however, then their *possibility* within human existence
—i.e., their ontological or existential possibility, for nothing
has been said thereby about their ontic possibility—must be
demonstrable.

Indeed, when faith affirms, for example, that it is impossible for man to be righteous before God through his works,
that he has therefore necessarily missed the possibility of laying
hold of his authenticity in the decision that essentially belongs
to his existence, the impossibility that is meant is an ontic or
existentiell one. And to speak of such an impossibility is only
possible and meaningful if one can speak ontologically or
existentially about the possibility of " righteousness."[7] To say
of an animal that it is impossible for it to be rightwised by
works of the law is clearly meaningless because righteousness
is not an ontological possibility for it.[8]

In a certain sense, then, theology does " repeat " the analysis
of philosophy, insofar, namely, as it can only explicate its
fundamental concepts as concepts of existence on the basis of
an understanding of man's " being," and insofar as it is dependent on philosophy for the analysis of the meaning of
being. It could not do this if what were in question was a
" systematic " philosophy that proceeds " deductively " from
an idea of being that it presupposes. However, it can do it if
what is involved is a philosophical inquiry that, as pheno-
menology, points to its objects, i.e., attempts to bring the

phenomena themselves to self-manifestation. In this case, theology does not really learn from philosophy as such, it does not simply take over some philosophical system of dogma, but rather lets itself be referred by philosophy to the phenomenon itself; it lets itself be taught by the phenomenon, by man, whose structure philosophy seeks to disclose.

A philosophy would be unusable if it undertook to ascertain the " meaning " of human existence in the sense of trying to show that the latter is " meaningful " (or, on the contrary, as in Nietzsche, that it is " meaningless "). It would then try to take from the concrete man the question as to his " meaning," a question that is posed uniquely to him and can only be answered by him as an individual person; it would try to give a universal answer to man's question, " What is truth?" which as his question is a question of the moment. On the other hand, a legitimate philosophical analysis of human existence shows precisely that it is the concrete man himself who must alone pose the question about his " meaning," the question, " What is truth?" and give an answer to it. And just this is what it means for such an analysis to exhibit the " meaning " of human existence, i.e., to show what man means, what *meaning* " being " has when one speaks of man.

If philosophy by no means deceives itself into thinking that its work as inquiry leads to absolute knowledge,[9] then naturally theology also ought not to suppose that philosophy provides it with a normative ontology with which it is then able to work as it pleases. And this it will not suppose precisely when it is willing to learn from philosophy to look at the phenomena themselves. On the contrary, it will then expect that, by radicalizing and criticizing itself, philosophical work will always be able to exhibit the phenomena better and more clearly—wherewith, of course, theology will also recognize that it itself has always to learn and to relearn. But this recognition can be a stumbling-block only to a theology that has forgotten that it also is inquiry and imagines that, for its part, it is able to achieve absolute knowledge.[10]

In the sense indicated, then, theology does indeed " repeat " the work of philosophy; and it must repeat it if what happens in the Christian occurrence that is realized in faith, in " rebirth," is not a magical transformation that removes the man of faith from his humanity.[11] It must do it if existence in unfaith is both annulled and preserved in existence in faith. If, through faith, existence prior to faith is overcome *existentiell* or ontically, this still does not mean that the existential or ontological conditions of existing are destroyed. Theologically expressed, faith is not a new quality that inheres in the believer, but rather a possibility of man that must constantly be laid hold of anew because man only exists by constantly laying hold of his possibilities. The man of faith does not become an angel, but is *simul peccator, simul justus.* Therefore, all of the basic Christian concepts have a content that can be determined ontologically prior to faith and in a purely rational way. All theological concepts contain the understanding of being that belongs to man as such and by himself insofar as he exists at all. Thus theology should indeed learn from philosophy—precisely from that philosophy " which confesses as its deepest determination ' to serve the work of Dilthey,' which is to say, man's understanding of himself *qua* man."[12]

If Kuhlmann asks me, then, " Is the term ' future ' as Bultmann's theology understands it identical with what the philosopher Heidegger discovers as ' authentic possibility of being '?"[13] then I reply, Yes, indeed!—namely, in a formal or ontological sense. And just as I can clarify *conceptually* what Christian eschatology is when I know what in general " future " can mean for man, so also I can only clarify the concept of " sin," for example, by referring to the concept of guilt as an original ontological determination of existence.[14] In saying this, I by no means deny that I only know what sin is in faith. On the contrary, the more certainly the concept of guilt is grasped in its ontological content the more clearly it can be said theologically what sin is. I would make a mistake only if

I supposed that I could rationally deduce sin from guilt or could demonstrate the datum of sin in a rational way. In fact, I am even willing to accept in a positive sense Kuhlmann's reproach : " The decision of faith becomes a ' project' of the guilty being that I already am."[15] Indeed it does; for it is only so that the formal ontological meaning of the decision of faith could be defined, and it must be defined in this way if the decision of faith is to be an actual movement within man's existence. And I am able to give a clear conceptual statement of what " love " means in a Christian sense only on the basis of the " care "-structure of man's nature.[16]

Now I concede to Kuhlmann that in the works of mine to which he refers the explication of theological concepts is incomplete and that I was interested one-sidedly in the task that has for its subject the connection of theological work with existential analysis. But what I *cannot* concede to him is that the theological explication of existence in faith may not fall back on the philosophical analysis of man. On the contrary, I affirm that this is precisely what theology *must* do if it at all wants to clarify existence in faith in a conceptual way, i.e., if it wants to be a science and not merely a sermon. That there has to be theology as a science in addition to preaching is, to be sure, neither to be deduced from an idea of science nor to be established by the philosophical analysis of existence. For the latter, theology is indeed " superfluous." Theology can have its basis only in the man of faith. Only faith can motivate applying oneself to a science that undertakes a conceptual interpretation of existence in faith, and so theology can only be a movement of faith itself.

But what else should it be? What other basis can it have? It seems to me that the chief weakness of Kuhlmann's remarks is that one cannot tell from them how he himself thinks of the motive and object of theology as a science. Insofar as he speaks of its object, he speaks, in my opinion, only of the object of preaching. In a similar way, I still have never been able to see, in spite of all my efforts, what motive Grisebach has, *as a philosopher,* to be constantly having his say in our theological work.

I will not go into here what can or does lie behind faith's practical compulsion to develop a theology, but may refer to my essay "*Kirche und Lehre im Neuen Testament.*"[17] However, Kuhlmann can easily convince himself by consulting any dogmatics, old or new, that *every* theology is dependent for the clarification of its concepts upon a pretheological understanding of man that, as a rule, is determined by some philosophical tradition. Thus, for example, whether Christ is made understandable in terms of the concept of (divine) nature or religious and moral personality or the concept of a historical fact; or whether redemption is understood as a cosmic process, as a transformation of nature, as a moral and religious process, or as an experience; or whether faith is interpreted as holding things to be true or as trust, as obedience or as numinous experience; or whether the concept of sin is interpreted in terms of nature or of ethics—always the concepts that must guide the interpretation are concepts in which the "natural" man understands himself and his world. And how could it be otherwise if what is being talked about has to do with man and if what is said is to be understood—if none of these things is to remain a mere *x*? Even preaching is guided by a specific understanding of man, even if it does not need to make this understanding conceptually explicit. Theology, however, does have to make it explicit, since its task is to stand guard over preaching's purity and understandability.[18] It can fulfil its task only if it inquires after concepts that express the being of man in the most appropriate and "neutral" way possible. And if it does not ask philosophy for these, this is a mere fake. For then it is either uncritically dependent upon some older philosophical tradition or else itself engages in philosophical work—in which case the results are usually inferior enough!

I by no means imagine that by these remarks I have dealt exhaustively with the theme "Philosophy and Theology";

rather I have simply sought to indicate the direction in which an adequate treatment of it is to be found. Precisely at this point, however, new questions arise, especially the question of a so-called " natural theology," i.e., the question how we are to understand from the standpoint of faith, both positively and negatively, philosophy's ontological or existential analysis of human existence as an ontic or *existentiell* undertaking on the part of man—which is, of course, a different question from the question of the results of this analysis for ontological or existential understanding.[19] Since " ontological understanding cannot be neatly cut off from ontic experience,"[20] this question must become acute; and it is understandable that Kuhlmann's polemic against my theological work as being pseudophilosophical corresponds to a polemic directed by certain philosophers against Heidegger, which charges that he has abandoned the soil of pure ontological analysis and speaks pseudotheologically. But I do not have to defend Heidegger against such a charge.

I propose now to make use of what has been said by once again taking up Kuhlmann's charge and, to be sure, by dealing with the central formulation of that charge with reference to the concept of revelation—wherewith the question concerning " natural theology " will again present itself.

Kuhlmann fears that revelation is profaned by my procedure. Revelation becomes " the clarification, perhaps the definitive clarification, of one's own profane—or is it rather always already graced?—existence." For " if in order to understand what revelation is I must always already have a 'preunderstanding' of it, then indeed the 'hearing' of revelation itself becomes 'profane.' But then there is also no longer the possibility of understanding 'the word that is written' as 'holy'; for this 'word' says nothing more than what I already knew in my profane self-understanding."[21]

First of all, consider an analogy! A friendless person who consciously or unconsciously, avowedly or unavowedly longs for friendships knows what friendship is—and yet does not know it either. If such a person succeeds in finding a friend, what "more" does he then know than he already knew in his friendless self-understanding? Will he be able to define the concept of friendship in a new and better way? Of course not! —at least not in principle, even if in practice he is *perhaps* now able to talk of friendship more easily and richly. The very fact, however, that any such talk of friendship (i.e., as may be the result of an actual friendship) can be understood by any other friendless person shows that the knowledge of friendship is also open to a person who is actually friendless. What "more," then, do I know when I stand in an actual relation of friendship? Nothing!—at any rate, nothing more *about* friendship. What "more" I do know is that I now know my friend and also know myself anew, in the sense that, in understanding my friend, my concrete life in its work and its joy, its struggle and its pain, is qualified in a new way. In knowing my friend in the *event* of friendship, the events of my life become new—"new" in a sense that is valid only for me and visible only to me, that indeed only *becomes* visible in the now and thus must always become visible *anew*. However well I can know in advance and in general what a friend is, and also know that friendship must surely make my life new, the one thing I can never know in advance and in general is what my friend is to me.

And so it is indeed that the "word" of proclamation tells me "nothing more than what I already knew [or could have known] in my profane self-understanding." What "revelation" means in general cannot be any more exactly and completely specified by the man of faith than by any man of unfaith. Every man, because he knows about death, can also know about revelation and life, grace and forgiveness. What "more," then, does the man of faith know? This—that revelation has actually encountered him, that he really lives, that he is in fact graced, that he is really forgiven and will always be so. And he knows this in such a way that by faith in the revelation his concrete life in work and in joy, in struggle and in pain is newly qualified; he knows that through the *event* of revelation the events of his life become new—"new" in a sense that is valid only for the man of faith and visible only to him, that indeed only *becomes* visible in the now and thus must always become visible *anew*. The only new thing that faith and faith alone is able to say about revelation is that it has become an event and becomes an event. And what theology can do is, on the one hand, to say the very same thing and, on the other hand, to undertake the conceptual explication of such speaking about the event of revelation, to the end that the man of faith will have a critical knowledge of himself and that preaching will actually speak of revelation and faith.

If the revelation of which faith and theology speak is an event (and, to be sure, a specific event), then the "hearing" of revelation is indeed "profane" insofar as it is perceptible as a human process and insofar as it can be made understandable ontologically as a movement within man's existence.[22] The hearing receives the title "holy" only through its object, the revelation that is actually occurring, to whose occurrence it itself belongs.

If the revelation of which faith and theology speak is an event, then it is not an "original mode of being," "a way of existing that stands open to man 'in and of himself.'"[23] Nor is grace "a disposable quality of the natural man."[24] The knowledge about what revelation is in general and man's knowledge about his dependence on revelation (or the denial of this) is indeed a knowledge on the basis of the "*lumen naturale.*" And this knowledge has no need of the "clarification" of the gospel, however certain it is that from the hearing of the gospel such clarification of the natural man can actually be derived and can be appropriated by philosophy— just as an actual friendship can also actualize the "preunderstanding" of friendship and further its conceptual explication.

Whatever the man of faith acquires through such "clarification," however, then stands open also to the understanding of unfaith. This is so, on the one hand, because ontological analysis will become all the more certain and complete the richer the ontic experience and, on the other hand, because every ontic experience (as an experience of man) has the ontological conditions of its possibility in the human structure and therefore can be understood as possible on the basis of this structure. Thus it is also possible that Heidegger's ontological analysis can be fructified by Kierkegaard's explicitly Christian understanding of man without Heidegger thereby becoming a theologian or Kierkegaard turning out to be a philosopher.

What is the situation, for example, in understanding Paul's doctrine of the righteousness of faith, which is an explication of the man of faith's self-understanding? Is this doctrine understandable only to faith, or also to unfaith? Must I, in order to interpret it, be sure that I believe or that I will believe? Is the understanding of it that I may possibly acquire a guarantee to me that I believe? Must I therefore present myself to my readers and hearers as one who is also a man of faith? And should I say to the person who understands my interpretation, "You have faith"? Or if this is all nonsense, may one then no longer interpret the Scriptures? In a word, exegesis presupposes the *lumen naturale*; otherwise it is meaningless.

Finally, however, it must be said that there is also given to faith through revelation and the gospel a definitive "clarification" of profane existence that is not visible to philosophy. It is a "clarification," namely, that does indeed permit "profane" existence to appear as "always already graced." Of course, philosophy can even "understand" this in the formal sense, just as well as it can understand that in an actual friendship my eyes are opened with respect to my past so that I recognize what was genuine in it and what was not. But only the man of faith understands (in the ontic or *existentiell* sense) profane existence as graced. This does not mean, however, that "the *humanum* has again become *theos*,"[25] but rather that the natural man is again discovered as a creature of God.

II

In order now that this discussion may be something more than merely negative and polemical or programmatic and abstract, I propose to consider a concrete problem from the complex "philosophy and theology" or "ontological analysis of man and theological understanding of man," viz., the problem, "the historicity of man and faith." In doing this, I will, to be sure, no longer be engaged in discussion with Kuhlmann, but with Friedrich Gogarten; for such a discussion has the prospect of leading to positive results because Gogarten's remarks on this theme grow out of the original motive of theological inquiry and not out of interest in the purely formal question of scientific procedure. I hope it will be clear that my discussion with Gogarten is not directed *against* him, but rather is intended to inquire somewhat further *with* him in the direction of his own inquiry. That I stand together with him in this direction is no accident, for I largely owe it to him that this is my situation; and so it is that what I am able to say is also an expression of gratitude for what I have learned from him. I will set Gogarten's interpretation of history over against the understanding of historicity that has been worked out by Heidegger. (That I am not any less indebted to the latter I hardly need to say.)

To be a man—if I may briefly summarize for our purpose the results of Heidegger's analysis—is something that uniquely belongs to the individual; and the being of man is a "possibility of being," i.e., the man who is involved in care for himself chooses his own unique possibility. This choice is a genuine resolve only when it is a carrying out of the "resolution" that grows out of man's seeing in death his properest possibility and letting himself be thrown back by death into the now—of understanding the now from the standpoint of death and thus resolving in the situation.[26]

Like Heidegger, Gogarten also is concerned to achieve an original understanding of history and historicity in opposition to the vulgar understanding—specifically in his discussion with Troeltsch. But there would appear to be an opposition between Heidegger and Gogarten. For, on the one hand, the "being toward death" in terms of which Heidegger makes understandable what is meant by "resolution" plays no role at all for Gogarten. On the other hand, the concept of the "neighbour" cannot be found in Heidegger, whereas for Gogarten it is precisely the encounter with the neighbour as "thou" that constitutes historicity. For Heidegger man is limited by death; for Gogarten he is limited by the thou. To be sure, Heidegger does say that our being related with other persons determines the actual possibilities of resolve; however, resolution itself is not based in our relation with others, but in our temporality, i.e., our finitude, our being toward death.

Is there, then, a double possibility for understanding man's historicity? If so, how are the two interpretations related? Can the one proposal be "built into" the other? Or must one or the other be designated as false? The relation is difficult to judge because up to now Gogarten has not given us a clear and thorough analysis. If we confine ourselves to his remarks in the book *Ich glaube an den dreieinigen Gott,* then it would seem that he views man in much the same way Heidegger does; for he points out that history stands under the law of "transitoriness" and then adds the statement that it is the sphere of "decision."[27] However, he immediately goes on to interpret "decision" as decision in face of the thou, whereas for Heidegger it is a decision for a possibility of my own existence.

Of course, this need not be in opposition to Heidegger; for in the latter's view also man's concrete situation is determined by being related with others so that every actual decision is made in the face of the thou. Furthermore, Gogarten's "decision" admits of being interpreted in such a way that in deciding for the thou man lays hold of a possibility of his own existence. Even so, however, the "thou" is understood by Gogarten differently from the way Heidegger understands "the other." For Gogarten, namely, it is the thou that first discloses the transitoriness of my existence and constrains me to decision, while for Heidegger the other is first authentically disclosed, i.e., is divested of his characteristic as an instance of "the one," by my knowing myself under the eyes of death as placed in decision. For in knowing about his own coming to an end, man for the first time genuinely understands his relation with others, in that, by knowing about his own solitude and freedom, he understands the others accordingly and sets them free for their possibilities. Moreover, it would not be clear from Heidegger's "being in relation with others" why, as Gogarten thinks, the reality constituted by the relation of I with thou must from the outset be described as full of contradictions and oppositions.[28]

But we must now add still a further difference, namely, that for Gogarten the encounter with the thou contains two possibilities (and only these two) that play no role whatever for Heidegger—*hate and love*. For Heidegger, the other becomes authentically visible as the other because I know myself in resolution and thereby have a true understanding of the being with others in which I am always actually involved. For Gogarten, on the other hand, the thou with whom I am bound from the beginning only becomes visible in love, i.e., in the acknowledgment of his claim on me; prior to such acknowledgment he is not visible to me as thou, as neighbour, because I stand over against him in hate. It would seem, then, that if one and the same phenomenon is seen in both of these interpretations, then Heidegger's "resolution" must be interpreted as "love." Can this be done?

It is certainly not forbidden simply because existential

analysis cannot consider in principle the specific thing upon which the individual man resolves. For it would be a misunderstanding to suppose that with "love" there is given a concrete "what" of resolve. On the contrary, "love" designates a "how" of human existence, a mode of being in which it is authentically historical. Just as, according to Heidegger, man resolves in a particular situation, so also, according to Gogarten, does the man who loves love the concrete thou in a specific action. Whereas for Heidegger it is resolution that makes the choice, for Gogarten it is love.[29]

But now if love does not refer to the concrete "what" of a resolve—since, rather, it is *in* love that such a "what" is discovered—does love perhaps belong to the possibilities that present themselves in the inheritance over which man takes charge? For in the case of these possibilities also what is meant is not a concrete "what"; on the contrary, it is only on the basis of a decision for one of them that such a "what" can be found. These possibilities (e.g., to exist as a statesman, a philosopher, a scientist, a citizen, or a hermit) are clearly something "more general" than the concrete "what" of a resolve and yet something "more concrete" than resolution. Is love, then, such a possibility of authentically existing?

At first glance it might seem so, i.e., that in laying hold of love man chooses one of the many possibilities for existing authentically—namely, love—and rejects the rest.[30] According to Gogarten, however, love is not one possibility for existing authentically among others, which could only be rejected if man chose to lay hold of love. On the contrary, love is the *only* possibility of authentic existence. Only in love is man historical. Only where a thou encounters the I and is ackowledged in his claim by the I in love does anything at all really happen—*what* happens being left open. For Heidegger, on the other hand, resolution as such constitutes man's historicity, and it is left open which of his possibilities man lays hold of. Therefore, if there is to be a unity between Heidegger and Gogarten, we must be permitted to say that only where the I decides for the thou, acknowledging his claim in love, is resolution actually realized. The possibility of saying something like this, however, falls outside of existential analysis; for this would not be an ontological statement; it speaks about the factual. But does this mean, then, that the possibility of saying this is utterly excluded? Manifestly not! From the standpoint of existential analysis, we are entirely free to make such a statement as a statement about the factual, about an ontic experience.

In point of fact, Heidegger speaks as an ontologist and therefore has neither the occasion nor the right to speak of love. Gogarten, on the other hand, speaks as a theologian of the ontic; and it is in this sphere alone that love, in the radical sense in which he understands it, is to be found.

In Gogarten, there is an intersecting of the ontological concern to clarify the concept of historicity and the theological concern to show that history really occurs only where faith works through love. Therefore, if he does not succeed in achieving perfect clarity, the lack of clarity in his remarks is precisely proof that theological work is dependent upon existential analysis. Gogarten's real concern is theological, namely, to show that actual history only occurs where the I hears the claim of the thou. But in order for this statement to be at all understandable, it is obviously necessary first to clarify what history and occurrence mean in the formal or ontological sense, i.e., it is necessary to make clear what is meant by historicity as a characteristic of human existence. Thereby—insofar as the being of man is defined as a " possibility of being "—it would also be made clear that man can exist in both an " authentic " and an " inauthentic " historicity; and only then would the theological affirmation be clear that man is only genuinely historical in faith and in love. For this affirmation states that genuine historicity, which is an ontological possibility of man as such, only occurs ontically under a specific ontic condition that cannot be further understood ontologically.

This condition is specified by Gogarten when he says that love is possible only in Christ. What does this mean? Since love does not mean a concrete " what " of resolve, upon which man can simply decide, but rather is the " how " of resolve in which such a " what " is first discovered; and since, on the other hand, love is not (like historicity) a characteristic of man as such (what Heidegger speaks of as an " existential "), but rather is an ontic determination of resolve—since both of these things are true, what is meant by Gogarten's statement is that I am able to take charge of my own factual being there as one who loves only if I myself am already loved, and that the fact that I am already loved is what is promised to me in the proclamation of Christ and thereupon appropriated by me in faith.

Obviously an ontological analysis of existence cannot raise any objection against this statement. For just as little as such an analysis can give consideration to the fact of Christ, the fact of the proclaimed word, so little has it any occasion to deny this fact. It would have to object only if the attempt were made by theology (i.e., by a pseudo theology) to find a place for the Christian proclamation in man's ontological constitution and thus to interpret Christianity as an " existential " of human existence. It cannot object, however, precisely if it exhibits the ontological possibility of something like a word that encounters man and wills to be heard and obeyed and that ontically qualifies his existence as a word that is either heard or rejected. The claim of faith that there is only *one* word that has this power is not discussible for ontological analysis, and the assertion that this word is the word of God is for it absurd, for it knows only man and nothing beyond him. On the other hand, however, the claim of faith that the word of the proclamation is the word of God and therefore is spoken to man from the beyond does not at all mean that this word does not at the same time encounter us as a phenomenon of human existence. That it is the word of God is not to be seen, but only to be believed; and to be able to show what this means, what is meant therefore by "the word became flesh," is precisely an indirect result of existential analysis.

The "exclusiveness" that theology claims for the word of proclamation and thereby for the Christian man (i.e., for the man of faith and love) as alone genuinely historical may not be falsely interpreted to mean that the Christian man is in any way exempt from the ontological conditions of human existence. According to Heidegger, man freely chooses his possibility of existing authentically. This freedom of choice is not taken away from the man of faith because for him love is now the *only* possible possibility. For love does not mean an inherited possibility for existing authentically which has been freely chosen and in which the man who is to resolve necessarily exists; on the contrary, such a possibility is first chosen *in* love. The man of faith remains fully responsible; he has to take charge of his "thrownness" (which he understands as creatureliness) and to resolve in his actual being-there. Choice is not taken from him; he stands under the demand to choose in love.[31]

Furthermore, the claim of the man of faith that he alone is free does not compete with the ontological exhibition of man's freedom for his possibility of existing authentically; for Christian freedom is freedom from sin. Therefore, it is the judgment of faith that wherever the freedom of man that is exhibited ontologically realizes itself ontically without doing so in faith and love, it is not freedom. Similarly, it claims that wherever resolution realizes itself ontically in that an actual man, being shattered by death, lets himself be thrown back upon his being-there and resolves in the situation and thus for himself, it is really *a resolution of despair*.

For resolution is understood ontologically as meaning that it is in it that man, whose being is a possibility of being, lays hold of a possibility of his existence through a particular resolve. What faith and theology say and show is that in this possibility of being (which in its ontological character is not in dispute) there is always present in fact a *necessity of being,* insofar as in every actual choice in which man chooses a possibility of existing authentically he in fact always chooses what he already is—that he never gets rid of his past and therefore is never free. For this reason, however, he is also never genuinely historical insofar as historicity means the possibility of an actual i.e., a new occurrence.

If for faith, all of the ontic resolution, freedom, and historicity of the man of unfaith is illusory, and it all really exists only in faith and in love, then the question necessarily arises how the faithless man is at all able to see these characteristics of human existence in existential analysis. Now, doubtless the man who has death in view resolves upon a possibility of his existence; but the resolve is a resolve of despair and the possibility is always only the one possibility of being what he already is. Precisely in this resolve of despair, however, man understands what resolution, freedom, and historicity are. And it is just for this reason that faith can say of existence before faith that it stands in hate, in sin. It does not stand in a neutral sphere so that if it is to be moved to love, it must first undergo a miraculous transformation. Love is not *caritas infusa,* but rather is from the outset an ontological possibility of human existence of which man dimly knows. Faith is from the outset an ontological possibility of man that appears in the resolve of despair. It is this that makes it possible for man to understand when he is encountered by the kerygma. For in willing to resolve man wills to believe and to love.

If, then, there is to this extent no conflict between Heidegger and Gogarten, i.e., between ontological analysis of man and the theological interpretation of existence in faith, but if, on the contrary, theology is able on the basis of existential analysis to interpret faith and love in their formal ontological essence as resolution, there nevertheless would seem to be a final point where there actually is a conflict.

According to existential analysis, man's resolution is based in his being limited by death, i.e., in his temporality as a being towards death. According to faith, on the other hand, the resolution that is to be understood as love has its basis in man's being limited by the thou, who is visible to existential analysis only as " the other," while to faith he becomes visible in love as " the neighbour." But now by seeing that man is actually limited by the thou, faith and love make clear that being limited by death only holds true of one who does not stand in love. Because, namely, I do not see that my neigh-bour limits me, because—in hate—I am bent on realizing my-self, death becomes the limit for me. For him who knows himself loved, however, it becomes clear that the actual limita-tion of the I is given by the thou, and death forthwith loses its character as the limit. The question concerning death becomes superfluous for him who knows (*existentiell*) that he is there to serve the neighbour.

Is there, then, after all, a theological correction to be made of the ontological analysis of man, and is theology itself to propose something like an ontology that is to compete with the philosophical one?

No! For in existential analysis death as the limit of human existence is significant merely for answering the question con-cerning man's existence as a totality.[32] The ontic phenomenon of death is only one striking phenomenon in which man's limitation clearly displays itself. And its significance in this regard can also be taken over by another ontic phenomenon that similarly allows man's limitation to become visible—namely, by love. For " to be sure, nothing at all depends on the word itself, though *everything* depends on understanding what the analysis of human existence has sought to expose by means of the reality that is thus denoted."[33] Precisely this is the question : if " the problem of existential analysis is solely to expose the ontological structure of man's being toward an end,"[34] then cannot the encounter with the thou clarify this ontological structure equally well as death?

That existential analysis sees in death the phenomenon in

terms of which it can understand man in his totality rests on its having to seek for a phenomenon that, so to speak, limits man from the outside and that he himself is not able to give. For man cannot in his care-structure, his " being out ahead of himself," know any end of existence that constitutes him as a totality. However, if the analysis is not to engage in empty speculations about " something outside " man, it has to be able to exhibit the limit that constitutes him a totality as something within his existence, as encountering us in man himself. The one phenomenon that satisfies these conditions is death.

Now if theology instead gives this function to the proclamation that is encountered in existence and, in unity with it, to the encounter with the thou who becomes understandable as a thou through this proclamation, it does not say that the existential analysis of death is " false " and that the man of faith would no longer experience his limitation in death. Death stands before even the man of faith. If it has " lost its power " for him, this simply means that faith (and, accordingly, theology also) sees that death means an either/or for man in the sense of judgment and grace (and therefore in the sense of a qualification of man as a totality of which existential analysis can know nothing), which is decided in faith. Thus theology recognizes the intimate connection between death and the revelation of God. For it sees, on the one hand, that God encounters the natural man in death[35] and, on the other hand, that the encounter with revelation means nothing more and nothing less than death for the natural man—that love is an absolute surrender of the I and only as such " overcomes " death.

Thus the determination that the man of love acquires from the thou is exactly analogous to the threefold determination of man by death, which is made visible by existential analysis :

(1) " So long as man is, there is a not yet that he will be, a something that is constantly outstanding that belongs to him." Precisely so, however, does the man of faith and love understand himself (cf. Phil. 3 :12-14; Rom. 13 :8).

(2) "The coming to an end of the particular being that as not yet reached its end (or the actual elimination of that which is outstanding) has the character of no longer being-here." Correspondingly, the man of faith understands that he first receives his existence from the thou; if the particular claim of the thou that stands before me were completely eliminated, then I would no longer be I.

(3) "The coming to an end involves a mode of being for the concrete man that is absolutely unique to him." Correspondingly, the man who loves knows that the neighbour is uniquely *his* neighbour and that he cannot appoint another to do his loving for him.[36]

Thus, in the same way as in relation to death, the man who has to render love to the thou " stands before himself in his properest possibility of being" and " in thus standing before himself all relations in him" to death " are dissolved."[37]

However, being limited by death so far from simply ceases for the man of faith that it rather constantly appears and must constantly be overcome in faith and in love. Therefore, the characteristics that determine existence in faith are all to be made conceptually understandable only on the basis of existential analysis. As *faith* is coming under the eyes of God, so *love* is the resolution that lays hold of the situation, and *hope,* the being ahead of oneself in care, in which one is concerned for himself, but in which this " for himself," while not destroyed, is left in the hands of God. And by the same token, *joy* is nothing other than the anxiety that motivates man (as the latter is anxious about " nothing," so joy rejoices in " nothing ") in a specific modification, namely, as " overcome."

PAUL*

I. SOURCES

The sources for a historical knowledge of Paul are essentiall
his genuine letters; these include Romans, I and II Corinth
ans, Galatians, Philippians, I Thessalonians, and Philemor
These letters come from a limited period in his life and,
occasional writings, contain only a few notices and intimatio
about his life; on the other hand, they give a rich picture
his views and intentions. So far as the outer course of his li
is concerned, Acts provides much good material in its source
even if alongside of these it also provides legendary traditio
As far as possible, its information must be controlled by Paul
own letters. The later Christian tradition, to which the spur
ous Pauline letters in the New Testament already belong, co
tains only a few reliable statements in addition to legenda
information. Paul is not mentioned at all in heathen liter
ture, although he is perhaps referred to in certain Jewi
writings.[1]

II. LIFE

1. *Background and Training.* Paul was the child of a tr
Jewish family of the tribe of Benjamin (Rom. 11:1; II Cc
11:22; Gal. 2:15; Phil. 3:5). According to Acts 22:3 (
9:11, 21:39), he was born and raised in Tarsus in Cilicia a
thus came from a Hellenistic city in which there was
mingling of Oriental and Greek populations. Tarsus was si
nificant as a commercial city and was also a place where Gre

* "Paulus," Religion in Geschichte und Gegenwart, iv (2nd e
Tübingen: J. C. B. Mohr, 1930), 1019-45.

cience (and especially Stoic philosophy) was carried on. If Paul speaks of himself in Phil. 3:5 as a "Hebrew of Hebrews," this can be taken to suggest that his family had strictly preserved its Palestinian character (especially the Aramaic language) in the Diaspora. Whether his parents actually migrated to Tarsus from Gischala in Judaea—and, indeed, whether he himself was born in Gischala (Hieronymus)—is uncertain and is hardly confirmed simply because in Acts 23 : 16 ff. the son of his sister appears in Jerusalem. In fact, it seems rather improbable, if Acts (22 :28, cf. 16 :37) is correct in handing down that he was born a Roman citizen and had the civic rights of a citizen of Tarsus (21 :39). If he was born a Roman citizen, then he had the name Paul (the only name he ever uses in his letters) from birth, while his Jewish name was Saul. Moreover, this means that he cannot have belonged to the lower social classes. In any case, his letters show that he was a Hellenistic Jew, i.e., that in his training Jewish tradition and Greek culture were combined. And if his scientific development was not anywhere near as comprehensive as that, say, of Philo, he still had mastered the Greek language to a high degree; not only are many of the techniques of rhetoric and of popular philosophy (" diatribe ") familiar to him, but he is also acquainted with certain concepts and ideas of Stoic philosophy (e.g., the concepts of "conscience," "freedom," and "duty"). He obviously had enjoyed a systematic training in Jewish scribism, as is evident not only from his having belonged to the company of the Pharisees (Phil. 3 :5; cf. Gal. 1 :14), but especially from the style of his thinking, his argumentation, and his exegesis. According to Acts 22 :3, he had studied in Jerusalem with Gamaliel the elder. But this is hardly correct, since one must surely conclude from Gal. 1 :22 that prior to his conversion he had never resided for any length of time in Jerusalem (although this naturally would not exclude occasional trips for religious festivals). As a rabbi Paul practised a trade (according to Acts 18 :3, he was a tentmaker), for he frequently makes reference to his work (I

Thess. 2.9; I Cor. 9;6 ff.; II Cor. 11:12). His world of idea
gives evidence of an acquaintance with heathen cults and wit
Oriental and Gnostic mythology. To what extent this stem
from the views that he acquired in his youth or from his late
travels cannot be said; it would have been mediated to him i
part through his Jewish connections, among whom, in add
tion to scribism, apocalyptic and mythological speculation
were also carried on. In any case, his christology did not gro
entirely from Christian ideas, but rather presupposes the cor
cepts of a mythological-apocalyptic expectation of Messiah an
redeemer in which he already lived as a Jew.

2. *Conversion.* So far as the pre-Christian period of Paul
life is concerned, we know for certain only that as a Pharise
he was a zealous champion of the law and of the scribal trad
tion (Gal. 1:13 f.; Phil. 3:6). It appears likely from Ga
5:11 that even as a Jew he engaged in missionary activit
among the heathen, apparently with the point of view that
characterized in Rom. 2:19 f. In his zeal he became a pe
secutor of the Christian community (Gal. 1:13, 1:23; Ph
3:6; cf. Acts 9:1 ff., 22:4 f., 26:9 ff.). Since he cann
have resided in Jerusalem prior to his conversion (see abov
II, 1), this persecution cannot have taken place in Judaea; an
his participation in the death of Stephen is a legend—a jud
ment that is also confirmed by a literary-critical investigation o
Acts 7:58-8:3. From Gal. 1:17 one must infer that th
scene of the persecution was either in or around Damascu
Moreover, the character of the persecution is considerab
exaggerated in the account in Acts; for what was involve
could not have been a carrying out of sentences of death, b
only beating with rods and expulsion from the synagogue-
or, in other words, the same kind of persecution that Paul hin
self subsequently experienced as a Christian missionary (
Cor. 11:24). But why did Paul persecute the church? Natu
ally, for him also it was scandalous that Christians proclaime

a crucified one as the Messiah (I Cor. 1:18 ff.) and claimed that the time of salvation was already breaking in. But while in the judgment of Jews this would indeed be madness, it would not be a crime that was deserving of punishment. The Christian message first became a crime when, with the preaching of the crucified one, the validity of the law was also called in question. Thus when Paul characterizes himself in Gal. 1:13 f. as a persecutor of the church and at the same time as one who was zealous for the law, he shows that he had come to know Christianity in a form in which it already stood over against the law in a critical way and to some extent had actually overcome it. This is also evident because for him the question concerning the acceptance of the Christian message is identical with the either/or decision between the law and Jesus Christ. And it is further confirmed because we know of different forms of Hellenistic Christianity, all of which to some degree pose this either/or and yet are not determined by Paul's characteristic teaching concerning the law. Therefore, Paul first came to know Christianity in its Hellenistic form; and he became a persecutor because he could not help seeing it as an attack on the law that was the holy will of God and "the embodiment of knowledge and truth" (Rom. 2:20).

It was as a persecutor that Paul experienced his conversion; and to be sure, as a psychic process this conversion was a vision of Christ (Gal. 1:15; I Cor. 9:1, 15:8; there is very likely an allusion also in II Cor. 4:6), which has been coloured over with legendary features by Acts (9:1 ff., 22:4 ff., 26:9 ff.). In view of the complete lack of biographical reports, nothing at all can be said about how this process is to be made psychologically understandable and thus how it was prepared by Paul's inner development. In particular, it is nothing other than sheer fantasy when one depicts the impression that was made on him by the persecuted Christians; and that he even saw Jesus and was impressed by him is also to be read out of II Cor. 5:16 only by fantasy. Paul himself had no interest in

his personal development, but only in the theological mean
ing of his conversion; and it is solely the latter that we are in
position to know. Especially may one not understand Rom
7:7-25 as a biographical document of Paul's inner develop
ment; for the "I" of these verses is as little the individua
"I" of Paul as is, for example, the "I" of I Cor. 13:11. O
the contrary, Paul is there presenting the situation of the Jev
under the law in the light of the real meaning of that situa
tion as it is disclosed to the eye of faith. Moreover, the phras
"kicking against the goads," in Acts 26:14 does not refer t
an inner struggle, but rather is a widespread proverbial ex
pression that means that man cannot withstand the divine. I
is completely clear from Paul's letters that his "conversion"
was not a conversion of "repentance," in which after lon
suffering under an afflicted conscience and inner resistanc
he finally succeeded in confessing his guilt before God an
thereby inwardly set himself free. For as one who has bee
converted, he does not look back on his past with a feeling c
shame, as though it had been a time in which he was sunk i
guilt, but rather views it with a feeling of pride (Gal. 1:13 f.
Phil. 3:6). He has not been freed from a burden, but rathe
has sacrificed a proud past (Phil. 3:6 ff.). That he was
persecutor does not impress him as guilt, but merely provide
a measure of the grace of the God who has called him (I Co.
15:9 f.). His conversion also does not appear to him as a
enlightenment that emancipates him from an illusion, fror
the unbearable burden of works of the law and a false idea c
God. For he never doubts that up to the time of "fulfi
ment," the way of the law was commanded by God and w
meaningful (Gal. 3:23 ff.; even Rom. 7:7 ff. is a defence c
the law, not an attack on it!). Thus he knows nothing abou
the law's being a burden from the standpoint of the Jew
subjective experience; and at no time in his Christian polem
against the law does he represent faith as an emancipatio
from such a burden. Nor is what is meant by the "anxiety" i

which man exists prior to faith the subjective feeling of anxiety that is caused by false religious ideas (see below, III 2). Faith is not the emancipation of a man who is yearning for freedom from chains that he himself experiences as oppressive; rather it is the resolution to surrender all that was man's pride, all self-glorification, all " boasting." This means, however, that Paul's conversion was the resolve to surrender his whole previous self-understanding, which was called in question by the Christian message, and to understand his existence anew. If God had already permitted the time of salvation to break in by sending the Messiah, then the way whereby man himself sought to achieve righteousness by means of works of the law was called in question. If God himself had introduced salvation by sending the Messiah and permitting him to be crucified, then he had destroyed the Jewish way of salvation and had thereby passed judgment against everything human, which had reached its highest point in Judaism. Thus what Paul was asked by the Christian proclamation was whether he was willing to see in a historical fact like the person and destiny of Jesus the breaking in of the time of salvation, the new creation that was being introduced by God. He was asked whether he was willing to acknowledge in the cross of Jesus the judgment against the previous self-understanding of the pious Jew and whether he was thus willing to understand himself anew and to accept the judgment of " sin and death " against his previous life. And this he affirmed in his conversion.

3. *Career as Apostle.* A. Paul apparently knew himself called to be an apostle by his conversion (Gal. 1:15 f.) and immediately engaged in missionary activity in Damascus and Arabia. After a brief visit to Jerusalem, he then worked in Syria and Cilicia (Gal. 1:21) and resided for a time in Tarsus, in order thence to be fetched by Barnabas to Antioch, where Hellenistic Jewish Christians who had been driven from

Jerusalem had already established a congregation (Acts 11:19 ff.). Since as a result of this Hellenistic mission there arose a Gentile Christianity that did not accept the law and specifically did not accept circumcision, a discussion with the primitive community, which remained faithful to the law, became inevitable. This took place at the so-called Apostolic Council, for which Paul and Barnabas went up to Jerusalem. They sought to see to it that the Gentile Christians' freedom from the law was acknowledged and thus were able to preserve the unity of the two early Christian groups; this was especially expressed by the determination that there should be a collection taken in the Gentile Christian congregations for the " poor " at Jerusalem (Gal. 2:1-10; the presentation in Acts 15 is legendary). Since, however, the question concerning the intercourse in mixed congregations (especially at table) of Jewish Christians who were faithful to the law and Gentile Christians who were free from it was apparently left undiscussed, there subsequently arose a conflict between Paul and Peter in Antioch, which also led to Paul's falling out with Barnabas (Gal. 2:11 ff.). Later on, also, Paul's mission was occasionally interfered with by " Judaizers," i.e., by Jewish Christian missionaries who demanded from converted Gentiles an acceptance of the law, or at least, of circumcision. Paul struggled against such " Judaizers " in Galatia. However, the opinion, which has been influential ever since F. C. Baur, that throughout the whole field of Paul's missionary activity there was a constant struggle between Paulinism and Judaizing Christianity is false. To be sure, in II Corinthians also Paul has to struggle with Jewish Christian adversaries; however, they clearly are not preachers of the law; and whether he is fighting against " Judaizers " or rather against Jews in Phil. 3:2 ff. is disputed. In any case his polemic in Romans is not directed against " Judaizers," but rather takes issue in principle with the Jewish position of legalistic piety.

The mission field that Paul undertook to serve after the

Apostolic Council can be determined from Acts, which is frequently confirmed by statements in the letters. He first preached in Cyprus and in Pamphylia, Lycaonia, and Pisidia in Asia Minor (Acts 13 and 14, which are falsely placed before the Apostolic Council in ch. 15). Then, a subsequent journey led him from Syria-Cilicia clear across Asia Minor (the Galatian congregations were founded at that time; Acts 16) to Troas and thence to Macedonia (Philippi and Thessalonica) and back to Achaia. In Corinth, then, he tarried for a longer period and from there also established other congregations (Acts 15:40-18:22). After what seems to have been a short return trip to Antioch (Acts 18:22 f.), he once again undertook a large-scale mission for which Ephesus was his headquarters. From there, after a trip through Macedonia to Corinth, he again went up to Jerusalem to deliver a collection (Acts 18:23-21:16). There, at the instigation of the Jews, he was arrested by the Romans because of a riot and then (the record is not clear) was brought to Rome for sentencing (Acts 21:17-28:31). Acts closes with the statement that he was imprisoned in Rome for two years. So far as the outcome of his trial is concerned, nothing certain is known; however, it is firmly fixed in the tradition that he died the death of a martyr. This is evidenced already by the intimations in Acts (especially 20:22 ff., 21:10 ff.), and it is specifically narrated in I Clement (ch. 5), which is apparently of the opinion that Paul, like Peter, was executed under Nero. According to I Clem. 5:7, before he died, Paul also preached in Spain, just as he says he had planned to do in Rom. 15:24 f. Whether he actually did so, however (to do so he would have had to be freed from the Roman imprisonment that is reported by Acts), or whether the Spanish journey is a legend that has grown out of Rom. 15:24 f. is a matter of dispute. It is certain, however, that he did not do any further work in the East, as is assumed by those scholars who argue for the Pauline authorship of the Pastorals in order to be able to maintain the statements that are contained in these letters concerning journeys that cannot be assigned to his career prior to his (first) Roman imprisonment.[2]

B. Paul was not the first nor was he the only missionary of the apostolic age. Already before him, Hellenistic Jewish Christians, among them especially Barnabas, had engaged in missions to the Gentiles (Acts 11 :19 ff.), and in Damascus as well as in Antioch there existed Christian communities. Moreover, Paul did not found the congregation at Rome, any more than he established the Christianity of Alexandria, whose origins are in general unknown to us. Thus in addition to him and his fellow workers, there were both before and alongside of him a whole host of missionaries who are now forgotten. Whether some one of them envisaged the missionary task in the same way that Paul did, to carry the gospel to the ends of the earth until Christ returns (Rom. 15 :17 ff.), we do not know. In any case, Paul himself was sustained by a consciousness of this task; and he supposed that he was fulfilling it by founding congregations in the important cities, whence the faith might then be spread to the surrounding countrysides. His work as a missionary was his " boast," which, to be sure, was wrought by Christ; and he was proud of having only preached the gospel where it had not as yet been heard (Rom. 15 :20; II Cor. 10 :15 f.), and also proud that he had renounced the right of the apostle to be supported by the congregations (I Cor. 9 :15 ff.; II Cor. 11 :7 ff.). All the same, however much he looked upon his work as a missionary as his life-task and however certain he was that the results of his mission had been prodigious—in his own conviction, the greatest of all (I Cor. 15 :10)—it is not in his accomplishments as a missionary that his real significance lies. Nor does it lie in the fact that he not only won the Gentiles to the faith, but also organized viable congregations and inwardly and outwardly strengthened them by his letters and visits. In this respect, there may well have been others who were his equal. Moreover, his real historical accomplishment is not that he fought for and won freedom from the law for Gentile Christianity, even if his part in this was a prominent one. For there is little doubt that this also would have happened without him, even as it had been prepared for before him and was actually carried out alongside of him. Writings like Hebrews, Barnabas, and I Clement, which in one sense or another, although in an un-Pauline sense, are free from the law, show that in this connection there were several possibilities; indeed, this is even shown by the so-called " Apostolic decree," which was not concluded by Paul and the earliest apostles at the Apostolic Council, as Acts reports, but rather was afterwards agreed upon by the Jewish community and the Hellenistic Christians and then subsequently communicated to Paul (Acts 21 :25). In this respect, the way had also been prepared by Hellenistic Judaism through reinterpreting the law and easing its requirements for proselytes. Thus there was hardly a danger that the Christian communities in the Greco-Roman world would become legalistic Jewish sects. However, there was considerable danger that they would become a passing phenomenon of Hellenistic syncretism, like the other religious communities that grouped themselves around the cult of some Oriental redeemer-deity. An essential part of Paul's accomplishment consists in his having joined the Christian communities into a firm unity and in seeing to it that there was no break with the mother community in Jerusalem. By teaching the individual churches to understand themselves as members of the one ecclesia and by helping those who had faith in Jesus Christ to see themselves as the true Israel, he gave the new religion a historical consciousness of itself as a church and also endowed it with the power that indwells such a consciousness. The Christian congregations were not only bound together, like the mystery congregations, by the same cult and the same theological or mythological ideas, but rather by the conviction that they stood at the end of a closed and unified history and thus also by a strong feeling that they belonged together and to Jerusalem. It is for this reason that Paul puts so much importance on what seems to be the most trivial stipulation of the Apostolic Council—namely, the collection; hence also his endeavour to bind the congregations together, not only by exchanging news and greetings between them, but also by impressing upon them their ties with Jerusalem (Gal. 2:10; I Cor. 16:1 ff.; II Cor. 8 and 9; Rom. 15:25 ff.). Thus, to a high degree, Paul's significance consists in his having given to Christianity not the consciousness of being a new "religion," but rather the consciousness of being a "church" in a sense that was unknown in the Hellenistic world. Nevertheless, this consciousness of being a church is but a recasting of the Jewish inheritance; for in Judaism also the idea of the church as the people of God was very much alive. And there undoubtedly were other Christian missionaries of Hellenistic-Jewish background who were also sustained by such a church consciousness (cf. again Hebrews, Barnabas, and I Clement), so that here, too, it is impossible to speak of an exclusive accomplishment of Paul. If, however, his accomplishment actually does tower above that of others, this is not only because the idea of the church was determinative in his work, but especially because as a writer he surpassed everyone else in quality and influence. Even if his letters are only occasional writings, still, in form as well as content, they are the surpassing monuments of early Christian literature (with the sole exception of John), which almost immediately were read in the church way beyond the congregations for which they were written, were subsequently collected together, and were also frequently imitated. However, even with this we still have not spoken of Paul's real significance. For this lies in the fact that as a *theologian* he gave to the Christian faith an adequate understanding of itself. However much his thought still moved within the mythological ideas of antiquity, still, on the one hand, he extricated Christian thinking from the realm of mythology and speculation and made it into an unfolding of the understanding of man, the world, and God that is given in faith itself; he based Christian knowing on our being known by God and defined its proper object as that which has been "bestowed" on us by God through grace (I Cor. 2 : 12); thus he understood knowing in its unity with the whole Christian life, so that knowing proves its legitimacy by realizing itself in unity with the obedience of faith and love as *existentiell* thinking. On the other hand, he also demonstrated the indispensability of such thinking for the life of faith and love, by showing that it preserves for this life a correct self-understanding, so that the latter does not fall away and is not led astray, whether by Jewish legalism or by the speculations of pneumatics and Gnostics. Paul finally performed the greatest service for the freeing of faith from the law and for uniting the congregations into a church because he gave a firm conceptual expression to the necessities that others also had more or less clearly recognized. This expression gave strength to the self-understanding and self-consciousness of the Christian community and determined Christian theological thinking forever after, again and again saving it from falling away into a false understanding of faith. And Paul's theology acquired such significance even where its propositions were passed on without their meaning's really being understood in its fullness, as was in fact immediately the case with his disciples and imitators; even as truths that were only half or badly understood they carried their corrective in themselves.

III. THEOLOGY

1. Presuppositions: A. *Paul's Personality and Conversion.* If we are concerned to inquire about the actual content of Paul's theology, then it would be wrong to go back to his "personality" in order on that basis to understand his theology. For in the first place, a picture of his personality and his character can only be obtained by reconstructing it on the basis of having first understood his theological and non-theological statements; and so one deceives himself if he imagines that he

can understand what Paul says by understanding his personality. In the second place, however, what one customarily
refers to as the "character" of a man is not something outside
of his work to which one can refer it in order to explain it;
his "character" is as little this as, conversely, his work is
something that is detached from his "character." Rather a
man first acquires his "character" in his work, and his work
is a presentation of his "character." Thus it is certainly
correct to say that the prominent features in a picture of Paul
are his concern with his subject and his passion, which
together combine to make for a radicalism in thought and
judgment. However, in saying this, one is not speaking about
presuppositions from which his work has grown, but rather is
characterizing that work itself. If, on the other hand, one
means by the question concerning Paul's character the natural
dispositions that were a given condition of his work, then
indeed it is possible to say something about these on the basis
of his letters; but what is said can never be of any use in
making the content of his work understandable. For that Paul
was temperamental, was given to brooding, had a sensitive
feeling for life, was touchy, etc. are all things that he shared
in common with countless other men. Therefore, while to
draw this kind of a picture of his character can offer an
æsthetic fascination, it is of no consequence whatever in understanding the subject matter with which he was concerned.

Likewise, it is a popular error to try to derive Paul's theology from his conversion experience. For this experience also
can only be reconstructed by having first understood what he
says. Thus the question about the actual content of his conversion is a question about his theology itself. His conversion
was neither a conversion of repentance nor one of enlightenment (cf. above, II *2*). And if one, by viewing it from the
standpoint of the psychic course of his life, can speak of it in
general as "a break in his development," this still does not say
anything about its meaning. For what happened when Paul
was changed from a persecutor into a faithful man was, in his

view, only an extreme instance of what happens in principle whenever a man is smitten by the "word" and resolves to believe it, surrendering his old self and obediently placing himself under the grace of God. This is clearly shown by Phil. 3:4-16 and II Cor. 4:3-6. Indeed, Paul demands such a "break" from every man, although it is characteristic of him, in contradistinction to Hellenistic mysticism and pietistic and Methodist religiousness, that he says nothing about the psychic conditions of the "break" or about the forms of experience in which it takes place.

The presuppositions of Paul's theology which must be considered in order to understand it all have to do with the *actual subject matter* of his thought. Whoever would understand him must, on the one hand, become acquainted with the understanding that he had of himself (and thus also of God and the world) as a Jew under the law, and likewise with the word of the Christian proclamation that encountered him and constrained him to a yes or no decision. On the other hand, one must acquaint himself with the world-views and the traditional modes of thinking and forming concepts in which Paul lived and in terms of which (or in opposition to which) he developed his new understanding of faith. It is only in this way that one can translate his statements into a modern conceptuality and yet at the same time avoid modernizing re-interpretations. In fact, of course, both types of presuppositions overlap; for the Jewish faith in God as well as the Christian kerygma were naturally expressed in a specific contemporary conceptuality.

B. *The Early Community and Jesus.* It is impossible here to present the Jewish faith in God and the Christian kerygma (cf. above, II, 2). However, the one thing that must be emphasized is that Paul's theology cannot be understood as a further development in the "history of ideas" of the preaching of Jesus. It is not with the preaching of Jesus that he begins, but rather with the kerygma of the early community, the content of which is not Jesus' proclamation, but Jesus himself. It is the message that Jesus of Nazareth, the rabbi and prophet, the one who was crucified, has been raised by God and made Messiah; that he will shortly come as the "Son of Man" in order to hold judgment and to bring salvation. At the same time, it says that the community of his followers knows itself to be the congregation of saints of the end-time, the elected Israel, which is in possession of the Spirit, the promised gift of the last days. Therefore, the early community did not detach itself from the ordinances of life of Israel, but rather continued to move in them in the way that had been taught by Jesus, whose sayings it preserved. To be sure, it did define itself as a unique congregation within Judaism (without, however, segregating itself from the cult of the temple) by baptism, which it understood as the purifying bath for the penitent and those who were sanctified for the breaking in of the time of salvation. It also met together for common meals, although there was as yet no talk of cultic veneration of Jesus Christ. It is this community and its kerygma that is a basic presupposition of the theology of Paul. On the other hand, the preaching of Jesus is such a presupposition only insofar as it signified radical Judaism in the spirit of the old prophetic proclamation. Paul neither heard Jesus' preaching itself, nor did he permit it to be mediated to him by the first disciples, in relation to whom he knew himself to be completely independent (Gal. 1:1, 1:11 ff.). To be sure, he did take over some of the sayings of Jesus (whether genuine sayings, or sayings created by the community) from the Palestinian tradition, namely, bits of regulation having to do with congregational order (I Cor. 7:10 f., 9:14), which he, of course, regarded as words not of the "historical Jesus," but of the exalted Lord (cf. I Cor. 7:25). Perhaps I Thess. 4:15-17 also stems from traditional sayings of Jesus; but this is hardly true of I Cor. 11:23-5. It is also possible that certain sayings of the Lord are echoed in Paul's moral instruction (e.g., Rom. 12:4, 13:9 f., 16:19; I Cor. 13:2); however, what is involved here is precisely a type of moral instruction which, with Jesus as well as with Paul, to some extent came from Jewish tradition or the Jewish spirit. In any case, Paul's real doctrine of salvation, with its anthropological and soteriological ideas, is not a continuation of the preaching of Jesus. This is clear, for example, from the fact that he never once appeals to a saying of Jesus in support of his teaching about freedom from the law. And if in his letters he never makes reference to the tradition concerning Jesus' life (outside of I Cor. 11:23, where what is really involved, is the basing of a cultic feast in the destiny of the cult deity), then one may not say that he must have proceeded very differently from this in his missionary preaching and must have told a good deal about Jesus' life. (Nor may one appeal in support of such a statement to Gal. 3:1; for what is meant there is the preaching of the cross, as is indicated in Gal. 3:10 ff., I Cor. 1:18 ff., and elsewhere.) Whether Paul knew much or little of the tradition about Jesus' life, the content of that life as that of a teacher, a prophet, a miracle-worker, or one who had been crowned with thorns plays absolutely no role in his preaching of salvation. For him, the significance of Jesus' person lies in the latter's having been sent as the Son of God in human form in order through his death and resurrection to free men from the law and sin (Gal. 4:4 f., etc.).

However, just as little as one may say that Paul's theology represents a development in the history of ideas of Jesus' preaching, so little, of course, may one say that, from the standpoint of the history of ideas, it stands in opposition to Jesus' message—as though the latter's piety, say, was a joyous faith in God the Father, whereas Paul's religion is to be characterized as an austere faith in redemption. Looked at in terms of the history of ideas, the proclamation of Jesus and that of Paul are essentially the same. Thus their idea of God is the same: God is the Judge and also the God of grace; and similar also is their view of man, who is obligated to obey the will of God and as a sinner is dependent on God's grace—who can exhibit no merit before God and also can make no claims on him. Neither for Jesus nor for Paul is God the immanent law of the world or the hypostatization of an eternal Idea of the Good. Rather he is the one who stands before man as he who comes in judgment and grace; and for both men God deals with man in history. The difference, however, is that Jesus proclaims a final and decisive act of God, the Reign of God, as coming or, indeed, as now breaking in, while Paul affirms that the turn of the aeon has already taken place and, to be sure, with the coming, the death and the resurrection of Jesus. Thus, for Paul, it is Jesus' cross and resurrection that are the decisive event of salvation through which the forgiveness of sins, the reconciliation of man with God is effected, and with which, therefore, the new creation is introduced. Consequently, while the person and history of Jesus do indeed constitute a presupposition of his theology, they do not do so from the standpoint of their historical or ideal content, but rather as the act of God, as the occurrence of the revelation of salvation. Paul does not teach other and new *ideas* from those that Jesus teaches, but rather teaches us to understand an *event* in a new way. This he does by saying that the world is new since and because Jesus has come; now the reconciliation between God and man is established and the word that proclaims this reconciliation is instituted.

c. *The General Conditions in the History of Religion.* Outside of Paul's rabbinic training (cf. above II, *1*), the presuppositions from the history of religion that must be considered in relation to the formation of his theological concepts and his explication of the kerygma are the following: (1) *The preaching of the one God and his judgment* that was characteristic of the propaganda both of Hellenistic Judaism and of pre-Pauline Christianity. Under the influence of the Greek enlightenment, there had taken place in Hellenistic Judaism a new conceptual formulation of monotheistic faith, together with a total interpretation of the world in the manner of the philosophy of religion and a critique of polytheism and its cult as well as the moral life of the Gentiles. This tradition was directly taken over by Christianity; and Paul also stands within it when he makes use of the Stoic theory of a natural knowledge of God (Rom. 1 :18 ff.) or varies somewhat a Stoic formula concerning the divine omnipotence (Rom. 11 :36; I Cor. 8 :6), or when he applies the concepts of "conscience" (Rom. 2 :15, etc.), "duty" (Rom. 1 :28), "virtue" (Phil. 4 :8), "nature" (I Cor. 11 :14, etc.), or even when he interprets the heathen gods as demons (I Cor. 10 :10) or as "elemental spirits of the world" (Gal. 4 :3, 4 :9). In all probability such ideas played an even larger role in his actual missionary preaching; thus they are presented also in Acts 14 :17, 17 :23 ff. (2) *The discussion concerning the law* in Hellenistic Judaism and in pre-Pauline Hellenistic Christianity. Here, too, there is a unified tradition running from the former to the latter, which attempts to demonstrate the moral character and universal scope of the divine demand. Insofar as this tradition practised allegorical reinterpretation of the narratives and laws of the Old Testament, Paul also stands in it (cf., e.g., I Cor. 9 :9 f., 10 :6 ff.); however, insofar as it made a distinction between moral demands and cultic-ritual ones, he has left it behind, although he is still affected by it, as is shown by I Cor. 7 :19. (This is probably a saying that Paul quotes and then modifies in his own sense in Gal. 5 :6, 6 :15.) (3) *The Kyrios-cult and the sacraments* in pre-Pauline Hellenistic Christianity. If the early Palestinian community had expected Jesus the risen one as the coming Son of Man and if, accordingly, its messianic faith was essentially eschatological, there had already developed prior to Paul in the Hellenistic Christian communities in Syria (which did not participate in the Jewish temple cult and the ordinances of life that emanated from it) a cultic veneration of Christ as the "Lord." He was known to be present in the congregation's worship, dispensing supernatural powers to those who belonged to him. Baptism was understood in the sense of the Hellenistic mysteries as a sacrament that mysteriously unites the baptized person with Christ and thus grants him a share in the latter's death and resurrection. And the common meals of the early community became the "Lord's Supper," which likewise brings about sacramental communion with Christ. Naturally, the form of the kerygma corresponded to this, and already prior to Paul there were represented different interpretations of Jesus' death, which in part expressed the ideas of an atoning or covenantal sacrifice and in part the ideas of a cosmic process and a sacramental *communio*. This can be learned from the remarks concerning baptism in Rom. 6:3 ff. and the saying concerning the Lord's Supper in I Cor. 11:23-5, which already combine different interpretations, as well as from the tradition to which Paul refers in I Cor. 15:3 and, likewise, for example, from the theology of Mark. For the rest, we can no longer prove which of the concepts that Paul uses to interpret Christ's death and resurrection were already in use prior to his time; it is clear, however, that the frequently encountered ideas of "for us," of an atoning sacrifice (Rom. 3:25), of reconciliation (Rom. 5:11; II Cor. 5:18 ff.), of a ransom (Gal. 3:13, 4:4 f.; I Cor. 6:20, 7:23), and of substitution (Gal. 3:13; II Cor 5:14 f.) all stem from this sphere in which the Jewish ideas of sacrifice and the notions of the Hellenistic mysteries were combined and from which Paul's formulations came to him. (4) *Gnosticism and pneumaticism.* In the syncretism of the Hellenistic-Oriental world and, of course, hardly ever sharply separated from the mystery cults (which, having originally been vegetation cults, celebrated the dying and rising of a deity in which the faithful were vouchsafed a share), there was a religion of redemption which had migrated to the West from Iran, combined itself with certain astrological ideas, and found its historically significant expressions in "Gnosticism." The cosmological and soteriological ideas of this religion give expression to a dualistic understanding of human existence. They teach, first of all, the heavenly origin of the soul, which has been banished to the body and the world of the senses, and then, second, the soul's redemption by a divine being, who disguised himself in human form, took upon himself all the misery of earthly life, thereby deceiving the demonic rulers of the world, and then after having brought revelation to "his own" through doctrines and rites, once again was exalted to the heavenly world, whither his own will subsequently follow him. According to the Gnostic or the pneumatic, whoever believes this revelation has knowledge and freedom. Hence his intense self-consciousness and peculiar way of life, which could lead either to asceticism or to libertinism. That such Gnosticism and pneumaticism had already prior to Paul or contemporaneously with him penetrated the Christian congregations is shown by his struggle against the pneumatics in Corinth. With them, apparently, such Gnosticism had been combined with Jewish theology, very much as also happened with Philo. But these Gnostic ideas had already influenced Jewish apocalypticism and in this way had also influenced Paul. For as much as he fights against the consequences of such pneumaticism, he still appropriates Gnosticism's concepts (e.g., the contrast between "spiritual" and "psychic," the concepts "knowledge," "freedom," or "authority") and makes use of its mythology in his own doctrines. Thence stem the ideas of "this aeon" and the "coming aeon," the idea of Satan as the "god of this aeon" (II Cor. 4 :3 f.), of the "rulers" (I Cor. 2 :6) and other spiritual powers. Thence also the notions of Adam as the first, and Christ as the new "man" (Rom. 5 :12 ff.; I Cor. 15 :21 f., 15 :44 ff.), of the giving of the law by angels (Gal. 3 :19), of Christ's descent in the disguise of a man (I Cor. 2 :6 ff.; Phil. 2 :6 ff.; II Cor. 8 :9), and of redemption as a mighty cosmic drama (I Cor. 15 :24 f.; Rom. 8 :18 ff.).

2. *Content:* A. *Theology and Anthropology.* For Paul, *God* is not a metaphysical being and thus is not an object of speculation, but rather is the God whose action does not take place primarily in cosmic occurrences, but in relation to man in history. On the other hand, he does not understand *man* as an isolated being within the world, but rather always sees him

in his relation to God. Therefore, it follows that what God
and man mean for Paul can only be understood together as a
unity and that his " theology" can be presented as anthropology.

And the same thing is true of his " christology "; for he also
does not understand Christ primarily as a metaphysical being
about whose " natures " he speculates, but rather understands
him and his work as God's act of salvation in relation to man.
Of course, one may not make a division between a " physical "
anthropology that describes how man is " in himself " and an
" ethical " anthropology that expresses how he stands in relation to God. For as Paul understands him, man is never what
he is outside of his relation to God; and even general anthropological concepts like " body " and " soul " are decisively determined for Paul by man's standing before God. However,
there *is* a division that arises because man has acquired a new
possibility for relation with God through the revelation in
Christ, namely, faith. Therefore, the arrangement must be as
follows : (1) man prior to the revelation of faith; and (2) man
under faith. It must be noted, however, that the being of
man prior to faith first becomes visible in its true lineaments
only from the standpoint of faith itself and that it is from
this perspective alone that it can be understood.

B. *Man prior to the Revelation of Faith.* 1. With the
word " man " Paul can, of course, occasionally refer to one
being in the world among others (e.g., angels; cf. I Cor. 4 :9;
15 :36 ff.); but his more precise use of language is such that
the title " man " characterizes man in his relation to God and,
indeed, in such a way that before God all the differences and
advantages of which individuals could boast disappear (Rom.
3 :28 f.; I Cor. 1 :25; Gal. 1 :1). " Man " designates man in
his humanity before God. And this God before whom he
stands is not a cosmic being that is separate from him; to be
sure, there may also be such a being, but insofar as *God's*
being is spoken about, it is not a being that is merely on hand
but rather a " being for us," so that in a precise sense God

alone " is " (I Cor. 8 :4-6). Man's being in relation to God is primarily a being claimed by God as the Creator. When Paul makes use of the Stoic theory of a natural knowledge of God (Rom. 1 :20 ff.), it does not serve him in order to conclude to God's being *in* the world and to the divinity of the world and the security of man by reason of divine providence, but rather in order to conclude to God's being *beyond* the world, to the world's creatureliness and to God's claim to be honoured by man. Correspondingly, "world" for Paul means "creation" (Rom. 1 :20; I Cor. 3 :22). And, to be sure, it can mean the totality of what is created by God as that which surrounds man and concerns him; but it especially refers to the world of man himself (Rom. 3 :19, 11 :12; II Cor. 5 :19, etc.), although not in the sense of a total class of beings on and within the world, but rather as a community of creatures who are responsible to God. Insofar as men have withdrawn from this responsibility, have denied their creatureliness, and have made themselves independent of God, they are called " this world." This world (or " this aeon," as Paul can also say in order to express the notion that it is provisional) is at enmity with God and seeks its own glory; therefore, it stands under God's wrath and will be judged by him. That this " dualism," which is several times expressed in Gnostic terminology, is not meant in the cosmological sense of Gnosticism is shown by the counterconcept " new creation," with which Paul refers to the men who are reconciled and are faithful (II Cor. 5 :17; Gal. 6 :15). Thus " world " does not refer to men as a " what," but rather as a " how," as a " how " of their life and, to be sure, as a " how " that they themselves have created by turning away from God. As such it is a power that always already encompasses each individual, encountering him and taking him along with it, so that he cannot isolate himself from it (by believing, say, in his soul that has tragically fallen from the world of light and is imprisoned in " this world " or by imagining his free spiritual personality). And this " how " manifests itself in the " care " (I Cor. 7 :29 ff.) in which each man takes his life in his own hands and wills to secure it. From "care," then, grow "boasting" and "confidence," which base themselves on anything that by man's estimation or accomplishment, passes for a work. Precisely this pride, whether it is based on national or social advantages or on wisdom or works of the law is rebellion against God before whom no man may boast (Rom. 2:17, 2:23, 3:27; Cor. 1:29, 3:21, 4:7). The height of illusion is that man thinks he can separate himself from the "world" and bring himself to a being beyond it. The Jew who wills to earn "righteousness" before God is fallen under this illusion, even as is the pneumatic who imagines that he can become a "perfect one" by means of his "wisdom." The counterpart of such boasting and confidence is "anxiety" (Rom. 8:15) such a man is in fact a slave. For in his care and putting confidence in worldly values and accomplishments he lets these become lord over him, and because they are all transitory (I Cor. 7:31), he himself falls under death; by understanding himself in terms of the transitory and the provisional his being is not authentic, but rather has fallen subject to what is passing away. In the mythological way of thinking of his time, Paul sees such an existence as an enslavement to spiritual powers, Satan and his hosts. Indeed, he can even speak of the law as having been given by such spiritual powers insofar as man understands the law as a pretext for his own accomplishments; and he can also speak of the service of worship as a veneration of the "elemental spirits of the world" (Gal. 3:19 ff., 4:8 ff.). Nevertheless, how little these mythological notions have a speculative character, how little Paul wants to "explain" something by them, but rather makes use of them simply in order to express a certain understanding of human existence, is shown, for example, by his not tracing sin back to Satan (Rom. 5:12 ff., 7:7 ff.) and by his saying that such powers are no longer really of any concern to the man of faith because for him they no longer even "are"

(I Cor. 8:4 ff.); i.e., they no longer mean for him the lord-ship over the world under which he is fallen, but simply the quality of the world to tempt him; Satan is the "tempter" (I Cor. 7:5; I Thess. 3:5).

2. It is on this basis that the individual anthropological concepts, like "body," "soul," and others, are also to be understood. They do not refer to *parts* of man, individual members or organs, but rather always mean *man as a whole* with respect to some specific possibility of his being. For this reason, Paul can also use almost every one of these concepts in the sense of "I" (cf., e.g., I Cor. 6:15 with 12:27; or I Cor. 13:3 with II Cor. 1:23, 12:15), and so also, the concepts can many times seem to flow into one another. One may not, for example, permit himself to be misled by I Cor. 15:35 and attempt to understand "body" as the form of man and "flesh" as his matter. In this passage, this meaning is of course present; but it is a mistake to take this passage as one's starting point because Paul here lets himself be misled by his adversary into speaking apologetically. Passages in which he speaks calmly, like Rom. 1:24, 6:12, 12:1; I Cor. 13:3, all clearly show that "body" for him does not mean "form" but rather refers to the whole man and, to be sure, insofar as, for others as well as for himself, man can be the object of observation and action. "Body" designates man insofar as something can be done to him or can happen to him, indeed, insofar as he is always exposed to such happenings and never freely has himself at his own disposal—and thus, for example, can become ill and die. Man is "body" in his temporality and historicity. That "body" is not thought of "dualistically" is made especially evident when Paul affirms the resurrection of the body; i.e., to have a body for him is something that belongs to man as such, and he is as anxious about the prospect of being without a body as if it meant nothingness (II Cor. 5:1 ff.). Thus the body is not some part of a man in which the soul or the real I is stuck.

And if man yearns to be free from "this body of death" (Rom. 7:24), he yearns to be freed from himself as he now is, to be "transformed," as Paul elsewhere puts it (II Cor. 3:18; Phil. 3:21; Rom. 8:29). The extent to which Paul has at the same time formulated this thought in terms of mythological ideas is unimportant, if one sees what the understanding of existence is that is hereby expressed.

So also "soul" is not a something *in* man—say, his better self—but rather is the whole man himself insofar as he is alive, is a living being (I Cor. 15:45). Therefore, "soul" for Paul is neither the bearer of spiritual life in the Greek sense nor our immortal self, the heavenly stranger in a darksome body, in the sense of Gnosticism; rather it is the vitality, the "life" (Rom. 11:3, 16:4; Phil. 2:30), which also belongs to animals in contradistinction to lifeless instruments (I Cor. 14:7). Precisely as such a vitality, however, the soul is not immortal, but mortal; it does not at all signify man's authentic being. But, of course, "soul" can also be the "I," for man is a living being (II Cor. 1:23, 12:5; I Thess. 2:8). As in the Old Testament, "every soul" means "every man" (Rom. 2:9, 13:1).

Insofar as the life of man is a conscious life, Paul can occasionally refer to it as "spirit" (I Cor. 2:11; Rom. 8:16; to be distinguished, of course, from the Spirit of God, the Holy Spirit, that is also referred to alongside of it!). And once again "spirit" also can mean simply "man," or "I" (Rom. 1:9; I Cor. 16:18; II Cor. 2:13; and in formulas of greeting). But the real word that Paul uses to refer to man as conscious is "mind"; it designates man insofar as he understands or knows something and, to be sure, insofar as he knows about his own possibilities and understands himself (e.g., Rom. 14:5). Since, however, man's being is a being before God, the knowledge about his own possibilities is at the same time the knowledge of the claim of God, of what man ought to do (Rom. 1:20, 7:23). And, further, since the specifically human knowing about oneself does not have the character of a theoretical, neutral confirmation that something is so, but rather also has the character of laying hold of a possibility, of willing (Rom. 7:15 ff.), it follows that "mind" can either be a correct or a false self-understanding. The mind of the heathen is base (Rom. 1:28 f.); their minds are blinded (II Cor. 4:4); on the other hand, the mind of Christians is renewed (Rom. 12:2). Paul can also speak of the mind as the "inner man" (Rom. 7:22; however, one may not draw on II Cor. 4:16 to explain this, for what is spoken of there is the man of faith!). But what is meant by this is not something like a better self "in" man; for in Rom. 7:13 ff. the "mind" or the "inner man" is as much the "I" or self as is "flesh" (cf. below, III, 2, B, 3). The wretchedness of man that is presented here does not consist in his better self's standing over against his worse material corporeality, but rather in his self's being split, in I standing over against I. Indeed, the essence of the unredeemed man is to be thus split.

In order to refer to man as one who has knowledge of himself, i.e., of his possibilities before God, and thus a knowledge that can also go astray, Paul likewise makes use of the Old Testament expression "heart" (e.g., Rom. 2:5, 8:27; II Cor. 4:6) and the Greek expression "conscience" (Rom. 2:15; I Cor. 8:7 ff., 10:25 ff., etc.).

What has been given now by this clarification of Paul's basic concepts is not anything like a "physical" anthropology; for the concepts "body" and "soul" refer to man in respect of his creatureliness, while the concepts "mind," "heart," and "conscience" speak of him in his responsibility before God.

3. If man as having a body is withdrawn from his own disposal and always stands in the context of a history, then, for Paul, there is only a twofold possibility for the determination of this history—by God or by sin. He expresses this either/or by means of the contrast between flesh and Spirit.

And, to be sure, the being of man prior to faith is determined by the "flesh." This word means, first of all, the animated flesh of the body. But, then, just as "body" refers to man himself as object of an action or as subject of a happening, so also "flesh" refers to him in his pure being on hand in which he can become an object. Hence the concepts body and flesh can to a certain degree mean the same thing (II Cor. 4:10 f. I Cor. 6:16); illnesses and marks are in the body as well as in the flesh (Gal. 4:13 f., 6:17; II Cor. 12:7). And as "body" can be the "I," or self, so also can "flesh" (II Cor. 7:5) Thus flesh is not a part of man, but man himself as he is actually found—as well or ill, as belonging to a nation or to a family. Abraham is the father of the Jews "according to the flesh," while Christ "according to the flesh" is a descendant of David (Rom. 4:1, 1:3, 9:5). The natural life of man is a life "in the flesh" (II Cor. 10:3; Gal. 2:20; Phil. 1:22 ff.), and whatever belongs to such a life, like food or means, is called "fleshly" (Rom. 15:27; I Cor. 9:11). But in close connection with this, "flesh" acquires yet another meaning which becomes clear when it is said that the man of faith no longer exists "in the flesh" or "according to the flesh." As the characteristic of a certain type of demeanour (boasting knowing, walking, etc., I Cor. 11:18, 5:16, 10:2), "according to the flesh" does not designate man as he appears to others, but as he understands himself, namely, on the basis of what he is found to be, of what is immediately evident (Rom. 2:28). "To be according to the flesh" means "to be intent on what is fleshly" (Rom. 8:5). This does not mean to be determined by what is fleshly in the sense of the life of impulse or of the senses, but rather to be determined by anything in the entire sphere of what is immediately evident whether this be national advantage, legal correctness, the accomplishments of the man who exists under the law, or human wisdom. All of this is "flesh" (Phil. 3:4 ff.; Gal 3:3; I Cor. 1:26); therefore, works righteousness is included under the concept as surely as are vices. No man can get out of the flesh as existence in what is immediately evident; but the question with which he is faced is whether he will understand himself in terms of it and put his " confidence " in it—whether as one who is situated in the flesh he also wants to walk according to it (II Cor. 10:3). To understand oneself in terms of the " flesh," however, is " sin "; for sin is the care, boasting, and confidence of the man who forgets his creatureliness and tries to secure his own existence. It reaches its acme in the Jew; for to pursue one's own righteousness means precisely to put one's confidence in the flesh (Phil. 3:4-9); it is similar, however, with those who are "wise according to the flesh "; for they, too, do not honour God, but boast of themselves (I Cor. 1:18-31). Sin is falsely wanting to be oneself; and there is the deep connection between the flesh and sin that the man who thus wills to be himself can only do so by understanding his existence in terms of what is on hand, what has been accomplished, what can be grasped and proven—in short, in terms of the " flesh." And so also there is a connection between flesh and sin *and* " death "; for each man understands himself in terms of what is transitory, what is fallen under death, and so death is already at work in him (Rom. 7:5). For everyone, on the other hand, who no longer understands himself on the basis of the flesh, or of what is visible, but rather understands himself on the basis of the invisible, and walks accordingly, flesh, sin, and death have come to an end (Rom. 8:9, 6:2, 6:10 f.; Gal. 5:24; I Cor. 15:56 f.). Thus, for Paul, flesh is neither matter in the Greek sense, i.e., the material that has to be given shape by spirit as the power of form, or the life of the senses that must be educated, nor is it matter in the sense of Gnosticism (even if he is influenced by the latter's terminology) i.e., the inferior, evil realm of the senses, which is opposed to the soul. Rather it is the world of what is on hand, which first becomes the sphere of sin through the attitude of man, just as the creation only becomes " this world " through men's falling away from God.

But now Paul does not look upon sin as something acci-dental, which is present here and there or even in most places; rather he views it as the attitude that man necessarily has since the first sin of Adam; i.e., he sees that every man is already guided by a false understanding of human existence and that the man who wants to free himself from this world only becomes the more entrapped in it because he but repeats the primal sin of wanting to be himself. In order to illustrate this fact of sin's sovereignty, Paul makes use of the Gnostic myth of the primal man and interprets it in terms of the con-trast between Adam and Christ (Rom. 5 :12 ff.; I Cor. 15 :20 ff., 15 :44 ff.). And from the crossing of his own ideas with the notions of the myth there arise confusions that cannot be considered here. The one thing that we must note, however, is that he never traces sin back to something that is not yet sin; rather sin has come into the world through sin, although it has thereby become an absolute and all-dominating power (Rom. 5 :12). Even in Rom. 7 :7 ff. sin is not referred to the flesh as matter or as a mythical power, but rather to the sinner, to the man who lives according to the flesh. What Paul means becomes clear when it is recognized that for him the sole way of becoming free from sin is forgiveness; i.e., if man has sinned, then he *is* a sinner. What has happened in his past is not an individual fact that has now been left behind, but rather is present in that it qualifies him as guilty before God. Neither man nor mankind can become free from the past by their own self-will; on the contrary, they bring the past with them into every present. However, because sin is guilt before God there is also the possibility that God will free man from the past, that man will become new. But this can only become clear when the final factor that determines the existence of man prior to faith has been taken into consideration.

4. The " law " means that there is a fact in the existence of the sinful man that, in spite of his false understanding of himself, again and again makes audible to him the claim of God. This fact is given in the concrete demands that always

encounter man and point out to him that he does not belong
to himself. From the standpoint of his Christian understanding of the law, Paul sees that these concrete demands actually
grow out of man's constantly being bound together with other
men at whose disposal he ought to place himself. For it
seems to him that the final meaning of all of the specific requirements of the law is that man should love his neighbour
as himself (Rom. 13:8 ff.; Gal. 5:14, cf. 6:2). That the
Gentiles also hear such demands is indicated by Paul in the
letters that we have only in Rom. 2:14 f. Thus it is with
reference to the Jews that he develops his detailed consideration of man's situation under the law, because being himself a
Jew, he naturally assumes that the true embodiment of the
law is the law of Moses. From this it becomes clear, first of
all, that for him the law of God is not the eternal moral law,
not the Idea of the Good that springs from the human spirit
as the idea of its perfection and at the same time is its norm.
Rather the law is the whole complex of concrete, historically
given moral and ritual demands that encounter the Jew in his
actual historical community. It is characteristic of Paul that,
unlike the prophets and Jesus, he does not distinguish between
cultic-ritual demands, formal-legal demands, and moral demands; for man prior to faith, the law is the " letter " that
kills (II Cor. 3:6) even in its moral demands. Paul does not
criticize the law from the standpoint of its *content,* but with
respect to its *significance* for man; i.e., he criticizes it as it
appears from the standpoint of the Jewish understanding. In
the law, man is confronted by the demand of God, obedience
to which would bring life, for God is the Judge (Gal. 3:12;
Rom. 2:10, 2:13, 10:5). Moreover, the demand of the law
is also valid for the Christian, for it is once again taken up in
the commandment to love; and for the Christian also God is
the Judge (I Cor. 1:8, 3:12 ff.; II Cor. 5:10, etc.). Therefore, the situation of man prior to faith is not so frightful
because the law is inferior, but because man does not fulfill it,
because at best he wills it, but does not do it (Rom. 7:11 f.).

Nevertheless, Paul not only says that man *can* not be right-wised by the law, but also that he *should* not be rightwised by it. And he also says that although the law is indeed the holy will of God, which is valid also for Christians, it still is something provisional that is done away with for the man of faith (Rom. 7:1-6, 10:4). The apparent contradiction is simply resolved. Since in fact every man is a sinner (Rom. 3:9-20), it is an illusion to want to earn righteousness by works of the law, as the Jews suppose they can do. For what is evident in such a supposition is not only that they regard sin as an individual work that can also be abstained from or, in any case, can be compensated for, but also that they understand obedience to the law as the accomplishment of individual works of which they can boast before God. In other words, they are not obedient at all in the genuine sense; and the law ought not to meet men in the way in which it meets them. The way of the law, when it is understood as a means for earning righteousness, is false. Thus the sin of the Jews is the failure to appreciate that man owes God an absolute obedience and therefore is dependent on him, on his forgiving grace; the real sin is " boasting." And insofar as it is precisely the law that provokes this extreme possibility in the man who has a false self-understanding, the law is what allows him thus to founder, so that he can understand what grace is in case it encounters him. So the law becomes the " taskmaster to bring us to Christ" (Gal. 3:24) and finds its end in him (Rom. 10:4). So also, in accordance with God's plan, sin has increased so that grace might increase all the more (Rom. 5:20; Gal. 3:19). Precisely because under the law man is driven to his most extreme possibility, there also develops under it an understanding for Christ. Therefore, the unity of man in the history that leads through his sin and redemption is clear. Redemption is as little a magical transformation of his " nature," or his endowment with a higher " nature," as it is enlightenment. It is forgiveness, through which he is brought from bondage to freedom, from anxiety to joy, and

om disobedience to obedience. And equally clear is the unity
f the will of God that encounters man in law and grace; for
ist as the law demands obedience, so also does the message
f God's gracious act (cf. below, III, 2, C).

However much Paul's doctrine of the law is polemic in
character, it is by no means something occasional and second-
ry, but rather contains his central thoughts. This becomes
pecially evident when he struggles against the Gnostic pneu-
atics in Corinth on the basis of the same fundamental ideas.
s the Jews use the law in order to boast, so also do the
neumatics use the gospel and imagine that they are able
hereby to lift themselves above the ranks of a sinful humanity.
hey forget that man himself does not build his life, but that
verything that he has has been received as a gift (I Cor.
:7) and that he may boast of nothing save of the Lord (I
or. 1:31). Jews and pneumatics alike repeat the world's
rimal sin of not honouring God as God (Rom. 1:21).

c. *Man under Faith:* 1. Like every man, Paul knows that
uman life is governed by the image of salvation, by an ideal,
state or a condition in which all of man's questions and
rievances and anxiety have ceased—or, in purely formal
erms, that it is governed by the image of man's authenticity.
nd he fully agrees with Judaism in understanding this
uthenticity as "righteousness." Man ought and wants to be
righteous"; as righteous he can stand before God, and the
ious Jew hungers and thirsts for the day in which God will
ronounce him righteous in the judgment. As for Judaism,
righteousness" for Paul is primarily a forensic and eschato-
ogical concept; i.e., it does not mean, first of all, man's moral
prightness, a human quality, but rather the position that he
as in his relations with and before others, and pre-eminently
efore God in the judgment. His righteousness is his "accept-
nce," which is granted to him by others and especially by
God. Paul entirely agrees with Judaism that man can finally
eceive this acceptance only from God in the last judgment.
Rom. 2:13, 3:20, 4:3, 4:6, etc.). However, he differs from

E.F. F

Judaism at two points: (1) He says that God's eschatologi
sentence of judgment *has already been passed,* namely, in
death and resurrection of Christ; we are already righteous
we have faith in this act of salvation (Rom. 4:25, 5:1, 5:
etc.). This does not mean that the faithful have a new qual
that they are ethically perfect, or that, their guilt having be
cancelled, they must now take care for themselves. Rather
simply means that God accepts them as they are. On the ot
hand, this does not mean that God merely regards the faith
man " as if " he were righteous; on the contrary, by accepti
me, God takes me to be a different person than I am; and i
(in faith) let go of what I am in myself, if I affirm God's ju
ment and understand myself in terms of him, then I really
a different person, namely, the one that he takes me to be.
Judaism regarded fulfilment of the·law as the condition
God's eschatological verdict; according to Paul, howev
God pronounces the faithful man righteous entirely with
conditions (Rom. 3:21 ff., 10:4 ff.; Gal. 2:16 ff., et
Thus, for him, righteousness is not something that is merit
but rather is utterly the gift of God. Consequently, he ref
to it in contrast to one's "own" righteousness, i.e., the
ceptance merited by one's own accomplishments, as
"righteousness of God," i.e., the acceptance that God fre
gives. Its sole basis is in God's freedom and grace, and
Paul can also speak of the "reconciliation" that God
established (Rom. 5:10 f.; II Cor. 5:18 ff.).

2. The meaning of the saving act of God through which
actualizes righteousness for men is forgiveness. Howev
according to Paul, this forgiveness is carried out by God in
death and resurrection of Jesus Christ as the Son of God w
became man (I Cor. 1:18 ff., 15:3; Gal. 3:1; Phil. 2:6
Rom. 3:24 f., 4:24 f., etc.). Thus, for Paul, Christ is sig
ficant neither as teacher and prophet nor as example and he
His humanity and his destiny come into question only inso
as in them he realizes his obedience, *and,* to be sure, this is
obedience of the pre-existent Son of God (Phil. 2:6

om. 5:18 f.). However, the idea of pre-existence for Paul
not a speculative theory about a divine being, nor does it
and in the context of a cosmological mythology, as it does in
nosticism (even if materially this is whence it stems).
ather it has the significance of saying that what has happened
Christ is not a human or earthly event in the continuum
such earthly occurrences, but rather is the act of God. In
hat has happened in Christ, *God* has acted, God's act of love
is taken place. This act, however, is completely unapparent,
d it also is not made apparent by different images, drawn
om cult and myth, in which Paul describes it (cf. above, III,
c). These all say only one thing, that the historical fact of
e cross is God's judgment against sin and the world and
at therefore whoever accepts this judgment in faith is free
om sin (Rom. 6:10 f.; Gal. 6:14). And so also can one
elieve in Christ's resurrection; for however much Paul thinks
the latter also as a cosmic event, he still endeavours to
nderstand it as an occurrence in which the believer himself
articipates. He tries to understand it as the making possible
a new humanity that is not caught in what is provisional
d in death, but rather has the future and *life* (I Cor. 15:
-2; Rom. 5:12 ff., 8:29).

In actual fact, faith does not relate itself to historical or
smic processes that could be established as free from doubt,
it rather to the *preaching* behind which faith cannot go and
hich says to man that he must understand the cross as God's
t of salvation and believe in the resurrection. Only in
reaching is the cross God's saving act, and therefore the
reaching that is based on the cross is itself God's act of
lvation and revelation. Faith comes from preaching (Rom.
:10-17), and God's act of salvation is the institution of the
word" of reconciliation (II Cor. 5:18 f.). It is in the
reaching of the gospel that the righteousness of God is
vealed (Rom. 1:17); and in the preaching of the apostle,
hat is encountered is the word of God itself (II Cor. 5:20),
r the actual speaking of Christ (Rom. 15:18). This preach-

ing of God's saving act, however, is not a communicatic
about events that one can also establish outside of faith
rather in speaking of God's act of salvation, it at the san
time addresses the conscience of the hearer and asks hi
whether he is willing to understand the occurrence that it pr
claims as occurring to him himself and thereby to understar
his existence in its light. For this reason, preaching has th
possibility of working death as well as life (II Cor. 2:14-1
4:1-6). Thus the event of preaching is itself the eschatologic
event of salvation (II Cor. 6:1 f.).

As the preaching has its basis in what has happened
Christ, so also does the "church." For Paul, "church" is th
community of the faithful, the central point in the life
which is the worshipping congregation; and, to be sure, it
the community of all those who are called by God, which
represented in each individual congregation. As the cor
munity of those who are called, it is constituted by th
"word," and likewise by the sacraments of baptism and th
Lord's Supper, which, like preaching, make the salvatio
event something present and thus are also a kind of proclam
tion (cf. I Cor. 11:26). Therefore, the church is neither
association that constitutes itself nor a crowd of pneumat
individuals. As established by Christ and the word, it is itse
an eschatological fact; those who belong to it are the "saints
of the last days who are already taken out of "this world
Since the last days have been introduced by Christ, the chur
is nothing other than the continuation of the Christ-event.
is his "body" (I Cor. 12:12 ff.), and he is its "Lord," i.
the one to whom the individual comes to belong in baptism
Cor. 6:11, 12:13 f.; Gal. 3:27 f.), at whose table one ea
the "Lord's Supper" (I Cor. 10:21, 11:20), and who
present with all his power in the congregation (I Cor. 5:
The congregation is "in him" (Rom. 12:5; Gal. 3:28);
acknowledges him as its Lord and at the same time as t
Lord of all (Rom. 10:9; I Cor. 12:3; Phil. 2:11). So als
then, does each individual belong to Christ, since he is ba

tized in him (Rom. 6:3; I Cor. 12:13; Gal. 3:27); he is "in him," i.e., he belongs to him (Gal. 3:28 f., 5:24; Rom. 8:9, 14:7 ff.), he belongs to the new world as a "new creation" (II Cor. 5:17). Thus the meaning of the salvation-occurrence is that the act of God that takes place in Christ continues in preaching and in the church, that the "world" has come to an end, and that the time of salvation has already become a reality for faith. Just how what is wrought by his occurrence can actually be understood as the possibility of a new human existence must now be made clear by an elucidation of the concept of faith.

3. "Faith," first of all, is the obedient hearing of the word of proclamation. It is "obedience" because it is the subjection of oneself to the act of God that is proclaimed and realized in the word (Rom. 1:15, 10:3, 11:30; cf. Rom. 1:8 and I Thess. 1:8 with Rom. 15:18, 16:19; further, II Cor. 10:5 f. with 10:15, etc.). As obedience, faith is the exact opposite of a "work," and Paul takes great pains to show that faith is not a "condition" of salvation in the sense of an accomplishment (Rom. 3:28, 4.5 f., 9:31 f.; Gal. 2:16, 3:2, etc.). But although it is not an accomplishment, it is an *act* of genuine obedience, in which man radically renounces his own existence and gives glory to God alone (Rom. 3:27, 4:20 f.). Therefore, faith for Paul is not a psychic state or a spiritual attitude, as it is for Philo. Nor is it trust in God in general. Rather it is obedience towards a specific act of God that is proclaimed to man. It is faith *in* . . . , namely, in Jesus Christ, i.e., in the saving act of God that has occurred in Christ. Thus it is not "piety," but rather a specific "confession" (Rom. 10:9). And since the righteousness that is awarded to it (cf. above, III, 2, C, 1) is not an individual attribute, which the believer obtains and possesses, but rather is the acceptance that is awarded to it by the judgment of God, faith is never closed, but is always simultaneously "hope." Indeed, the proclamation does not say that the image of God's wrath is false, but rather that whoever believes escapes from

his wrath. But the wrath itself abides (Rom. 2:5, 2:8, 5:9; I Thess. 1:10); for it is not God's "attribute" or his "affect," but his rule as Judge; and God's grace has its character precisely in that he is and remains the Judge. It is the grace of the Judge, i.e., it is forgiveness; and it can only be understood as grace where God's verdict as judge is simultaneously seen with it. If for the faithful, anxiety is a thing of the past, this is not so with the "fear of God," which rather belongs to faith itself (Rom. 11:20 f.,; II Cor. 5:10 f.; Phil. 2:12 f.) Only so is the "trust" that also belongs to faith (Rom. 4:5, 4:17, 4:20, 6:8) genuine trust, in which man utterly looks away from himself and completely surrenders himself to God (II Cor. 1:9). Faith is also a "knowledge" in that it knows about the saving act of God that is proclaimed to it. However it is not knowledge in the sense of speculation about some historical or cosmic event, but rather a knowledge in which the man of faith also knows about himself and understands himself anew, in that he understands the saving act as a gift and himself as one to whom it has been given (I Cor. 3:12) God's revelation in Christ is not the communication of knowledge as such, but rather an occurrence for man and in man that places him in a new situation and thereby also opens up to him a new understanding of himself (cf. especially II Cor. 2:14-4:6). Thus his knowing has its basis in his being known by God (I Cor. 8:2 f., 13:12; Gal. 4:9). So it is that faith is the new possibility for existence before God; it is created by God's saving act, is laid hold of in obedience, and manifests itself as confession and hope, as fear and trust—in short, as a new understanding of oneself. That faith actually is such a new possibility of existence comes to expression when Paul can say not only that the righteousness of God was 'revealed (Rom. 1:17, 3:21), but also that faith was revealed (Gal. 3:23-5).

In its unity of obedience, confession, and hope, of fear and trust, faith as a new self-understanding is not the once fo all resolve to join the Christian religion or a once accepted world-view. Rather it has reality only as the *obedience of faith that is always new*. However much such faith may begin with a foundational resolve and confession, the existence of the faithful man is not at all the simple state that is thereby established or the natural development that is thus begun. For if it were, faith as an act would become a process in the past and would be understood as a " work," which by its very essence it is not. It is only faith if it always remains faith, *i.e.*, if the individual with his entire existence always realizes his obedience anew. This comes to expression (1) when Paul again and again admonishes his hearers to examine themselves and to stand fast in faith (I Cor. 10:12, 11:28, 16:13; II Cor. 13:5; Rom. 14:4, 14:22; Gal. 5:1, 6:3 f., etc.), inasmuch as fear of God belongs to faith (Rom. 11:20 f.; Phil 2:12, etc.); (2) in the statements concerning the individual possibilities of faith; *i.e.*, faith can be weak or strong (Rom. 14:1, 15:13 f.; I Thess. 3:10; II Cor. 10:15, etc.), and from it can arise both this judgment and that (Rom. 14:2, 14:22 f.). Thus the man of faith also still stands in a life in which it is necessary to judge and to act, and all this should be determined by faith (Rom. 12:6), for otherwise it is sin (Rom. 14:23). So, then, faith also " abides " (I Cor. 13:13); for no future can be imagined in which the Christian could understand himself otherwise than as having his basis in the saving act of God; the same thing follows (3) from the fact that the relation to the Lord that is acquired through faith and baptism is also thought of as a determination of one's entire life (Gal. 2:20). To die with Christ in baptism means a life-long crucifixion with him (Rom. 6:6; cf. Gal. 5:24, 6:14), so that henceforth his life and sufferings are at work in the ministry and sufferings of the man of faith (Rom. 8:17; II Cor. 1:5, 4:7 ff., 13:3 f.; Phil. 3:10). If this consciousness of being bound to the Lord occasionally found expression with Paul himself in mystic or ecstatic experiences (II Cor.

12:12 ff.), still being "in Christ" is in principle not mystic ism, but rather precisely life in the new historical possibilit that is determined by Christ. One "stands fast" in the Lor just as he "stands fast" in faith (I Thess. 3:8; Phil. 4:1 and as there are levels of faith, so also are there levels of bein, in Christ (Rom. 16:10; I Cor. 3:1, 4:10) and individuall different ways of manifesting one's life in him (I Thess 5:12; Rom. 16:2, 16:8, 16:12, 16:22; I Cor. 15:58 16:19, 16:24; Phil. 1:13, 2:1, 2:5, 4:21; II Cor. 2:17 12:19; Philem. 8). In life and in death, the man of fait belongs to Christ (Rom. 14:7-9; I Cor. 15:18; I Thess. 4 16), and this communion, which can also be designated a Christ's being in the believer (Rom. 8:10; II Cor. 13:3, 13 5; Gal. 2:20, 4:19), is never completed, but is a constan striving forward; it is the determination of a life that is fre from the past and open for the future (Phil. 3:12-14) becaus it is no longer dominated by the will to be oneself (Gal. 2:1 f.).

4. Paul can designate this new life in still a different wa and thereby further describe it by the concept of the "Spirit. Just as "flesh" signifies the determination of life by what on hand (cf. above, III, 2, B, 3) so "Spirit" signifies its dete mination by what is *not* on hand, not produced, not disposabl —by what is invisible, miraculous, and solely the object c faith. In the popular image of the Spirit with which Pau makes contact, the idea of "miracle" as a power that dete mines man's existence is already laid out, although it thought of somewhat primitively in that remarkable phen mena, and especially psychic ones, are understood as mirac lous and wrought by the Spirit. Paul radicalizes this idea l showing that all the phenomena that can be grasped on th plane of what is on hand are ambiguous and as such do ne attest the Spirit of God. This they do only when they stan within a specific life-context (I Cor. 12). The only mirac is that which transforms man in his entire existence and, e

course, also attests itself in all of the concrete expressions of his life. Therefore, for Paul, Spirit is the "how," the determination of the new life, which is not produced by man himself, but is given to him. Thus, on the one hand, Paul speaks of the Spirit as the gift that is given to the faithful man (Rom. 5:5; I Cor. 2:12; II Cor. 1:22, etc.), the gift of the last days in which the final consummation is already guaranteed (Rom. 8:23; II Cor. 1:22, 5:5); on the other hand, he speaks of it as the determination of the new life, which must be laid hold of in faith and which proves itself in the concrete way in which one leads his life (Gal. 5:25; Rom. 8:12-14). Spirit is the determination of heart and conscience, of walking and striving, of joy and of love (Rom. 5:5; Gal. 4:6; Rom. 9:1, 8:4-11; Gal. 5:16; Rom. 14:17, 15:30). The life of the man of faith is one of being led by the Spirit (Rom. 8:14), a constant bearing of fruit and being transformed (Gal. 5:22 f.; II Cor. 3:18). Since this new possibility of life that is designated by "Spirit" must be expressly laid hold of, and since, further, it is faith that is the laying hold of it, Paul also does not refer faith to the activity of the Spirit, but rather, conversely, refers the reception of the Spirit to faith or to baptism. This clearly shows that he has no need of the wonderful or the miraculous for the purpose of explanation (Gal. 3:2, 3:5, 3:14; II Cor. 1:21 f.). Insofar however, as the resolve of faith must maintain itself as the determination of one's entire life, a life in the Spirit and a life in faith are one and the same. And as faith brings one into communion with the Lord, so this communion with the *Lord* is nothing other than being determined by the *Spirit*. Hence Paul can say that where in the Old Testament "Lord" is spoken of, what is meant is the "Spirit" (II Cor. 3:17). Lord and Spirit almost coincide (II Cor. 3:17 f.; Rom. 8:9-11, 9:1, 15:18; cf. Rom. 8:8 f. with I Cor. 15:5; Phil. 2:6, etc.); both terms designate the new eschatological mode of existence in which the faithful stand.

Both designate the " freedom " of the faithful (II Cor. 3 :
17; Gal. 5 :1). This freedom is (1) *freedom from sin* (Rom
6 :18, 6 :22, 8 :2), i.e., not a sinless state, but rather the opening up of the possibility of new life through forgiveness; it is
freedom for God's claim, for the imperative (Rom. 6 :11 ff.
Gal. 5 :13 f.; I Cor. 5 :7 f.), which did not exist before
(Rom. 7 :13 ff.), but exists now (Rom. 7 :4 ff.). Thereby it is
also (2) *freedom from the law* (Gal. 2 :4, 5 :18, 5 :33; Rom
6 :14, 7 :1 ff.; II Cor. 3 :7-18, etc.) and (3) *freedom from men*
and their standards (I Cor. 7 :21-3, 9 :1, 9 :19, 10 :29; Gal
3 :28) and, finally, (4) *freedom from death* (Rom. 8 :2)
which receives its power precisely through sin and the law
(I Cor. 15 :56).

The new covenant is the covenant of " life " (II Cor. 3 :7
18), and Romans 5 seeks to establish, in face of the claim of
Judaism, that faith actually has the righteousness that is the
substance of eschatological salvation because it has life, because it can live in hope. Faith has life not as a state in
which dying has ceased, but as hope (Rom. 8 :18-39), so that
precisely every distress must serve as a confirmation of faith
because it brings to mind that everything here and now, all
that is simply on hand, is provisional (Rom. 5 :3 f., 8 :19 ff.
II Cor. 5 :1 ff.). Thus the believer who actually puts his hope
in God alone (II Cor. 1 :8 f.) is raised above all the powers of
natural life, yes, even above life and death themselves (I
Cor. 5 :6-9; Rom. 14 :7-9; I Cor. 3 :21 f.). This never means
however, that he has salvation as a possession that is at his
disposal or that he is perfected and can boast. On the contrary, he can boast solely of God and of what God gives him
(I Cor. 1 :29, 3 :21; Rom. 5 :11, 11 :17 f.) and, in a para
doxical way, of the cross of Christ and of his own nothing
ness (Gal. 6 :14; Rom. 5 :3; II Cor. 11 :16-12 :13); for in
this he becomes certain of the power of the Lord, which is
made perfect in weakness (II Cor. 12 :9 f., 4 :7). Indeed, he is
not his own lord, but rather has his freedom precisely in that
he no longer belongs to himself, but to another (I Cor. 6 :19

7:22; Rom. 7:4-6, 14:17-19; II Cor. 5:14 f.; Gal. 2:19 f.), that he obediently stands at the disposal of God (Rom. 6:13). Everything belongs to him because he belongs to Christ (I Cor. 3:22 f.). Therefore, his freedom is not the right to indulge every caprice; for precisely such capriciousness would once again make him a slave to what is on hand, from which he has now become free.

If for the believer everything worldly and on hand that he encounters turns out to be radically indifferent, inasmuch as nothing can be held against him, this indifference neverthe-less immediately disappears before the question of the indi-vidual's concrete responsibility (I Cor. 6:12, 8:1 ff., 10:23). Service of Christ realizes itself in actual life as *service to the neighbour,* of whom precisely the man who is free, and only he, should and can make himself a genuine servant (I Cor. 9:19-22, cf. 8:9; Rom. 14:13 ff., 15:1 ff.; Gal. 5:13). Such service is the fulfilment of the "law of Christ" (Gal. 6:2); it is "love," which is the fulfilment of the law (Gal. 5:14; Rom. 13:8 ff.), the love in which faith manifests itself as the determination of one's life (Gal. 5:6) and in which knowledge has the criterion of its genuineness (I Cor. 8:1 ff.); the love that is higher than all of the other Spirit-wrought phenomena of the Christian life (I Cor. 12:31, 13:1 ff.); the love in which the new creation becomes a reality (cf. Gal. 5:6 with 6:15) and which therefore never ends (I Cor. 13:8 ff.). Naturally, for one who stands in love, an "ethic" is no longer necessary, however much brotherly admonition, such as Paul himself practises, can point out to another his responsibility and show him what he has to do (I Thess. 5:11 f.; Rom. 12:8, 15:14).

All this, this life in the Spirit, in freedom and love, which is based in the faith that no longer seeks itself, but gives all glory to God, remains understandable and realizable only to him for whom the "glory of God" is indeed the final motive and the final goal. It is to the glory of God that Christ is confessed as Lord (Phil. 2:11); and the same thing is true of the life of the congregation (Rom. 15:6; II Cor. 1:20), our eating and drinking (I Cor. 10:31), the work of the apostle (II Cor. 4:15), and the works of love of the faithful (II Cor. 9:11-13). To God's glory, Christ accomplished his work (Rom. 15:7); for even as we belong to him, so also does he belong to God (I Cor. 3:23), and in the end he will relinquish his reign to God so that God may be all in all (I Cor. 15:28).

ROMANS VII AND THE
ANTHROPOLOGY OF PAUL*

The much discussed problem of Rom. 7 is generally seen to
lie in the question, "Who is the I who speaks here?" "Is it
man under the law, or is it the man of faith?" And further,
"If it is the man who stands under the law, is it man under
the law in general, or is it specifically Paul who here speaks
of his own development?" It seems to me that these questions
have been sufficiently discussed and that there can be no doubt
as to the answer : the situation characterized here is the general
situation of man under the law and, to be sure, as it appears
to the eye of one who has been freed from the law by
Christ. The most recent monograph that, to my knowledge,
has this problem for its theme—namely, that of W. G. Kümmel—has dealt with these questions with exemplary circum-
spection and care and with correct judgment.[1]

However, a further problem that arises just at this point
does not seem to me to have been given its due in the preceding discussion. What exactly is the split in man's existence
under the law that is portrayed in Rom. 7 :14 ff.? According
to vss. 15-20, it is the fact that willing the good is constantly
brought to nothing by the doing of evil. According to the
usual interpretation, this means that man would fain fulfil the
law as God's holy and good will (vs. 12), but in fact does not
fulfill it, that he never gets beyond good intentions. The
"wanting" or "willing" ($\theta \epsilon \lambda \epsilon \iota \nu$) of vss. 15-18 is directed
toward fulfilling the "commandments" ($\epsilon \nu \tau o \lambda \alpha \iota$) of the
"law" ($\nu \delta \mu o s$); and, correspondingly, the "bringing about"
($\kappa \alpha \tau \epsilon \rho \gamma \alpha \zeta \epsilon \sigma \theta \alpha \iota$, vss. 15-20) or "doing" ($\pi o \iota \epsilon \hat{\iota} \nu$ vss. 15-21;

---

* "Römer 7 und die Anthropologie des Paulus," Imago Dei, Festschrift for Gustav Krüger (Giessen: Alfred Töpelmann, 1932), pp.
53-62.

πράσσειν, vss. 15, 19) that take place in fact are to be understood as transgression of the commandment; and "agreeing with" (συνφάναι, vs. 16) or "delighting in" (συνήδεσθαι, vs. 22) are to be understood as saying yes to the demand of the law or to the commandment. Thus man is split because the "sin" (ἁμαρτία) that expresses itself in "desire" (ἐπιθυμία) constantly overpowers his good will. Consequently, Ovid, *Metamorphoses* VII, 19 f. seems to be a parallel: "*video meliora proboque, deteriora sequor.*"[2] Is this interpretation tenable?

Must not one, in order to carry it out, weaken the "doing of evil" (πράσσειν of κακόν) to a failure to fulfil the law fully and constantly, whereas it clearly means a doing that is absolutely and in principle perverted? For can Paul disregard the fact that in many cases the Jews actually did fulfil the law, as indeed he even bears witness concerning himself in Phil. 3:6: "as to righteousness under the law blameless"? For even if Rom. 7 is not Paul's personal confession, but rather a description of Jewish existence in general, it still must be applicable also to his existence as a Jew. But is it thus applicable if the split that it describes is really that between the affirmation of the law's demand by the will and its violation in action?

But the main issue is this: that which, according to this interpretation, must be the Jews' really sinful character is not at all what Paul elsewhere holds it to be; what elsewhere appears to him as the Jews' real sin is here completely left out of account!

Of course, it goes without saying that transgression of the law for Paul is sin. And Jews are just as guilty of this sin as are Gentiles (Rom. 3:19). However, the peculiar guilt of the Jews is not merely the "self-contradiction" (Rom. 2:17-24) that they who are guilty before God through their transgressions also appeal to the law—from which one might conclude, then, that "the act of renunciation with which Paul began to believe" was "merely the simple act of repentance."[3]

This would lead to the consequence that the law remains in force and that righteousness through Christ is allotted to him who seriously intends to obey it and, in face of his sins, gives evidence of real repentance.

But the antithesis, " faith " ($\pi\iota\sigma\tau\iota\varsigma$) vs. " works of the law " ($\check{\epsilon}\rho\gamma\alpha$ $\nu\acute{o}\mu o\nu$) goes way beyond any such view. Paul's " repentance " (and it is characteristic that in this context he never speaks of repentance) does not at all consist in acknowledging as a believer his earlier transgressions, but rather in condemning his earlier zeal for the law and his fulfilment of it (Phil. 3 :4 ff.), just as in general he does not hold the Jews' fault to be their transgressions, but rather their zeal for the law (Rom. 10 :2 f.). To be sure, whenever they suppose that in God's eyes they are superior to the Gentiles, they must be made conscious that as transgressors of the law they are not a bit better (Rom. 2 :17-24). However, Paul nowhere argues against the way of the law with the thought that this way leads to despair, nor does he anywhere praise faith as a way out of a split that is awakened by the conscience. His fundamental reproach is not that the way of the law is wrong because, by reason of transgressions, it fails to reach its goal (that is the position, say, of IV Ezra[4]), but rather that the *direction* of this way is perverse and, to be sure, because it intends to lead to " one's own righteousness " (Rom. 10 :3; Phil. 3 :9). It is not evil works or transgressions of the law that first make the Jews objectionable to God; rather the intention to become righteous before him by fulfilling the law is their real sin, which is merely manifested by transgressions. And that it does thus become manifest is the divine purpose of the law, which is to increase sin (Rom. 5 :20 f.; Gal. 3 :19, 21 :4; cf. Rom. 4 :13-16). The " knowledge of sin " that comes through the law (Rom. 3 :20) consists in man's being led by the law into concrete sins that show that he sins because he *is* a sinner. For the converse does not hold, that he first becomes a sinner because he sins. This is also the clear sense of Rom. 7 :7-13, as will shortly become still clearer.

But what is the Jews' real sin? What constitutes the perversity of the way of the law? The first question Paul asks after he sets forth for the first time the doctrine of "the righteousness of God" based on "faith apart from the law" (Rom. 3:21-6) is: "Then what becomes of boasting?" (vs. 27). "Boasting" or "putting confidence in the flesh" (Phil. 3:3 f.) characterizes the Jews' attitude under the law and, to be sure, precisely because he makes the law that demands obedience into a means of "boasting." Thus "faith" for Paul is not (in the Jewish sense) the confidence in God's gracious forgiveness that is based in repentance and that brings the sinner back to the way of the law that he has abandoned by his transgressions; nor is the movement of the will that is contained in "faith" the characteristically Jewish attitude of repentance that turns away from transgressions; rather it is "obedience" (ὑπακοή), i.e., primarily the subjection of oneself to the new way of salvation by God's "grace" (χάρις) and the renunciation of "one's own righteousness," the turning away from "works" (ἔργα). Faith is not the self-condemnation of one's old life as a life spotted by transgressions and therefore a condemnation of that which already could be and was condemned in and by existence under the law itself (IV Ezra); rather it is the sacrifice of what, from the law's standpoint, was "gain" (Phil. 3:7-9), i.e., was *affirmed* by existence under the law. Accordingly, the law is no longer valid for the faithful who are uncircumcised, and to take it upon oneself is to fall back into the "flesh" (Gal. 3:3).

I hold it to be completely impossible that in Rom. 7:14 ff. this basic idea, which is the characteristically Pauline idea, is to be forgotten in favour of the reasonable insight: "*video meliora proboque, deteriora sequor.*" But I believe that it may also be shown quite simply—at any rate, as soon as one recognizes that the anthropology presupposed by the usual interpretation is not that of Paul—that the meaning of Rom. 7:14 ff. is completely different.

This non-Pauline anthropology—I will refer to it in brief as the subjectivistic anthropology—presupposes that the "willing" of which Paul speaks is the willing that is actualized in the individual acts of will of the subject who is lord of his subjectivity; in short, it presupposes that the willing is *conscious*. This presupposition is false. For man is not primarily viewed by Paul as a conscious subject; the propensities of man's willing and doing which give him his character are not at all the strivings of his subjectivity. Rather, according to Paul's view, human existence transcends the sphere of consciousness. This is clearly expressed when he holds that man wills and acts under the domination either of "flesh" or of "Spirit" (e.g., Rom. 8:5 ff., 8:12 ff.; Gal. 5:16 ff.) and that *tertium non datur*. From the standpoint of a subjectivistic anthropology, these "powers" under which man stands can only be understood as mythological entities or else interpreted in the sense of a naturalistic dualism. I hope that the interpretation of Rom. 7 will show that these "powers" in truth designate the possibilities of historical existence.

Thus it seems to me clear, first of all, that the "willing" of which Paul speaks is not a movement of the will that lies in the sphere of subjectivity, any more than—as is clear without any question—are the "thinking" and the "mind" of Rom. 8:5-7, 8:27 and the "desiring" of Gal. 5:17.[5] Rather this "willing" is the trans-subjective propensity of human existence as such. This statement will, I think, become completely evident when it is shown to what object this "willing" is directed. But before this is shown, there is yet another misunderstanding that often influences exegesis that must be removed.

It is by no means the case, namely, that in the split that is portrayed in Rom. 7:14 ff., the doing of evil goes back to "flesh," whereas the willing of good springs from a power that is alien to "flesh," but impotent against it, i.e., from the "mind" (νοῦς) or the "inner man" (ἔσω ἔνθρωπος).[6] Rather man is "of the flesh" precisely because he is charac-

terized by the split between willing and doing. In him, in his
"flesh," dwell both things, his willing as well as his doing
(vs. 18). Just as his willing and doing are not distributed
between two subjects—say, a better self and his lower impulses—but rather are both realized by the same I, so also are
"flesh" and "mind" (or the "inner man") not two constituent elements out of which he is put together. Man *is*
the split.[7]

However, one may reply, the portrayal still shows that the
I can distance itself from the indwelling sin, that is can deny
the responsibility for "bringing about" the very thing it hates
(vss. 17, 20). Indeed it does! But it is precisely this apparently contradictory portrayal, in which—in complete analogy
to Gal. 2:19 f.—on the one hand, the distance of the I from
the subject is emphasized, while, on the other hand, the I is
affirmed to be the only subject (vss. 14 f., 20)—it is precisely
this portrayal that permits us to recognize the peculiar character of the split. What is involved is not a warfare between two
subjects that simply stand there in their separateness, any more
than it is a relationship of tension between two forces. Man
is precisely a split and a warfare because he ought not to be it,
may not be it, and, indeed, *sub specie* his authenticity, cannot
be it, i.e., because human existence is concerned with its
authenticity and yet constantly fails to find it.

Indeed, it is completely clear that the "I" (ἐγώ) that dis-
tances itself from "sin," i.e., the "inner man" or the "mind,"
is man insofar as he knows about his authenticity and—consciously or unconsciously—is determined and driven in his
entire existence by his concern for it. For Paul it goes without
saying that to know about one's authenticity and to be determined by the claim of God are one and the same thing, for it
is only as one who is righteous before God that man is what
he should and can be.[8] It is precisely because man is a being
who is concerned with his authenticity, which he intends to
realize in all his doing, but which he can also fail to realize
in all his doing (and, according to Paul, in fact does fail to

realize)—it is because man is this kind of a being that he is also this peculiar split. In all his doing, *he* acts because in all his doing he intends to achieve his authenticity; but insofar as he fails to achieve it, it is precisely *not* he in his authenticity who acts!

In saying this, I have in essence already said what the object of "willing" is about which we are inquiring. But it is by no means the case that this can only be gathered from the text indirectly. On the contrary, it can be seen quite directly that the object of "willing" is not the fulfilling of the "commandments," but "life" (ζωή). What is really willed in all our doing is "life"; but what comes out of all our doing is "death" (θάνατος). This will become completely clear from the context.

For how does the context develop? It suffices to point out that 1:18-3:20 has shown that prior to the revelation of the "righteousness of God" both Gentiles and Jews stood under "God's wrath," i.e., were fallen into death. Then, in 3:21-31 it is affirmed that God has now disclosed the "righteousness of God" as the way of salvation, while in ch. 4 the scriptural proof for this affirmation is brought forward. Characteristically, the God to whom faith is directed is designated in vs. 17 as "life-giver." The arrangement of what follows, then, is only understandable if one remembers that for Paul, as for Judaism, "righteousness" is the substance of eschatological salvation, that therefore his paradoxical affirmation is precisely that this eschatological salvation is already present. Thus ch. 5 begins: "Therefore, since we are rightwised. . . ." The questions that must immediately arise for Jewish thinking—and thus also for that of Paul—are such questions as these: "Where then is 'salvation'?" "Where is 'life'?" "What about death and sin, which still seem to be present and in view of which the presence of 'righteousness' seems to be illusory?"

The discussion of these questions dominates chs. 5-8 and, to be sure, in such fashion that in ch. 5 the theme is death and life, while in 6:1-7:6 it is sin and "sanctity"; and further, that the treatment of the first theme is the presupposi tion for treating the second, because death and sin, on the on hand, and life and "sanctity" (in 7:4 "bearing fruit fo God"), on the other, belong together. This becomes eviden precisely in 7:1-6, where the inner connection of "law" an "sin" is made clear, so that no one can conclude from th discussion in ch. 6, which shows the connection of death an sin and life and "sanctity" and the Christian's freedom from sin, that the "law" could be preserved after sin has beer brought to nothing. According to vs. 5, the law belongs witk sin and leads to death. The man who has been freed from sir (ch. 6) is precisely the man who has been freed from th law, who has been placed in the status of "the new life of th Spirit" (7:6). The circle is really closed; for if 6:1-23 (ir accordance with the way of raising questions that is determina tive from 3:21 on) shows that sin is disposed of with th law, then at the conclusion of the demonstration in 7:1-6 thi thesis is converted: the law is disposed of with sin. The poin that is reached, then, in 7:6 is taken up again in 8:1. The two great themes of 5:1-7:6 are now dealt with once more in a new form and in reverse order: in 8:1-11, freedom from sin, and in 8:12-29, freedom from death, and, to be sure, in such fashion that the connection of the two themes becomes clear. Thus the second theme appears at the end of the first as its consequence (8:10 f.), whereas the first appears at the beginning of the second as its presupposition (8:12 f.). I do not need to show here how through this repetition the two themes and their connection appear in a new light or how their arrangement is worked out in detail. It is sufficient to say that the whole thing confirms the thesis that the present is salvation and life, inasmuch as the future is already given to the man of faith with the salvation that is present.

But what is the meaning of the interlude in 7:7-25? It is usually held, and rightly so, that this section is an apology for the law;[9] it is an effort to forestall concluding from the connection of " law " and " sin," which is asserted in 7 : 1-6 (and especially in vs. 5), that "the law is sin " (vs. 7). And, to be sure, the motive of this apology is not really piety or the thought that the reader will be shocked, but rather the clear insight that the character of sin as guilt would have to be surrendered if acknowledgment of the law as the demand of God with reference to which man becomes guilty breaks down.

The " apology " is developed in 7 : 7-13 in such a way as to show that the sin that already slumbers in man is awakened by the " commandments " of the " law." It is precisely God's good will that leads to man's death as a result of the " sin " that inwardly dominates him. This statement is further clarified in vss. 14-25 in that the manner in which " law " and " sin " determine man is illumined. But with this not only is the negative purpose achieved of forestalling the false conclusion, but at the same time the positive thought of vss. 1-6 is once again taken up : vs. 5 is shown to be correct by making clear the connection of " law " and " sin," so that 8 : 1 is as much the answer to the question raised in 7 : 24 as it is the resumption of 7 : 6.

The guiding thought that must now be established for the interpretation of the details is that what is ultimately at issue in the passage is eschatological salvation, and that the two eschatological possibilities are " life " and " death." Thus in 7 : 5 the theme of 7 : (7-)14-25 is formulated with complete clarity : " While we were living in the flesh, our sinful passions, aroused by the law, were at work in our members to bear fruit for death." Service of the law is viewed from the standpoint of what comes of it—namely, death ; and the point that is further elaborated in vss. 7 ff. is already concisely stated here : death is the result of service of the law because by means of the law the " sinful passions " (in vss. 7 f. " desire ") are actualized.

In vss. 7-13 what is emphasized is that the result of the way of the law is death : the " commandment "[10] that should have led to life led to death (v. 10)—which is explained in vss.

11-13 (in correspondence with vs. 5) to mean that the law was the means for sin to bring death about (vs. 13). Just as in vs. 5 there was talk of "sinful passions," so in vss. 7 f. there is talk of "desire." It is characteristic that nothing is said about "transgression" of the law, about παράβασις. Indeed, it remains completely uncertain whether and to what extent in serving the law there is transgression of the "commandments." What is emphasized is that by means of the "commandments" desires are awakened; and these are awakened whether the commandments are transgressed or fulfilled. Man is a sinner even if he fulfils the commandments. That Paul has in mind the service of the law as such and not merely trangressions of it is clearly shown by vs. 6. For the "being discharged from the law" of which he speaks does not mean primarily making transgressions impossible, but rather (as is shown by the ὥστε-clause that follows) termination of "service under the old written code," and therefore freedom from service of the law as such. (In II Cor. 3 :6 f. also, the fruit of service of the law is said to be death, and in II Cor. 3 :13 freedom from such survice is again designated as καταργη-θῆναι of the νόμος.) This is completely clear : according to the movement of thought from 3 :21 on, the only thing that can be meant in 7 :1-6 is freedom from legalism as such, i.e., the bringing to nothing of the law as the way of salvation by "works," and not merely the cancellation of "transgressions."

This, then, is to be maintained for vss. 14-25. Just as vs. 13 has said that and why the result of serving the law is death, so vs. 24 concludes with the question, "Who will deliver me from this body of death?"; and it is in keeping with this when the character of existence in faith is defined in 8 :1 f. : "For the law of the Spirit of life in Christ Jesus has set me free from the law of sin and death." In this new existence, then, the demand of the law can also find fulfilment, i.e., when the direction of the way of the law is turned around.

Thus it should be clear what is meant by "I do not know what I am bringing about" (ὃ γὰρ κατεργάζομαι οὐ γινώσκω,

vs. 15)—namely, man does not know that his "service under
the old written code" leads to death, just as according to II
Cor. 3 : 14 f., the Jews do not know the meaning of service of
the law because their "minds" are hardened and the law is
covered with a veil. Thus for the first time the words "I do
not know" are given their clear and important meaning,
whereas in the usual interpretation they always have to be
interpreted artificially; e.g., "I do not know how it happens
that my good intentions are always followed by transgression"; or "My actions are actually incomprehensible" (Lietzmann).[11] Therefore, the "bringing about" exactly as in vs.
13, where it is said of sin—is just as trans-subjective as is
"willing" (see above); i.e., it refers not to the empirical deed
of transgression, but rather to the result of doing, which for
existence under the law is the outcome of *every* deed—namely,
death.

But now the split that is portrayed in vss. 15-20 should also
be clear : the object of "willing" is "life," whereas the
result of "doing" ($\pi o\iota\epsilon\tilde{\iota}\nu$ and $\pi\rho\acute{a}\sigma\sigma\epsilon\iota\nu$) is "death." "Life"
is the "good" ($\dot{a}\gamma a\theta\acute{o}\nu$) or the "right" ($\kappa a\lambda\acute{o}\nu$); while
"death" is the "evil" ($\kappa a\kappa\acute{o}\nu$, vss. 19, 21). That these
entities can appear as the objects of $\pi o\iota\epsilon\tilde{\iota}\nu$ and $\pi\rho\acute{a}\sigma\sigma\epsilon\iota\nu$, even
though "life" and "death" are not "made" or produced, is
due to the intentionally sententious and antithetical formula-
tion. And that $\pi o\iota\epsilon\tilde{\iota}\nu$ and $\pi\rho\acute{a}\sigma\sigma\epsilon\iota\nu$ must be interpreted in
accordance with $\kappa a\tau\epsilon\rho\gamma\acute{a}\zeta\epsilon\sigma\theta a\iota$, is shown by the fact that the
latter constantly recurs (vss. 17, 18, 20); and this word means
here what it usually (though not always) means for Paul—
namely, "to bring about" or "to obtain by work" (cf. vs.
13). Therefore, the words $\pi o\iota\epsilon\tilde{\iota}\nu$ and $\pi\rho\acute{a}\sigma\sigma\epsilon\iota\nu$ are chosen in
order to bring to pointed expression the inner contradiction
between willing and actually doing, between what is basically
intended and what is in fact done. Everything that is done is
from the beginning directed against its own real intention.
This is the split! Therefore, it is the same split that was
formulated in vs. 10 in this way: "the very commandment

that promised life proved to be death to me." *This* is the riddle whose solution is seen by the insight into sin that is made possible by faith—that in serving the law the law's true intention is in fact perverted. It is also clear now what is meant by " agreeing with " or " delighting in " the law (vs. 16, 22)—namely, not a specific agreement with its concrete demands, but an affirmation of its fundamental intention to lead to life.[12]

Paul's whole conception becomes clear if, as is now possible, we ask what is to be understood by " sin," if it is something that is already present in man that can be awakened by the " law." The " law " encounters man as the claim of God, " Thou shouldst (not)!" i.e., it wants to take from man the disposition of his own existence. Therefore, sin is man's wanting to dispose of his existence, to raise claims for himself, to be like God.[13] Inasmuch, then, as this " sin " brings " death," it becomes evident (1) that the man who wants to be himself loses himself; instead of the " I," " sin " becomes the subject (vs. 9); and (2) that being a self nevertheless belongs to man, for in losing himself he dies (vss. 9 f.); but also that his self is not realized when he himself tries to lay hold of it by disposing of his existence, but only when he surrenders himself to the claim of God and exists for him. This would be " life " for him; then he would exist in his *authenticity*.[14] It is precisely through his willing to be himself that man fails to find the authenticity that he wills to achieve; and this is the deficit of sin (vs. 11). But just because the will to be authentic is preserved in the false will to be oneself, even if only disguisedly and distortedly, it is possible so to speak of the split in man's existence that the authentic I is set over against the factual one.

For this reason, what is portrayed in vss. 7-13 is not " the psychological process of the emergence in man of individual sins " (Lietzmann), but rather the process that is at the basis of existence under the law and that lies beyond subjectivity and psychic occurrences. Because man is a self who is concerned with his authenticity and can find it (as that of a creature) only when he surrenders himself to the claim of God, there is the possibility of sin. Because from the beginning the claim of God has to do with man's authentic existence, there is the possibility of misunderstanding : the man who is called to authenticity falsely wills to be himself.

Finally, because what is involved in Rom. 7 :7-25 are transsubjective processes it is possible to understand Rom. 7 in its unity with 5 :12-21. But concerning this I can say nothing further here, just as I must also forego developing additional consequences—positive insights as well as new questions— from what has been said.

THE TASK OF THEOLOGY
IN THE PRESENT SITUATION*

Ladies and gentlemen! I have made a point never to speak
about current politics in my lectures, and I think I also shall
not do so in the future. However, it would seem to me un
natural were I to ignore today the political situation in which
we begin this new semester. The significance of political
happenings for our entire existence has been brought home to
us in such a way that we cannot evade the duty of reflecting
on the meaning of our theological work in this situation.

It should be emphasized, however, that what is at issue here
is not the defence of a *political* point of view; nor can our
purpose be either to repeat the " happy yes " to political events
that is spoken all too quickly today or—depending on how we
stand with respect to these events—to give voice to a sceptical
or resentful criticism. Rather we must look at these events
simply from the standpoint of their immense possibilities for
the future and ask ourselves what our responsibility is *as
theologians* in face of these possibilities.

Since, as theologians in the service of the church, we have
to develop the basis and meaning of Christian faith for our
generation, the first thing we must do is to reflect on what is
in principle the relation of faith to nation and state, or the
relation between the life of faith and life in the political order
This relation is determined by faith's being directed to the
God who is Creator and Judge of the world and its Redeemer
in Jesus Christ. This means that the relation of God to the

* " *Die Aufgabe der Theologie in der gegenwärtigen Situation,*"
Theologische Blätter, xii (1933), 161-6. (Bultmann himself explains
in a footnote to the original title: " The following remarks were
made as an introduction to my lecture on May 2, 1933.")

world and therefore of faith to life in the world, and thus to political life, is a peculiarly two-sided one.

God is the *Creator*; i.e., the world is *his*; it is *his* gift that encounters us in the world in which we stand, in its goods and tasks, in its beneficent and frightening phenomena, in the events that make us both rich and poor. God is the Creator; this means that he is not the cause ($\alpha i\tau i\alpha$) to which thought refers the world, or the source ($\dot{\alpha}\rho\chi\dot{\eta}$) in terms of which the happenings in the world can be grasped in their unity and lawfulness by the understanding. Rather that God is the Creator means that he encounters us as Lord in our concrete world, in the world that is determined historically, in our actual life in the present. Faith in the Creator is not a philosophical theory or a world-view that one has in the background of his concrete experience and action, but rather is something that we are to realize precisely *in* our experience and action as obedience to our Lord. That God is the Creator means that man's action is not determined by timeless principles, but rather by the concrete situation of the moment.

This situation acquires its concreteness by means of a variety of factors. Included among them are what we speak of as the "ordinances of creation." By means of such ordinances we are not men in general who have to cultivate their humanity, but rather are this man or that man who belongs to this people or to that; we are male or female, parent or child, young or old, strong or weak, clever or dumb, etc. Also included in such ordinances of creation is our nationality and the political ordinance of the state, in which alone nationality can become the object of our concern and action. We do not need to reflect here on the place that nation and state occupy in the order of priority of the claims that encounter us; nor do we need to ask whether it even has meaning to speak of an order of priority here or whether such ordering of claims is precisely a question that can only be decided in the concrete moment. For the present it suffices to recognize that faith in God and nationality stand in a positive relation, insofar as

God has placed us in our nation and state. It suffices to under
stand—in the words of F. K. Schumann—that "nationalit
means being subject to an original claim; that to stand in
nation or to be a member of a nation means to share a commo
destiny, to subject oneself to the claim of the past, to let one'
own existence be determined by others, to be responsible fo
a common future, to receive oneself from others and thus als
to be able to sacrifice oneself in return."[1] It suffices to know
that faith in God the Creator demands this of us.

But with this not everything has yet been said. For God i
the *Creator,* i.e., he is not immanent in the ordinances of th
world, and nothing that encounters us as a phenomeno
within the world is *directly* divine. God stands beyond th
world. Therefore, however much faith understands the worl
as his creation, indeed, precisely *because* it understands th
world as his creation, it acquires a peculiar relation of dis
tance to the world—the relation, namely, to which Paul refer
by the peculiar phrase ὡς μή :

> I mean, brethren, the appointed time has grown very
> short. From now on, let those who have wives live as
> though they had none, and those who mourn as though
> they were not mourning, and those who rejoice as though
> they were not rejoicing, and those who buy as though
> they had no goods, and those who deal with the world as
> though they had no dealings with it. For the form of this
> world is passing away. (I Cor. 7 :29-31)

This does not mean that faith has a negative relation to th
world, but rather that the positive relation that it has to i
and to its ordinances is a *critical* one. For faith knows tha
God the Creator is also the Judge of the world. It knows tha
men always forget that the world's goods and ordinance
summon man to service, point him to his tasks, and are no
given for his possession and gratification. It knows tha
human striving, both individual and collective, is always dir
ected toward disposing of the world and contriving securit
for the self. It knows that man forgets his creatureliness an

wills to understand himself as the lord of his life. And through such sinful perversion of man's own self-understanding the ordinances of creation also become ordinances of sin, and, to be sure, all the more so, the more man veils the sinful tendency of his will and looks upon the ordinances in which he is placed as though they were directly divine. Everything, possessions and family, education and law, nation and state, can become sin at man's hands; i.e., it can become a means for pursuing his own interests and disposing of his existence.

Therefore, all of the ordinances in which we find ourselves are *ambiguous*. They are *God's* ordinances, but only insofar as they call us to service in our concrete tasks. In their mere givenness, they are ordinances of *sin*.

In order to make this clear I need only remind you how different are the positions of the Old Testament prophets and Jesus with respect to justice. In an age that imagined it satisfied its duty to God by pompously carrying on the cult and that permitted unrestrained self-will to rule the common life, the prophets proclaimed the demand for justice and righteousness as the demand of God. For justice puts a check upon man's self-will. Think, for example, of some of the laws to which Jesus makes reference in the Sermon on the Mount. The law regulating divorce insures the wife against the arbitrariness of the husband, in that it places the latter under certain limits of justice. The *jus talionis* (" an eye for an eye, a tooth for a tooth ") limits the thirst for revenge to an extent that is bearable for political life. Likewise, the commandment, " You shall love your neighbour and hate your enemy," puts a check on the blind hate that sees the enemy in every adversary, and gives legal recognition to the concept of the " neighbour." On the other hand, Jesus' own " But I say to you " opens our eyes to how human sin turns justice to its own ends, how the restraints of justice are interpreted as concessions : " I *may* divorce my wife," " I *may* seek revenge," " I *may* hate "—in short, by preserving a formal legality I can at the same time leave room for my self-will. Thus Jesus protests against ordinances of justice that have become ordinances of sin. Everyone who dismisses his wife is an adulterer! If anyone strikes you on the right cheek, turn to him the other also! Love your enemies!

This does not mean that Jesus demands anarchism; for his protest is against ordinances of justice only insofar as they have become ordinances of sin. A life of justice that is determined by the thought of service and fulfils the original purpose of justice to bind man to his fellow men is not touched by his polemic. On the contrary, he affirms that God demands justice and righteousness.

The situation is such, however, that every ordinance of justice has the double possibility of being placed either in the service of sin or in the service of God. All ordinances are ambiguous, and our understanding of the ordinances in which we find ourselves is always already conditioned by the history out of which we come. And all our human history is likewise ambiguous. At one and the same time it presents us with a great inheritance of possibilities for free and noble action *and* temptations to act slavishly and meanly. All history conceals within itself both deeds of heroism and sacrificial courage *and* the war of all against all. All history is infected with sin, and from the beginning every human action is guided by that sinful self-understanding in which man wills to pursue his own interests and to dispose of his existence. Consequently, the power for every great and good deed must be acquired by overcoming the self. No state and no nation is so unambiguous an entity, is so free from sin, that the will of God can be read off unambiguously from its bare existence. No nation is so pure and clean that one may explain every stirring of the national will as a direct demand of God. As nature and all our personal relations with one another have become uncanny as a result of sin, so also has nationality. From it emerge deeds of beauty and nobility; but there also breaks out of it the demonry of sin. Every state and every nation bears within itself not only the possibilities and tasks of the good and the beautiful, but also the temptations to the evil and the mean.

In a day when the nation has again been generally recognized as an ordinance of creation, the Christian faith has to prove its critical power precisely by continuing to insist that the nation is ambiguous and that, just for the sake of obedience to the nation as an ordinance of creation, the question must continue to be asked what is and what is not the nation's true demand. Indeed, precisely in this time of crisis we are sensible that we must once again seek and find the true meaning of possessions and the family, the true ordinance with respect to the sexes and age levels, and the true meaning of authority and education. And so also it is necessary to ask what is the true and normative meaning of the nation. To be sure, there is given to man an original knowledge of such matters, which we can speak of as an "instinct" of nationality. However, in this instance, as everywhere else, this original instinct is obstructed and spoiled, warped and distorted by the history of sin out of which we come.

Christian faith must be a critical power in the present discussion, and it must prove its essentially *positive* character precisely in its *critical* stance. How can it do this? Well, it can do it because it knows not only about sin, but also about *grace*—because it knows God not only as the Judge, but also as the Redeemer, who through Jesus Christ restores his original creation. Redemption through Jesus Christ means the forgiveness of sins through the revelation of the love of God, and therefore also means the freeing of man to love in return.

Only he who knows the transcendent God who speaks his word of love to the world in Christ is able to extricate himself from this sinful world and to achieve a perspective from which the world's ordinances can really be known as ordinances of creation—i.e., as ordinances for which he must gratefully rejoice and in which he must silently suffer and serve as one who loves. He alone has a critical perspective over against the

loud demands of the day, in that he measures the good and
evil in such demands by asking whether and to what extent
they serve the command of love. And he alone also has a
critical perspective with respect to himself, which enables him
to ask whether his own action is really selfless service.

Such a critical perspective will never permit the struggle
for state and nation to become a struggle for *abstractions*.
For we may never overlook that state and nation are made up
of concrete human beings who are our neighbours. Like
humanity, nationality is always in danger of losing its concreteness and becoming a mere abstraction. Is our present struggle
on behalf of the ideal of nationality a struggle for an abstraction or for something concrete? The criterion for each one of
us is whether, in his struggle, he is really sustained by love,
i.e., by the love that not only looks to the future in which it
hopes to realize its ideal, but also sees the concrete neighbour
to whom we are now bound in the present by all the commonplace ties of life. To be sure, every struggle involves severity
and demands sacrifice. But the right to demand sacrifice and
to exercise severity belongs only to him who sees his neighbour
in those who are affected by what he does! He alone will
discover the kind and manner and also the limit of his action.
The only man who can truly serve his nation is he who has
been freed to love by receiving the love of God in Christ.

Ladies and gentlemen! There cannot be the slightest doubt
that this is the meaning and the demand of the Christian faith,
and that these are the thoughts that the theologian has to
advocate. For what I have said is simply taken from the
thoughts of the New Testament and the Reformers. Thus
while it may be comforting or disturbing, this is in any event
the way it is; and it is not my task to expound how we might
wish things to be, but only how they actually are, according
to the teaching of the church.

We have attempted in face of the immense possibilities that
are now open to us to understand our responsibility as it
becomes clear to us through the critical power of the Christian

faith. We must not close our eyes to the fact that with these possibilities we are also presented with temptations; indeed, it is precisely our duty as theologians to point this out, so that the joy over the new situation will be pure and the faith in the new possibilities, honourable.

Will we preserve the power of our critical perspective and not succumb to the temptations, so that we may work together for Germany's future with clean hands and believe in this future honourably? Must I point out that in this critical hour the demonry of sin also lies in wait? "We want to abolish lies!" so runs a great and beautiful slogan from the recent demonstration of German students. But it also belongs to lying to hide the truth from oneself. And I want to show quite openly by referring to three examples what our responsibility is as protagonists of the new Germany in face of these temptations. The examples are "the advance laurels," the practice of denunciation, and the use of defamation as a means for winning the struggle.

The first example is comparatively harmless. If Adolf Hitler, in a very gratifying decree, exhorted us not to change the old names of streets and squares, then the new Marburg town council should be ashamed of itself that, at its first session, it could find no more urgent a duty in the new situation than to give new names to some of our streets and squares. Indeed, the matter is not nearly as harmless as it may first appear. For by means of such a process of awarding laurels in advance one feeds a peculiar feeling of security that is not to be confused with "faith" in the future. Faith involves *seriousness,* and seriousness knows what Hitler again emphasized in his speech yesterday, that we are only at the beginning and that infinitely much is still required of us in the way of patient work and a willingness to sacrifice. And I hardly need to point out how quickly such light-minded security will turn to disillusionment when our leaders demand sacrifice. As over against this temptation of light-mindedness we have to emphasize the seriousness of the task.

The second example is much worse, and the government's repeated demonstrations against the practice of denunciation is sufficient evidence of the danger that lurks here. I happen to know, for example, that the Minister of Religious Affairs receives daily baskets full of denunciations; happily, I also know that these find their well-deserved places in the waste basket! But the issue here is not only the eventual result of the denunciations; rather the worst of it is that such a practice of informing against others poisons the atmosphere, establishes mistrust between fellow countrymen, and suppresses a man's free and honest word. "We want to abolish lies"— fine, but it also belongs to this that one respects the free word, even when it expresses something other than what he wishes to hear. Otherwise one educates men to lie.

This already brings us to the third example. The defamation of a person who thinks differently from you is not a noble means for winning a struggle. And once again I may appeal to a statement of Hitler, that those who think differently should not be suppressed, but rather won over. By defamation one does not convince his adversaries and win them to his point of view, but merely repulses the best of them. One really wins only by a struggle of the *spirit* in which he respects his adversary. As a Christian, I must deplore the injustice that is also being done precisely to German Jews by means of such defamation. I am well aware of the complicated character of the Jewish problem in Germany. But, "We want to abolish lies!"—and so I must say in all honesty that the defamation of the Jews that took place in the very demonstration that gave rise to this beautiful sentiment was not sustained by the spirit of love. Keep the struggle for the German nation pure, and take care that noble intentions to serve truth and country are not marred by demonic distortions!

But there is yet this final word. If we have correctly understood the meaning and the demand of the Christian faith, then it is quite clear that, *in face of the voices of the present, this Christian faith itself is being called in question*. In other words, it is clear that we have to decide whether Christian faith is to be valid for us or not. It, for its part, can relinquish nothing of its nature and claim; for " *verbum Domini manet in aeternum.*" And we should as scrupulously guard ourselves against falsifications of the faith by national religiosity as against a falsification of national piety by Christian trimmings. The issue is either/or!

The brief words of this hour can only remind us of this decision. But the work of the semester will again and again bring the question to our attention and clarify it in such a way that the requisite decision can be clearly and conscientiously made.

HOW DOES GOD SPEAK TO US
THROUGH THE BIBLE?*

" How does God speak to us through the Bible?" Who asks
that? Would someone who is certain *that* God speaks through
the Bible ask such a question? Why should he want to know
how? If it were asked as a purely theoretical question, it
would be a useless, even a frivolous game. For what God says
to us through the Bible is in the form of *address*. It can only
be listened to, not examined. The man to whom God really
speaks through the Bible hears what God says to him and acts
accordingly, and he has just as little time and reason to
ponder over the *how,* as has a son to submit the style of his
father's words to theoretical examinations. In doing so, he
would forget to hear rightly.

Or does the question come from a doubter, who has heard
from others that God speaks through the Scriptures and who
wants to know how this is possible, how it can be understood?
We shall not help him if we think that we must first of all
explain *how* God speaks, so that he can convince himself of
the *fact*. We cannot first of all prove the *possibility* of God's
speaking through the Bible in order that belief in its *reality*
may naturally follow.

No! The question of *how* God speaks to us through the
Bible has no sense unless we ask at the same time *what* God
says to us through the Bible. And we have good reason for
putting this question. We have a reason even if we do not
doubt the *fact* that he speaks. For the conviction *that* he
speaks might be only a theoretical conviction, only a dogma
with which we reassure ourselves. And with such a conviction

* " How Does God Speak to Us through the Bible?" *The Student
World,* xxvii (1934), 108-12.

we might be deaf to what God really says to us through the
Scriptures. Perhaps we are interested in the Bible and read it,
always assuming that it is God's word, but all the same in no
other way than we read other serious and devotional books
with a view to enriching our spiritual knowledge, with a view
to the upbuilding of our philosophy of life and to confirm the
thoughts—also the Christian thoughts—that we already have.
If this is so, the question : how does God really speak to us
through the Bible? should stir us and make us think. If this is
so, we are, however, not so much concerned with the " how "
of *God's* speech, but with the " how " of *our listening.* How
should we listen? Unless we find the true answer we cannot
help those who ask in doubt, sceptics or seekers, how God
speaks.

How then should we hear? Which is the right way to prepare? The first condition for readiness is this : we must silence
all other voices; everything we say to ourselves, everything
other people say to us. For we want to hear what *God* says to
us. And if we take this seriously, there is room for but one
voice. For God's voice sounds from beyond the world. If we
wish to hear it, we must be prepared to let it challenge everything in us and everything in the world : our instincts and
desires, our ideals and enterprises, all everyday and ordinary
things, but also everything extraordinary and noble. If we
wish to hear God, we must give up everything to which we are
attached, everything that binds us. If we wish to come before
God, we must be prepared to look into nothingness, into
death. For God does not grant life except after first having
demanded death. His word is the word of creation, creat-
ing out of nothingness; before him all that we ourselves are
and have must be wiped out. The everlasting life, which God
wishes to grant through his word (John 6:63, 6:68), he
grants to the *dead* and in doing so wakes them (John 5:24).
Are we prepared to realize that without this word we are
dead? That through this word we shall be " born again,"
that we shall be " newly created " (John 3:3 ff.; II Cor.

5 : 17)? Do we want to expose ourselves to this word that is sharper than a two-edged sword (Heb. 4 : 12 f.)?

Those only who are thus ready to hear the word of the Bible will hear it as God's word. Yes, because they hear it with this readiness, they hear it already as God's word. For the call to this preparedness is already the call of God through the Bible. The readiness to listen will increase through it; i.e., the word of the Scriptures teaches men to recognize ever more clearly what is the "beyond" and the "here," death and life, flesh and Spirit, God and man. Why does hearing the word make one ever readier to listen to it? Why does hearing it lead to an ever clearer recognition of human nothingness and God's greatness? Because it teaches us to understand that the word of *judgment* is at the same time the word of *grace,* that God demands the death of man in order to grant him life, that God in his mercy sent us Jesus Christ, that his mercy surrounded us before we were aware of it. For God's word teaches us to consider our nothingness and the death in us, as our *sin,* as the revolt against him who is our life, while we, the rebels, wanted to live by and for ourselves. And the radical readiness that we receive through the Scriptures for the Scriptures is the submission to God's word as the word of forgiveness.

Is that possible? Is the promise of the Scriptures that God has forgiven us and received us in his mercy through Jesus Christ a word that we can believe as God's word?

If we still ask these questions, we are obviously not yet rightly prepared. For they indicate that we still consider the Bible as an ordinary book which we may study like other books in order to profit by it. If we ask for plain convincing reasons why God speaks actually here, in the Bible, then we have not yet understood what God's sovereignty means. For it is due to his sovereign will, that he has spoken and speaks here. The Bible does not approach us at all like other books, nor like other " religious voices of the nations," as catering for our interest. It claims from the outset to be God's word. We did not come across the Bible in the course of our cultural studies, as we came across, for example, Plato or the Bhagavad-Gita. We came to know it through the Christian church, which put it before us with its authoritative claim. The church's preaching, founded on the Scriptures, passes on the word of the Scriptures. It says : God speaks to you *here*! In his majesty he has chosen *this* place! We cannot question whether this place is the right one; we must listen to the call that summons us.

Only thus do we rightly understand the word of judgment and grace. For the word does not teach the nothingness of human things and the mercy of God as general and abstract propositions. The realization of the nothingness of human nature can easily go together with human conceit, and the knowledge that God's nature is grace may be combined with desperation. But when in the preaching of the church the word addresses *you,* it shows you *your* nothingness, *your* sin, and tells you that God is merciful to *you* and has loved you from all time.

The Scriptures teach this as God's word addressed to you, ever more clearly, and *again and again.* For no one has ever heard it enough. One does not come to know this in the same way that one grasps an enlightening thought, nor so that one knows it once for all. God's word is not a general truth that can be stored in the treasure-house of human spiritual life. It remains his sovereign word, which we shall never master and which can only be believed as an ever-living miracle, spoken by God, and constantly renewed. How should he who has heard it once not listen and hope, strive and pray, that he may hear it again?

Belief in this word is the surrender of one's whole existence to it; readiness to hear it is readiness to submit one's whole life to its judgment and its grace and, since our life is always trying to evade the word, readiness always to hear it anew. This does not mean that one takes a " biblical philosophy of life " from the Bible, by means of which one can find a reason for one's life, from which one can lay down hard and fast rules of conduct, and which supplies an infallible solution for the riddle of destiny. Nay, far more : if the way of faith leads from glory to glory (II Cor. 3 :18), it is so just because it remains a way through perplexity and darkness (II Cor. 6 :4 ff.). Glory is that which is granted from beyond—granted to the faith that hears God's word ever anew.

The word of God never becomes our property. The test of whether we have heard it aright is whether we are prepared always to hear it anew, to ask for it in every decision in life; whether we are prepared to let it intervene in the moment of decision; to let it convince us of our nothingness, but also of God's mercy, freeing us from all pride—" and what hast thou that thou didst not receive?" (I Cor. 4 :7)—but also from any faint-heartedness—" as having nothing, and yet possessing all things " (II Cor. 6 :10)!

We are constantly under the temptation not to listen to God's word any more. It is drowned for us by the noise of the world, by the quiet stream of everyday life with its soothing murmur, by the call of pressing duties and cares, or the stunning fury of fate. Which call sounds the louder, the manifold and varied voices of the world or the voice of God?

Or could a word of God possibly resound out of these many voices of the world, out of our duties and destinies, out of nature that surrounds our lives, out of history that forms them, and could this not complete the word received through the Bible? Yes. God speaks here too—but enigmatically, incomprehensibly. God's voice can be *understood* only by him who lets the word enter into him every time it speaks to him out of the Scriptures. For without the criterion of this word, which has only one interpretation, all these other voices are uncertain in their meaning. If we listen only to them we shall go astray. Are we not constantly being misled by these manifold and varied voices? Do they not constantly tempt us to become the masters of our own lives? We need then to have the word of judgment and grace continually repeated to us.

The readiness to submit one's whole life to God's word, to hear God's word ever again, i.e., to hear it anew each moment, is at the same time the *readiness to love*. When God's word frees us from ourselves and makes us into new beings through his love, it sets us free to love others. We abide in him only if his words abide in us (John 15 : 7), if we keep his commandments (John 15 :10). And his commandment is love (John 15 :12).

How does God speak to us through the Bible? As the sovereign Lord, who demands death and brings life, who claims our whole existence for his will, who sets us free to love. Are we ready to hear?

FAITH IN GOD THE CREATOR*

Hence, as to the eating of food offered to idols we know that an idol has no real existence and that there is no God but one. For although there may be so-called gods in heaven or on earth—as indeed there are many gods and many lords—yet for us there is one God, the Father, from whom are all things and for whom we exist, and one Lord, Jesus Christ, through whom are all things and through whom we exist. (I Cor. 8:4-6)

I

The specific question with which Paul deals in this chapter is for us a thing of the past. It is the question whether a Christian may eat meat that has been sacrificed to idols. There were different ways in which a Christian of that period could find himself in the situation of eating such meat. The meat of the animals sacrificed in the temple was afterwards sold on the market. Or it would be set before a Christian, say, who was invited to a meal with heathen relatives or friends. Consequently, for Christians of that day this was frequently an urgent question. Many judged that one could eat such meat without hesitation because the gods to whom it was offered were not real gods at all and therefore the meat sacrificed to them was no different than ordinary meat. On the other hand, there were others who were anxious : even if the idols are not really gods, there nevertheless are evil demons! And does not a Christian pollute himself if he handles things that belong to their realm?

The answer that Paul gives is this : in principle, the first group is correct. The so-called god to whom the meat is

* "Der Glaube an Gott den Schöpfer," Evangelische Theologie, I (1934-5), 175-89. (This was originally a sermon delivered at the academic worship service at Marburg on July 1, 1934.)

sacrificed means nothing to Christians; moreover, the sacrificial meat is as harmless as any other, and Christian freedom does not need to let itself be limited by heathen superstition. However, Christian freedom has its own limit in loving consideration for the anxious brother who is unable to free himself of the thought of the gods' evil power and is afraid of pollution. In consideration for him, the strong man also should decline to eat, so that the weak brother is not led to do something with a bad conscience that he would not do by himself through his own insight.

Thus Christian freedom has its limit in love for the brother. Or, better said, it does not really have its limit in love, but rather thereby precisely manifests itself. For this freedom is the inner freedom of leaving undone as well as of doing. Therefore, one should leave undone whatever offends the brother and tempts him to act against his conscience.

Thus what we learn from Paul's dealing with this question that for us is a thing of the past is how Christian freedom and love belong together, how freedom is an inner attitude that can express itself in leaving undone as well as in doing, and how its exercise is to be made dependent upon its effect on others.

II

But we have not turned to this chapter today because of this teaching about how Christian freedom is to be exercised, but rather because of the few verses that have been read, in order to learn from them wherein Christian freedom has its *basis*.

This basis lies in *faith in God as the Creator*. We all have occasion today to reflect on this basis of Christian freedom, inasmuch as " faith in creation " has become a battle slogan in the struggle within the church. Many ask : " Has not the Christian church placed much too little emphasis on the idea of creation?" " Has it not improperly permitted the first article

of God the Creator to recede behind the second article of
Christ the Redeemer?" "Must not we today reflect anew on
the faith in creation?"

Whatever is the case with the other questions, this last one
is certainly correct. We must indeed reflect anew on the faith
in creation; and as Paul makes this faith into the critical
principle of his discussion of the (for us) antiquated question
of meat sacrificed to idols, so must we today accept it as the
critical principle for dealing with the concrete questions of
our time. And our text should be especially helpful in this
reflection inasmuch as in it the second article is placed immediately after the first one: "Yet for us there is one God,
the Father, from whom are all things and for whom we exist,
and one Lord, Jesus Christ, through whom are all things and
through whom we exist."

Thus it is clear that for Paul both statements belong together and cannot be played off one against the other. The
only question is how their relation to one another is to be
understood.

What does it mean that God is the Creator? "We know
that an idol has no real existence (Luther: "that an idol is
nothing") and that there is no God but one" (vs. 4).

The first thing that Paul emphasizes is the nothingness of all
other beings that pass for divine. If he says that there are no
such beings, then what he says in the following sentence (vs.
5) makes clear how this is meant: "For although there may
be so-called gods in heaven or on earth—as indeed there are
many gods and many lords. . . ." Thus there are such beings
as beings that somewhere and somehow exist. But on the
other hand there are no such beings as *divine* beings, i.e., as
powers that could lay claim to our worship or place us under
obligation. *For us* they do not exist, because "for us there is
only one God the Father" (vs. 6). Only he places us under
obligation, only he can lay claim to our worship.

Paul knows very well that there are many gods and lords

i.e., that there are many powers in the world which claim us and whose claim is accepted by many men as divine. What kind of powers? Ancient men generally and therefore Paul also pictured the powers to which human existence is exposed as personal beings, i.e., they thought of this world as the realm in which gods and demons hold sway. There are uncanny demons whose raging desire is at work in man's impulses and sensuality; but there are also exalted spirits, spirits of the stars, whose law regulates everything that happens on earth; there are gods of life and fertility out of whose fullness come all the sprouting, blooming, and ripening of the fruits of earth and all the vitality of the world of animals and men; there are deities that are the custodians of law and order and that hold in their hand the destinies of nation and state; and there are pure spirits that set the rules of human thinking and impose responsibility upon human willing.

Now have all of these ceased to be powers for us? If we really want to grasp what Paul means, we must not get hung up on the images in which ancient thought tried to make human existence understandable, but rather must reflect on the actualities that are intended in such images. Certainly for us the images of bands of demons and divine figures have come to an end. But have the powers also come to an end whose efficacy and claim once found expression in these images? By no means!

Wherever the reality that sustains our life and determines our willing is seen to lie in any of these powers, the many gods and lords still hold sway. This is true whether the power in question be the unbending action of natural laws or the vital impulse of the life of nature that reveals itself brightly and attractively or awfully and shockingly in natural structures and processes and in the multiformity of nature's species. It is true whether the power be the world of ideas and ideals, of the timeless spirit, out of which unfold the norms of the good, the true, and the beautiful, or rather the *nomos* of nation and state. Wherever the ultimate reality that gives meaning to our life and demands our worship is seen to lie in these powers, the many gods and lords still hold sway.

If in times past, when idealism and positivism were the dominant modes of thought, modern man's idol was the Absolute Spirit or the law of nature, today it is the vital power that is at work in natural life and gives form to the *nomos* of nation and state, which, indeed, is frequently identified with it.

But Paul says of all these powers that they are nothing in face of the one and only God. He does not say that they are simply nothing and that therefore they could have nothing to do with us; rather he says that they are nothing divine, that they do not have anything *decisive* to do with us, that they are not what constitutes the basis and meaning of our life.

Thus the first thing that is expressed by the Christian idea of God as the Creator is that *God stands beyond all the great powers of nature and history and of national and spiritual life,* in whose realm we exist, who lay claim to us and further us and demand our devotion. Here, in *this* realm, God is not to be found! If we serve these powers we do not yet thereby serve God : if we give them the glory we refuse it to God the Creator. He is beyond them. He is their source; for from him are all things.

But if they are from him—do they not then bear the stamp of his being? Do they not then reveal his " eternal power and deity " (Rom. 1 : 20)? Do they not then compel us to worship, and in worshipping them, do we not bow precisely before their source, their Creator?

Here the spirits divide, and we must try to recognize the decisive point. It is clear that Paul says both things—first that everything is from God, and therefore the powers also and then, second, that these powers are nothing before him. These two statements belong together in the Christian faith in creation. And if it is correct that we can recognize in every created thing the stamp of the Creator's being and the trace of his rule, this is only correct so long as we become aware at the same time of the nothingness of every created thing.

How are we to understand this? We must become clear that to say of anything in the world that it is God's creature is at the same time to say that in and of itself it is nothing. What is created does not have its own existence. The world as God's creation is not like the work of an artist, which, when once he has created it, stands alongside of him and has its own existence and, after he is long since in his grave, still remains and shows to subsequent generations what kind of a spirit inspired him. On the contrary, God's creation is a creation out of nothing; and to be God's creature means absolutely and in every present to have one's source in him, in such a way that were he to withhold his creative will the creature would fall back into nothing. Thus to be God's creature means to be constantly encompassed and threatened by nothingness.

> *When thou hidest thy face, they are dismayed;*
> *When thou takest away their breath, they die*
> *And return to their dust.* (Ps. 104:29)

We understand the world as God's creation only when we know about this nothingness that encompasses every created thing; only when, beyond all the importance that the creatures can acquire for us, we do not forget the final unimportance that stamps them as creatures; only when, beyond all of the world's beauty that may charm us, we do not forget the shadow of nothing that lies over every splendid thing and constantly seeks to remind us of its transitoriness; only when, beyond all of the sublimity of historical figures and accomplishments, we do not forget the final harmlessness of all of man's efforts in face of the eternal, before whom a thousand years are but as yesterday when it is past (Ps. 90:4); only when, beyond all of our esteem for the nobility of human greatness, we do not forget that before God even the noblest and greatest is but a man who is encompassed by nothingness.

But we will better understand this if we attend to the

second statement that stands alongside of the first. "Yet for us there is one God, the Father, from whom are all things *and for whom we exist.*" Like everything that is created, we are from him and exist for him, i.e., he is our whence and our whither. We are encompassed by him, we have our being from him, and we have it for him, we belong to him.

What does this mean? It does not mean a theoretical worldview that holds that human existence is to be referred back to the existence of God as its cause or substance and that because our existence stems from his it is endowed with his nature, so that we now bear divine being within us. Rather it means, first of all, that we are creatures, that we are dust and ashes, that in ourselves we are nothing. It means that in ourselves we have no permanence and nothing whereupon we could base our own right and our own claims, nothing that we ourselves can assert as the meaning and worth of our life. We are encompassed by the same nothingness that encompasses the entire creation; we are suspended in nothing.

"No!" you may say. "We are in the hands of the Creator!" Certainly we are. But as soon as we forget what that means, as soon as we forget that it is through his creative will that we are what we are and are nothing in ourselves, as soon as we forget to give thanks to him for our existence and to give him the glory (Rom. 1:21)—so soon are we in fact nothing.

And this is precisely what happens when we worship the creation instead of the Creator (Rom. 1:25). And do we not constantly do this, or at least constantly stand under the temptation to do so, even if we no longer have anything to do with images of idols and sacrifices?

What is it that gives our life, as we commonly understand and lead it, its reality and its meaning? Nothing other than precisely devotion to those powers of nature and history which, if they do not point us to their source, are nothing in themselves. What actually claims all our thinking and acting from morning to night? Are we mindful that, when our thinking and acting are guided, blessed, or shaken by our life in nature, this nature that dispenses power and joy to us, but also brings us grief and suffering—are we mindful that it does not provide the basis of our true existence, that it may not lay claim to our true willing, may not carry away our passions in joy and grief? Are we free of the arrogance and thoughtlessness to which the gifts of nature seduce us? Are we free of the care and anxiety that grow out of binding our life to nature?

Or are we mindful that, when our thinking and acting are taken in claim by the projects and duties of civic and political life, by the ideals of our nation and its history, we can participate in all of this only with an inner reservation—that none of it is the claim of God if it is not understood from the standpoint of its source in him? Are we acquainted with that peculiar distance from life of which Paul speaks?

> Let those who have wives live as though they had none, and those who mourn as though they were not mourning, and those who rejoice as though they were not rejoicing, and those who buy as though they had no goods, and those who deal with the world as though they had no dealings with it. For the form of this world is passing away. (I Cor. 7:29-31)

Or does the noise of joys and sorrows, of business and of duties, of plans and ideals drown out our knowledge of the dark, uncanny nothing in which we are suspended—the knowledge that, like shipwrecked sailors abandoned in infinity, we are left to swim in the infinite depths and must surely be lost if God does not sustain us?

This, then, is the primary thing about faith in creation: the knowledge of the nothingness of the world and of our own selves, the knowledge of our complete abandonment. "Therefore," Luther says in the Large Catechism, "if we had faith in this article, it would humble us, it would terrify us." Yes, this is the kind of faith that is involved. For such knowledge is only true and authentic when it is not mere knowledge or an occasional feeling, but rather actually places its stamp on our attitude, our willing and acting—when we really abandon ourselves to God by existing for him and giving him the glory.

This knowledge does not mean to speak of God as the first cause of all beings and to affirm the efficacy of this first cause everywhere in nature and history or to search after it and gaze upon it with astonishment. It is easy to look with wonder and reverence upon the fullness and power of natural forces and to marvel at the richness of history. But this still is not reverence for God the Creator. Perhaps such astonishment and such wonder also have a rightful place in the faith in creation; but this can only be when they are raised on the basis of a knowledge of one's own nothingness. It is on such a basis that the praise of the Creator is raised in Ps. 104, which we have heard from the altar, and in Paul Gerhardt's morning hymn about the "Golden Sun," which we have sung. Such knowledge stands at the beginning of faith in creation and without it this faith is spurious, i.e., is a worship of the creature instead of the Creator.

III

But now is this knowledge by itself already Christian faith in Creation? Of course not! For such knowledge can also arise among the heathen when they lose confidence in their gods and when the question concerning the true meaning of human life is seriously raised.

> *Creatures of a day! Are we really?*
> *Or are we really not?*
> *A dream of a shadow is man.*
>   (Pindar, *Pyth.* VIII, 95 f.)

> *Life's but a walking shadow.*
>   (Shakespeare, *Macbeth*, V, 5)

> *We are such stuff*
> *As dreams are made on, and our little life*
> *Is rounded with a sleep.*
>> (Shakespeare, *The Tempest*, IV, I)

And this knowledge of the nothingness of all human efforts can even become a kind of resigned and consoled thinking that rises above the noise of the day:

> *Attending the most anxious dream is*
>> *A secret feeling*
> *That everything signifies nothing,*
>> *Even if we were still to be so oppressed.*
> *In our weeping there plays*
>> *Propitiously a smile.*
> *But I would fain think,*
>> *Thus should it always be.**

Such knowledge becomes Christian faith in creation only because *the second article stands alongside of the first.* We not only have one God, the Father, from whom are all things and for whom we exist but also *one Lord, Jesus Christ, through whom are all things and through whom we exist.*

What does it mean to say that all things are through him? In speaking in this way, Paul makes use of a formula that was present in the world-view of the educated Gentiles of his time and gives it a specific meaning. Wherever the idea of a God who is beyond the world had been thought—and this had

---

* *Den bängsten Traum begleitet*
  Ein heimliches Gufühl,
Das alles Nichts bedeutet,
  Und wär' uns noch so schwül.
Da spielt in unser Weinen
  Ein Lächeln hold hinein.
Ich aber möchte meinen,
  So sollt' es immer sein.
    (Freidrich Hebbel, *Dem Schmerz sein Recht*, II)

been done by several thinkers—the question arose how such a transcendent, eternal, and spiritual God could have anything to do with this transitory, material, and corporeal world in which we live. If he is beyond the world, and yet has not completely abandoned it, this is only possible because there is a transition or mediation between this world and the world beyond. Thus there arose the theory of an intermediary being who effects this transition by mediating between God and the world. There is a Son of God who gathers into himself whatever divine forces are at work in the world, who, so to speak, brings the high God near to the world, and in whom the high God becomes evident. What is this Son of God? Well, the truth of the matter is that he is nothing other than an abstraction, a personification of the forces and laws that are at work in the world, a creature of thought.

But Paul nevertheless seizes upon this idea. Yes, there is a mediator between God and the world who brings God near to us, in whom God becomes evident to us, and through whom the world becomes God's creation for us. If we know him, we know God; and if we do not know him, we do not know God. But how does he bring God near to us? How does God become evident to us in him? Is he a personification of all the world's laws and vital forces? By no means! He is an individual man like us in whose action God acts, in whose destiny God is at work, in whose word God speaks. He has died on the cross—for us; and he now lives in eternity—for us! And only when we understand this do we understand that God is the Creator; and so it is through him that the world becomes God's creation—for us!

How this is possible, however, can only be understood when we understand the last statement : " and through whom we exist." In saying " we " here, Paul speaks of Christians who believe that in Jesus they experience the action of God and that through him they have gained their existence.

But how have they gained it? Paul has said earlier in his

letter that Christ has been made by God " our wisdom, our righteousness and sanctification and redemption." This is said to men who think that they must and can become wise by their own thinking, righteous and holy by their own doing, and redeemed through their own power, i.e., free from that which is master of us all, from the commonplace. Thus it is said to men who do not exist through Christ, but rather through themselves, who see in themselves the basis and meaning of their existence. Christ is *made* our wisdom, our righteousness and sanctification and redemption—i.e., he does not simply enlighten us concerning it. For the view that we can and should gain the basis and meaning of our existence by our own power is not simply an error that might be corrected by enlightenment, but rather is nothing other than *sin*.

For just this is sin : to forget that we are creatures—yes, even to misuse the idea of creation by saying that God is in us, that we sense in ourselves divine and creative forces, and by undertaking in the strength of such forces to shape our lives and to build the world. And this sin, this forgetting of his own nothingness, is precisely what really delivers man to nothingness, to death. If he no longer sees God, then all he sees around him is nothing. But he flees from this sight and hides his nothingness from himself. Yet, whoever hides his nothingness always seeks life in the creation instead of from the Creator. And all of those powers that are nothing in themselves thereby acquire their power over him. And because he cannot bear the sight of nothing, he clothes these powers with the splendour of divinity and pays them his worship. In return, they pay him with nothingness, with death.

God has made Christ " our wisdom, our righteousness and sanctification and redemption," i.e., through him God has brought sin and death to nothing. In the cross of Christ, God passes judgment against all of the world's greatness and pride, against all of its wisdom, righteousness, sanctification and self-redemption. To have faith in the crucified one means to permit oneself to be crucified with him, to permit this judgment also to be passed against oneself. To have faith in the cross of Christ means to be prepared to let God work as the Creator. God creates out of nothing, and whoever becomes nothing before him is made alive. Whenever the cross really leads me to the knowledge of my own nothingness and to the confession of my sin, I am open for God's rule as the Creator who forgives me my sin and takes from me nothingness, death. Thus Christ as the one who leads us to God, the Creator of life, is our Lord, through whom we exist. And so it is that the second article stands alongside of the first. The first article leads to the second, and the second leads back to the first.

Luther said once:

This is the supreme article of faith of which we speak: I believe in God the Father almighty, Maker of heaven and earth. And whoever honestly believes this is already helped and is once again brought back to the place whence Adam fell. But few are they who go so far as to believe fully that he is the God who makes and creates all things. For such a man must be dead to everything, to good and bad, to death and life, to hell and to heaven, and must confess in his heart that he is able to do nothing by his own power.

What we are to learn from the cross of Christ is to go so far as to believe precisely this; and it is for this reason that Christ is our Lord, through whom are all things and through whom we exist.

I V

It is in such a faith as this that Christian freedom is based. For such faith knows that nothing in the world can ultimately claim me and also that nothing in the world can destroy me. The man of faith is free from anxiety because he fears God, and for the rest, fears nothing in the world. He is now free to marvel at God's creative power in nature and history:

> *O Lord, how manifold are thy works!*
> *In wisdom hast thou made them all;*
> *And the earth is full of thy creatures!* (Ps. 104:24)

The man of faith is free for the tasks of the day because in the inner distance of having as though he had not he is free from tension and anxious care:

> *Evening and morning*
> *Are his care,*
> *Blessing and increase,*
> *And prevention of ill*
> *Are his works and his works alone.**

The man of faith is free for love, which opens his eyes to what God requires of him in the moment.

The powers of the world tempt man today as always to surrender his freedom, and they promise him dominion over the world if he will but fall down and worship them. But faith knows that such worship is idolatry. And what about idolatrous sacrifices? Does not this question that for us has become a thing of the past still have an urgency, albeit in a different form? Of course it has! For the question is always urgent, whether and in what way we as Christians can participate in an intercourse with the world—its creations and its enjoyments, its judgments and its ideals—that is understood and carried out by others as service of the worldly powers. Our participation depends on our becoming clear ourselves and also seeing that no misunderstanding arises in the minds

---

* *Abend und Morgen*
  Sind seine Sorgen,
  Segnen und Mehren,
  Unglück verwehren
  Sind seine Werke und Taten allein.
          (Paul Gerhardt, " *Die güld'ne Sonne* ")

of others, that for us these powers are not ultimate powers, that beyond them stands the creative power of God that forbids us to fall down and worship them because all glory belongs to him as the Creator. For everything that we do in the worldly realm can be done in two senses : either as a tribute to the worldly powers or, in faith in God the Creator, as a service of love. Amen.

JESUS AND PAUL*

I

. According to Alfred Rosenberg,[1] the " great personality of esus " has " been misused " by ecclesiastical Christianity. Whatever its original form, the great personality of Jesus Christ was immediately after his departure burdened and amalgamated with all the rubbish of Near Eastern, of Jewish and African life."[2] Specifically, the teachings of Paul consti- ute " the Jewish spiritual matrix, so to say, the Talmudic- Oriental side of both the Roman and the Lutheran Church."[3]

The perspective that is expressed in such statements is not new. It was earnestly discussed by the theological research of he preceding generation after it had been particularly brought o attention by Wilhelm Wrede's *Paulus* (1905). According o Wrede, Paul should " be considered the second founder of Christianity "; as " the real creator of a Christian theology," it was he who " made Christianity into a religion of redemp- ion." For him, Christianity is such a religion of redemp- ion because what redeems man " in no way lies within him," but rather lies " outside of him in a divine work of redemp- ion that has once for all procured salvation for mankind." Paul's whole innovation consisted in the way he made these saving facts, the incarnation, death, and resurrection of Christ, the foundation of religion."[4] According to Wrede, this Christian doctrine of salvation has the character of a myth.

The judgment of Arnold Meyer was similar.[5] Unlike Paul, Jesus had no doctrine of universal sinfulness; he did not demand faith in an act of atonement for sin, in his death and resurrection, but required only trust in the power of God. For

* " Jesus und Paulus," Jesus Christus im Zeugnis der Heiligen chrift und der Kirche. Beiheft 2 zur Evangelische Theologie Munich : Christian Kaiser Verlag, 1936), pp. 68-90.

217

Jesus, there was no need of a mediator between God and man. "If one understands by Christianity the faith in Christ as the heavenly Son of God . . . then it was principally Paul and not Jesus who founded such a Christianity."[6]

Wrede, Meyer, and others pointed to the distance between Jesus and Paul in the conviction that authentic Christianity is the religion of Jesus. And it was with this same conviction that Adolf Harnack had in 1900 sketched the "essence of Christianity" on the basis of Jesus' proclamation. "In this complex—God the Father, providence, man as child of God, the infinite value of the human soul—the whole gospel is expressed."[7] This becomes clear in the Lord's Prayer. "According to this prayer, the gospel is existence as a child of God extended to the whole of life; it is an inner union with God's will and God's Reign and a joyous certainty in the possession of eternal goods and protection from evil."[8] The essential elements in the gospel—and they are to be separated from the "husk" of Jesus' picture of the world and history—are "timeless."[9]

2. We must be grateful to these researchers. The earnestness and honesty of their inquiry inevitably compelled Christian faith to a more and more radical self-examination with respect to its authentic nature. However, it is not necessary for us to go into the details of the discussion as it was carried on then, since the question has been raised today in a new way.[10] This has been due largely to the "history of religions school," which has relentlessly furthered the process of self-examination. It has pointed out that the "Christ-myth" has its origins in contemporary mythology. The figure of the Messiah-King as well as the image of Son of Man (and connected with it the doctrine of the two aeons), comes from the messianic mythology of Judaism. On the other hand, the ideas of a saviour-god who dies and is once again brought to life, and of sacraments (baptismal bath and holy meal) through which the mystes acquire a share in the destiny of the deity—these ideas come from the mystery religions. Furthermore, it is

from Gnosticism that we get the idea of the heavenly redeemer and his incarnation and exaltation, which prepare the
way for the faithful to return to their heavenly home. Thus
the historical study of the Christian doctrine of salvation seems
to signify its destruction. But it also seems to leave the way
open to return to the simple gospel of Jesus![11]

Thus, for researchers like Wilhelm Bousset and Wilhelm
Heitmüller, it is clear that the historical phenomenon that has
hitherto been called "Christianity" includes the Pauline
doctrine of salvation, that "Christianity" in its traditional
sense is the religion in which man's relation to God is mediated by the person of Christ. Therefore, they conclude, the
religion of the historical Jesus was not "Christianity"; Jesus
was not the "first Christian." Christianity only exists where
there is faith in Christ, or faith in God through Christ.

What is the implication of this? Does it mean a return to
Jesus and the abandonment of the Pauline doctrine of salvation? If so, we would clearly have to abandon what has
hitherto been called Christianity. However, one would hardly
be permitted to shrink back from such an implication if its
presuppositions were correct. Nor may any Christian, and
especially any theologian, hesitate to consider this possibility.
For such consideration can only serve to clarify what is really
at stake, what Christianity authentically is. Moreover, one
might perhaps be prepared to pay the price of renouncing
"Christianity" if he could be sure that by so doing he would
be acting in accord with Jesus' own real intention.

I I

1. If the demand to abandon Christianity couches itself in
the slogan, "Return from Paul to Jesus!" then the meaning
of Christianity must be made clear by considering Paul's relation to Jesus. And the first thing to note is that it is a sure
result of research that Paul's theology is not dependent on

Jesus' proclamation, that Paul was not Jesus' disciple, either directly or through the mediation of the original disciples. Indeed, he himself sharply rejects such mediation (Gal. 1:1) and affirms that he has received his gospel directly by revelation (Gal. 1:11 f.). Naturally, he was acquainted with the kerygma of the church, else he could hardly have persecuted it. But what was the kerygma with which he was acquainted? In a word, it was the message that God had raised the crucified Jesus of Nazareth and had made him Messiah, i.e., the king of the blessed end-time who will come to hold judgment and to bring salvation.

All of this Paul naturally knew. But even here we already have a Christ-myth and not the "simple gospel" of Jesus that was expressed in the latter's own proclamation. By this proclamation Paul is as good as completely untouched; in all essentials it is irrelevant to him.[12]

But the question remains how the actual subject matter of Paul's theology is related to Jesus' proclamation; i.e., we must still ask whether or to what extent the above-mentioned presentations of the opposition between Jesus and Paul are correct. We must still inquire whether, by abandoning Paul, it is possible to get back to a proclamation of Jesus that is free of mythology and that contains timeless truths that would also enlighten men today.

2. Research in the history of religions has given us a better understanding not only of the theology of Paul, but also of the proclamation of Jesus; and the result of this research is to make clear that *it is not possible by returning to Jesus to obtain a Christianity that is free from mythology.*

The error of the above-mentioned presentations lay in not doing justice to *Jesus' eschatological message,* i.e., the proclamation in which Jesus and Paul are in complete accord and which says that the old aeon has reached its end, that it is now the last hour, that the Reign of God is at hand, indeed, is already breaking in, and that the Son of Man will come as

dge to bring destruction to sinners and salvation to the
ghteous.[13]

To be sure, the demand made by Harnack and others to dis-
nguish between "kernel" and "husk" is not in itself an
correct demand. Since it is clear that Jesus' expectation of
1 imminent end of this world was a mistake—even today the
on of Man has not yet come on the clouds of heaven—the
1estion is in order whether his entire proclamation is thereby
allified, or whether there are motives in it that still retain
eir validity. The only issue is what is kernel and what is
1sk. If one can say in general that the "husk" is the picture
= the world that Jesus shared as an ancient man and as a child
= his people and time, what is the "kernel"? More exactly,
hat is the idea of God, the view of man and his relation to
od, that is contained in Jesus' eschatological message? Fur-
.er, what is the meaning of Jesus' view of the now, of the
our of his appearance, allowing that for him the meaning of
.is now would naturally be objectified in the garments of a
assing cosmology? And connected with this, finally, what is
.e meaning of his claim?

It is out of the question to say with Harnack that Jesus' pro-
amation of the Reign of God comprises two poles: on the
1e hand, it is God's outward rule and as such is something
ature that is still coming, while, on the other hand, it is
mething inward and already present—namely, wherever
an inwardly unites himself with the living God.[14] According
Harnack, insofar as God's Reign is the latter, it is a spiritual
ality, "a power that sinks within a man and can only be
1derstood inwardly"; it is a rule "that grows steadily and
lently like a seed and bears fruit."[15] But to speak in this
ay is obviously impossible; for in Jesus' view the Reign of
od is not God's rule in the human soul. Nor is it possible
> say that it is God's spiritual reign in the community of
.ose who are bound together by obedience to his will, so that
.s Reign would be erected within history precisely in this

community. Both kinds of statement are a misunderstanding
of Jesus. According to his proclamation, God's Reign
indeed the sovereignty of his will, but it is a reign that is pe
fectly realized throughout the entire world and over eve
man—namely, by God's own act at a specific time. And th
time is now immediately at hand; indeed, it has already broke
in with the coming of Jesus himself. It is with reference
this imminent Reign of God that he teaches his disciples
pray: "Thy Reign come!" And this petition is a petition f
redemption from this corrupt and evil world.

For what is presupposed by the idea of the Reign of G
and the expectation of it is a total understanding of the wor
and man and history of a very special sort. The expectation
the Reign of God is indissolubly connected with the idea
the two aeons into which the history of the world is divide
and therefore contains a specific judgment concerning th
world—namely, a condemnation of it. This means that th
world is evil, or, mythologically expressed, that it is under th
rule of Satan and the demons. It is because of this, of cours
that Jesus' ministry takes the form of a struggle against th
demonic powers. Expressed in nonmythological terms,
means that the men with whom Jesus has to do are an "adul
erous and sinful generation" (Mark 8:38; cf. Matt. 12:3
12:41 f., 12:45); they are "evil" (Matt. 7:11). Even Jesu
himself refuses to be called "good"; for "no one is good b
God alone" (Mark 10:18). To be sure, Jesus did not teac
any doctrine of original sin. Nevertheless, there is present
his message the judgment that men on the whole are co
demned, even if in individual matters they are able to d
good (Matt. 7:11). Do you suppose that those who peris
because of violence and misfortune are especially evil men
"I tell you, No; but unless you repent you will all likewi
perish" (Luke 13:1-5). In other words, Jesus says nothin
other in his call to repentance than Paul tries to make clear
his theology by means of theoretical argument.

Jesus' eschatology is naturally based on faith in creation, i.e

the conviction that God has called the world and man into
ing and therefore is their sovereign Lord; that man belongs
God and is accountable to him as Judge. For the meaning
this faith in creation is not that God is present in the world
something that can be disposed of, or that man can rejoice
the divine spark in his soul or the divine life in his nation.
ther it means that God addresses man through the world
d demands of him fear, reverence, and obedience.

God's demand removes man from his own disposal, his own
ans and purposes. And while Jesus, to be sure, does not
mand asceticism, he does require sacrifice. For both him
d his hearers the preaching of "love" does not mean libera-
on from an unbearable burden of legal prescriptions; it can-
t be heard, so to speak, with a sigh of relief: "Therefore, I
not need to torment myself any longer with an abundance
laws or to know how much is required! I no longer need
torment myself inwardly with scruples and doubts whether
have done enough or whether I have not again and again
come guilty! What is at issue is not such externals, but
ther one's intention—the fact that one incessantly strives!"
ertainly the reduction of the commandments of the law to
e moral demands of the decalogue (Mark 10:19) or to the
vofold commandment of love (Mark 12:28 ff.) *is* a libera-
on from a burden. But it is so in a wholly other sense than is
pposed by the modern man for whom it would of course be
ost inconvenient and burdensome to be placed under the
emands of the Jewish law. For the pious of Jesus' day, the
w was in general not a burden, but a matter of pride; and
or the man who was raised in them, the habits of Jewish
stom were not at all inconvenient.

The first thing to recognize is that the demand of love does
ot require less of man than the law, but rather more. It
ally removes him from his own disposal and places him
nder God's sovereign will. This is clearly shown by the
ntitheses in Matt. 5, which make the point that it is not the
orrect fulfilment of the law's demands of justice that proves

man's obedience to God. With all his correctness, he can sti
be a sinner; and God wants the whole man with his comple
and undivided obedience. Wrath, lust, lax intention, inn
dishonesty, vengefulness, and calculation—all these, and n
merely transgression of the law, are what make man evil. N
can one say that what is involved in this juxtaposition
justice and God's demand is simply the specifically Jewis
law, whereas some other justice that sprang from the mor
consciousness of man or of a particular nation would not
opposed to the demand of love, but would be in harmon
with it. By no means! For the legal prescriptions that Jes
mentions are not specifically Jewish, nor do they have to d
with ceremonial or ritual demands; rather they are demands
justice such as everywhere spring from man's moral co
sciousness: the prohibition of murder and manslaughter an
of adultery and perjury; the law regulating divorce; the *ju
talionis*; and the demand for national solidarity. Therefor
the antitheses are intended to be a matter of principle: Go
demands more than justice. Indeed, all justice is meaningle
if it is not understood from the very outset as a means to a
end, as standing in the service of God's *real* demand, th
demand of love. And in this respect also Paul is in comple
accord with Jesus: the real demand of the law is love, in whic
all the other commandments are summed up (Gal. 5:14; Rom
13:8-10); the whole law is fulfilled in one word, you shou
love your neighbour as yourself!

This is indeed a liberation from an intolerable burden, i
sofar as man is once again given back his own responsibilit
insofar as he is no longer dependent on human authoriti
who must first explain God's will to him; insofar as he
placed above justice and beyond it; and insofar as he does n
have to ask concerning all possible duties, but only concernin
his one obligation and what it requires of him in the immed
ate moment. Therefore, it is a liberation only for the ma
who understands that he is inwardly liberated when som
thing greater is demanded of him, when what is demanded

he himself. For the average Jew, however, as for the average man, this does not signify liberation, but rather bondage. For him, external correctness, blind obedience to an authority is much easier—in spite of all the inconveniences it frequently brings with it—than radical personal responsibility before God. The natural man's real response to the reduction of the law's demands to the commandment of love is not to breathe a sigh of relief, but to be terrified. And whoever does not know this terror neither senses the seriousness of the demand nor understands the meaning of liberation.

Therefore, Jesus' turning to the condemned and sinful, to the tax collectors and the harlots, by no means expresses a relaxation of the strictness of the law's demand. Indeed, it expresses precisely the opposite. For the truth of the matter is that those who are condemned are not worse than those who are correct and self-satisfied, but rather are better. They better satisfy the claim of God—though this is true, of course, only when they "repent," i.e., when they become aware of their nothingness in God's presence. When Jesus juxtaposes the repentant publican to the self-satisfied Pharisee, or the "prodigal" son to the correct elder son, he makes clear who the real sinner is—namely, the one who does not see the seriousness, the radicalness of God's demand; who supposes that he is able to stand in God's presence because of his correctness and accomplishments, and does not understand that God demands the *entire* man. It is just this, however, that is understood by the man who beats his breast, saying, "God be merciful to me a sinner!" (Luke 18:13).

But exactly this is also the view of Paul—namely, that all that the man who is correct and self-satisfied looks upon as his gain is really his loss (Phil. 3:4 ff.); that the basic sin of man is to want to boast before God, to take pride in his accomplishments. The only difference is that Paul explicates theoretically in the form of a "philosophy of history" what Jesus presents without such theoretical reflection. This Paul does by showing that in God's intention it is precisely the

E.F.   H law's true meaning to lead man to the knowledge of his nothingness before God, " so that every mouth may be stopped, and the whole world be made accountable to God " (Rom. 3:19). But it is precisely this being struck silent in God's presence that Jesus also points to as man's only appropriate attitude : " And when you have done all that is commanded you, say, ' We are unworthy servants; we have only done what is our duty ' " (Luke 17:10). Thus Jesus also retorts ironically to the man who thinks that because of his greater accomplishments he can claim more from God than another to whom God has been gracious, " Do you begrudge my generosity?" (Matt. 20:15).

However, the reduction of the will of God to the commandment of love may also appear liberating because it seems to direct man's eyes to the world and not to require of him that he know of anything beyond the world; i.e., it seems to leave man in his own sphere by simply pointing him to his fellow men. To suppose this, however, would be an error. For the commandment to love the neighbour is indissolubly connected with the commandment to love God, and, to be sure, in the conviction that one cannot see the neighbour as one should if one does not have God in view; or that one does not at all know what the good for man is—and this one must know if he is to love him—if he does not know that this world is finite, provisional, and incomplete. The world for Jesus is not complete, and the responsible man stands before God. Therefore, the fear of God goes hand in hand with the love of man, and this gives to man a split or reserved position in relation to this world.

Man should fear him who can destroy both body and soul in hell (Matt. 10:28). To be sure, this fear is not anxiety. In fact, it is precisely what gives man freedom from anxiety, the freedom from the fear of men, of those who kill the body, but cannot touch the soul. Whoever fears this God knows that he who even cares for the sparrows has also numbered all the hairs of our heads (Matt. 10:29 f.). This does not mean, of

course, that God directs everything " for the good " in the way
that *we* picture the good and desire it; rather it means that
we are inescapably in his hands. Whoever fears this God
knows that he need not be anxious; if God clothes the grass
of the field with a glorious beauty, shall he not all the more
take care of man (Matt. 6:25 ff.)?

But the admonition to be without care always has as its
condition the fear of God. It is not an admonition to thoughtlessness or blindness in face of misery and suffering, but rather
points man to his limits. How ridiculous the presumption to
take one's life into one's own hands in anxious care! " And
who among you by having care can add one cubit to his
stature?" (Matt. 6:27). Can man dispose over time? How
can he suppose that by having care today he can free the next
day of care? The morrow will come and bring its own cares
(Matt. 6:34). Can man imagine that by having care for the
means of life he is able to secure his life? " You fool! This
night your life is required of you!" (Luke 12:20). The
words concerning the lilies of the field and the birds of the
heaven do not admonish man to act with a light-hearted
optimism, but rather point him to his limits; they show him
his pitiable condition. And here, too, this is a liberation for
the man who becomes aware that this is his condition. Only
he who is free from " presumptuousness " is free from anxiety
(Kierkegaard). Whoever fears God can confidently give everything into his care. But God is not simply he who frees man
from care, so that he can feel at home in his world and settle
down in comfort.

If the man who should completely belong to God in fact
stands in the world, oppressed by its necessities and tempted
by its gifts, he is constantly in danger of losing himself in the
world and forgetting that he is confronted with an either/or.
"No one can serve two masters; for either he will hate the
one and love the other, or he will be devoted to the one and
despise the other. You cannot serve God and mammon "
(Matt. 6:24). " If your eye causes you to stumble, pluck it

out; it is better to enter the Reign of God with one eye than
with two eyes to be thrown into hell" (Mark 9:47). "How
hard it is to enter the Reign of God! It is easier for a camel
to go through the eye of a needle than for a rich man to enter
the Reign of God!" (Mark 10:24 f.). "No one who puts
his hand to the plough and looks back is fit for the Reign of
God" (Luke 9:62). "Do not lay up for yourselves treasures
on earth . . . but lay up for yourselves treasures in heaven.
. . . For where your treasure is there will your heart be also"
(Matt. 6:19-21).

In all of this Jesus does not demand asceticism, even if he
does demand renunciation and sacrifice for the sake of God
and the neighbour. The rich man who supposes that he has
already fulfilled God's commandments is put to the test to see
whether he is able to give up his riches or whether he is
inwardly bound to them (Mark 10:17-22). It is also valid
under certain circumstances to renounce marriage for the sake
of God's will (Matt. 19:12). And similarly, breaking with
one's family may also be required. "If any one comes to me
and does not hate his own father and mother and wife and
children and brothers and sisters, yes, and even himself, he
cannot be my disciple" (Luke 14:26). The parables of the
treasure hidden in a field and the pearl of great price show
that man must be ready to surrender everything for the sake of
the Reign of God (Matt. 13:44-6). Jesus does not demand,
however, the renunciation of possessions and family as a
matter of principle. His disciple Peter, for example, was
married. And asceticism with respect to eating is just as alien
to him as sexual asceticism. Indeed, he himself is chided as
"a glutton and a drunkard" (Matt. 11:19). Nor does he ever
preach anarchism; rather he takes it for granted that justice
and the state are the forms of man's life in the world.
"Render to Cæsar the things that are Cæsar's, and to God the
things that are God's" (Mark 12:17). But what is it that
belongs to Cæsar? Money! And what belongs to God? The
whole man! Jesus does not raise the question whether in-

directly, in the course of obedience to God, man might not also be obligated to do more to Cæsar than simply pay taxes. However, this question can only be raised and answered if it is first acknowledged that man completely belongs to God. And to make this clear is what Jesus takes to be his vocation; he does not understand it as his task to give instructions concerning life within the world. "Who made me a judge or divider over you?" (Luke 12:14). In the circle of his disciples, another ordinance is in force than that of the world:

> You know that those who are supposed to rule over the Gentiles lord it over them, and their great men exercise authority over them. But it shall not be so among you; rather whoever would be great among you must be your servant, and whoever would be first among you must be slave of all. (Mark 10:42-4)

But what else is this attitude to the world than what Paul also requires when he speaks of the attitude of " as though not "?

> The appointed time has grown very short. From now on, let those who have wives live as though they had none, and those who mourn as though they were not mourning, and those who rejoice as though they were not rejoicing, and those who buy as though they had no goods, and those who deal with the world as though they had no dealings with it. For the form of this world is passing away, and I want you to be free from anxieties. (I Cor. 7:29-32)

Therefore, just as little as one can flee from the mythology of Paul to a nonmythological proclamation of Jesus, so little can one return from Paul's critical judgment of the world and man to Jesus' more optimistic view, or from Paul's transcendent God to the immanent God of Jesus. Both men are in complete accord. For Jesus, just as for Paul, God stands beyond the world as Creator and Judge, and this world itself is perverted and fallen under the domination of evil powers. Likewise, Jesus also shares Paul's expectation of an act of God that will bring the present corrupt course of the world to an end and redeem the pious from it. Blessed are the poor, the hungry, and the mourners! Blessed are all who look for the Reign of God that is to come, for it is theirs! Thus whoever finds Paul offensive and uncanny must find Jesus equally so. For what Paul expressly says, namely, that the gospel is a scandal, is exactly what is shown by Jesus' proclamation, ministry, and destiny.

III

1. Or could it be, as has often been said, that the difference between the two men lies in their views of the grace of God? Is it not the case that, for Jesus, God simply as such is always and utterly gracious, so that man can always be confident of his grace and can always have recourse to it, whereas, for Paul, there is need for an especial arrangement of God, namely, the reconciling work of Christ, in order that he can be gracious? And in keeping with this, is not " faith " for Jesus nothing other than simple trust in God, whereas, for Paul, it is faith in Jesus Christ, the crucified and risen Lord? Does this not disclose a fundamental difference between the two men?

So it may appear; but it is only an appearance. For, in the first place, Paul takes it completely for granted that God has always been the God of grace; that it was always his grace when the sun rose on the evil and the good and the rain fell on the just and the unjust. Paul never questions this nor could he have ever doubted it. Indeed, he speaks of the time before Christ as a time in which God was patient, forbearing, and kind (Rom. 2 :4, 3 :26). To be sure, he is also of the opinion that men did not recognize this kindness of God, but rather were blinded by misunderstanding; they did not permit it to drive them to repentance, but lost themselves in thoughtlessness and self-satisfaction.

In the second place, however, Jesus is of the opinion that God's grace is not something that can be taken for granted, but rather is such that it can only be promised to man by God himself. If the sinner is honest and knows himself to be a sinner, he can only end in despair; for the more honest he is, the less God's forgiveness can appear to him as something he can take for granted. He can only wait and see whether God will forgive him. He does not have such a distance from himself in the consciousness of his sinfulness that he already stands there pure in his better self. On the contrary, it is precisely his better self that condemns him. The sinner as such does not know of God's grace, for if he did his knowledge of sin would be falsified. To be sure, he may have a knowledge of God's grace in general; but the decisive question is whether he knows the " for me "—exactly as in our human relations with one another the person who is guilty does not have the pardon of the other simply on the basis of his remorse, but rather only when the other actually pardons him. His trust in the pardoning kindness of the other may be ever so great— and yet he knows that he would nullify it for himself were he to reckon on it. He can only confess and trustfully ask; and he knows that he has to take this humiliation on himself. But Jesus says nothing other than this in the parable of the " prodigal son " (Luke 15 :11-32). The son who condemns himself rises and goes to his father to confess his guilt, and thus may hear the father's forgiving word. And in a similar way, Jesus portrays the publican who dares not lift up his eyes to heaven, but can only beat his breast, " God, be merciful to me a sinner!" (Luke 18 :13). However, to all such who do speak this way Jesus promises the forgiving grace of God.

But Paul says nothing else than that in Jesus God has unmistakably spoken his word of forgiving grace for everyone who will take refuge in him. That is, *for Paul, Jesus Christ is the forgiving word of God.* Thus it is only natural if he assumes that the condition for receiving grace is to hear this word in the place where God has spoken it. It would have struck him as comic were anyone to have said that this places a limit on grace or makes asking the forgiveness more difficult. Indeed, he would have insisted that precisely the opposite is the case, that it really makes such asking easier. For in Christ God's love has become visible. In Christ, the grace of God is freely offered to each and all!

But is not precisely this binding of God's grace to the person of Jesus a limiting of it of which Jesus himself knew nothing? While it is true that Jesus did not demand faith in his own person, he did demand faith in his word. That is, he made his appearance in the consciousness that God had sent him in the last hour of the world. But this means that the decision to which he summons men by his proclamation is the definitive decision; that precisely the fact that he now summons men to repentance is the final proof of God's grace; that his coming is God's grace in the last hour; that insofar as anyone hears his word, God's salvation is now freely offered to him. Indeed, Jesus demands decision with reference to his ministry:

> The blind receive their sight and the lame walk, lepers are cleansed and the deaf hear, and the dead are raised up, and the poor have good news preached to them. And blessed is he who takes no offence at me! (Matt. 11:4-6)

> Whoever acknowledges me before men, the Son of Man also will acknowledge before the angels of God; but he who denies me before men will be denied before the angels of God. (Luke 12:8 f.)

> Behold, something greater than Solomon is here. . . . something greater than Jonah is here. (Luke 11:31 f.)

If Paul, like the earliest community, saw in Jesus the Messiah, he did nothing other than affirm Jesus' own claim that man's destiny is decided with reference to his person.

But this meant for Paul that by sending Jesus God has made an end to the old age of the world.

The turn of the aeon to which the pious looked forward, the liberation and redemption from the old and corrupt course of the world, has become a reality in Jesus Christ. " But when the time had fully come, God sent forth his Son, born of woman, born under the law, to redeem those who were under the law, so that we might receive adoption as sons." (Gal. 4:4 f.). Everyone who hungers and thirsts for righteousness should let himself be told that whoever believes in Jesus Christ now receives this righteousness as a gift of God; for it is precisely in Jesus Christ that God's verdict as Judge, which either damns man or acquits him, has been spoken. Therefore, " if anyone is in Christ," i.e., affirms his claim, subjects himself to his lordship, " he is a new creation; the old has passed away, behold, the new has come " (II Cor. 5:17). The time of salvation that was looked forward to so ardently is present : " Behold, now is the acceptable time; behold, now is the day of salvation!" (II Cor. 6:2).

2. And in saying this we have pointed to the real difference between Paul and Jesus. Jesus looks to the future and points his hearers to the *coming* Reign of God, which, to be sure, is coming even now, is already breaking in. Paul, on the other hand, looks back and points to what has already occurred. For him, the turn of the age has already taken place, the day of salvation is already present! [16]

To be sure, Paul is of the opinion that the consummation is yet to occur, that Jesus Christ will still return as judge and consummate the Reign of God. But the decisive thing God has already done, and the faithful even now have the possibility of being new creatures and belonging to the new age. [17]

3. But does not Paul's doctrine of redemption say more than this? Does it not speak of Christ's cross and resurrection as saving facts in a way that cannot be understood and accepted by men today?

It can hardly be denied that Paul does indeed speak of the

cross of Christ in terms and concepts that we today must designate as mythological. And, as we said above, research in the history of religions has shown that these concepts come from certain Oriental mythologies that for us are definitely a thing of the past. But, then, every man speaks in the language of his age, and what we have to do is to discover the fundamental idea that lies behind these mythological statements. It alone signifies a genuine question of decision for us that we cannot avoid.

Paul's basic idea is that in the cross of Christ God has pronounced judgment on the world and precisely by so doing has also opened up the way of salvation. Because a crucified one is proclaimed as Lord of the world, it is demanded of man that he subject himself to God's judgment, i.e., to the judgment that all of man's desires and strivings and standards of value are nothing before God, that they are all subject to death. If God has reconciled the world to himself through the cross, then this means that he has made himself visible in the cross and, as it were, says to man, " Here I am!" All of man's accomplishments and boasting are at an end; they are condemned as nothing by the cross.

But the cross cannot be separated from the *resurrection*; i.e., precisely he who accepts as valid for himself the judgment that is spoken in the cross, who, as Paul puts it, lets himself be crucified with Christ, experiences the cross as liberation and redemption, and is able to believe that, by giving Jesus up to the cross, God thereby led him into life—a life in which all share who let themselves be crucified with him. It is precisely death that frees us for life. Therefore, Paul looks upon everything that was gain to him—namely, the national advantages of which he could boast and his irreproachable life and striving under the law—as loss, " so that," as he says, " I may know him [*sic* Christ] and the power of his resurrection, and may share his sufferings, becoming like him in his death, that if possible I may attain the resurrection of the dead " (Phil. 3 :7 ff.). " Those who belong to Christ have crucified the flesh

with its passions and desires" (Gal. 5 :24). "But far be it
from me to glory except in the cross of Christ, by which the
world has been crucified to me, and I to the world" (Gal.
6 :14).

If someone asks today whether this is not empty speculation
and pure fantasy, he is not the first to raise this question. The
Letter to the Romans clearly shows that even in his own lifetime this question had been submitted to Paul and, indeed,
that he himself had raised it : "You assert that with Christ
the old world has come to an end and the new world has
begun, that God's verdict as Judge has already been spoken.
And you also assert that in faith you are already a new creation and even now have righteousness. But where is this
resurrection life of which you boast? Where is the righteousness and the freedom from sin that belong to the new life?"
Paul replies to this question with the theological argument
that he develops in Romans 5 and 6, which is intended to
show that and how the new life is present. We cannot reproduce this argument here or attempt to explain it. But we can
point to certain passages that one might characterize as confessions of Paul, in which it becomes clear how he experiences this resurrection life precisely in abandoning himself to
death, in renouncing his own power and boasting.

But we have this treasure in earthen vessels, to show that
the transcendent power belongs to God and not to us. We
are afflicted in every way, but not crushed; perplexed, but
not driven to despair; persecuted, but not forsaken; struck
down, but not destroyed; always carrying in the body
the death of Jesus so that the life of Jesus may also be
manifested in our bodies. For while we live we are
always being given up to death for Jesus' sake, so that
the life of Jesus may be manifested in our mortal flesh.
(II Cor. 4 :7-11)

Thus he goes his way "through honour and dishonour,
through slander and praise,"

treated as impostors and yet true; as unknown and yet

well known; as dying and behold we live; as punished
and yet not killed; as sorrowful, yet always rejoicing; as
poor, yet making many rich; as having nothing, and yet
possessing everything. (II Cor. 6:8-10)

His bodily sufferings seem to hinder him, and he prays to the
Lord to free him from them. But he hears the reply, " My
grace is sufficient for you, for my power is made perfect in
weakness!" "Therefore," he continues,

I will all the more gladly boast of my weaknesses, that
the power of Christ may rest upon me. For the sake of
Christ I am content with weaknesses, insults, hardships,
persecutions, and calamities; for when I am weak, then
I am strong. (II Cor. 12:8-10)

From this, the meaning of the cross and the resurrection
becomes evident, and all the theological-mythological discussion about them can be put aside, provided only that this
meaning is grasped. Faith in the cross and resurrection is not
the acceptance of some irrational mythological doctrine, but
rather is primarily submission to the judgment of God, the
renunciation of all boasting. Thus Paul defines faith as
"obedience," i.e., as precisely the acknowledgment of the
way of the cross as the way of life. As such obedience, it is
also trust in God's power as Creator to give life to the dead.
Therefore, Paul says, for example, in II Cor. 1:9 that a
situation of danger in which he despaired of life itself occurred "so that we would put our confidence not in ourselves, but in God who raises the dead." This is exactly the
point Luther makes, when he says that God does not grant life
except after having first demanded death. Faith is the trust in
God that arises precisely where to the eyes of man there is
nothing but darkness, but death. But such trust presupposes
the obedience that is willing to surrender to death all that is
one's own.

Now does such a faith as this make us unfit for life? Paul
did not mean that the faithful are to flee from life (I Cor.
5:10). It was not his view that the faith in which man stands

alone before God tears him out of his relations with his fellow men. On the contrary, the man of faith is to rejoice with those who rejoice, and weep with those who weep (Rom. 12:15). He may have a part in the world's joys and sorrows, and he may marry and conduct business—though, of course, in the peculiar distance of "as though not," i.e., without being inwardly bound to anything that is passing away (I Cor. 7:29-31). In all of his conduct within the world he is guided by "love." For self-surrender through the cross means positively that the man who no longer wills to be for himself exists for others. Since what has been opened up to him in the cross is the liberating love of God, the love of Christ also compels him to serve his fellow men (II Cor. 5:14), and his faith is active in love (Gal. 5:6).

Finally, we must say a word about "the sacraments." As even the fathers of the ancient church correctly recognized, the Christian sacraments are ceremonies that have a formal relatedness to the sacramental rites of the mystery religions. And much that Paul has to say about them is completely cast in the conceptuality of the mysteries' theology. Still, for him, the meaning of baptism and the Lord's Supper does not consist, as it does for the mysteries, in their being means whereby those who participate in them are infused with mysterious powers and thus deified and made immortal. Rather the meaning of these rites is simply that it is precisely through them that the once for all salvation-occurrence in Christ's death and resurrection is made present and actual for the individual, so that it may be personally appropriated by him. Since for Paul the salvation-occurrence is the decisive act of God that puts an end to the old world and establishes the new one, it cannot possibly become an event of the past like other historical events. Rather it stands, as it were, outside of time and is valid for every future in an eternal present. However, this eternal presentness of God's decisive act is appropriated by the individual precisely in baptism and the Lord's Supper. By means of such ceremonies he makes his own personal con-

fession to what God has done. Baptism places him who receives it under the cross of Christ, so that his life becomes one
of crucifixion with Christ and he no longer belongs to himself, but stands at the disposal of God. And in the Lord's
Supper, he confesses the crucified one; by celebrating it, he
proclaims Christ's death (I Cor. 11:26).

But baptism and the Lord's Supper are only a special means
of re-presenting the salvation-occurrence, which in general is
re-presented in the word of preaching. With the cross, God
has instituted the office of reconciliation or the word of reconciliation (II Cor. 5:18 f.); in other words, the preaching
itself belongs to the salvation-occurrence. It is neither a narrative report concerning an event of the past that once occurred,
nor is it an instruction having to do with questions of world-
view; rather what is encountered in it is Christ himself, i.e.,
the address of God. " So we are at work for Christ in such a
way that God makes his appeal through us : Be reconciled to
God!" (II Cor. 5:20). Therefore, Christian doctrine is not a
religious world-view that can be discussed and developed, but
rather is one and the same word of proclamation that preaches
the cross as God's judging and liberating act and asks everyone whether he is willing to submit to the cross and understand himself in terms of it. The church only exists where
the faithful are assembled around this word. Therefore, the
church is neither a religious association nor a sociological
phenomenon, but rather is in its essence invisible, namely, as
the community of those among whom God creates life—and
rules. And this is true, even if the church is also the visible
community of the faithful, recognizable through word and
sacraments. The church no longer belongs to this world, and
human standards and distinctions have no validity in it. Of
it, it is true that " there is neither Jew nor Greek, neither slave
nor free, neither male nor female; for all . . . are one in Christ
Jesus " (Gal. 3:28).

One cannot flee from Paul and return to Jesus. For what
one encounters in Jesus is the same God who is encountered

n Paul—the God who is Creator and Judge, who claims man ompletely for himself, and who freely gives his grace to him vho becomes nothing before him. All that one can do is to go o Jesus *through* Paul; i.e., one is asked by Paul whether he is villing to understand God's act in Christ as the event that has lecided and now decides with respect both to the world and o us. Paul was aware that the preaching of the cross is a candal and a folly. The question that it puts to us is whether ve are ready to become aware of our nothingness before God ind to receive life in the midst of our death. It asks us vhether we are prepared to understand the meaning and goal of our life not in terms of our own world-views and plans, out on the basis of the Christian proclamation that encounters is as the word of God.

THE SERMON ON THE MOUNT AND
THE JUSTICE OF THE STATE*

The question concerning the relationship between the demands of the Sermon on the Mount and the justice of the state is essentially the question of the understanding of the six great antitheses in Matt. 5:21-48, in which Jesus sets over against what "was said to the men of old" his "But I say to you." Not only should there be no murder and adultery, but even anger and evil desire are forbidden; divorce is not limited by, say, specific legal conditions, but is entirely ruled out; not only perjury, but swearing as such is prohibited retaliation against injustice is not regulated by the principle of "an eye for an eye," but ought not to take place at all love is demanded not only for the "neighbour" (i.e., one belonging to the same social group), but even for the enemy.

The meaning of these antitheses is simply that the demand of *God* is set over against *justice and law*; for the propositions that are rejected are propositions of Jewish justice. However inasmuch as in Judaism justice is explicitly understood as the demand of God, the more exact meaning of the antitheses is that God's demand is not exhausted by the demand for justice Therefore, it is not justice as such that is under discussion Jesus does not set over against an inferior and antiquated justice some new and better justice, but rather attacks the view that a man who satisfies what justice requires is thereby already righteous before God. God demands *more* than justice demands and can demand; for while the latter always allows the human will a certain amount of free play, God claims man's will in its entirety.

In order to understand this it is necessary to recall that

* "*Die Bergpredigt Jesu und das Recht des Staates,*" *Forschungen und Fortschritte,* xii (1936), 101-2.

justice among the Israelite people was developed and affirmed in its character as divine demand in the prophetic movement. Over against a piety that sees the fulfilment of the divine demand in the cultus, the prophets proclaim justice and righteousness as the will of God. The meaning of justice for them is that it checks man's self-will and binds the life of the community with ordinances that protect each person from the oppressions of others. Thus murder, adultery, and perjury are forbidden under pain of punishment; thus also there are the laws concerning divorce, retaliation, and love of neighbour; for these regulations likewise are in the first instance restrictions: a husband may not arbitrarily dismiss his wife, but is bound by specific conditions; the injured party may not seek revenge with complete freedom, but is restrained by the *jus talionis*; the concept of the "neighbour" (i.e., the fellow member of the social group) is given legal recognition and one is obligated to the neighbour by the duty of love.

However, man understands all this in such a way that with a formal fulfilment of the law he makes room for his own self-will. His limitation by the law at the same time contains a concession: he *may* divorce his wife, he *may* hate, he *may* avenge himself. Indeed, the whole realm of inner disposition or attitude (anger, desire, falsehood) is not at all comprehended by the law; for the latter can have to do only with the "what" and not with the "how" of action. From the standpoint of justice, the question of the extent to which my action corresponds with the commandment becomes essentially a question as to the "what" or the matter of action. In fact, obedience or disobedience to the law has to be publicly demonstrable.

Now Jesus speaks in a situation in which it has become clear that the law, whose fulfilment the prophets had demanded as obedience to the will of God, can be fulfilled without a man's actually being obedient, i.e., that one can fulfil the commandment in a formal way without really submitting to God's will. Jesus' demands arise out of the knowledge that one cannot fulfil the will of God up to a certain point, but rather that God demands the whole man. In this sense he sets his "But I say to you" over against the ordinances of justice.

Therefore, if the meaning of the antitheses is that the demand of justice is still a long way from the demand of God, the question remains whether the demand for justice as such stands in contradiction to the divine demand. Clearly this is not an implication of Jesus' actual words. And for other reasons, also, it is impossible to ascribe such an idea to him. For he holds fast to the authority of the Old Testament, which in large part contains just such legal demands. And even if the famous sayings that he has not come to abolish the law and that not a letter of the law shall perish (Matt. 5 : 17-19) are words that were subsequently put into his mouth by the church, they still correctly convey his total attitude, insofar as his criticism was not directed against what was in the Old Testament as such, but against the practice of justice by the "scribes" (i.e., the jurists).

Nevertheless, it is understandable that again and again the impression could arise that the implication of the Sermon on the Mount is to negate justice as such. The truth in such an impression is this : when the prohibition against retaliation and the commandment to love, even to the point of loving the enemy, are established as divine demand, then the implication is that justice—not, to be sure, simply as such, but rather as the individual's laying claim to justice for his private interests—does indeed contradict the divine demand. What God demands is not the renunciation of justice in the sense of the ordinances that regulate the community, but rather the renunciation by the individual of *his* rights in the concrete moment, i.e., of his use of the ordinances of justice to further his own interests against the neighbour.

At the same time, the idea is also implied—though without being explicitly stated—that justice has a legitimate meaning when it stands in the service of the demand of love, or, in practical terms, when it serves the community. This implication was clearly seen by Luther.[1] Moreover, with the idea that justice receives its meaning from the demand of love there is also given a criterion for criticizing and further developing positive justice; and this is true however little Jesus himself was interested in any such further development of it.

Finally, however, it is clear that the Sermon on the Mount does imply the idea that justice *ought* not to be at all. If there were no anger and hate, evil desire, falsehood and lovelessness—and there ought not to be such attitudes!—then the regulations of the law that are directed against the deeds to which these attitudes give rise would not be necessary. To be sure, without ordinances the human community clearly could not live. But the essential thing about the ordinances of justice is that they are ordinances of coercion, that they are combined with the force that is indispensable for their establishment. But coercion and force are necessary as a result of the evil that in actual fact is constantly at work in the human community. And just as this evil ought not to be, so also there really ought not to be ordinances of justice. However, the abolition of justice is not for Jesus a political programme, nor is it a possibility that can be realized by man at all. On the contrary, it will happen automatically when the " Reign of God " is realized. Therefore, in Jesus' sense, the state's ordinances of justice are something provisional in face of the future of God's Reign. True human community grows out of a deeper ground than the ordinances of justice—namely, out of man's willing obedience to the demand of God.

THE MEANING OF THE CHRISTIAN FAITH IN CREATION*

I

Everywhere in the world there are creation myths, tales that tell how the world that surrounds men has arisen and especially how man himself has come to be. And everywhere it is told that the source of the world and man lies beyond them in a higher power or creator deity—and this is so regardless of how consistently the idea of "beyondness" is thought in the frequently childish stories.

One customarily refers to such creator deities as "gods of origination." And to them is referred not only the mere existence of man and the world, but especially the *ordinances* of life, i.e., religious and secular law and the mores in which man finds himself and by which he knows himself to be bound. This already points to the real meaning of the faith in creation that is expressed in these myths.

For in its origin, the meaning of such faith is not that of a scientific theory that wants to explain rationally how the world and man have arisen. It is not merely curiosity and intellectual need that account for the existence of the creation myths. Rather the meaning of faith in creation is threefold.

1. It grows out of wonder at the riddle of the world that encompasses man as the *uncanny*. Man knows that he is not originally at home in the world, but rather is anxious in it. And it is just this anxiety and the striving that arises from it to illumine the darkness that surrounds existence and to become lord over the uncanny that is the origin of the creation myths. In the first instance, rational understanding stands in

* "Der Sinn des Christlichen Schöpfungsglaubens," Zeitschrift für Missionskunde und Religionswissenschaft, li (1936), 1-20.

the service of this striving. Man must accept his existence with its troubles and danger whether he wants to or not. He does not dispose of his source, but it disposes of him. His whence and his whither are a riddle. And when he attempts to lighten the darkness by his primitive tales, he does not locate his source in himself, but beyond himself; he knows that he is dependent on a higher power, which he represents to his imagination in pictures of higher beings that are often fantastic.

In such knowledge he knows that he is not free, but bound. And precisely in this bondage—and, as it were, with a sigh of relief—he becomes lord over his original dread, but only in the sense that he attains his security by becoming part of an authoritative order. He is reassured only through obedience to an authority, through obeying ordinances which he does not comprehend as self-engendered or deduce from an understandable principle, but which he simply accepts as given and to which he subjects himself even though they are not understood. The deity in which faith in creation believes is not the terrifying, the " numinous," the " *tremendum*," but, on the contrary, the power that banishes the " *tremendum*."

Countless statements in the Old Testament give clear expression to such an obedient and confident faith in creation :

Thy hands have made and fashioned me;
Give me understanding that I may learn thy command-
ments. (Ps. 119:73)

Know that Yahweh is God!
It is he that made us, and we are his;
We are his people, and the sheep of his pasture . . .
Give thanks to him, bless his name!
For Yahweh is good;
His grace endures for ever,
And his faithfulness to all generations! (Ps. 100:3-5)

2. Faith in creation, as is evident from what has already been said, is not a theory about the past. It does not have its meaning by relating what took place at some earlier time and no longer concerns man in the present, but rather speaks precisely about man's *present* situation. It tells him how he is to understand himself *now*; and the reference to the past is only for the purpose of teaching him to understand his situation in the present, i.e., to understand that he is not permitted to raise questions about the " why," to make claims, but rather is abandoned to a higher will.

Just as God once created man, so also does he constantly fashion him in his mother's womb in a wondrous way (Ps. 139 :13); and just as he once breathed the breath of life into man, so also does he do the same again and again (Job 33 :4). If God withdraws his breath, then men return to dust (Ps. 14:29); if he sends it forth, they are again created, and he renews the face of the earth (Ps. 104 :30).

" Woe to him who strives with his Maker,
An earthen vessel with the potter!
Does the clay say to him who fashions it, ' What are you
*   making?'*
Or ' Your work has no handles'?
Woe to him who says to his father, ' What are you begetting?'
Or to his mother, ' With what are you in travail?' "
Thus says Yahweh,
The Holy One of Israel, and his Maker:
" Will you question me about things to come,
Or command me concerning the work of my hands?
I made the earth,
And created man upon it;
It was my hands that stretched out the heavens,
And I commanded all their host!" (Is. 45 :9-12)

Yet, Yahweh, thou art our Father;
We are the clay, and thou art the potter;
We are all the work of thy hand. (Is. 64 :8)[1]

3. The creation stories do not understand man in terms of the continuum of the world-whole which lies open to observation; i.e., they do not understand him as a cosmic being, as an organic member of the whole. His existence is not derived from the cosmos; the world could exist without him. Human existence is not something necessary to the whole, but rather is pure facticity, contingency, or caprice. That man is in the world is due to an *event,* to the creation of God; it is not to be deduced from the eternal necessity of a cosmic continuum. Therefore, to a certain extent, man stands at a distance from the cosmos; he does not essentially belong to the world, but the world is there for him, like a house or a room. In other words, man is not understood in terms of the world, but rather the world in terms of man. Without the world man is not, and yet he is not of the world or for it, but it is for him; it is given to him for his life and action. Thus in Gen. 1 the earth is given over to man by God as the field of his dominion, and in Gen. 2 God places man in the garden of paradise in order to watch over it and to cultivate it. And so also in Ps. 8 : 6 it is said :

> *Thou hast given him* [sic *man*] *dominion over*
> *The works of thy hands;*
> *Thou has put all things under his feet.*

In this threefold meaning, then, faith in creation is the expression of a specific understanding of human existence.

II

Modern science has destroyed the old creation stories, even that of the Old Testament. But has it thereby also destroyed the faith in creation? The decisive question in this connection does not have to do with the results of science, but rather with its way of raising questions, with its presuppositions, with the understanding of human existence which these presuppositions contain.

Since modern science has grown out of the science of the Greeks, the latter may well be taken as an example of science in the attempt to answer our question.

According to Aristotle, Greek science begins with " wonder." Originally it does not serve intellectual curiosity, but rather the questions of human existence, which wants to understand itself in its world in order to be able to act justly and to fulfil the meaning of life. For this reason, it inquires, on the one hand, concerning the $\dot{\alpha}\gamma\alpha\theta\dot{o}\nu$ (the good), i.e., that " for the sake of which " everything is and ought to be; and, on the other hand, concerning the $\dot{\alpha}\rho\chi\dot{\eta}$ (the source) in terms of which the world can be understood as a unity. It is only through such understanding that man can find his way in the world by acquiring a direction for his thinking and acting. Insofar as science inquires concerning the source in order to understand human existence, it clearly holds fast to the question that is originally determinative in the faith in creation. By means of the light of research, it seeks to banish the darkness, the demons of the uncanny.

The decisive question, then, is whether science as it progresses imagines that it becomes lord over the uncanny and solves the riddle, or whether it remains conscious that the riddle and the uncanny constantly belong to the very essence of the world and man. In other words, the question is whether science thinks that man's original dread rests only on an illusion, on false and childish ideas, on an insufficient development of human capacities, so that it will be removed by the results of research and the development of technology—so that, by means of scientific enlightenment and technical progress, man's anxiety about life will be taken from him and the world and his existence will be made clearly understandable and controllable. Or will science recognize that its way is unending, that it does indeed have its meaning in giving man light for a part of the way and helping him to bear the responsibility for his actions, but that it can never solve the riddle of the world, can never explain the source of his existence, and can never wipe out his dread in face of the darkness—in face of suffering and death, destiny and the responsibility for life?

True science not only originates in "wonder," it is constantly encompassed by wonder. It knows that new riddles loom behind every riddle that is solved. It knows that its meaning cannot be to spread enlightenment by means of its results, but that it is constantly underway and constantly struggling; it knows that its significance for human existence does not really lie in its results, but in its intellectual work as such—that work through which man becomes conscious of his humanity in contradistinction to nature and becomes capable of human community and fit for the establishment of human life in the midst of a reign of natural forces that constantly destroy the works on his hands. Greek science was aware that it could not give a rational account of human existence: "The limits of the soul you could not discover, though you traversed every path; so deep is their ground" (Heraclitus, Fr. 71).

Science only comes into conflict with the idea of creation when it imagines that it is able to solve the riddle of the world and human existence by means of its results—when it tries to replace the awe that is "humanity's noblest part" with an optimistic prudence. What contradicts the idea of creation is a so-called "scientific world-view" that reassures man, i.e., that tries to deceive him about the essential uneasiness of human existence. Such a view is a deceitful means for reassuring man precisely when the original questionableness of his existence breaks in upon him. It deceives him when it tries to persuade him that his destiny, his responsibility and guilt, his suffering, and his death are not a riddle with which each of us must deal as an individual and which make clear to us that we do not dispose of ourselves—when, in other words, it tries to persuade him that everything is just an "instance" of the universal world-process that follows its own laws, and that it can all be grasped by the understanding as soon as these laws are understood.

Greek science did not make this mistake; it held fast to the first motive of the faith in creation. But did it also preserve the second motive, the idea that the source of the world, the ἀρχή, which it tried to understand, is not something past, but rather something present—something that even now determines human existence? Yes, it is precisely here that Greek science performed its great service, i.e., by recognizing that the question concerning the source that was alive in the old myths is not exhausted by the superficial question concerning origin in time, that the source does not lie behind us as something long past, but rather is eternally present. Greek thinking understands ἀρχή in the double sense of "beginning" (*initium*) and "source" (*principium*). For it, the question concerning the ἀρχή is the question concerning that out of which the world and man always rise and which always constitutes the basis of the law, the authority, the order, in accordance with which thought and action must be directed in order to be true and good. For the ἀρχή is the ἀγαθόν. To this extent, the second motive of faith in creation is also alive in Greek science. And it is alive in every other science that so inquires concerning the source that the latter is not only cause and beginning, but also law and goal.

But Greek science took yet another step—the step that all idealistic science takes with it—when it claimed to see the ἀρχή in the power that is also the peculiar power of man himself, namely, mind or the spirit—the thinking, measuring, shaping spirit. Thereby the world is understood in terms of the idea of the τέχνη, of an artifact, and thus from the standpoint of man's capacity to shape things, to give form to matter in purposeful ways. In other words, the world is a cosmos, a work of art. And just as the source of what man himself forms and produces resides in the images in his mind or spirit, in accordance with which the artisan or the artist gives the individual things their concrete shapes, so also does the source of the cosmos reside in Spirit as the sum-total of all the Ideas.

This means that the source of the world and of man is the same source, and, indeed, is the power that man bears within himself. This power is not something mysterious that cannot be disposed of, but rather is bright and shining spirit—i.e., the mind that measures things and orders them and that has purposes and gives to things their forms. "Geometrical proportion is mighty, both among gods and among men" (Plato, *Georgias,* 508 a).

And this means, further, that the ἀρχή, the source, is something that is at man's disposal, though not, of course, in the sense that human life is abandoned to subjective caprice; for the source and the order that has its basis in it stand beyond the subjectivity of the individual. However, they do not stand beyond what every individual can recognize and develop as his true nature; they do not stand beyond the human spirit. Insofar as he is spirit, man, so to speak, bears within himself the source of the world. But this means that *the idea of creation is surrendered*: God no longer stands beyond the world and man as the Creator, but is immanent in the world as its law and is also immanent in the human spirit: "*Deus in nobis.*" Insofar as he is spirit, man himself, so to speak, helps to constitute the authority of the divine order of the world. True faith in creation, on the other hand, affirms that man is subject of a power that lies beyond him and that cannot be disposed of—not even in his thinking; that he is called into being by this power, abandoned to it, and placed under its authority—an authority that he does not help constitute through his spirit.

And what about the third motive of faith in creation, the fact that in it the world is understood in terms of man? It might seem that here the world is indeed understood in terms of man, insofar as the source of the world is seen in the spirit

that is also man's spirit. In truth, however, man is here understood precisely in terms of the world. For what is viewed as
his nature is what can be understood as the power of universal
lawfulness; it is not the peculiar, individual life that each
man has to live by himself and that acquires its distinctive
form through his unique decisions and his particular destiny,
but rather is precisely something universal, the spiritual capacity that in principle is the same in everyone. Man is understood as a part of the cosmos; he is not seen in his historicity.
It is the universe and the eternal, not the singular and the
temporal that constitute his nature. It is not history and
destiny that give him his form, but the timeless laws of the
cosmos.

Thus Greek science preserved in whole or in part genuine
motives of the faith in creation; but it also surrendered decisive motives of that same faith. All modern science stands
under its influence, especially the idea of science of idealism.
And in all of us who stand in this scientific tradition there is a
conflict between this science and the faith in creation, insofar
as we try to hold fast to Christian faith and thus also to faith
in creation. But what does the Christian faith in creation say?

III

The Christian faith in creation affirms that man is not at
home in the world, that here he has " no lasting city." It
affirms that he is under an illusion when he imagines that he
can dispose of himself and can outwardly and inwardly secure
his life. It points out to him that he has not brought himself
into existence and does not dispose of his end. It reminds him
that human life stands under the shadow of death. But it
does not have to be the thought of death itself that makes us
uneasy; rather we all know that time is slipping away from us
and that we cannot hold on to a single moment.

This is something that no one fully imagines,
And is much too dreadful for anyone to bemoan:
*That everything slips and trickles away.**

aul tells us that "the form of this world is passing away"
Cor. 7:31). And we all know the saying of Nietzsche:

Misery says, "Begone!"
But every pleasure wants eternity,
Wants deep, deep eternity.†

Ve cannot achieve the eternity of pleasure, we cannot hold
st to time, we cannot banish death. The uncanniness, the
ddle, the anxiety, the dread, the uneasiness are not foolish
aginings that could be removed by enlightenment, but
ther belong essentially to our life. One does not become
rd over the dread of death simply by considering death
mething natural, an instance of the universal necessity of
ing. Someday I will die, and I cannot look at my death as an
stance of dying in general, so that if I can explain the latter
terms of the world's order, I am reassured. Each of us dies
s own death and has to come to terms with death for himself.
And so life also is *my particular life*. It is not an instance
the processes of life in general, but is entrusted to me to
ve. I have my destiny with which I alone have to come to
rms in joy and sorrow, in gratitude and terror. I live in my
cisions in which I myself am at stake, either to win my self
to lose it. I have my guilt and my remorse. And as my life
uncanny because I am a temporal being subject to death, so
so is it uncanny because it is *a historical life*. There are no
niversal standards that relieve me of the concrete responsibi-
y of deciding myself. Who knows whether he has decided
ghtly? Who knows what the right authority is? Who knows

* *Dies ist ein Ding, das keiner voll aussinnt,*
   und viel zu gravenvoll, als dass man klage:
   das alles gleitet und vorüberrinnt.
                     (Hugo von Hoffmannsthal)
† *Weh spricht: vergeh!*
   Doch alle Lust will Ewigkeit,
   Will tiefe, tiefe Ewigkeit.

whether he has really been obedient and has not lived und
illusions? In the deed of decision, man's being is at stake—
i.e., in the *moment* whose content can never be deduced from
the universal, but which is always a concrete, individu
moment that demands action, decision. What man himself
—i.e., has become in his temporal-historical existence—is
stake in this decision. He can win his self or lose it, but l
has to act. He cannot determine from universal laws what h
to happen now, what ought to be done. To be sure, he ca
determine, to a certain extent, the possibilities of action; an
he ought to do this as far as he can. But the choice amon
these possibilities is always a venture; and no God and n
Spirit can take away from him the venture and the responsib
lity for his choice. There is always the threat of " Too late!
of not being able to restore what is lost.

Man's historical existence has this character because it on
takes place *with others,* in relation to whom one must mak
concrete decisions. Man stands in a historical world in whic
he is bound together with concrete human beings. It is i
relation to *them* that he is responsible, not to some univers
law or Idea. In this responsibility he wins his true dignit
because in it he ventures himself and, through surrender, wir
himself. Through these concrete bonds there arise the poss
bilities that give to my life its richness, or else destroy it. Fc
in this existence with others there is either trust and love c
mistrust and hate. Here one either gives himself to the othe
or refuses himself; he either hears the other's claim or ignore
it. And none of this, through which man becomes rich c
poor and determines his character one way or the other—non
of this happens according to rules that are at the disposal c
thinking; it cannot be calculated, but rather constantly de
mands action, venture, surrender. Thus, in all of this, man
constantly *insecure.* Our mutual ties are not something at ou
disposal, but rather always stand in danger. Love is possesse
neither in giving nor in receiving in the way in which on

ossesses an insight or a conviction. It is not methodically
arned and developed, but only grows in the concrete en-
ounter with its decisions, when I hear the other and exist for
im by giving and from him by receiving. And when once
ove has appeared, it is not simply there, nor does it develop
ith the immanent necessity of logical thought. Rather it
develops " only through constantly new tests and decisions;
only *is* in that it is constantly laid hold of anew by con-
antly hearing anew the claim of the thou. There is no
iendship and no marriage that is secure and unendangered;
ach of them rests on the basis of the uncanny.

> *Ah, we know ourselves so slightly,*
> *For a God holds sway within us.**

Thus human life is insecure; its course is not at man's dis-
osal. The man who is entrusted to himself does not have
imself in hand. His life rests on the basis of a riddle, of the
ncanny, and is constantly threatened. It is a life in time sub-
ct to death, in history faced with decisions, and with others
a responsibility.

Such knowledge is included in the Christian faith in crea-
on, and without it—whether it be brought to clear conscious-
ess or not—there is no such faith. It is not a knowledge,
owever, that could prove faith in creation to the under-
anding; for it is not at all a knowledge that has been ac-
uired by the understanding or that proceeds from rational
ases. Rather it has grown out of reflection on human exist-
nce. Whether everyone so discovers his nature when he re-
ects on it must be left to him. All the Christian proclama-
on can do is to point it out to him and ask him if he under-
ands himself in this way, if he is willing to acknowledge that
is is true of him. Without such an acknowledgment, how-
er, i.e., without the acknowledgment that man is a being
ho lives in time, in history, and in responsible relation with

---

* *Ach, wir kennen uns wenig,*
  denn es waltet ein Gott in uns. (Hölderlin)

others and therefore is insecure and not at his own disposal—
without this acknowledgment, there also is no faith in God th
Creator.

Therefore, we say that such knowledge is included in th
Christian faith in creation. But what does the Christian fait
in creation say beyond this? What it says becomes clear in th
specific judgment that it makes about the uncanniness b
which human life is always threatened. It affirms that th
uncanniness has its basis in *sin*.

By " sin " we understand what the old dogmatics referred t
as *" superbia"*—namely, that man wills to be himself b
himself and for himself. Precisely through such willing th
world acquires for him the character of the uncanny because
will never let him be as one who wills to be himself by him
self and for himself. To be sure, being a self is what being
man means; but being a creature means that one does nc
exist by himself and for himself, but rather by another powe
and for it. If, according to Christian faith, God has create
man, then this means that man receives his selfhood fror
God and can only be himself by receiving it, i.e., by acknowl
edging that he exists by or from God. And this means at th
same time that he exists *for* God. For wherever I receiv
myself as a genuine gift from the thou, I not only am *fron*
him, but also am *for* him; and I know that my being permitte
to be for him is precisely the highest meaning of his gif*
Were I to try to dispose of the gift as something that I my
self, by myself and for myself, had under my power, then
would break the bond of love and the love of the other woul
become a reproach to me. It is a universal human experienc
that no one wants to be indebted to the other for his existenc
but rather endeavours to seclude himself in the illusion tha
he exists by himself and for himself.

That man ought not to be himself from himself and for him
self, but rather from God and for God is shown by the fac
that God has not created him as an isolated subject, but ha

placed him in relation with his fellow man. It is in this context that he is to understand and show that he is himself from others and for others. And he actually can understand this; for there are moments given to every man when it dawns on him that he lives his highest life from others and for them. Of course, a glance at the historical reality in which we live shows that each of us, from the beginning, wants to exist only from himself and for himself. Everyone seeks to secure his life and to dispose of as many goods as he can; and the more he succeeds in acquiring the more he desires. And even the protest against such a striving that again and again makes itself heard only confirms that everyone first seeks his own and that life becomes a *bellum omnia contra omnes*. We no longer first listen for the claim of the other, but rather ignore him in self-seeking and thoughtlessness, in "representing our own interests." That no humane social life is possible without the justice of the state and the coercion that carries it out, and that none of us would trust himself in a society that was not bound by ordinances (i.e., by an arrangement in which each grants to the other a tolerable number of claims in order to secure his own)—both show what we think of man. And what if we perhaps want to think of ourselves as exceptions? What if we want to say that we have to see to our interests because others are seeing to theirs? All we succeed in doing is to confirm that we all come out of a history that, from the beginning, is determined by the understanding that each seeks his own right and his own advantage. We live in a world in which everyone wants to look out for himself; we come into every now as those who always want to be themselves by themselves and for themselves.

This poisoning of our life that no one can escape and no one can remove is what is meant when the church speaks of *original sin*. One may make ever so many criticisms of the traditional mythological setting of the doctrine of original sin and talk idly about man's original goodness, but in actual fact

I

each one of us acknowledges that the doctrine is true, namely, in his judgments concerning the concrete men with whom he has to deal and in his relations with them. We mistrust one another from the beginning, and in our mistrust there is at the same time resistance against others, refusal to have anything to do with them, hate.

And it is just in this that the real uncanniness of the world and life has its basis—namely, that all the striving for meaning and authenticity, for the right act and the right decision, for mutual love and trust in our relations with one another is reared on the ground of a sinful existence and thus is threatened by nothingness. For what is the really uncanny element in responsibility and decision? It is not that we can be deceived by an erroneous judgment; for we could come to terms with that if we only knew that we might have a good conscience. No, what really torments us is whether we may have a good conscience. And what is uncanny about our social relationships in work and friendship and in love and marriage? Is it not that an unreserved devotion is seldom if ever realized and that we also do not believe in the unreserved devotion of others?—that a final reservation and a final mistrust are always at work and thus also a secret anxiety? The fact that anxiety thus penetrates our life is a sure sign that the uncanniness of the power of sin is the background against which our life is set; for " there is no anxiety in love, but perfect love casts out anxiety " (I John 4 : 18).

The world is uncanny in consequence of sin; and the question concerning the Creator only has meaning for Christian faith when it is raised in the knowledge of sin's uncanniness, i.e., when it is bound together with the confession that, of ourselves, we cannot at all understand the world as God's creation, but rather live in a world that is constituted by man himself and by his sin.

But in saying this, the idea of creation seems to become a theory concerning the past : indeed, God once created the world, but ever since sin began to exercise dominion, the world's character has been determined by it; indeed, God once created man after his own image, but ever since man fell into sin, it is meaningless to speak of him as God's creature; and so the doctrine of the church affirms that, with Adam's sin, man loses the character of an *imago Dei*.

In truth, however, precisely the fact that the sinful world is uncanny for man attests that God has created him. His relation to God is that he stands guilty before him as a sinner. His sin is precisely that he denies his creatureliness by willing to be himself from himself and for himself. But just because this makes the world uncanny for him, the uncanniness rests on his being a creature of God; and thus precisely the world's uncanniness attests to God as the Creator. Man is God's creature—though, to be sure, one who does not understand himself in his creatureliness. But this does not make him any the less a creature; and his creatureliness becomes evident precisely in the consequence of his not wanting to be a creature. Just in making himself independent, his dependence becomes evident. In making himself independent of God he becomes dependent on the power of evil; for there is no evil in itself, but only because there is God. For the man who does not accept it as he should, the goodness of God becomes evil. God's goodness is precisely that man should be himself and receive his selfhood from God his Creator as a creature. If he refuses to do this, then precisely his selfhood, which he has received from God as a possibility, becomes evil for him. Thus even in our human relationships the person who refuses to receive anything from others and to exist from them allows the very thing that they can give him to become evil. It is a constant reproach to him and the power that he hostilely opposes.

That the world is uncanny for man shows that he is God's creature and that his being a creature continues to determine him whether he knows it or not. The uncanniness that enters the world through sin and persistently encompasses man is, as the New Testament expresses it, *the wrath of God*. Because this wrath of God stands over man, he is abandoned to God's power.

But, of course, only faith can thus understand the matter. For from the standpoint of unfaith, the uncanniness of the world, the wrath of God, is nothing more than uncanny, demonic, destructive power. To see the power of *God* in such power would mean that one already understood his abandonment to this power as due to God. And to experience the power of the *Creator* in God's wrath would mean that one already understood the wrath as his *grace*.

Naturally, faith in God as the Creator is not the theoretical insight that man's creatureliness becomes a curse to him because he rebels against it, so that if one were once to have this insight, uncanniness would be banished and wrath transformed into grace. Rather faith in God the Creator *can* grow out of such an insight if it is connected with genuine submission to God's wrath. It is out of such a *"resignatio ad infernum,"* as the mystics and Luther tell us, that faith in the Creator can arise as the faith that precisely in his wrath God displays his love for me because his wrath is what holds me to him.

But how can such faith in the Creator as faith in God's grace arise? If wrath is accepted as judgment through genuine submission to it, still faith in creation is not simply the dialectical inversion of one's knowledge of wrath. How, then, does faith arise?

When in human relations the love of another person has become a curse to me through my refusal of it, how does it again become love for me? If I take seriously my guilt toward the other person and am pained by it, then the presupposition may be created for my relationship to him once again to become pure. But the matter is not settled simply by my saying that I acknowledge my guilt and may therefore again encounter him as though nothing had happened. All I can do is to ask for his forgiveness; and only his forgiveness—whether through his word or through an act that is eloquent without words—can once again give his love back to me as his free gift.

So also, in knowing my sin and submitting to God's wrath, all I can do is to ask for forgiveness. And where does God speak his word of forgiveness? For I clearly cannot have recourse to an *idea* of God's grace, if grace can only encounter me as a free gift and cannot be an idea that I dispose of in my thinking. There can be grace only as event.

Yes, the heart and soul of Christian faith is that God has spoken his forgiving word to sinners in Jesus Christ and that this word is valid also for me and indeed is presently spoken to me in the proclamation of the church. For the Christian church is neither a religious association nor the place where the religious ideals and forces of a natural community have come to self-consciousness and expression; rather it is the place where the word of divine forgiveness is spoken in commission and heard in faith.

Thus genuine faith in creation is at the same time faith in God's forgiveness; and conversely, Christian faith in God's forgiveness is at the same time faith in God as the Creator. Therefore, Luther says:

This is without doubt the supreme article of faith of which we speak : I believe in God the Father almighty, Maker of heaven and earth. And whoever honestly believes this is already helped and is once again brought back to the place whence Adam fell. But few are they who go so far as to believe fully that he is the God who makes and creates all things. For such a man must be dead to everything, to good and bad, to death and life, to hell and to heaven, and must confess in his heart that he is able to do nothing by his own power.

This kind of a faith in creation is not a theory about some past occurrence such as might be depicted in mythological tales or cosmological speculation and natural scientific research; rather it is faith in man's present determination by God. However, it is not a conviction about an ἀρχή that is constantly present in the world-process, the rule of which I can rationally investigate and with reference to which I can understand all individual phenomena. Rather it is an "*existentiell*" knowledge, i.e., a knowledge of myself as a rightwised sinner that has an effect on my existence and that must constantly be laid hold of anew. The world does not lose its uncanniness simply because it is explained in terms of a reassuring world-view, but only because I take refuge in the grace of God. If uncanniness has its basis in sin, then it remains a constant threat and constantly overcomes me as soon as I try to lead my life by and for myself and forget that I only receive it by and for God. This means that I am constantly tempted, that I must constantly experience God's wrath, and that I must constantly take refuge in his grace. *Faith in the Creator can never be possessed once for all as a reassuring insight, but must constantly be won and realized anew.* For if, in receiving forgiving grace, I receive my selfhood as a being from God, then I must at the same time understand and realize it as a being *for* God, i.e., as *a life in love* that I have to fulfil in my personal relations with others.

From this it also becomes clear how the third element in faith in creation appears in its Christian meaning—the thought, namely, that man as the creature of God is not to be understood in terms of the world, but that the world is to be understood in terms of man.

Just as God, in the narrative in Gen. 1, gives man dominion over the world of aminals, so man as the creature of God is lord over the entire world; i.e., it stands at his disposal insofar as he has faith in God his Creator. Luther, for example, has described the way in which such disposition is to be exercised in his explanation of the first article in the Large Catechism. Man is to dispose of the world to the glory of God. This means, on the one hand, that his relation to the world is

always determined by the peculiar "as though not" that is
spoken of by Paul:

> Let those who have wives live as though they had none,
> and those who mourn as though they were not mourning,
> and those who rejoice as though they were not rejoicing,
> and those who buy as though they had no goods, and
> those who deal with the world as though they had no
> dealings with it. (I Cor. 7:29-31)

On the other hand, however, this freedom over the world is
determined by love.

> I am lord over everything, but I will not be enslaved by
> anything. I am lord over everything, but not everything
> builds up. Let no one seek his own good, but the good
> of his neighbour. Knowledge puffs up, but love builds
> up. (I Cor. 6:12, 10:23, 10:24, 8:1)

To exist from God and for God means, in practice, to exist
from the neighbour and for him; in such an attitude man is
himself and is free from the world. If, as in Greek science,
man is understood in terms of the world, then the nature of
the world is seen to lie in its *lawfulness,* which is at work in
man as well as in the cosmos, so that man can be considered a
member of the cosmic whole. If, however, in the Christian
faith in creation the world is understood in terms of man,
then the world is *the concrete world* with which man is in fact
surrounded. And just as man is not man in general, but
rather a concrete man, this or that man, standing in a very
specific historical situation, so also is his world a historically
determined one, and his fellow men are his concrete, historically determined neighbours.

This means that man's action is not determined by timeless
principles, but by the concrete situation, by the moment. Even
love is not an ethical principle that gives specific answers to
the question, "What should I do?" and from which specific
rules can be deduced. Rather the command to love tells me
that I as one who loves should know what the concrete

moment requires of me. Naturally, in order to be able to bear the responsibility for my action precisely as one who loves, I must conscientiously consider all the possibilities of acting that are open in the moment, as well as all the consequences of my action. Love does not act blindly. Nevertheless, the choice among the possibilities, the decision whose risk no one can take from me, should be made in love.

Thus to understand the concrete moment as one who is faithful and loving is the Christian freedom from the world in which man as creature of God has the world at his disposal.

This concrete moment is always determined, however, by what are usually spoken of in more recent theology as "ordinances of creation." What is meant by this phrase is not the eternal laws of the world-process, which can be understood in their unity and coherence in terms of the $\dot{\alpha}\rho\chi\dot{\eta}$, but simply the conditions that make my world and my situation a concrete one and keep me from understanding myself and my neighbours as men in general, i.e., from supposing that we have to regard one another solely with respect to the eternal nature of the human spirit.

That I stand in ordinances of creation and have to act in them means, for example, that I am a man or a woman, am old or young, strong or weak, clever or untalented, well or ill, German or French, etc. All of these specifications determine my moment, and I cannot ignore them. My conduct toward another is actually determined by my being father or son, brother or spouse, by my belonging to a specific nation and to a specific class, and by my having my particular responsibility either as a youth in relation to my elders or as an elder in relation to the young. There is no moment in our personal relations with one another that is not determined by such concrete conditions.

The use of the phrase "ordinance of creation" is not yet permanently established, and little depends on the words. In any case, the moment is further determined by what we speak of as the political situation. One can ask whether we ought also to designate a situation's being determined by concrete forms of justice and the state as an ordinance of creation. The attempt has been made at this point to speak of an *indirect* ordinance of creation. For if the ordinance of the state, with its justice and coercion, has its source in sin, then we must clearly say that it does not belong to the real ordinances of creation. If, on the other hand, however, the wrath of God that stands over the sinful creation has its basis in God's not letting the created world go, then the ordinances of the state that set bounds to the uncanny, to evil, are also to be designated as ordinances of creation.

This means, however, that Christian action may not be guided by the vision of a utopia in which there is no state, no justice, no coercion, but rather has to acknowledge that the ordinance of the state is an ordinance of the sinful creation. And the Christian doctrine of the state may not attempt to reduce the latter to a *humanitas* that is determined by eternal principles or to a nationality that is constituted by the divine powers of blood and soil. Rather in the knowledge of the power of evil, it must affirm the authority of the state with its justice and coercion.

However, the "ordinances of creation" and, to be sure, the "direct" ones as well as the "indirect" ones are *ambiguous* in consequence of sin. It is impossible to read off unambiguous demands as demands of God from the natural conditions that determine our immediate situation. What follows for me because my situation is determined by my sex, my age, my family ties, my being a part of my nation, etc., is something that I myself have to discover in love. For, on the one hand, man is distinguished from the animals precisely because his action is not unambiguously regulated by natural impulse, but rather must be ventured in responsible freedom; and, on the other hand, all natural conditions and relations are only present in a concrete historical form, and our history is a history that is qualified by sin. Thus we always have to discover what is required of us by the demands that are given through our being part of the ordinances of sex and age and family and nation. No nation is so unambiguous an entity that one can explain every stirring of the national will as a demand of a divine ordinance. Nor is nationality a purely natural thing that is given in one's blood; rather it is something that, though it has a natural basis, arises in history; and through history every nation is given the possibility of evil as well as of good. What is to be considered the law of a nation in a particular case is in fact left to the responsible decision of the individuals who belong to it. And in a day when nationality has again appeared as an ordinance of creation, the Christian faith has to prove its critical power by also insisting that the nation as something simply given is ambiguous and that, precisely for the sake of obedience to the nation as an ordinance of creation, the question must continue to be asked what is and what is not the nation's true demand. Just as faith in creation is only possible on the basis of faith in redemption, so also can a man truly serve his nation only if he has been set free to love by receiving the love of God in Christ.

Also ambiguous is the "indirect" ordinance of the state with its justice and coercion. The presupposition for the responsible exercise of the state's coercive power is always the knowledge that it has its basis in evil and thus the knowledge of God's wrath; and the only thing that can be peculiar to the Christian state is that, in addition to this, it also knows about sin and forgiveness. Therefore, every idolatrous deification of the state is excluded—i.e., every notion that the state has its basis in man's good will or that it is a creation in which human greatness and dignity erect themselves a throne. What is required is an understanding of the service of the state as a service of love. Coercion stands in the service of concrete men and therefore in the service of God.

Thus the Christian faith sees the uncanny in evil, over which man does not become lord and which can only be overcome by faith in God's forgiveness, by the faith that works through love. Such faith, however, is not mere knowledge of

a dogma. The rational understanding of the Christian proclamation and the Christian faith in creation, which we have
here been at pains to develop, has to achieve its true meaning
in *existentiell* understanding. Thus Christian faith in creation
must constantly be won and realized anew in the decision of
the moment.

HISTORY OF SALVATION AND HISTORY*

The real theme of Oscar Cullmann's book is "the early Christian conception of time and history." It is placed under the title *Christ and Time*[1] because the author wants to show that early Christianity understood Christ as the mid-point of time, in relationship to which the whole of history, both before and after, is to be understood and judged. In the first instance, of course, Christ is the mid-point of the history of salvation, which takes place in the context of the general history of the world; but although it itself is also history, this history of salvation, this "Christ-line," provides the norm for judging history in general and does so, indeed, because the "history of salvation," the "biblical history" is the occurrence (or the act) of God's revelation. Hence all theology as a speaking about God's revelation is also "biblical history."

These statements raise difficult problems, which I for the moment put aside in order to trace the picture that Cullmann draws of the early Christian conception of time and history. It is in this conception that his interest really lies.

I

The first part of the book is entitled, "The Continuous Line of Salvation." It attempts to show that salvation is bound to a continuous occurrence in time that embraces past, present, and future and receives its structure from its middle point, the historical fact of the death and resurrection of Jesus.

* "*Heilsgeschichte und Geschichte,*" *Theologische Literaturzeitung,* lxxiii (1948), 659-66. (In its original form, this article is subtitled " A Review of Oscar Cullmann, *Christ and Time*.")

"Early Christian faith and thought do not proceed on the basis of the spatial contrast between the 'here' and the 'beyond,' but rather on the basis of the temporal distinction between 'formerly,' 'now,' and 'then'" (p. 38). This is first established by an inspection of the New Testament's "temporal terminology" ($\kappa\alpha\iota\rho\acute{o}\varsigma$, $\alpha\grave{\iota}\acute{\omega}\nu$, etc.) and then illuminated by pointing to the contrast between the Bible's linear view of time and the cyclical view of the Greeks. Accordingly, the New Testament also represents the future aeon as temporally future and thinks of the occurrence of the end-time as taking place in a temporal progression. Since God's lordship over time means that the past and the future are at his disposal, it includes the fact that he pre-exists and predestines and also anticipates the future in the present. Hence Christ is also to be understood as the middle point of history, and the Christ-occurrence, as the revelation of God's lordship over time as a whole. So also is the Holy Spirit and the sanctification of the faithful to be understood as an anticipation of the end in the present, and the church as the locus of the divine lordship over time. Embraced within the church, Christians receive a share in the gifts of the whole line of salvation and are enabled "even now to experience as something at work in themselves the future occurrence that is divinely anticipated and, on the other hand, to grasp the whole occurrence of salvation in its major stages and final direction" (p. 79).

The mid-point of the history of salvation, which in the expectation of Judaism is something future, has become past for Christians; whereas for Jews the mid-point coincides with the parousia, for Christians it falls in the midst of the time prior to the parousia (pp. 82 f.). From this new centre, then, not only the history of Israel, but also the time before the creation and the creation itself are understood as preparation for the redemption in Christ (pp. 90 f.). In the time after Christ "the time of salvation does not stand still" (p. 92); history must go on, namely, because, prior to the parousia, sin is not put aside (ibid). As a whole, the history of salvation is "prophecy (p. 97); and, to be sure, the picture of this history includes in its narratives about the beginning and the end of things processes that cannot be historically confirmed, but "objectively can only be the object of revelation and subjectively can only be the object of faith" (p. 98). The historical middle section does, of course, include facts that can be confirmed historically, but these facts are raised to the status of an object of faith in that things are affirmed of them which can fall under the competence of no historian, e.g., that Jesus is the Son of God, or that his death is an atoning death.

In relation to this picture of the history of salvation, the distinction between history and myth is meaningless, as is also the distinction between historical occurrences and occurrences of nature, for creation also is included in the history of salvation. The picture of history that is thus prophetically drawn or, better, revealed, is a christological prophecy, since it is drawn on the basis of Christ as the mid-point, and the whole occurrence therefore appears as a "Christ-line": "Christ the mediator of creation—Christ the Suffering Servant of God who fulfils the election of Israel—Christ the Lord ruling in the present—Christ the Son of Man who returns as the consummator of the entire occurrence and the mediator of the new creation. The pre-existent one, the one who yesterday was crucified, the one who today rules as a hidden Lord, the one who at the turn of the age will return—they are all one; it is the same Christ, but in the exercise of _temporally successive functions in the history of salvation_" (p. 109). This basic conception also corresponds to Jesus' understanding of himself. The movement of the history of salvation, which takes place in accordance with the principles of election and representation (p. 115), proceeds, first, as a "progressive reduction," since, with the purpose of saving all men, there is first chosen representatively an individual people, then a "remnant," and finally one (Christ); from him, then, the movement again progresses until it includes the many.

The theme of the second part is " The Once-for-all Character of the Epochs of Salvation." The *kairoi* that "make up the line of salvation" are "events that in their character of having happened once for all are always decisive" (p. 121). This is pre-eminently so in the case of the Christ-event, whose character of having happened once for all had become an offence even in early Christianity—so much so that the docetism that appeared already in Jewish Christianity sought to avoid it. The character of having happened once for all, however, also belongs to the history of salvation prior to Christ; and it may not be destroyed by false allegorizing of the type represented by the Letter of Barnabas and Wilhelm Vischer. Correctly understood, the Old Testament history is a preparation for the Christ-event, since it "is aimed at an incarnate and crucified Christ," or "temporally progresses toward the incarnation and crucifixion" (p. 136). The future also is to be understood with reference to Christ as a development in the history of salvation. Eschatology is "not put aside, but dethroned" (p. 139), insofar as the question concerning the "when" of the future "end" ($\tau\acute{\epsilon}\lambda o\varsigma$) is taken care of because Jesus Christ who has appeared already is that "end" (p. 140). Nevertheless, eschatology retains its "own significance in the history of salvation." The new thing that the eschatological future will bring is "that the entire world of the ʻflesh,ʼ of matter, will be seized by the Holy Spirit, the $\pi\nu\epsilon\tilde{\upsilon}\mu\alpha$" (p. 141). "So long as this final consummation is still outstanding, the Holy Spirit penetrates the whole of the body only temporarily" (p. 142).

Even the occurrence of the present is salvation-occurrence, insofar as it is the history of the church, which already stands in the new aeon or, better, since the parousia is yet to occur, stands in the "last" days, in the interim period, with which Jesus himself also reckoned. This significance of the present in the history of salvation is misunderstood by Kierkegaard with his concept of "contemporaneity" (p. 146, cf. p. 168). The present is the time of Christ's lordship as the one who sits at the right hand of God until his parousia. Thus it was not the future, but rather the present that was the object of early Christianity's chief interest (p. 152). The present salvation-occurrence, whose real meaning is constituted by the missionary proclamation of the gospel, is a sign of the end (p. 157). However, the present epoch of the church may not be freed from its relation to the mid-point and absolutized, as happens in Catholicism; the right relation to the past is guaranteed by the domination of Scripture, which also belongs to the centre, over tradition.

There follows in Part III, then, a discussion of the theme " The History of Salvation and the General Course of World Events." Since the dualism of creation and redemption is alien to the New Testament, the whole course of world events is included in the history of salvation; and precisely the " concentration " of this history serves the purpose of universal salvation by means of the principles of election and representation. From the mid-point of the history of salvation on, there takes place a process of progressive expansion, the bearer of which is the church. Its Lord is also the Lord of all; church and world surround him like two concentric circles (p. 188). As in the beginning all history of salvation was also world history, so also at the end the history of salvation will again become history of the world. The state, behind which stand the invisible spiritual powers of the cosmos, is also included in this process. Christ has subjected these cosmic powers, so that now the state, which is not essentially a phenomenon of the history of salvation, is placed within the divine ordinance and given its " christological foundation " (p. 205). If, then, the world is included in the salvation-occurrence, " denial of the world cannot be an adequate expression of the early Christian attitude " (p. 212). Insofar as the man of faith knows that the world is passing away he denies it; " insofar as he knows that it is the divinely willed context of the present stage of the history of salvation he affirms it " (p. 213).

The fourth and final part deals with " The Individual Man

and the Past Stage of the History of Salvation." The individual is placed in the history of salvation; it is aimed at
him (p. 217), and, to be sure, the past stage of that history
becomes effective for him on the basis of faith in the saving
significance of the facts of the past (pp. 218 f.). Such a faith
presupposes a sense of sin and guilt; for " only on this basis
can the history of salvation be related to the individual.
Indeed, the entire history is understandable only on the
basis of the sense of sin; for it is for the sake of human sin
that the whole occurrence is necessary," and the doctrine of
righteousness through faith is " nothing other than an application of the salvation-occurrence to the individual " (p. 219).
This " relation of the I to the history of salvation " finds its
expression in faith in one's own election—which faith includes
the conviction that " one already has a share in the history of
salvation in the most remote past, ' before the foundation of
the world ' " (p. 220). Thus the past stage of the history of
salvation is the believer's " own past "; " active participation,
to be sure, first makes its appearance in the church and therefore in the present stage of the history of salvation " (p. 221).
By virtue of the gift of the Holy Spirit, each individual in the
church has his particular service to perform; and not only the
apostolic office, but even " the most modest service in the community of Christ belongs in the history of salvation " (p.
224). The divine command that goes forth to the individual
is determined by the Christ-occurrence; i.e., the imperative
(the ought) has its basis in the indicative (the is). No new
commandments are laid down, but the old one should and
can be radically fulfilled in ethical decision in the concrete
situation on the basis of one's own judgment influenced by
the Spirit; and the " principle of application " in such decisions is love.

Since the future of the individual depends on the future of
the whole history of salvation, hope is directed toward the
latter's consummation, whereupon the physical resurrection of
the individual will ensue. The basis for this is the resurrec-

tion of Christ that has already taken place. This resurrection is already at work in the present (through the Spirit) in healing the sick and raising the dead, and it will also be at work at the last day in the physical resurrection of individuals, who then will receive a " spiritual body," i.e., a body that not only has the Spirit for its " principle," but also as its material (p. 241).

II

In its architectonic thrust and compact structure, this book is an impressive performance. Moreover, there is no question that Cullmann has focused upon an extremely significant motive in the early Christian pattern of thought, viz., the idea of a history of salvation, and has followed out its effects in the various areas of this pattern of thought with care and ingenuity, as well as with great powers of bringing things together into a unified picture. If one may conclude from his statement that "all Christian theology is in its inmost essence biblical history " (p. 23) that he thinks he himself has laid hold of the central theme of theology, then I, of course, must disagree. For as much as I would agree with the statement that the occurrence of salvation is Christian theology's real theme, as little could I see this salvation-occurrence in what Cullmann speaks of as the history of salvation. Is it not necessary, if we are to speak of the occurrence of salvation and the history of salvation, to determine clearly in what sense " occurrence " and " history " can legitimately be spoken of by theology?

I confess that the author's basic conception is not clear to me. I cannot see that for him " history " in the phrase " history of salvation " has any different meaning from what it has in " history of the world "; nor can I understand how the Old Testament history of salvation as history is in principle different from the history of the people Israel that is also open to the profane historian. For the meaning of "history" in the phrase "history of salvation" is not given any distinctiveness simply because certain marvellous and divinely caused things have also happened in the history of salvation. It seems, at least, that history for the author is nothing other than the succession of events in time (and, naturally, also in space); thus not even once is there a distinction made between truly historical processes and the events of nature. Obviously Cullmann wants to get beyond this when he says that the history of salvation as a whole is "prophecy" (p. 97)—as a whole! In its individual parts, namely, one must distinguish between the stories of the beginning and the end, which are *nothing but* prophecy, and the "historical parts" that lie in between, which, as they are presented in the early Christian writings, are "revealed prophecy about history" (p. 98). Does Cullmann identify himself with this early Christian view? It seems so. But, then, is the "history of salvation" something completely different from the general course of world history, namely, the *picture* that prophetic interpretation draws of world-historical processes? Does this mean, then, that it is not an *occurrence* at all? And does this also hold good of the stories of the beginning and the end, which are *nothing but* prophecy? Or did something happen at the beginning and will something also happen at the end that simply in happening is already the salvation-occurrence? I cannot find my way through this. Nor can I understand the following: the history of salvation is the history of revelation (pp. 26 f.), which means evidently, that in it the act of divine revelation takes place (pp. 23 f.). "Nowhere . . . is God's act more concretely revealed to man than in history, which, to speak theologically, in its inmost nature, presents the relation of God to men" (p. 24). Where and how, then, does God really reveal himself? *In* history, or *within* history?—Does "history" here mean history in general or the history of salvation and thus prophetically interpreted history? And what concept of revelation is presupposed? If history is first perceived as history of salvation, i.e., as the act of divine revelation, by means of " revealed prophecy about history," then is it necessary, if God's revelation *in* (or within) history is to be known, that there be a previous revelation *about* history? But where does this come from? And who receives it and in what way?

If theology is the unfolding of the knowledge that is given in faith as such, then only an occurrence that is experienced and laid hold of in faith could be designated as the salvation-occurrence or as the history of salvation. Is it not necessary, then, that an analysis of the concept of faith provide the foundation for a theologically tenable discussion of the history of salvation? Is it admissible, for example, to apply to the latter the concept of development? And if so, in what sense? Naturally, Cullman also has an idea of what is meant by faith in all that he says. But what idea is it when he writes that revealed prophecy " raises historically verifiable facts to the status of an object of faith " (p. 98)? Is it necessary to faith, then, " to grasp the work of Jesus Christ, the crucified and risen one, in its connection with the divine plan of salvation " (p. 137), or " to grasp the whole occurrence of salvation in its major stages and final direction " (p. 79)? What interest does faith have in understanding the cross of Christ not only as the salvation-occurrence that is valid for me, but also as the " midpoint " of the history of salvation (p. 219)? Does not the whole picture that Cullmann draws belong to the " mysteries," one of which is expounded in Rom. 11 : 25, or to the " wisdom " that is appointed for the " mature," which lies beyond the " folly " of the " word of the cross " that is the true basis of faith? It seems to me that he turns the theology of the New Testament into a Christian philosophy of history; and it is no wonder that he agrees with the basic conception of Ethelbert Stauffer's *Theologie des Neuen Testaments* (p. 26, n. 9), which also dissolves theology into philosophy of history.

Like the concept of " faith," the concepts of " salvation "

nd "world" must also be so defined that it is possible to
deal with the history of salvation and the history of the world
in an unambiguous way and thus express with clarity the
dialectical relation of yes and no to the world. Further, it is
necessary to work out an unambiguous meaning for sin and
justification and reconciliation, as well as for election and
representation, if such things are to be made clear as the
basic motives and principles of the history of salvation. And
so also is it alone meaningful to raise questions about the
relation of history and myth (pp. 94 ff.). For it is of course
clear that to someone who speaks of the history of salvation
as Cullmann does the distinction between history and myth
is meaningless. But from the basis that he chooses he does
not even have the possibility of discussing the problem.
Therefore, the criticism that he directs against my demythologizing exegesis does not even touch me; for on the basis of
his presuppositions, everything that he says is completely correct. The problem only arises when one asks what meaning
the concept "history" has in the phrase "history of salvation." Does one ask on the basis of a modern understanding
of history or on the basis of faith?

But I will not dwell any longer on such general considerations. I also want to refer only very briefly to some details in
which I likewise am unable to agree with the author. Is the
plural καιροί in the Pastoral Epistles (I Tim. 2:6, etc.) actually
a genuine plural, so that it designates "stages in the history
of salvation" (pp. 40 f., 42)? Hardly! Is it actually so certain
that Jesus combined the ideas of Servant of God and Son of
Man in order to designate his role in the history of salvation
(pp. 111 f.)? I do not believe so! May one really say, "It is
no longer to be disputed that Jesus looked upon his own
death as the decisive point in the divine plan of salvation"
(p. 149)? If so, why is it not to be disputed? There are still
weighty reasons that count against it, and there are perfectly
respectable investigators who feel the weight of these reasons.
Did Jesus really count on an interim between his death and

his parousia (pp. 149 f.)? I have not been convinced that h
did, even by Kümmel, to whom Cullman appeals. And ma
one assert that if this thesis should prove correct there is n
longer any substantial reason for denying the genuineness o
Matt. 16:18 (p. 150)? That is too much even for Kümmel
Rom. 2:14 ff. certainly is not intended to show that in th
judgment the heathen will be at no disadvantage relative t
the Jews (p. 182), but rather that God's judgment also justl
applies to the heathen, even though they did not have the la
of Moses. II Tim. 2:12 certainly does not speak of th
lordship of the church in the present stage of the history o
salvation (p. 187). It is painful to see that the grotesque mis
interpretation of " authorities " ($\dot{\epsilon}\xi o \upsilon \sigma i \alpha \iota$) in Rom. 13:1 f
recurs to the angelic powers (p. 194). How can it be decree
that the logion to Luke 6:5 that is handed down in Codex I
is " certainly genuine " (p. 227)?

But enough of this! Let us rather pass on to some mor
important critical comments.

1. First of all, Cullmann's method of, so to speak, carryin
up the statements of the various New Testament writings t
the same level seems to me to lead to an illicit harmonization
Indeed, one must immediately ask in which of the Nev
Testament authors the idea of the history of salvation plays an
role at all or at least any essential role. If it is to be found i
Paul, in Hebrews, in Matthew and, in a certain way, also i
Luke and Acts, it certainly is not to be found in John (eithe
in the Gospel or the Letters); and even among the former, i
functions in different ways. In any case, it is a gross over
statement to say that the entire New Testament presupposes
unified conception of the history of salvation (p. 112), an
the oldest formulations of faith do not seem to me to provid
proof of this.

Furthermore, the " body " of Christ as a designation of th
church is by no means a concept that is common to the whol
New Testament (for the earliest community it is unthinkable)
but rather is limited to the Pauline and deutero-Paulin

literature. Moreover, it is not a history of salvation concept at all, but rather stems from Gnosticism and is in opposition to the concept "people of God," which does presuppose the history of salvation. And this opposition—which is at the same time an opposition of spatial and temporal categories generally—may not simply be smoothed over.

Furthermore, is it really the case that the Pauline grounding of the imperative in the indicative is characteristic of the entire moral instruction of the New Testament? And must one not admit, even if he finds that the genuinely new understanding of Christian existence on the basis of faith is expressed in Paul's formulation, that this understanding is by no means reached everywhere? Is it really correct to say, in face of the deutero-Pauline literature, that the New Testament lays down no real catechetical principles and no general ethical rules (p. 230)? I do not deny that it is possible, yes, even necessary to exhibit a unified "theology" of the New Testament or, better, a unified motive of believing thinking that lies behind all of the New Testament patterns of thought. But this task is, in my opinion, set about in the wrong way if one imagines that he should exhibit the unity of what, in truth, are very different forms of thought. In that case, one is misled into a false harmonization, and the result is not a picture of New Testament theology as a historical phenomenon, but rather a biblical dogmatic in the old style. And I very much doubt that the proclamation of the church and its faith can be better served by such a theology.

2. The whole area of problems posed by the history of religions is all but completely ignored. The consequence is, first of all, that the influence of Jewish apocalypticism on the New Testament understanding of the history of salvation is underestimated. The truth of the matter is that the whole picture of the course of the history of salvation that Cullmann draws is by no means something specifically Christian, which has been drawn on the basis of the "mid-point" of the Christ-occurrence, but rather is simply the picture of Jewish apocalyp-

ticism. The only difference is that the bringer of salvation, which for Judaism is still expected, is believed to have been already present in Jesus of Nazareth. This may mean that the " mid-point " of the history of salvation is pushed back on the time-line (concerning this, see below), but the picture itself is by no means transformed thereby. It is not first for Christians (pp. 107 f.) that the " mid-point " is the starting-point for understanding history, but exactly the same thing is also true already for Jews; for apocalyptic pictures of history also are always drawn on the basis of the " end." Naturally, the connection of history and myth is also exactly as charac- teristic of the Jewish conception of the history of salvation as it is of the Christian one. In short, the Christian philosophy of history that Cullmann draws is nothing other than Jewish apocalyptic speculation, modified only by the " mid-point's " having been pushed back on the time-line.

The picture has, of course, been enriched by some new features : the eschatological bringer of salvation has at the same time become the mediator of creation, and the salvation that he is to introduce is not only salvation for the chosen people or for the community of his elect but also pacification, " reconciliation " of the entire cosmos, whose rebellious spirit- ual powers have been subjected to him; and he himself has become a cosmic figure. However, these features do not come from the tradition that thinks in terms of the history of salvation, nor are they by any means specifically Christian; they stem rather from Gnostic thinking, even as the idea of the church as the " body of Christ " is also of Gnostic origin (see above). One can see, for example, how the author of Eph. 2 : 11 ff. endeavours to connect the cosmological thinking of Gnosticism with the thinking that is expressed in the history of salvation; and the same thing is true of the author of Hebrews (cf. the studies of Schlier and Käsemann). It is also not the case that, as Cullmann supposes, the motive of Gnostic docetism is spiritualism and the flight from the his- torical once for all; rather (apart from the purely fabulous

lements in the myth) the motive of Gnosticism is the con-
usion of historical occurrences with those of nature; i.e., it
s not the misunderstanding of the significance of *occurrence
as such,* but rather the misunderstanding or misinterpretation
of the historicity of human existence. So also, then, the death
of Jesus is indeed a scandal for the early community and for
he thinking of Jewish-Christians; but it is not at all a scandal
or the thinking of Gnosticism and the so-called mystery re-
igions, and hence also not for specifically Hellenistic Chris-
ianity. On the contrary, for the latter it is precisely in the
erms of the mystery type of thinking that Jesus' death is
nterpreted. The verses from Col. 3:1-4, which place "the
different stages of the Christ-line of salvation in relation to
our personal life" (p. 218), are expressed throughout in the
sense of the mystery religions' mode of thinking. For the
mystes also salvation rests on a fact of the temporal past, even
if the latter is thought of as an event of the most remote past
rather than the most recent. If the myth is actually "timeless," it in any case is not so in the sense that it speaks of
what is timeless—and that is the decisive question here. It
does this neither in the mystery religions nor in Gnosticism. Is
not the logic of Rom. 5:12 ff. and I Cor. 15:12 ff. that of
Gnostic thinking, in that it is understandable only on the
basis of the idea of the primal man?

3. Since, as a matter of fact, eternity is represented in New
Testament thinking as a continuous time, Cullmann can
rightly designate Christ as the mid-point of the time-line.
However, he cannot designate him as the mid-point of history
or of the history of salvation. According to early Christian
thought, Christ is rather the end of history and of the history
of salvation. The appearance of Christ "when the time had
fully come" (Gal. 4:4) signifies the eschatological event that
puts an end to the old aeon. Henceforth there can be no more
history and also no more history of salvation, for the latter
has reached its end precisely in him. To be sure, the final
drama in which the eschatological events of the sending of

Jesus (or his coming), his death, and his resurrection will find
their conclusion is still to take place—apart, that is, from John,
for whom that drama (i.e., the parousia, the resurrection of
the dead, and the judgment) has already occurred and is now
occurring. Everywhere else, the parousia and everything connected with it is expected to take place in the immediate
future; and as a result of the *delay of the parousia* there
emerges for early Christianity (especially for that part of it
that was nourished by Jewish tradition) a most pressing problem—a problem the importance of which has been strongly
and rightly sensed by Albert Schweitzer and Martin Werner
and Fritz Buri, but which Cullmann endeavours to trivialize.
This he seeks to do by means of a comparison : just as the
decisive battle can already be fought in a relatively early phase
of a war and yet the war continue even though it is already
decided, so also is everything already decided by the Christ-
occurrence, and it matters not how long the consummation is
still outstanding (pp. 83 f.). But is this comparison convincing when the parousia that Paul expected during his own lifetime has now been delayed some 1,900 years? In any case, early
Christianity did not think so.

I do not know of any place in the New Testament where
Christ's cross and resurrection are conceived as " the middle
point and meaning of all that occurs," "first, in a purely
temporal sense, but then also as a point of orientation, i.e., as
a middle point that gives meaning to the whole course of
events that develops in time " (p. 86). On the contrary, the
meaning of the continuing course of events is not reflected
upon at all, not even by John, for whom the parousia, the
resurrection of the dead, and the judgment have already
occurred and for whom the subsequent course of time can only
be the further realization of such an eschatological occurrence, but no longer a " history of salvation." To say that
the essential point of the words, " the Reign of God is at
hand," does indeed have to do with chronology, only not in
the sense that the nearness of the end is emphasized, but

rather that a new division of time is proclaimed (pp. 87 ff.) is a tortured expedient in face of embarrassment. It is certainly correct, if one considers the later New Testament writings like the Pastoral Epistles and Acts, that the question concerning the "when" of the parousia in early Christianity gradually loses its importance; and one could acknowledge with a certain justice that Cullmann's construction is right to the point in relation to Acts. But this would only give evidence of the latter's temporal distance from Paul and its substantial distance from John. And what is manifested in it is not the consistent development of the history of salvation type of thinking, but rather its having been left behind. One may certainly say, following the Johannine interpretation of eschatology, that the question concerning the "when" of the parousia has lost its justification for a type of thinking that is consistent with faith. What one may not do, however, is to eliminate the problem that existed at this point for early Christianity and obscure the fact that John was the first one to draw this conclusion (although the way for it had been prepared by Paul).

4. Since Cullmann eliminates the problem that grows out of the delay of the parousia, another related and ultimately far more important problem scarcely comes into his view. This is the problem, namely, of the temporality of Christian existence. The faithful, those who have been freed from the world and its powers by Christ, those who are rightwised and bound together with him into one body, are "a new creation"; they are set free from the world and translated as "saints" into the eschatological mode of existence. But how can their eschatological existence still be understood as temporal being? An answer to this is not given simply by pointing out that the eternity of the new aeon also is represented as a time-line; from this it would merely follow that eschatological existence is an existence within time. But an existence within time is something other than the temporality of existence itself. Thus, we ask, how is the temporality of eschatological existence at all

capable of being represented? And this question is posed all
the more urgently because time still goes on and the parousia
is delayed! Temporal existence means to exist in constantly
new decisions, in constantly new encounters, whether with
men or with destiny. But how can there be any such thing in
the case of one for whom the decision has already been made
once and for all? How can there be destiny and temptation
through suffering and death for one who has died and is risen
with Christ? How can the elect be tempted by the world (or
by Satan)? How can there be an ethical imperative over one
for whom the law has come to an end?

Of all these questions only the last is at least touched upon
in the final part of the book; nowhere, however, is the problem presented in all its depth. It could only be brought to a
solution if the concept of faith and the relation of the act of
faith to the conduct of life were subjected to analysis and if the
concept of the Spirit, whose help as a supernatural power
Cullmann naturally invokes, were exactly defined.

I may add that if Cullmann had grasped the problem of
the temporality of eschatological existence, he would hardly
have attributed to me the intention of wanting by my demythologizing exegesis to eliminate " the temporal and historical element as a mythological garment " (pp. 30 f.). That
he has not grasped this problem, which Gerhardt Delling in
his book, *Das Zeitverständnis des Neuen Testaments* (1940),
at least sensed, is for me the most painful defect in this rich
and clever book.

ON BEHALF OF CHRISTIAN
FREEDOM*

ı the concluding issue of *Die Wandlung* for last year (Dec-
mber 1948), Erwin Gross had some important things to say
ɔout "the degeneration of the church into a religious party."
. is painful to see that the first response to his remarks, to my
nowledge, is the polemical article that has appeared in the
rst issue (pp. 65-72) of *Junge Kirche*,[1] which is now once
gain appearing after a year's interruption of publication. In
s lack of understanding of Gross's concern, this article is a
ıd confirmation of his thesis of the "great apostasy." This
.ck of understanding is all the more incomprehensible in
iew of the fact that, in the very next issue, *Junge Kirche* has
ublished an essay by Ernst Tillich that moves in the same
irection as Gross's remarks.

But what is Gross's concern? He wants to fight for the
enuine freedom of faith which he sees threatened, indeed,
lready abandoned in the present development within the
hurch. But what is this freedom? It is freedom by and for
race, and this means at the same time, for the freedom of
ïod. That is, it is release from all worldly conditions and
ıdical openness for encounters with God in all that comes.
urther, it is the renunciation of every security that a man
ıight acquire by assent to "right doctrine" or by appropriate
ractical conduct; it is the renunciation of every "standpoint"
y which he could make the free grace of God his possession.
ı other words, it is the renunciation of every "legalism";
ɔr every such security is a legalistic security. The genuine
reedom of faith is man's radical surrender to God's grace as
ıe sole means whereby he is saved from his factual insecurity,
is total lostness. But this grace "must necessarily appear to

* "*Für die Christliche Freiheit,*" *Die Wandlung,* iv (1949), 417-22.

285

the man who lives in legalism in the form of an offendin,
perplexing, and frightening annihilation" (Gross, p. 710
Thus freedom is the readiness to sink into the " abyss (
nothingness " (p. 708), or, to express the matter with Luthe
it is the readiness to go out into utter darkness.

The remarks of Gross which are sustained by this idea (
freedom can hardly be suspected of stemming from a " fal.
liberalistic point of view." And the genuineness of ar
criticism of them would have to be proven by acknowledgin
agreement with their basic concern and then showing th
their judgment of the situation in the church is in error. In
asmuch, however, as a criticism neglects to do this and instea
defames its opponent, it simply shows how correct Gross
diagnosis is.

For what is it that in his judgment is the danger into whic
the church of the present has fallen? It is the fact that a fal.
security is growing up in the church because a pietistic orth
doxy is at work to gain control, i.e., a kind of " churchiness
that is determined to silence all opposition and thereby to tur
the church into a " collective " that is made up solely (
" standardized church-Christians."

This is the tendency, according to Gross, of the laws reg
lating church elections, insofar as they make active particip
tion in the life of the congregation a condition of eligibili
for church office; for this leads, in turn, to setting up a cor
mission of ecclesiastically reliable persons who determir
whether or not this condition is fulfilled. *Junge Kirche*
angered by the fact that Gross compares this method with th
of Hitler in silencing all opposition within the state. B
unfortunately this comparison is not in " bad taste " ar
cannot be settled by referring to the fact that with Hitl
what was involved was " the absolute will to power," where.
the election laws are intended to see to it that " powers th
are alien to the church do not acquire a domination over
that would threaten its life." As if Gross also was not awa

this difference! But what he refers to is the similarity of *methods*—and to this the criticism in *Junge Kirche* seems mind. It does affirm, to be sure, that " the problem of eligibi-ty for office in the church is a grave and important prob-m " and promises that the latter is still to be discussed at ngth in *Junge Kirche*. But why then the angry tone of plemic, rather than the simple confession, indeed, the ready greement, that Gross is completely right when he points to e absurd consequence of the election laws : " They create vo classes in the church : passive and active members. The assive members have the right of church taxes [namely, to ay them], while the active members, have the [additional] ght to dispose of them!"

One may say that Gross exaggerates when he speaks of the pietistic orthodoxy " that " in high places as in low, with erics as with laymen, among the leadership as among the ongregations, exclusively holds the field in the evangelical urch in Germany and also consciously drives toward such xclusiveness " (p. 702). In fact, I myself hold this to be an xaggeration; for I am acquainted with certain very notable xceptions not only in " low " places, but even in " high " nes. But, ah, they are exceptions! And Gross has correctly elineated a powerful tendency that also frequently attains to tual domination. Does not even *Junge Kirche* admit this hen it publishes the above-mentioned essay by Ernst Tillich a which the following question is posed : " Are we deceived we get the impression . . . that precisely we who have xperienced two world wars and the complete collapse of uman truth have taken flight into an orthodoxy, the words, nought forms, and doctrinal propositions of which have lready become almost a holy language and constitute an area hat is unassailable by the thinking of the world?" (p. 67). Tillich also believes " that we must admonish ourselves with very means at our command of the danger of drawing back ito an orthodox church " (p. 71). Is it without reason that in Württemberg Hermann Diehm (regardless of how one stands with respect to his concrete proposals) again and again struggles against the domination of ecclesiastical bureaucracy, or that in Hanover Götz Harbsmeier likewise resists the clericalization of the church? Is it not almost everywhere the case that the "pure doctrine" that the Christian proclamation must indeed prove itself to be is falsely viewed as a dogmatic system in which old confessions are repristinated as doctrinal laws? Are not charges of heresy the order of the day? And are not efforts under way to make the free work of theology dependent on the bidding of ecclesiastical authorities? Is it everywhere understood that the traditional confessions of the ancient church and the Reformation can be nothing other than contributions to the discussion in the common effort to unfold for the present the knowledge that is given in faith?

Certainly one can say that in his struggle against "pure doctrine" Gross understands the latter one-sidedly in the sense of orthodoxy as church dogmatics and does not take into account that the effort to acquire "pure doctrine" must indeed be the constant concern of theological reflection. However, in saying this, one must guard against the illusion that such "pure doctrine" can ever be authoritatively fixed. "Pure doctrine" is an "eschatological" thing, i.e., something that is always distant from me and standing before me in the future and yet also all the time present—namely, nowhere else than in that genuine and free discussion in which the truth always manifests its power.

Thus, in the sense in which he understands it, Gross' struggle against "pure doctrine" is completely legitimate. What he opposes is the security of the standpoint, i.e., the kind of security that does not engage in discussion freely, but rather seeks to hinder it by doctrinal discipline. He is opposed to the self-deception that holds that every attack on the presently approved form of the church is a refusal of the church's claim and enmity against it and that the church not only has to endure such attacks, but must even bear them joyfully as the "cross" that is laid upon it. Precisely when the church interprets every genuine opposition in this sense and thereby makes itself deaf to all criticism, it proves that it has fallen into the security that is the security of legalism and denies the freedom of God. Then it has indeed turned its confession into a programme and become a party.

Junge Kirche completely misunderstands Gross when it engages in the tactics of presenting his criticism as an attack against the "Confessing Church." This misunderstanding is perhaps occasioned by Gross's protests against the church's critics' constantly having to put up with the question about their ecclesiastical (and political) past and also by his assertion that the "law of the old warriors" now rules the church and that thereby "the future is destroyed with the past" (p. 705).

Nevertheless, it should have been clear that if the church is really open for discussion, it has to ask concerning the material validity of the criticism that it encounters and may not seek to avoid such criticism by raising the question of the legitimation of the critic in the light of his ecclesiastical (or political) past. It is just this that Gross demands, and it is just this against which *Junge Kirche* transgresses in apparently fulfilling his demand. For what is the statement, "Also, we do not want to concern ourselves with Pastor Gross's ecclesiastical or political past," but an insinuation that his past is not unobjectionable?

That Gross's protest against the "law of the old warriors" is not directed against the Confessing Church that led the struggle for the confession in the years of the Nazi domination is evident not only because he himself was at the time very much involved in that struggle in Thuringia, but also because he says this law destroys the future *with the past*. For what does this mean? Wherever the conduct of the past is made into a claim to fame, wherever a right is derived from it, wherever, therefore, the past is made the basis of security, and freedom from it is surrendered by making the words with which it fought into a law and by ossifying the act of confessing into a fixed confession—there the past is in truth destroyed. The only person who remains true to the past is one who preserves a freedom for the future, i.e., who remains open to the freedom of God and therefore is conscious of the fact that God could also "pronounce against" the Confessing Church "and acknowledge the justice of the criticism" (p. 706).

Still, *Junge Kirche* sees quite correctly that the Confessing Church would destroy itself if it ever became a party, that it cannot possibly do this if it is to remain true to its own inner principle (p. 41). But what Gross is asking is precisely whether this condition is being fulfilled! Must not even the "old warriors" permit themselves to be questioned about the genuineness of their motives? Has *Junge Kirche* not noted that this question is raised by Tillich when he writes: "To all of us it was a miracle, i.e., simply an astounding and unexpected fact, that precisely in this evangelical church there were still to be found so many forces of genuine resistance. A sign perchance of the retarding influence of old institutions—certainly not the awakening of a new life?" (p. 70 f.). If the author gives us to understand his answer by the very way in which he formulates the question, he nevertheless raises it.

That *Junge Kirche* has fallen under the "law of the old warriors" is unfortunately shown by the content as well as the tone of its polemic. It is shown not only by the "bad taste," but also by the plain stupidity with which it appeals against Gross to the warriors of the Confessing Church who paid for their confession with their lives—as if the question were not precisely on whose side today those warriors would take their stand! It is always easier to adorn the tombs of the prophets of the past than it is to remain true to them in the matter with which they themselves were concerned. Compare Matt. 23:29-31.

> Woe to you, scribes and Pharisees, hypocrites! for you
> build the tombs of the prophets and adorn the monu-
> ments of the righteous, saying, "If we had lived in the
> days of our fathers, we would not have taken part with
> them in shedding the blood of the prophets!" Thus you
> give witness to the fact that you are sons of those who
> murdered the prophets.

Equally meaningless is the remark that "a surprising number
of men and women today hold important church offices who
were never members of the Confessing Church" (p. 41). Let
us set next to this the statement of Tillich: "We note with
surprise that those who then for the most part discredited the
church's small band of intrepid warriors have today appropriated to themselves that group's moral credit." Thus we
readily see that the citing of statistics here is meaningless.
And if *Junge Kirche,* in order, as it says, not to evade the
central question (p. 42) points out that Bishop D. Wurm is no
party man and that the "church party" impeached by Gross
does not dispose of a large propaganda apparatus and a large
press, it *does* evade his central question.

It confirms his charge that the church can indeed talk about
man's lostness and God's grace and the freedom of the
Christian man and yet at the same time know nothing about
them *existentiell*—that, having falling into legalism, it can
fail to see that its true nature "vanishes into nothing precisely
where it is most passionately affirmed" (p. 706). In fact, for
this state of affairs the polemic against Gross is an astonishing
documentation. It asserts that his attack is unjustified because
what he rightly demands is actually being fulfilled in the
church today—namely, discussion of the laws regulating
church elections and a theological discussion of right doctrine
in which doctrinal discipline is exercised internally rather than
externally.[2] Fine! But that all of this stands within the brack-
ets of a clerical concern for security is demonstrated by
Junge Kirche's own failure in the concrete here and now to
take up the discussion in a free and open way. It precisely does

not let its security be questioned and challenged by Gross, but rather dismisses him as an illegitimate critic.

How are we to understand that in the very next issue this polemic is followed by the article by Tillich I do not know. Did the author of the polemic have pangs of conscience? Or is *Junge Kirche* so utterly without direction as not to recognize the contradictions into which it has fallen?

MAN BETWEEN THE TIMES
ACCORDING TO THE NEW
TESTAMENT*

I

The meaning of the theme "Man between the Times" is at first simple to determine. For the primitive Christian community is conscious of standing "between the times," namely, at the end of the old aeon and at the beginning—or, at least, immediately before the beginning—of the new one. Thus it understands its present as a peculiar "interim." This is expressed with particular clarity in I Cor. 15:23-7. According to rabbinic theory, between the old aeon and the new will fall the reign of the Messiah; for Paul this reign is already present as the interim between Christ's resurrection and his parousia. In other words, the primitive community interprets its present according to the scheme of traditional Jewish apocalypticism, i.e., the scheme of mythological eschatology and its doctrine of the two aeons. But while Jewish apocalypticism lives in the consciousness that the old aeon is rushing toward its end and looks forward with hope and longing for the coming of the new one, seeking on all sides for the signs of its approach, the Christian community is convinced that the new aeon is already breaking in and that its powers are already at work and can be discerned.

The reason for this conviction is that, for the Christian community, the appearance of Jesus is a decisive event, that it believes in the risen and exalted Lord as the one whom

* "Der Mensch zwischen den Zeiten nach dem Neuen Testament," Man in God's Design. A Publication of Studiorum Novi Testamenti Societas (Valenc: Imprimeries Reunies, 1952), 39-59.

God has made Messiah or bringer of salvation and who, accordingly, will come (again) on the clouds of heaven to hold judgment and to bring in the new aeon of deliverance. Thus the early community expressed the decisive significance that lay for it in the appearance, work and destiny of Jesus in the forms of mythological eschatology.[1]

Accordingly, " man between the times " is, first of all, man waiting—waiting for the breaking in of the new aeon, for the parousia of Christ. Of course, pious Jews, and indeed not only those specifically in apocalyptic circles, were also waiting men. But the waiting of the Christian community has a different character from that of the Jews who are filled with longing for the aeon to come. This is so not only because the Christian community waits for the imminent breaking in of the new aeon with full certainty, while the Jewish apocalypticist asks complainingly, " How long, O Lord?" (IV Ezra 4 : 33), but also and especially because the Christian community is even now, in a certain sense, already freed from the old aeon and belongs to the new one. It understands itself as the community of the last days, as the true Israel—as is attested by its self-designation as ἐκκλησία, i.e., the *qahal Yahweh*—as the community of the " saints," or of the " elect." The Spirit, the promised gift of the last days, is already poured out in it, working miracles and raising up prophets. Those who belong to it are " sealed " with " the seal of the living God " (Rev. 7 : 2 f., 9 : 4), which places them under God's protection so that they will be spared the terrors of the last days. Perhaps this way of speaking in Revelation is not merely symbolic. If Erich Dinkler is correct in saying that the sign of the cross was an eschatological *sphragis* already in Judaism,[2] then it is easy to assume that the sealing was a real act whereby the person sealed was marked with the sign of the cross—perhaps at baptism, which already for Paul is a seal (II Cor. 1 : 22; cf. Eph. 1 : 13, 4.30).

This whole mode of thinking moves within the perspective and in the concepts of the myth; and it originally presup-

poses the conviction that the end of the world—the old aeon
—is immediately imminent. But can it be maintained when
this end is always further delayed? Can the faithful understand their present as an "interim" when this "interim" is
constantly extended, until finally it will soon be two thousand
years?

Already in the New Testament itself the delay of the
expected parousia is felt. That impatience exists, that despair-
ing questions are heard, is shown even by the synoptic tradition with its admonitions to watchfulness and its emphasis that
the day will come unexpectedly when no one anticipates it,
like a thief in the night (Matt. 24:43; par. Luke 12:39 f.;
Matt. 25:1-13. Cf. further Luke 12:35-8; Mark 13:33-7).[3]
The warning that the day will come unexpectedly, like a thief,
is also echoed elsewhere (I Thess. 5:2-4; Rev. 3:3, 16:15:
II Pet. 3:10).

It is clear that in many congregations disappointment has
arisen. Indeed, II Pet. 3:1-10 has to defend the expectation of
the parousia against serious doubts. The author seeks to
explain the delay of the parousia, on the one hand, by pointing
out that God has a different standard of time from ours—
for him a thousand years are as a day—and, on the other hand,
by referring to God's forbearance, which waits upon men's
repentance. For the most part, of course, it is sufficient to
refer to God's secret decree: No one knows the day and the
hour, not even the angels in heaven and, indeed, not even the
Son (Mark 13:32; cf. Acts 1:7; II Clem. 12).

Alongside of this, however, the conviction persists that the
end of the times has actually come. Now, "in these last days,"
God has spoken to us through Christ (Heb. 1:2). Now, "at
the end of the age" Christ has been revealed (Heb. 9:26;
likewise Herm. Sim. IX, 12:3). It is expressed even more
strongly in I Pet. 4:7 "The end of all things is at hand!"
So also Barn. 21:3: "The day is at hand!" and Ign. Eph.
11:1: "These are the last times!" But even these cries and
warnings attest that the certainty of standing in the last days

and immediately before the breaking in of the age of salvation has been shaken.

Nevertheless, it must be emphasized that the voices of admonition or, rather, the impatience and disappointment to which they attest, by no means characterize the total picture of the apostolic and post-apostolic period.[4] If I disregard here Christian Gnosticism and also the Fourth Gospel and the Johannine Epistles, then other documents show that the transition from a time of lively and excited expectation of the imminent end to a time that looks for the end in the indefinite future has been made in wide circles without any discontinuity or difficulty. Neither in Colossians nor in Ephesians, nor even in the Pastoral Epistles, does the expectation of an imminent end play any role or is there anything to be discerned in the way of disappointment at the delay of the parousia. And in Hebrews and the Shepherd of Hermas, the consciousness of standing in the last days plays no essential role, and Hermas especially presupposes as his readers a community in which the eschatological consciousness is no longer alive. The same is true of I Clement, which, to be sure, does intend to make clear the Lord's imminent arrival by means of the parable of the vine in chapter 23; however, the real interest of this parable is clearly not the nearness of the parousia, but rather the truth of faith in the resurrection of the dead (chs. 24-6). It is not otherwise in II Clement, which in 11:3 makes use of the same parable, but is really interested only in the truth of faith in resurrection and retribution and not in the imminence of the parousia. In any case, there is no sign of impatience or disappointment.

If the passionate expectation of the imminent end could again and again flame up in specific situations and under specific conditions, as Revelation and I Peter attest, it still remains that in the course of time this expectation understandably died away, only to live again in specific situations throughout the whole subsequent history of the church. However, what never died away—if one disregards Gnosticism and

he Gospel and Letters of John[5]—is the eschatological expecta-
ion as such, i.e., the expectation of the end of this world in a
great cosmic catastrophe, the parousia of Christ, the resurrection of the dead and the last judgment. But does this expecta-
ion with respect to the future still stand, as it did originally,
n correspondence with a judgment concerning the past, i.e.,
he time before Christ? Does it stand thus, namely, in such a
way that the present is understood as an "interim," as a brief
transitional span between the old aeon that is past or at least
has reached its end and the new future aeon? We today are
accustomed to speak of the coming "end of the world" and,
n so doing, give evidence that our relationship to the past
has become an entirely different one from that of the primitive
Christian community. For in our concept "world," the notion
of an interim period has disappeared; the break between the
time before and the time after the appearance of Jesus has
become obscured, and the "interim period" is viewed as of a
piece with the entire past. The peculiarly paradoxical charac-
er of the interim period as a time in which the powers of the
new aeon are already at work has disappeared.

But because this is so we are estranged not only from the
earliest Christian community, but also from the New Testament, from the apostolic and post-apostolic age. For in spite
of the delay of the parousia and the postponing of the end,
this age preserved a peculiar consciousness of the "interim"
and maintained a characteristic judgment not only about the
world as such, but also about the past age of the world prior
to Christ.

One must ask himself how it was possible that eschatology
did not completely disappear or did not live on merely in
. form in which universal (cosmological) eschatology is displaced by an individualistic one, i.e., one which does not expect a new aeon, but simply the continuation of individual
life after death. (There are, indeed, the beginnings of such a
view in the New Testament. Cf. Luke 16:22, 16:23, 16:43;
Phil. 1:23). One must ask how it was possible that even

with the passage of time a specific judgment about the past, the period before Christ, remained alive. One can adduce various reasons for this, but probably the deepest of them is that in the forms of mythological eschatology there is contained a specific understanding of human existence, and that precisely in the paradoxical notion of an " interim "—a time that is neither past nor future, and yet both—there is expressed an understanding of the paradoxical existence of man, i.e., of the man for whom the appearance of Jesus is the decisive event of his life.

II

1. If we inquire now about the understanding of existence that is contained in the notion of " interim," we disregard the men who did not come to faith in Jesus as the bringer of salvation. To be sure, they, too, stand in the " interim " between Jesus' appearance (or resurrection) and his parousia. However, they do not know it and in their unfaith remain the old in the old. That is, they do not at all stand *existentiell* in the " interim," because for them the old aeon is in no sense at an end. Rather they belong to it with their entire existence and thus are faced with the judgment in which it will be brought to nothing. They are qualified by the new aeon only insofar as, in the eyes of the faithful, they are already judged without knowing it.

We also need speak only briefly of Jesus himself. For him also, of course, it is true that he knows himself to be between the times. He knows that the power of Satan whom he saw fall like lightning from heaven is at an end (Luke 10:18) and in the power of the Spirit of God he casts out demon (Matt. 12:28 or Luke 11:20) because Satan's dominion i already broken (Mark 3:27). Therefore the Reign of God i already coming (Matt. 12:28; Luke 11:20). The prophetic promise of the time of salvation is now being fulfilled (Matt

11 :5). Nevertheless, he teaches his disciples to pray : " Thy reign come!" (Matt. 6 :10; Luke 11 :2) and points to the imminent coming of the " Man " (Mark 8 :38 or Luke 12 :8). Thus his present work stands in an " interim." This judgment concerning his present, however, springs out of his own sense of vocation; he derives it from himself, and, quite otherwise than with the later community, it is not based on the fact that he looks back to an event that is of decisive significance for him. It is possible, of course, that the appearance of John the Baptist and his preaching gave Jesus his original impulse as one of the signs of the time, to attend to which he summons his hearers (Luke 12 :54-6). If Matt. 11 :11-14 is not completely a product of the later community, but has behind it a genuine saying of Jesus, then he did in fact see the turn of the age in the Baptist's appearance. However, he does not look back to the Baptist, as the community subsequently did to him himself, as the figure through whom the old aeon has been brought to its end and the new aeon introduced.

If one inquires further how the existence of men in this interim period is viewed in Jesus' message, then the answer must be that Jesus himself places them in this " interim." This he does, on the one hand, by placing them under God's demand in so radical a sense that they can be saved only by a complete conversion and, on the other hand, by summoning them to this conversion, in which they can be certain of God's forgiveness because he is a God who has more joy over one sinner who repents than over ninety-nine righteous ones (Luke 15 :7). This certainty of the unconditionedness of the divine demand and the divine grace and the certainty that he, Jesus, has to proclaim these two realities as something new, unheard of, and definitive clothes itself for him in the mythological notion of the end of the old, and the beginning of the new aeon. That man stands in this " interim " expresses his paradoxical existence before God as the Judge and the gracious Father; for him who lets God be his God, the past is extinguished and the future is open.

2. That men have been placed in this paradoxical " interim " by Jesus becomes clearer if we consider now the self-understanding of those who have become certain of God's forgiving grace by reason of their encounter with Jesus or with the word that proclaims him—who see in him the revelation of God's grace and in his appearance the beginning of the new aeon.

Just this, that Jesus' appearance signifies the end of the old aeon and the beginning of the new one, is what is soon expressed with full clarity by Paul. "But when the time had fully come, God sent forth his Son " (Gal. 4 :4). "Therefore, if anyone is in Christ, he is a new creation; the old has passed away, behold, the new has come " (II Cor. 5 :17). The same thing is expressed by John in a different conceptuality : "The hour is coming and now is, when the dead will hear the voice of the Son of God, and those who hear will live " (5 :25). "And this is the judgment, that the light has come into the world " (3 :19). "Now is the judgment of this world, now shall the ruler of this world be cast out " (12 :31). But the Pastoral Epistles also know that the grace of God that once was hidden has now been revealed through the appearing of Jesus Christ (II Tim. 1 :9 f.; cf. Titus 1 :2, 2 :11). Thus, in some kind of conceptuality, it is proclaimed that through Christ the old aeon of sin has been brought to its end and the new aeon of salvation established. Ign. Eph. 19 :3 may serve as a last example : ". . . ignorance was removed, and the old reign was destroyed, for God was manifest as man for the newness of eternal life." Therefore, the beginning of the new aeon is not a cosmic catastrophe, but an event of history. One can say that mythology is historicized, or begins to be historicized.

But our question is, How is the existence of man understood as an existence in the " interim "? How is the paradox understood that the man of faith is taken out of the past and belongs to the future and yet does not stand in the future, but in the past—that he who still lives in the old world nevertheless already belongs to the new one? In what sense has he become different and in what sense is he not yet perfected? To what extent is the understanding of the "interim" developed in an adequate way and expressed with clarity? To what extent is it expressed in an inappropriate conceptuality and thus obscured or falsified?[6]

The answer to these questions is to be found, first of all, in the recognition that the past, the old aeon, is understood as the aeon of sin, and freedom from it, as freedom from sin. As soon as this is seen, the existential meaning of the mythological statements concerning the turn of the age at once becomes clear. For the past that is ended is not only a cosmic situation—although it is also this for mythological thinking—but rather my particular past in which I was a sinner. And the future for which I am freed is likewise my future.

This is most clearly expressed by Paul and John because they most profoundly grasp the nature of sin. That is, they understand sin not merely as the transgression of particular commandments, as moral failure, but rather as the basic attitude of the natural man who cannot bear to live in uncertainty before God, but longs to secure his existence and endeavours to create such security—whether by naïvely living out of the disposable world in care or sensual pleasure or by self-consciously seeking grounds for boasting before God in a formal legal correctness. Sin is to want to live out of one's self, out of one's own power, rather than out of radical surrender to God, to what he demands, gives, and sends.

It is from this sin that the grace of God frees the man who opens himself to it in radical self-surrender, i.e., in faith. Because man thereby no longer belongs to himself (I Cor. 6:19), he is free from care, free from anxiety about death, free from legal prescriptions and human conventions and standards of value. In short, he is free from himself as he actually is as he comes out of his past; he is a new creation in Christ (II Cor. 5:17). As a man of faith, he has passed from death to life (John 5:24). But—and this is the paradox—his

freedom is never a static quality; it never loses the character
of a gift that never becomes a secure possession, but must
rather constantly be laid hold of anew as a gift. But in what
does this constantly new apprehension consist? In nothing
other than the constantly renewed attitude of faith, i.e., in that
openness for what God demands and sends that can never be
taken for granted, but must always be realized anew.

A. It is, first of all, openness for what God *demands*. For
the law, which as the way to salvation, as a means of boasting
before God, has found its end in Christ, remains God's holy,
righteous, and good will (Rom. 7:12); and it is precisely now
that it can really fulfil its true intention of being a law that
leads to life (Rom. 7:10). Henceforth, the imperative is
based in the indicative. To be crucified and risen with Christ
does not mean the acquirement of a mysterious power of
immortality, but rather the freedom of a life lived in the
service of God. "So you also must consider yourselves dead
to sin and alive to God in Christ Jesus" (Rom. 6:11). This
means, however, "Let not sin reign in your mortal bodies, to
make you obey their passions. Do not yield your members to
sin as instruments of wickedness, but yield yourselves to God
as men who have been brought from death to life, and your
members to God as instruments of righteousness" (6:12 f.
cf. further I Cor. 5:7 f., 6:11; Gal. 5:24).

Likewise with John! The dialectical relation of indicative
and imperative is expressed in the discourse about the vine
when it is said that the branch that bears no fruit is pruned
away, but that the branch's bearing fruit depends on its connection with the vine and that this connection is not first produced by the bearing of fruit (15:2-6). Jesus is the light of
the world, and whoever follows him will have the light of
life (8:12). But faith in him as the light is only genuine when
it proves itself by walking in the light. "If we say we have
fellowship with him while we walk in darkness, we lie and
do not do the truth" (I John 1:6). "He who says he is in the
light and hates his brother is still in the darkness" (I John

2 : 9). For John, the imperative is the command of brotherly
love, which is a new command because it has its basis in the
love of God for men that is bestowed in Jesus. Whoever
responds to this divine love in love for the brother, in him
God abides, and love is perfected (I John 4 : 12); he has really
passed from death to life (I John 3 : 14).

In a certain sense, John expresses the paradox—or the dialectic—even more clearly than Paul, because he makes clear
that the freedom from sin through the divine forgiveness is not
a once for all act, but that one's entire life stands under forgiveness. Whereas Paul is satisfied again and again to incul-
cate the imperative that is based in the indicative, John points
out that freedom from sin and walking in the light stand in a
paradoxical unity with the confession of sin : " If we say we
have no sin, we deceive ourselves, and the truth is not in us.
If we confess our sins, he is faithful and just, and will forgive
our sins " (I John 1 : 8 f.).

At this point, of course, a split soon develops. For if sin is
not understood in its depth, then the freedom from it also
cannot be grasped as freedom from its power, as freedom from
the old self, but only as the cancellation of guilt and punishment that man has incurred because of sins committed before
baptism. And if it is not understood that the Christian life is
a constant living under forgiveness, then there develops a
striving after moral sinlessness, a perfectionism, which is in
principle indistinguishable from Jewish legalism. Once again
it is up to the power and effort of man to stand in the day of
judgment and to gain the grace of forgiveness by his own
works.

But with this the problem of sins committed after baptism
becomes an urgent problem. Can the Christian who has fallen
back into sin after he has been baptized still repent? This is
denied in Heb. 6 : 4-6, 10 : 26-31, 12 : 16 f.; and, to be sure,
what is first of all in mind is clearly the sin of apostasy from
the faith (6 : 4-6), to which are added, then, other grievous
sins (" deliberate " ones, as they are called in 10 : 26), fornica-

tion and the like (12 : 16 f.). On the other hand, it is re-vealed to the author of the Shepherd of Hermas that God has once again and for the last time granted the possibility of repentance. However, this naturally could not be a generally valid and definitive solution of the problem. Rather the development finally leads to the ecclesiastical institution of penance, in which, to be sure, the recognition is to some extent preserved that the life of the man of faith again and again requires repentance and forgiveness, but in which for-giveness is not understood as freedom from the power of sin, but rather as the remission of guilt.

The same process can be observed with respect to the con-cept of the Spirit. The paradox of the " interim " is clearly expressed in the primitive Christian belief that the commun-ity has received the Spirit, which is then appropriated by the individual in baptism. Indeed, the Spirit is the " first fruits " or the " earnest " of the future salvation (Rom. 8 : 23; II Cor. 1 : 2, 5 : 5); it is the eschatological gift that already places him who is filled with it in eschatological existence—albeit within the provisional situation of the " interim " that is still a dwelling in the earthly tent of the body, a tarrying in an alien land, far from the Lord, a life of faith rather than of vision (II Cor. 5 : 1-8), a life of suffering in which, in our need and sighing, the Spirit teaches us how to pray as we ought (Rom. 8 : 18, 8 : 26 f.).

In mythological thinking, the Spirit is represented as a mysterious, so to say, magic-working power. Its miraculous effects, the so-called charismata, are in the popular view special deeds of power and abnormal psychic phenomena. Paul does not at all deny this view; but for him the charismata of the first rank are the gifts of brotherly service in the edification of the community; and the Spirit especially signifies for him the power and the norm of the moral life. This does not mean that the Spirit is thereby denied its character as something miraculous. Rather, for Paul, a morally pure life is itself a miracle—a miracle that is given to the baptized as those who are crucified and dead with Christ and thereby freed from their pasts. And just as the Spirit is the power, so also is it the norm of the new life. To be crucified with Christ means to be dead to sin and alive to God in obedience (Rom. 6:11); "those, however, who belong to Christ Jesus have crucified the flesh with its passions and desires" (Gal. 5:24). Therefore, here, too, it holds good that the imperative is based in the indicative: "If we live by the Spirit, then let us also walk by the Spirit" (Gal. 5:25).

It is not otherwise with John, if for him the "Counsellor" or the Holy Spirit is the power of the word that is at work in the community, purifying (15:3) and obligating it. The paradox is clearly formulated in I John 3:24: "All who keep his commandments abide in him, and he in them. And by this we know that he abides in us, by the Spirit that he has given us."

Was this understanding of the Spirit, and with it the understanding of the paradoxical "interim," preserved? What remains is, first of all, the notion that the possession of the Spirit is evidenced by special gifts and actions; and this notion is increasingly concentrated in the thought that particular persons are distinguished by possession of the Spirit—without, of course, in any way prejudicing the conviction that every Christian has received the Spirit on the occasion of his baptism. However, this universal possession of the Spirit is, so to say, latent. It guarantees participation in the future salvation (Eph. 1:13 f., 4:30), but it is no longer the power that determines the believer's existence. This does not hold good for all of the writings nor is it everywhere the case to the same extent; but the individual differences cannot be pursued here in any detail. To be sure, there is still talk in the deutero-Pauline literature of the Spirit of wisdom and knowledge (Eph. 1:17), of the Spirit as the power by which the inner man is strengthened (Eph. 3:16), of the word of God as the sword of the Spirit (Eph. 6:18), and of the Spirit of power, love, and self-control that God has given us (II Tim.

1 : 7). The " renewal " that is effected by the Holy Spirit in Baptism provides the basis for moral exhortation (Titus 3 : 5 f.); and the community has obtained its character by the sanctification of the Spirit (I Pet. 1 : 2). However, these are only scanty and feeble echoes of Pauline statements. Perhaps the unity of indicative and imperative, and therewith the paradox of the " interim," that is given in the idea of the Spirit is still preserved to some extent in Ephesians and I Peter; but it is scarcely still at work in the Pastoral Epistles and Hebrews, in I Clement, Ignatius, and Hermas.

However, the concentration of the possession of the Spirit in particular persons leads—in the controversy with a disorganized pneumaticism—to the consequence that the leaders of the congregations are held to be spiritual persons by reason of their office. (Is this already evident in II Tim. 1 : 14?) The Spirit becomes the endowment of the office bearer; it is imprisoned, so to say, in the ecclesiastical institution. This can be illustrated by the development of the concepts " holy " and " charisma." Already in the Pastoral Epistles the charisma has become an endowment of office that is mediated by ordination (I Tim. 4 : 14; II Tim. 1 : 6). And finally the persons who hold office become priests. " Holiness " becomes an attribute of the church that is borne by the holders of office. When Paul designates the church as the temple of God that is holy (I Cor. 3 : 16 f.), the concept " holy " has for him primarily the negative meaning of being free from the world and therewith of being under obligation. The same meaning is involved in the admonition in I Pet. 2 : 5 : " And like living stones be yourselves built into a spiritual house, to be a holy priesthood." The element of being under obligation is dropped, however, when the community is called the " holy temple in the Lord " in Eph. 2 : 21. And in Eph. 5 : 26, holiness is understood as sacramental purity : Christ has given himself up for the church " so that he might sanctify her, having cleansed her by the washing of water with the word, that . . . she might be [as one would say in the terminology of sacrifice] holy and without blemish." It is already a liturgical convention when Ignatius refers to the church as "holy" in the introduction to his letter to the Trallians; and the designation "the holy church" is already quite familiar to Hermas (Vis. I, 1 :6, 3 :4; IV, 1 :3). The church, so to speak, has the Holy Spirit at its disposal in its institutions and mediates it by the sacraments. The paradox of the "interim" hardly any longer characterizes individual existence or does so only through the mediation of the church in which the "interim" is, as it were, conserved. For the church is a structure that does not belong to the world, but nevertheless sets itself up within it.

B. The paradox of the "interim" becomes just as clear when one considers the attitude of faith with respect to what God *sends*. We understand by this the concrete conditions of life in which the man of faith stands and the destiny, culminating finally in death, that encounters him.

As those who are new creations and exist eschatologically, the faithful are freed from the world. They are no longer citizens of this world, but belong to a commonwealth that is in heaven (Phil. 3 :20). How can it still occur to them to set their minds on earthly things (Phil. 3 :19)? As Christ suffered outside the city, so should Christians "go outside the camp" because they bear his ignominy; "for here we have no lasting city, but seek the city which is to come" (Heb. 13 :13 f.). Here on earth Christians are strangers (Heb. 11 :13; I Pet. 1 :1, 2 :11; Herm. Sim. 1 :1).

However, now in the interim period, the faithful also live in concrete life relationships, in callings, in social situations, as married persons, as buyers, etc., and this all takes place in a city and in a state. What is to be their stand with respect to all of this? Well, they certainly cannot get out of the world (I Cor. 5 :10)! Moreover, they ought not to try to change the relations in the world or their own situation. "No, let everyone lead the life which the Lord has assigned to him, and in which God has called him" (I Cor. 7 :17). "Everyone should remain in the state in which he was called" (7 :20).

The slaves are to remain slaves (7:21-4), the married are not to separate, and while the unmarried do better to remain single, marriage still is no sin (7:26-8). One should also share in the joys and sorrows of others, rejoicing with those who rejoice and weeping with those who weep (Rom. 12:15). And one may likewise participate in the general business of the world—although, of course, in the distance of the "as though not" (I Cor. 7:29-31).

It is in this attitude of "as though not" that Christian freedom from the world consists. "I am lord over all things, but not all things are helpful. I am lord over all things, but I should let nothing become lord over me" (I Cor. 6:12). It is a freedom that has the right to dispose of everything in the world, but for which everything worldly has lost its power of motivation. This holds good in the positive sense and also in the negative sense, that there is nothing simply as such that the Christian has to avoid; for in itself nothing is unclean, but all things are clean (Rom. 14:14, 14:20; cf. I Cor. 10:26). The only motive of action is love, which as complete surrender presupposes freedom from the world. "Let no one seek his own good, but the good of his neighbour" (I Cor. 10:24; cf. Phil. 2:4). And in unity with this is the motive of the glory of God: "So, whether you eat or drink, or whatever you do, do all to the glory of God" (I Cor. 10:31). Thus freedom can express itself precisely in the renunciation of one's right of disposal: "For though I am free from all men, I have made myself a slave to all" (I Cor. 9:19). "For I have learned, in whatever state I am, to be content. I know how to be abased, and I know how to abound; in any and all circumstances I have learned the secret of facing plenty and hunger, abundance and want" (Phil. 4:11 f.).

Nowhere else, however, is the paradoxical character of freedom that corresponds to the paradox of the "interim" as clearly grasped and formulated as it is by Paul. After him, one finds a decline—not, of course, in John, but the Johannine literature is not under consideration here because its interest is not directed to this complex of questions.

In Colossians and the Pastoral Epistles, the knowledge is preserved that there are no ritual or ascetic commandments for Christians. Yet the polemic against such an opinion proves that there were Christian circles that held ritual or ascetic commandments to be binding. In the Pastoral Epistles the participation of Christians in civic life is also presupposed as a matter of course, although there still is nothing said about their responsibility for the state. However, the congregation prays for the state " so that we may lead a quiet and peaceable life, godly and respectful in every way " (I Tim. 2 :2). Here, as everywhere else, distance from the world is understood one-sidedly as distance from a life of vice. By such distance the community should do credit to the Christian faith in the eyes of unbelievers (Col. 4 :5; I Tim. 3 :7, 6 :1; Titus 2 :5, 2 :8, 2 :10; I Pet. 2 :12, 2 :15, 3 :1, 3 :16)—an idea that as such is not un-Pauline (cf. I Thess. 4 :12). However, precisely in such an exhortation there is presupposed an agreement between the standards of Christian and heathen morality that keeps the peculiar character of the Christian relation to the world from ever standing out. In fact, the Christian moral exhortations—e.g., those of the *Haustafeln* (or schedules of household duties) and the mandates of Hermas—are indistinguishable from non-Christian ones. One can say that the ethical instruction is specifically Christian only where it is characterized by the exhortation to suffer patiently (Heb. and I Pet.) and by a sharply negative attitude with respect to the world (Heb.; I Pet.; Herm. Sim. 1). But neither the ethic of civic virtue nor that of flight from the world is characterized, as it is with Paul, by the dialectic of the " as though not "; and the paradoxical concept of freedom has been lost. It is still echoed only in I Pet. 2 :16 in the admonition to " live as free men, yet not as such who use freedom as a pretext for evil, but as servants of God." One can also find an echo of the Pauline concept in Ignatius : The slaves " should not be puffed up, but should rather endure their servitude to the glory of God, that they may obtain [what they therefore do not yet have] a better freedom from God. They should not strive to be set free at the expense of the community, lest they be found the slaves of lust." How the dialectic is surrendered here, because freedom is something only future, is shown in Ign. Rom. 4 :3 : " They [*sic* Peter and Paul] are free; I, however, am until now a slave. But when I have suffered [martyrdom], I shall be Jesus Christ's freedman and will rise in him free. Now, as one who is bound, I am learning to desire nothing." Elsewhere, the concept of " freedom " is not found in Ignatius at all and, indeed, it is found neither in Colossians and Ephesians and the Pastoral Epistles nor in I Clement and Hermas.

The development can now proceed in different directions. Freedom as freedom from the world can be understood either undialectically in the sense of the Gnostic libertinism against which Paul already had to struggle in Corinth, or just as undialectically in the sense of asceticism, as it developed, say, in the Eucratites and, ultimately, in monasticism. Or, finally —and equally undialectically—freedom can be understood in a moralistic sense as freedom from vice. The ancient Catholic church that rejected libertinism combined renunciation of the world as a matter of principle and freedom from vice in a peculiar way. And because it developed a double morality— holding that certain ascetic commandments are binding on monks and clerics—it in a certain way preserved for the church as a whole the element of the interim—only, of course, in a depraved form.

The faithful hope for the resurrection of the dead and the vanquishing of death as the last enemy at the parousia of Christ (I Cor. 15 :26). Their life is a future one; now it is still hidden with Christ in God. (Col. 3 :3). Nevertheless, it is also something present; for in baptism they have died and risen with Christ. As through Adam death came into the world, so through Christ life has come (Rom. 5:12 ff.). Christ has abolished death and brought "life" and "immortality" to light through the gospel (II Tim. 1:10). The man of faith has passed from death to life (John 5:24). But this presence of life here and now is a paradoxical kind of presence; for the faithful still dwell in a mortal body and are subject to all the sufferings to which it is heir.

But in what way is life present? The first answer is that it is present for faith as the life of Christ who is the risen one. Given with his resurrection is the resurrection of all who belong to him. It is precisely this that Paul says when he appropriates the conceptuality of the Gnostic anthropos-myth: the whole line of humanity instituted by the primal man is determined by him; Adamic humanity is dominated by death, Christian humanity, by life (Rom. 5:12 ff.; I Cor. 15:20-3). Therefore, the present life is, so to speak, an *aliena vita,* or, as Col. 3:3 puts it, it is hidden with Christ in God.

But how is this present life that is given only to faith effective in the believer's concrete existence? It is effective in hope! That hope is a power that determines the believer's existence is expressed in Rom. 5:2-5: "We rejoice in our hope of sharing the glory of God. But more than that, we rejoice in our sufferings, knowing that suffering produces endurance, and endurance produces character, and character produces hope." Even if this is a circle—out of hope comes hope —it is nevertheless clear that hope is a vitality that, by bearing up in affliction and endurance, becomes conscious of itself and, as it were, comes to itself and discovers its *existentiell* meaning. I Peter and Revelation especially show how this hope produces life.

But, naturally, the paradox of this life of hope that is expressed in the words, "we rejoice in our sufferings" is elsewhere only feebly echoed—as, for example, in I Pet. 2:19 f.: "For it is grace when one, because he knows God, endures pain by suffering unjustly. . . . If when you do right and suffer for it you take it patiently, that is grace with God." Aside from the fact that what is at issue here is specifically innocent suffering and not suffering in general, hope in I Peter, as in Revelation, is throughout one-sided, in the sense that what is hoped for is that the sufferings of the present will be followed by a future in which there will be no suffering. Hope is no longer the power to understand the sufferings of the present in a positive way, namely, by laying hold of the paradoxical presence of life precisely in such sufferings.

But it is just this that is the case for Paul. Just as death for him is not merely the prospective event of dying, but is experienced as a present power in suffering, so also is life not only something prospective in the future, but rather something that is effective in the present. He has, so to speak, anticipated the future death by dying with Christ—to be sure, in the sacrament of baptism; but dying in baptism for him is not only a sacramental act, but at the same time an act of faith that receives the dying of Jesus into one's own life, so that Christ's resurrection life is also received as one's own. Paul glories in the cross of Christ, by which the world has been crucified to him and he to the world (Gal. 6:14). His life is stamped with dying in order that he "may know him and the power of his resurrection, and may share his suffering, becoming like him in his death, that if possible [he] may attain the resurrection from the dead" (Phil. 3:10 f.).

It is in this readiness for death that faith is peculiarly fulfilled—the faith that is man's radical self-surrender, his radical openness to God. Thus Paul can welcome suffering; for by bringing him to nothing it makes room, as it were, for God—for his life-giving power to become effective. This is faith in the God who gives life to the dead and calls into existence the things that are not (Rom. 4:17), the faith that, in suffering, pronounces the sentence of death over ourselves, so that we do not "rely on ourselves, but on God who raises the dead" (II Cor. 1:9). Paul has the treasure that God has given him in an "earthen vessel," i.e., in a mortal body, "to show that the transcendent power belongs to God and not to us" (II

Cor. 4:7). Likewise, by understanding his suffering as dying with Jesus, Paul carries about in his own body Jesus' death, so that the life of Jesus may also be manifested in his body (4:10 f.); and so he can describe his life in forceful paradoxes (I Cor. 4:12 f.; II Cor. 4:8 f., 6:9 f.) that all culminate in the words, "as dying, and behold we live!" To glory in the cross of Christ means at the same time to glory in one's own weakness (II Cor. 11:30, 12:9 f.), for "power is made perfect in weakness" (II Cor. 12:9).

Freedom from sin and freedom from death belong together and together constitute the freedom of the Christian man: on the one hand, there is the dying with Christ as the crucifixion of passions and desires (Gal. 5:24) and the being dead to sin and alive to God in obedience (Rom. 6:11 ff.), while, on the other hand, there is the surrender to the death that is at work in one's mortal body in suffering, in order thereby to experience God's life-giving power and to share in the resurrection life of Christ.

The paradox of life in death is also brought to forceful expression by John: "I am the resurrection and the life; he who believes in me, though he die, yet shall he live, and whoever lives and believes in me shall never die" (11:25 f.).

Later, the paradox is also echoed in the Letter to Diognetus, in its characterization of Christians :"they are put to death and they are made alive" (5:12); "when they are punished they rejoice as men who receive life" (5:16). Elsewhere, however, the paradox is lost—at least in the Pauline sense. It is apparently preserved when the presence of life is understood as a sacramental quality in the manner of thinking that is characteristic of the mystery religions. The person baptized has received the Spirit through his baptism and by possessing it is assured of future resurrection or immortality. Such a view could, of course, appeal to Paul: "If the Spirit of him who raised Jesus from the dead dwells in you, he who raised Christ Jesus from the dead will give life to your mortal bodies also through his Spirit which dwells in you" (Rom. 8:11). The viewpoint of the mysteries is presupposed by Paul in Rom. 6:1 ff., just as it is in Hellenistic Christianity; however, he interprets the future life of resurrection that is guaranteed by the sacrament as something that is already present and proves itself in moral action. This Pauline interpretation is still maintained in his school (Col. 3:1 ff.; Eph. 2:1 ff.; Titus 3:1 ff.), but a purely sacramental understanding of baptism is present in Hermas: the righteous ones of the Old Testament can participate in salvation only because they are baptized in Hades; "they had need to come up through the water that they might be made alive, for they could not otherwise enter the reign of God unless they put away the mortality of their former life" (Sim. ix, 16). The clearest expression of the sacramental presence of life is that of Ignatius, when he designates the bread of the Eucharist as "the medicine of immortality," and as "the antidote that we should not die, but live forever in Jesus Christ" (Ign. Eph. 20:2).

Alongside of this sacramental understanding of the presence of life stands the moral one; i.e., the notion that life is present is preserved in the view that the new behaviour of the Christian as one who has been brought from death to life is the proof of his really being alive. And this view also could appeal to Paul: "So you must consider yourselves dead to sin and alive to God in Christ Jesus" (Rom. 6:11). However, the Pauline dialectic is given up; for the idea is no longer that the Christian is now alive because he is dead *to* sin, but rather that *after* he was dead *in* sin he has now been made alive through baptism or forgiveness (Col. 2:13; Eph. 2:1, 2:5, cf. 4:18, 5:14).[7] Only in Col. 3:1 ff. is the paradox preserved, when, from the fact that Christians have died with Christ and their life is still hidden with him, the imperative is derived: "Therefore, put to death what is earthly in you" (vs. 5)!

But the other Pauline line of thought in II Cor. 4:7 ff., 6:9 f., 12:9 f.—the "as dying, and behold we live" theme— is nowhere to be found. It seems to have been forgotten that it is precisely in suffering and dying that the life of Jesus is revealed and the power of God made perfect. When suffering and death are nothing more than an affliction that will one day be followed by a time of happiness, then the "interim" in which man now stands in the present has been deprived of its *existentiell* meaning.

This whole analysis teaches us that an anthropology in accordance with the New Testament misses the mark if it describes the nature of man as something static and simply inquires about its constituent elements and properties. Rather what it must do is to present the dialectic of human existence. In this way, the requirements set forth by C. H. Dodd[8] will be fulfilled—namely, (1) to understand the specific difference between New Testament anthropology and a Greek or Hellenistic one; and (2) to recognize the determination of man by history.

IGNATIUS AND PAUL*

For Ignatius, Paul, "the sanctified one," "the one of good report," "the right blessed one" (Ign. Eph. 12:2) is an apostolic authority. Ignatius cannot compare himself with Paul (Ign. Rom. 4:3), but he yearns to follow in the latter's footsteps (Ign. Eph. 12:2). And he in fact does follow in Paul's footsteps insofar as, like him, he also writes letters to Christian congregations and likewise several times makes allusion to or actually cites the Pauline letters. However, I do not intend to give evidence for this by citing statistics; nor is it my purpose to exhibit the influence of Paul on Ignatius and to show how at particular points the latter either further develops or transforms Pauline conceptions.[1] Rather my intention is to inquire concerning Ignatius' understanding of Christian existence and to compare it with Paul's.[2]

I

It seems to me that, with the exception of Ignatius, none of the Christian writers after Paul (and John)—either among the authors of the later New Testament writings or among the Apostolic Fathers—has understood the Christian faith as an *existentiell* attitude. This must be said even of the authors of Colossians, Ephesians, and I Peter, where one is perhaps most likely still to find traces of such an understanding. None of them has understood the paradox of Christian existence—the being in between past and future, the simultaneity of "already" and "not yet"—in the exemplary way in which Paul

* "*Ignatius und Paulus,*" Studia Paulina, in honorem Johannes de Zwann septuagenerii (Haarlem: De Erven F. Bohn N.V., 1953), pp. 37-51.

xpresses it in Phil. 3 :12-14.[3] Therefore, none of them, with
he exception of Ignatius, has so clearly recognized the unity of
ndicative and imperative that for Paul characterizes Christian
xistence. This is all the more noteworthy because there is an
ssential difference between Ignatius and Paul.[4]

To be sure, in a certain sense, the paradox of Christian
xistence as an existence between past and future is main-
ained in all of the early Christian writings—namely, insofar
s in all of them (1) the appearance of Christ, his death and
is resurrection, is understood as the decisive event that has
ut an end to past history and also puts an end to the past life
f the individual when the work of Christ is appropriated in
aptism; and (2) the completion of the eschatological occur-
ence is expected to take place only in the future. But the
ecisive question is whether the " interim " between past and
uture is simply a chronological determination, or is also a
haracteristic of Christian existence. And this depends upon
vhat is understood to be the past that is done away with in
aptism and, further, upon whether or how the eschatological
uture is thought to be something that determines the believer's
resent existence.

On the whole, i.e., for most of the writers in question, the
ast that is already brought to a close is understood as life in
gnorance of God and in vice[5]—a conception that, to be sure,
s in itself not un-Pauline,[6] but also is not the distinctively
auline view. For Paul understands the past primarily as an
xistence under the power of flesh, sin, and the law, i.e., he
ooks upon the fallenness of the natural man as something
nuch more radical than anything that could be sufficiently
escribed as ignorance of God and immorality. After Paul,
owever (always, of course, with the exception of John), it is
ust this radicalness that is lost. This is evident not only
ecause the Pauline antithesis of " flesh " and " Spirit " plays
n increasingly more restricted role, and where it is encoun-
ered scarcely any longer has the depth of meaning of the
auline conception, but also because the concept of " free-

dom " hardly appears at all—at any rate, not in the Pauline sense.[7] And it is especially evident because the freedom from the past that is procured by baptism is primarily understood as the forgiveness of sins committed before baptism and thus as something through which man has been given a new chance. A symptom of this is that here and there the problem of (grievous) sins committed after baptism can appear as a serious problem. Finally, this loss of radicalism is also evident because the admonitions to Christians to repent,[8] the call to good works, and references to the Judge who will accept men according to their works get the upper hand. Indeed, it is explicitly said that the responsibility of Christians is greater than that of the pious men of the old covenant.[9] The future salvation must be achieved by fulfilling the " commandments," the " ordinances," and the " injunctions." In short, man is once again made to rely on his own power; his radical fallenness is no longer seen. Nor is this in any way altered because there is also something said about the forgiveness that is always open to the sinner who confesses and, occasionally, also something about the help of the Spirit. It is symptomatic that the concept of " righteousness " loses its Pauline meaning and, in general, seldom appears in the forensic sense, but is mostly used with a moralistic meaning. The consequence is that a perfectionism develops.

In keeping with this, the future eschatological salvation is not, as it is with Paul, already present in a paradoxical manner, but rather is exclusively future—to the extent that it is not at work in the sacramental powers that are mediated by the church. Indeed, there is now and again talk about the eschatological " Spirit " that is theoretically given to all Christians in baptism and that displays itself in the charismata and also in the power of moral attitude and action. But the unity of the possession of the Spirit with the imperative (cf. Gal. 5:25! is not made clear. The believer's emancipation from the world is not understood as something positive, but rather as something negative. It consists in the renunciation of fleshly desires and vices and, in extreme cases, becomes the practice of asceticism. A symptom of this is that suffering no longer has, as it does with Paul, the positive meaning of permitting the power of the Lord to come into its own; it is not understood as a suffering in which the sufferer shares in the passion of Christ and therewith also participates in his body. Rather the suffering that is reflected upon is an innocent suffering that one has to bear in certain cases in imitation of Christ as one's example.[10] Suffering is merely a necessity that will one day be followed by the age in which there is no suffering.

II

Now, as compared with this general development, Ignatius represents a completely different type. To be sure, if one compares him with Paul, then one must see at once that his theology does not grow out of the way of raising questions that is typical of Paul and also is not developed in the same polemical direction as is characteristic of Paul's position in Romans and Galatians. It is hardly surprising that, just like Paul, he designates the substance of salvation as " [eternal] life "; however, it is characteristic that for him the designation " righteousness [of God] " has disappeared.[11] Only twice is here an echo of the Pauline " to be rightwised ": (1) when Ignatius says that his authority is " his [*sic* Christ's] cross, and death, and resurrection. . . . in these I desire to be rightwised by your prayers " (Phila. 8:2). That the influence of the Pauline doctrine of being rightwised by faith is present here can be inferred from the fact that to " cross," " death," and " resurrection " is added " and the faith that is through him "—a co-ordination that, to be sure, is hardly possible for Paul. (2) In Ign. Rom. 5:1 Ignatius cites I Cor. 4:4: " But I am not rightwised thereby " (namely, by the mistreatment which he is suffering and through which he is becoming more and more a " disciple "). Furthermore, the absence of the concept " righteousness " has its counterpart in the almost complete absence of the concept " sin."[12] The heresy against which Ignatius struggles is indeed called " Judaism."[13] But the " Judaizing " that he battles consists in certain ritual observances, like keeping the Sabbath, and not in the Jewish " zeal " to attain righteousness by fulfilling the law. The contrast between " law " or " works " and " grace " or " faith " is missing in Ignatius; and along with it, the Pauline ideas about the significance of the law in the history of salvation—indeed, Paul's whole history-of-salvation perspective—are also absent.[14]

Thus the connection of " righteousness " and " life " that is present in Paul (cf. Rom 5:21) is also missing, and instead of designating Christ as " righteousness and sanctification and redemption " (I Cor. 1:30), it is said in different phrases that he is " our true life " (Smyr. 4:1; cf. Ign. Eph. 3:2; Mag. 1:2) or that he is " the true life in death " (Ign. Eph. 7:2). The result of the work of salvation is " the abolition of death " (Ign. Eph. 19:3); for " death " and " life " are the opposites that govern Ignatius' thinking (cf. Mag. 5:1). Formulations like " whether life or death . . . all are yours " (I Cor. 3:22; cf. Rom. 14:7-9), are for him no longer possible. The Lord's Supper is spoken of as the " medicine of immortality " and the " antidote to dying"; it brings about " living in Jesus Christ forever " (Ign. Eph. 20:2). Those who have faith in Christ escape from death (Tral. 2:1); they are " above death " (Smyr. 3:2). If Ignatius can occasionally speak of " immortality," instead of " life," that in itself is not unPauline (cf. I Cor. 15:53 f.); nor is the concept " imperishableness " foreign to Paul (cf. Rom. 2:7; I Cor. 15:42, 15:50, 15:53 f.), even if it plays a much larger role in Ignatius.[15]

The thought that dominates Ignatius' mind is not the striving for righteousness, but the longing for life; and insofar as this is so, he is more closely related to John than to Paul. With the former he shares a preference for the concept

" truth " and " true." In place of the contrast " death-life,"
one can also find " death-truth " (Smyr. 5 : 1). Ignatius writes
to Polycarp because he is acquainted with his congregation's
fervour for the " truth " (Pol. 7 : 3). He addresses the Phila-
delphians as " children of the light of truth " (Phila. 2 : 1).
Christian living means " to live according to the truth " (Ign.
Eph. 6 : 2). Christ is " our true life " (Smyr. 4 : 1), or simply
" true life " (Ign. Eph. 7 : 2), and the goal of the faithful is
" true life " (Ign. Eph. 11 : 1; Tral. 9 : 2; cf. Ign. Eph. intro. :
" through true suffering "). To be sure, the Johannine antithesis " truth-falsehood " is missing in Ignatius, as is also the
antithesis " light-darkness," although " light " is found twice :
(1) the longing of Ignatius is, through martyrdom, to receive
the " pure light " (Ign. Rom. 6 : 2); and (2) the Philadel-
phians are addressed as " children of the light of truth "
(Phila. 2 : 1).[16]

III

But now how does Ignatius understand the " interim character " of the present? It is by no means merely a chronological
concept for him. Naturally, like Paul, he also lives in the
hope of a future salvation, i.e., the " resurrection ";[17] and as
he can call Christ our " life," he can also call him our
" hope."[18] But does he understand the resurrection of the
dead as an act in a future eschatological drama, if he can say
that Christ through his coming has awakened the prophets
from the dead (Mag. 9 : 2)? In any case, the picture of the
future of the apocalyptic tradition plays no role in his thought,
even if some of the old formulas can still be found.[19] There
is nothing said about the two aeons[20] and just as little about
the future parousia of Christ. Indeed, the parousia is the
appearance in history of Jesus (Phila. 9 : 2; cf. Mag. 9 : 2),
who " was made manifest at the end of time " (Mag. 6 : 1).
Precisely in his historical appearance the cosmic catastrophe

that apocalyptic eschatology looks for in the future has already taken place (Ign. Eph. 19). Whereas the eschatological picture of the future fades, one finds hope directed toward individual salvation, toward "eternal life," "immortality," and "imperishableness."[21]

The thought that with the historical coming of Jesus the cosmic catastrophe has already taken place is not a thought that as such is peculiar to Ignatius. It can be found—in addition to the exemplary statements of Paul (Gal. 4:4) and John (12:31, etc.)—also in Col. 1 and 2; and the designation of the coming of Jesus as his parousia has its parallels in II Tim. 1:10 and Titus 3:11. Nevertheless, for Ignatius, the paradoxical presence of the future salvation is understood in a much more radical way than anywhere else, with the exception of Paul and John—namely, not as a new chance to achieve salvation, but as actually at work in the existence of the faithful. They are "members" of Christ (Ign. Eph. 4:2; Tral. 11:2), or "branches of the cross" (Tral. 11:2); as those who are united in the ecclesia they are the body (Smyr. 1:2) of which he is the head (Tral. 11:2). Thus the whole life of the Christian takes place "in Christ."[22] Through Christ or in him the faithful have for the first time partaken of real existence (Mag. 10:1), while the existence of heretics is only a semblance (Tral. 10; Smyr. 2). But in that case, the resurrection is not only something future, but is paradoxically present. That the "passion" of Christ is our "resurrection" (Smyr. 5:30) and that the gospel is "the perfection of imperishableness" (Phila. 9:2) is to be understood in accordance with Smyr. 7:2: "in which [*sic* the gospel] the passion has been revealed to us and the resurrection has been accomplished." It is the same paradox as in Paul and John: through Jesus Christ death is already overcome and life is a present reality (Rom. 5:12 ff.; John 11:25 f., etc.). This means, however, that Ignatius has grasped the meaning of II Cor. 5:17: "the old has passed away, behold, the new has come." The description of the cosmic catastrophe in Ign.

Eph. 19:3 fully expresses this: "the old kingdom was destroyed, for God was manifest as man for the newness of eternal life."

The old that is now at an end is not simply a heathen life of vice, however certain it is that this also has passed away. Rather it is the dominion of death, whose "destruction" has now begun. Mythologically expressed, it is the dominion of "the prince of this world" (Ign. Eph. 19:1, etc.); but the sphere of his dominion is precisely the sphere of death. That man finds himself under a demonic constraint in this sphere is expressed in the way in which the end of the old is described: "all magic was dissolved and every bond of wickedness vanished away" (Ign. Eph. 19:3). Man's lostness prior to Christ is really understood by Ignatius as fallenness under a power over which he cannot become lord; and his emancipation from it does not mean that he is now made to rely on his own power and must henceforth take care for his salvation through his works, but rather that he now stands under a new power so that the future salvation is already present.

Like Paul, Ignatius can designate the contrast between the old and the new as a contrast between "flesh" and "Spirit." The Christians are "those who are spiritual" and stand over against "those who are carnal" (Ign. Eph. 8:2); and even when he forms the contrast "human-spiritual" (Ign. Eph. 5:1; cf. "according to men" in Tral. 2:1; Ign. Rom. 8:1), he speaks like Paul (I Cor. 3:1, 3:3). The great difference from Paul is that, for Ignatius, the "flesh" is not primarily the sphere of sin, but the sphere of transitoriness and death. He can occasionally speak of "material things" instead of "flesh" (Ign. Rom. 6:2; ct. 7:2). And the latter is the sphere of "what is seen" (Mag. 3:2), or of "the visible" (Ign. Rom. 3:3; Pol. 2:2)—which as expressions, of course, are also Pauline (II Cor. 4:18). However, the agreement between them arises because "flesh" is really conceived by Ignatius as a sphere of power and not merely as sensuality—and, indeed, as a sphere of power that, while it is primarily the sphere of death, nevertheless is not conceived in a simple undialectical way as a strange natural power that stands over against man and overwhelms him, but rather is understood as a sphere that he himself can allow (and prior to Christ actually has allowed) to become a power over him. For even after "flesh" has been done away with for the faithful, it still remains a temptation, so that the admonition to act "according to God" and to do nothing "according to the flesh" is constantly in order (Mag. 6:2); and the either/ or decision between making the "flesh" or the "Spirit" (or "the mind of God") the standard of one's judgment and behaviour still stands (Mag. 6:2; Ign. Rom. 8:3; Phila. 7:1).

What is characteristic for Ignatius is that for the faithful the sphere of the "flesh" as a power is brought to an end in such a way that it is, so to speak, neutralized; i.e., the "flesh" is made fit to be united with the "Spirit" by the fact that Christ has assumed flesh and made it his own, so that his "resurrection" is simultaneously "of the flesh" and "of the Spirit" (Smyr. 12:2). Even as the risen one, he is "in the flesh" (Smyr. 3:1) and therefore is "both flesh and Spirit" (Ign. Eph. 7:2). Thus the bishop also is "flesh and Spirit" (Pol. 2:2), and Ignatius desires for the congregations that they may be "a union of the flesh and Spirit of Jesus Christ" (Mag. 1:2, 13:2; cf. Ign. Rom. intro.) or that they may "remain in Jesus Christ, both in the flesh and in the Spirit" Ign. Eph. 10:3). He gives glory to God because the community at Smyrna is nailed to the cross, "both in flesh and Spirit" (Smyr. 1:1).[23] His thought receives an especially clear expression in Ign. Eph. 8:2. The sentence that formulates the contrast, "they who are carnal cannot do spiritual things, neither can they who are spiritual do carnal things," is followed by the affirmation "but even what you do according to the flesh is spiritual, for you do all things in Jesus Christ." Although such statements are unthinkable for Paul (cf., e.g., II Cor. 10:3), they nevertheless come close to

the meaning of Gal. 2:20 and Phil. 1:22, even if the real
Pauline paradox (cf. espec. II Cor. 4:7 ff.) is thereby surrendered. The Pauline view that flesh as a power is done away
with (Rom. 8:2 ff espec. vs. 9) receives the curious form in
Ingatius' thought that the flesh itself has been brought into
community with the Spirit.

But now, since for Ignatius "flesh" is primarily the sphere
of death, this view has its parallel in the other notion that
through the death and resurrection of Christ death and life
also have been brought together into a unity. And in this,
Ignatius once again comes close to Paul's way of thinking.
Certainly, death and life are opposites (Mag. 5:1). But in
him who chooses "to die through his [*sic* Christ's] passion,"
the "life" of Christ is also actual (Mag. 5:2); for his
"passion" is our "resurrection" (Smyr. 5:3).[24]

Just how this is to be understood becomes clearer when
another motif of Ignatius' thinking is considered—namely,
the significance of the church as a sacramental community that
is led by the bishop as the representative of Christ (Ign. Eph.
6:1; Tral. 2:1) and, indeed, of God himself (Ign. Eph. 5:3;
Mag. 3, 6:1; Phila. 3:2; Smyr. 9:1). No action of the
congregation may be undertaken without the bishop;[25] and no
"strife," "factiousness," or "heresy"[26] may destroy the
community's unity—all of which, of course, is also not un-
Pauline (cf. I Cor. 1:10 ff., 3:16). The salvation that is mediated through the sacraments is available solely in the church
constituted by the episcopal office.

Nevertheless, Ignatius' Christianity may not be dismissed as
mere sacramentalism. For what is peculiar about his thought
is that the whole life of the Christian is drawn into a sacramental unity with Christ and thereby receives a sacramental
character—namely, as participation in Christ's passion, death,
and resurrection.[27] The paradoxical nature of Christ as "both
flesh and Spirit," as "true life in death" (Ign. Eph. 7:2) is
also the nature of the faithful; in them also flesh and Spirit,

death and life are brought into unity. Thus man's becoming God corresponds to God's having become man (Ign. Eph. 7:2, 19:3). To be sure, Ignatius does not speak of "deification"; however, he does speak of "communing with God" (Ign. Eph. 4:2), "being full of God" (Mag. 14), and "being" or "becoming of God" (Mag. 10:1; Ign. Rom. 6:2, 7:1); and the formula "in God" alternates with "in Christ" (Ign. Eph. 1:1; Mag. 3:1; Pol. 6:1), while "God in us" (Ign. Eph. 15:3) corresponds to "Christ in you" (Mag. 12; Ign. Rom. 6:3). As the faithful are "bearers of Christ," so also are they "bearers of God" and "couriers of God" (Ign. Eph. 9:2; Phila. 2:2; Pol. 7:2).

This communion in Christ's death and resurrection that is produced by the sacraments stamps the entire life of the faithful. Symptomatic of this is that Ignatius can designate the faith and love through which the faithful are to let themselves be created anew as the flesh and blood of Christ with which they have become united (Tral. 8:1), and that he can say that those who are nailed to the cross of Christ are confirmed in love by his blood (Smyr. 1:1). Made alive again by the blood of Christ, the Ephesians have performed their appropriate work (Ign. Eph. 1:1). Thus the presence of life does not consist simply in the faithful acquiring through the sacraments some kind of a natural quality, but rather in their whole life acquiring a new movement: it stands under the imperative that is the organic fruit of the indicative. Again and again the twofold reference to faith and love serves to characterize Christian existence;[28] indeed, in the exhortation to be "renewed in faith . . . and in love" (Tral. 8:1), sacramentalism is expressly eliminated in that "faith" is defined as the flesh, and "love" as the blood of Christ. Many times Ignatius affirms that one must not only be *called* a "Christian," but must also *be* one (Mag. 4:1; Ign. Rom. 3:2); that the "Christian" is not lord of himself, but must be at the disposal of God (Pol. 7:3); and that we must "lead Christian lives" (Mag. 10:1) or act "according to the teaching of

Christ " (Phila. 8 : 2). " Christianity " is a great thing, " when it is hated by the world " (Ign. Rom. 3 : 3). The " destruction of death " that has begun with the incarnation of Christ (Ign. Eph. 19 : 3) is actualized in the demeanour of Christians.[29]

If one may say that Ignatius, like Paul, has understood participation in Christ's death and resurrection in its *existentiell* meaning, because he understands it as something that determines the way one leads his life, still he does not achieve the full depth of the Pauline understanding. It is due to his un- or, at least, only half-Pauline understanding of " flesh " that he does not understand being crucified with Christ primarily as the constant struggle against sin and its " passions " and " desires " (Rom. 6 : 6; Gal. 5 : 24, 6 : 14)—even if he does know the opposition between " according to the Lord " and " according to desire " (Pol. 5 : 3; cf. Ign. Rom. 4 : 3, 7 : 1; Pol. 4 : 3) and even if the statement " My lust has been crucified " is explained by the words " I have no pleasure in the food that is perishing or in the delights of this life " (Ign. Rom. 7 : 2 f.). Since " flesh " is primarily the sphere of transitoriness and death, insofar as it is " human flesh " (Phila. 7 : 2) and stands in opposition to God. (Mag. 3 : 2; Ign. Rom. 8 : 3) it is really only done away with by bodily death. Thus freedom is not, as it is with Paul, something that is already present but rather is something future that will first be realized in the resurrection (Ign. Rom. 4 : 3). Thus it is necessary " willingly to choose to die in his passion " (Mag. 5 : 2; cf. Ign. Rom. 6 : 1); and thus also the high point and the really worthy goal of the Christian life for Ignatius is the death of a martyr, in which he will for the first time really " imitate the passion of my God " (Ign. Rom. 6 : 3). Now he but begins to be a disciple (Ign. Eph. 3 : 1; Ign. Rom. 5 : 1, 5 : 3); then he will really be one (Ign. Rom. 4 : 2 f.; Ign. Eph. 1 : 2; Pol. 7 : 1).[30]

Of course, it is not really as though, prior to martyrdom, discipleship is lacking a certain element that has to be added in order to make it quantitatively complete. Rather even now

Ignatius is already potentially or latently the "disciple" he yearns to be, and he but longs to be it really and demonstratively. The "I am not yet perfect" (Ign. Eph. 3:1) or "I am not yet perfected" (Phila. 5:1) have no other meaning than the Pauline "Not that I have already obtained this or am already perfect" (Phil. 3:12). Ignatius knows full well that "being a disciple" is not a quality, is not a secure possession, and that, as long as the end is not yet reached, one must say "I am still in peril" (Tral. 13:3). All "boasting" and all "being puffed up" are excluded;[31] "for the deed is not in present profession, but is shown by the power of faith, if a man continue to the end" (Ign. Eph. 14:2, cf. 17:1). However, what is definitely un-Pauline is that Ignatius sees in martyrdom a kind of guarantee, that he does not simply accept it as ordained by the Lord, but, so to speak, makes it into a work that gives him security, and that he therefore prevails upon the Roman congregation to do nothing to hinder his martyr's death. If for Paul the death of Jesus is at work in his present apostolic life and ministry (II Cor. 4:7 ff.), for Ignatius it is an example to be followed: "Suffer me to imitate the passion of my God" (Ign. Rom. 6:3). For Paul this idea of *imitatio* is completely foreign.[32]

Apart from this, however, Ignatius knows of the Christian's paradoxical existence between the "already" and the "not yet," and he also knows that being a Christian does not necessarily mean being a martyr. He knows the dialectic of Christian existence and can speak to his readers as those who, on the one hand, already *are* "disciples" or "imitators of God (or of the Lord)" (Mag. 10:1; Ign. Eph. 1:1; Tral. 1:2), but, on the other hand, still should *become* such (Mag. 9:1; Ign. Eph. 10:3; Phila. 7:2). They can be characterized in the *indicative* as "being of God" (Ign. Eph. 8:1) and as "in all ways adorned by the commandments of Jesus Christ" (Ign. Eph. 9:2), but also in the *imperative* as those who should "in all things be sanctified" (Ign. Eph. 2:2). The paradox of

Gal. 5 :25 is genuinely paralleled in sentences like the following: "As you are perfect, so also may your counsel be perfect" (Smyr. 11 :3). "Let us therefore do all things as though he were dwelling in us, that we may be his temples, and that he may be our God in us" (Ign. Eph. 15 :3; cf. I Cor. 3 :16, 6 :19). "I know that you are not puffed up; for you have Jesus Christ in yourselves. And I know that when I praise you, your modesty increases the more" (Mag. 12).

CHRISTMAS*

Why is it that we light candles at Christmas and take joy in their splendour? Whatever the historical causes for this custom, they are no longer effective for us. But does this mean, then, that the splendour of the Christmas lights has become merely a festal ornament that somehow belongs to the joyous mood of the holiday? Is it dear to us because as we look at it memories are awakened—memories that reach all the way back to our childhood and are at once sad and happy? Certainly this is so. But is this the only reason or the decisive one?

Whoever is asked why we light candles at Christmas will surely say, if he reflects on it, that the answer is not far to seek; the lights that we kindle are a symbol of *the* Light—the Light that is spoken of in these lines:

> *The eternal Light there enters the world,*
> *And gives it a new appearance.*
> *It shines brightly in the middle of the night*
> *And makes all of us children of light*†

In that case, however, the splendour of the light not only makes us happy in an æsthetic and sentimental sense, but rather, as a symbol, has something to say to us—is, so to speak, a word addresssed to us. But what is it that this world would tell us? Just this, that "the eternal Light" wants to shine into our dark world.

Into our *dark* world? Something, then, is presupposed if we want to understand the meaning of "the eternal Light" that "shines brightly in the middle of the night"—namely, that we actually live in a dark world. But is this so difficult to

* "*Weihnachten,*" *Neue Zürcher Zeitung,* December 25, 1953.
† *Das ewige Licht geht da herein*
  gibt der Welt einen neuen Schein.
  Es leucht' wohl mitten in der Nacht
  und uns des Lichtest Kinder macht.

understand today? It would seem not. For even for those whose security in existence has not been shaken to the same degree as it has in the countries that have been directly touched by the world wars and their consequences, the threatening danger that hangs over us all is not hidden. I refer, of course, to the danger that grows out of political and economic confusions and to the other danger that goes hand in hand with it that arises out of the development of modern technology and its application to the weapons of warfare. Indeed, all that one needs to do today is simply to mention these things.

However, perhaps our situation is not without prospects; perhaps the earnest efforts of responsible men do not remain ineffective. Perhaps, therefore, we are not really " in the middle of the night" and our world is not *completely* dark, but rather is lighted up by a few rays of hope that break through the clouds of darksome fear. But who can deny that this world in which we live is *uncanny*? And is not an uncanny world finally a dark world, a world in which we really do not know which way to turn?

It may well be that we today are especially receptive to the meaning of the symbol of light. But we would deceive ourselves if we were to understand the darkness and uncanniness of the world as merely the characteristic of an epoch that is accidentally our epoch. Is it not rather the case that what has become especially clear and obtrusive in our time is simply the true nature of the world in *all* times—namely, its uncanniness? Was this not known in that old hymn with the words, " *media in vita in morte sumus* "? And is not what is said in the Christian hymn about " the eternal Light" that shines " in the middle of the night" valid for all times, even for times of security?

But what is it, then, that makes our world today so especially uncanny? The mythological images of the devil and of other demonic powers in which man's consciousness of the world's uncanniness was once embodied have faded for us today into mere symbols. And yet it is striking that we rather readily make use of such symbols, that we not infrequently speak of " demonic powers " that domineer men and involve them against their wills in entanglements and wars and lead them to acts that they do not foresee and do not will. Not infrequently we speak of the demonic power of technology, which, with all its accomplishments, also leads to consequences that terrify its masters. Are not these words also true here?

> *Whither do I suddenly see myself led?*
> *Behind me there is no way out, and a wall*
> *Raised up out of my own works,*
> *Towering before me, keeps me from turning back.**

But who permits technology to become a demonic power? And what is the reason more generally that men can, so to speak, be possessed by the things that they think they are able to dispose of, the things that they themselves cause and create? Why is it that men become possessed by the business of work, which is so necessary in order to maintain life, their own as well as that of the community? Why is it that the forces that are released in carrying on such work can become powers that keep the man who is possessed by them from doing what he really wants to do and—as can sometimes terrifyingly come home to him for a moment—also deprive him of his authentic life?

If we look at the total picture of an epoch, even our own, and look only at the men around us, we are at a loss for an answer; and we are also at a loss to know how the destructive tendencies of an age that is possessed can be brought to a halt. But we should first of all not look *around* us, but *in* us! We get no place when we say that the world in which we live is uncanny and dark, but only when we confess that in us ourselves it is also uncanny and dark. "The eternal Light . . . shines brightly in the middle of the night *and makes all of us*

---

* *Wohin denn seh' ich plötzlich mich geführt?*
Bahnlos liegt's hinter mir, und eine Mauer
aus meinen eignen Werken baut sich auf,
die mir die Umkehr türmend hemmt.

children of light!" We achieve a right understanding of "the eternal Light" only when we become aware that we ourselves have to become "children of light."

But should we not say, insofar as we reckon ourselves to belong to the community of the Christian faith, that we already *are* children of light—namely, by reason of our faith? If we do, then we have only very badly understood the meaning of the *eternal* Light. For the eternal Light never becomes a light that belongs to this world. That is, it can never become our possession, a quality of our nature, a property of our character. Always it can only be received—and only be received again and again—as *a gift.* Its rays can and must fall upon us again and again out of eternity, out of that which lies beyond our world.

Yes, it is true: we *are* children of light; and we are such because the Light of divine love and grace that has shone forth for the world in the birth of Jesus Christ always shines for us all. We *are* children of light; and we are such because —in our real selves—we stand before the eyes of God in the light of his grace. We ought not to imagine that we actually are what we appear to be in the eyes of others or even, indeed, in our own eyes. We ought not to imagine this, either in the arrogance of self-satisfaction or in the despondence of self-condemnation. Rather we should believe that our true life is hidden from us. Indeed, even now we are already "children of God," but "it does not yet appear what we shall be" (I John 3:2).

This is what the lights of Christmas want to tell us. We cannot tell it to ourselves, but must rather let it be told to us and simply hear it. This is the message of Christmas, the word that Jesus Christ speaks, the word that he himself is. We are not what we seem to be or what we imagine that we are. Rather we are what we never are here and now; but what we never are here and now—*precisely that is our true being.* This is the Christmas message, this is the Christmas faith.

The "eternal Light" makes us "children of light" by

kindling in us the light of faith. Because of such faith our present uncanny and darksome self need not and cannot any longer frighten us and cause us pain. But it also need not and should not any longer determine how we lead our life. Freedom from it can and should manifest itself in freedom over against everything in our life within the world that tempts and entices us, that makes us anxious and intimidates us—in short, everything that bears within itself the threat of taking possession of us. Thus faith also gives the world " a new appearance." And this, not only in the fact that the world loses its power over him who knows that his true self lies hidden beyond it, but also in the fact that such faith has the power to transform the world. Paul makes the statement that " faith is active in love." But it is precisely love that transforms the world—not, to be sure, in the sense that it contains within itself the programme for a better world order, but in the sense that wherever the light of love shines forth, a brightness and cheerfulness is diffused, a new atmosphere comes into being. Naturally, this never happens without struggle; but it is also never without its victory.

But now have we not also found an answer to the question that was left unanswered above, what the reason is for the fact that demonic powers arise out of the business of our work and domineer us? The reason for this always is *the individual man*. It happens because he loses the knowledge of his true self that lies beyond all of his pains and efforts and, so to speak, waits for him as a gift to which he should open himself. Thus, while Christian love also takes responsibility for the order of the world, its first concern is for the " neighbour," that is, for the ones who are concretely bound to us, who actually encounter us here and now, to help them so that their eyes are opened for the gift that also waits for them.

AUTOBIOGRAPHICAL REFLECTIONS*

I, Rudolf Karl Bultmann, was born on August 20, 1884, in Wiefelstede (in what was at that time the grand duchy of Oldenburg) as the eldest son of the Evangelical-Lutheran pastor Arthur Bultmann and his wife Helene (née Stern). My father came from a peasant family that had its farm in the vicinity of Bremen; his father, in turn, was a missionary, and he himself was born in Freetown, Sierra Leone, West Africa. My maternal grandfather was a pastor in Baden.

The first years of my life were spent in the country; and from 1892 to 1895 I attended the elementary school at Rastede, whither my father had been transferred from Wiefelstede. Then, from 1895 to 1903 I attended the humanistic gymnasium at Oldenburg, where after 1897 my father was pastor at the Lamberti Church. I look back with pleasure on my school years, both in the elementary school and in the gymnasium. What especially interested me while at the latter, in addition to the study in religion, was the instruction in Greek and in the history of German literature. I also avidly attended the theatre and the concerts.

Then in 1903 I passed the final examination at the gymnasium and began the study of theology at Tübingen. After three semesters there, I went to Berlin for two semesters and then finally to Marburg for two more. In addition to attending classes in theology, I heard lectures on philosophy and its history. And while in Berlin, I especially enjoyed the theatre and concerts and the museums. The theological teachers to whom I am particularly indebted were, at Tübingen, the

* "*Lebenslauf,*" Marburg. January 28, 1956. (This brief autobiographical statement, which was originally prepared by Professor Bultmann at our request, is published here for the first time.)

church historian Karl Müller; at Berlin, the Old Testament scholar Hermann Gunkel and the historian of dogma Adolf Harnack; and at Marburg, the New Testament scholars Adolf Jülicher and Johannes Weiss and the systematic theologian Wilhelm Herrmann. Johannes Weiss encouraged me to prepare him for the doctorate and to qualify as a lecturer in the field of New Testament.

Before I actually did so, however, I passed my first theological examination under the High Consistory in Oldenburg in 1907 and, largely for reasons of expediency, was engaged there for a year (1906-7) as a teacher in the gymnasium. When, then, in the autumn of 1907 I received a scholarship to Marburg (to the *Seminarium Philippinum*), it became possible for me to proceed to work toward my degrees and my qualification. In 1910 I was awarded my degree (*Lic. theol.*) with a work on *Der Stil der paulinischen Predigt und kynischstoische Diatribe,* the theme for which had been proposed to me by Johannes Weiss. The theme for my qualification research, *Die Exegese des Theodor von Mopsuestia,* was proposed by Adolf Jülicher. Upon the completion of it in 1912, I was qualified as a lecturer in the field of New Testament at Marburg and taught there as Instructor until the autumn of 1916. When in 1908 my teacher Johannes Weiss had been called to Heidelberg, he had been succeeded by Wilhelm Heitmüller, with whom I soon came into friendly association and to whom I am likewise greatly indebted. I also spent a great deal of time during these years in the home of Martin Rade. I was a zealous reader of the journal, *Die Christliche Welt,* of which he was the editor, and a member of The Association of the Friends of *Die Christliche Welt* and regularly attended its great annual meetings (as did my father also as long as he lived). There one met the theologians of free Protestantism and was introduced to the discussions that stirred theology and the church in the years immediately before and after the First World War. I myself have personally experienced a considerable part of the history that Johannes Rathje has de-

picted in his biography of Rade, *Die Welt des freien Protestant-
ismus* (1952).

In the autumn of 1916 I was called to Breslau as Assistant
Professor and was active there until 1920. It was there also
that I was married and that our first two daughters were born.
The last years of the war, as well as the ones that immediately
followed it, were hard times that laid many privations on us
and in which we saw a lot of need and misery. In 1917 my
youngest brother was killed in France. But we also experienced much friendship and help. It was in Breslau that I
wrote my *Geschichte der synoptischen Tradition,* which was
published in 1921.

In the autumn of 1920 I was called to Giessen as full
Professor and as the successor of Wilhelm Bousset. I look
back on the time there with particular joy, inasmuch as the
friendly interchange with my colleagues, and not only with
those of the theological faculty, was especially lively. In fact,
it was not easy to leave Giessen; but I was convinced that I
could not turn down the call to go to Marburg, which is, so to
speak, my scientific home, and so in the autumn of 1921 I
returned there as the successor of Wilhelm Heitmüller. I
have remained at Marburg ever since, having turned down a
call to go to Leipzig in 1930, and became emeritus there in the
autumn of 1951.

The years at Marburg were troubled ones in consequence
of the change in political affairs and the outbreak of the
Second World War in 1939. During the twenties the external
conditions of life were more and more improved; and in 1924
our third daughter was born. The work with the students,
among whom the motives of the Youth Movement of the beginning of the century were still alive, was highly satisfying.
Then came the time of the Hitler regime with its coercion and
its pernicious methods. Life in the university and in the community at large was poisoned by mistrust and denunciations.
One could enjoy mutual openness and growth through common participation in the world of the spirit only within a

small circle of like-minded acquaintances; and many Jewish friends were forced to emigrate. It was during the war, however, that the Nazi terror really pressed down upon us. In the course of it my sole surviving brother died in a concentration camp. When the Allies (in Marburg, the Americans) finally marched in, I, along with many friends, greeted this end of the Nazi rule as a liberation. To be sure, the years immediately after 1945 were not an easy time either, although our external needs were considerably lightened by good gifts from abroad; and we must always think with gratitude of those, partly known and partly unknown, who sent them. It cannot be denied that, at first, many blunders on the part of the occupation made the achievement of a new community life and healthy political relations more difficult. But a confident cooperation with the American occupation was nevertheless possible, inasmuch as there was never a lack of good will on both sides to overcome the difficulties. Especially must I always be grateful to the American university officials who worked for the reorganization of the University. Ideal conditions have not been reached even today, and much old resentment is still at work; but the burden that oppressed us from 1933 to 1945 has definitely been taken from us. New cares are awakened by the present political situation, but I will not go into such questions here, especially since I have never directly and actively participated in political affairs. I will simply try to give a survey of my theological work during the Marburg years.

When I first came to Marburg I taught alongside Adolf Jülicher and did so until his retirement in 1923. His successor was Hans von Soden with whom, until his death in 1945, I was bound together in personal friendship and constantly engaged in scientific discussion. The same is true of my relationship to Gustav Hölscher, the Old Testament scholar, with whom I had already worked at Giessen and who came to Marburg in 1921 as the successor of Karl Budde. I was likewise close to Walter Baumgartner, who at that time was an Instructor. The point of view of the theological faculty in those days was not a unified one, and the oppositions within it, especially the tension between myself and Rudolf Otto (the successor of Wilhelm Herrmann), stirred even the students and led to lively discussions. These became especially animated whenever theologians from other universities, like Karl Barth and Friedrich Gogarten, were invited to Marburg to lecture. They were also enriched by the fact, however, that the interchange between theologians and philosophers was very lively (just as it had been earlier in the days of Wilhelm Herrmann, Hermann Cohen, and Paul Natorp). This was particularly the case when Martin Heidegger taught at Marburg from 1922 to 1928. I soon entered into discussion with him, just as I had done previously with Nicolai Hartmann and was to do subsequently with Erich Frank and Julius Ebbinghaus. There was also fruitful co-operation with the instructors in philosophy who were interested in theology: Hans-Georg Gadamer, Gerhard Krüger, and Karl Löwith; and in this the New Testament instructors, Heinrich Schlier and Günther Bornkamm, also participated. I must especially mention, however, that I also owe very much to my friendly relationship with the classical philologist Paul Friedländer, who was also teaching at Marburg at that time.

So far as concerns the publications that grew out of my work at Marburg, I may refer to the bibliography that has been published in *Theologische Rundschau* (1954). In the years before the Second World War there were several occasions for travelling outside of Germany. I was invited to give lectures in the Scandinavian countries, in Holland, and in Switzerland. Then, after the war, in 1947, I was invited to Sweden for eight weeks by the Swedish Institute for Cultural Exchange; and I think back on this with particular gratitude. I experienced much human goodness, enjoyed the possibility of scientific discussion, and was able to acquaint myself with the foreign literature in my field from which we had been cut off during the war. A great experience was mine, then, in

1951 when I spent three months in the United States, whither
I had been invited by different universities and theological
schools. The opportunity to meet and to discuss with
American scholars was of great value to me.

All such discussion, both at Marburg and elsewhere, has
furthered me not only in my special field of New Testament,
but also in my theological thinking in general. I have personally lived through important shifts both in the history of
recent theology and in the history of modern philosophy—
shifts that stand in a peculiar parallelism. In 1919 Karl
Barth's *Römerbrief* appeared, and from the beginning of the
twenties his influence on theological work steadily grew. Then
in 1920 Gogarten delivered his lecture on *" Die Krisis unserer
Kultur "* to the annual gathering of The Friends of *Die
Christliche Welt.* From 1923 on there appeared the journal
Zwischen den Zeiten, which was edited by Barth, Gogarten,
and Thurneysen as the organ of this new theological movement, which soon came to be designated as the " dialectical
theology." I attempted to enter into discussion with this
theology, first, in the essay *" Die liberale Theologie und die
jüngste theologische Bewegung "* (1924) and then, later, in
the lecture *" Die Bedeutung der ' dialektischen Theologie ' für
die neutestamentliche Wissenschaft "* (1927).[1] I also con-
tributed to the journal *Zwischen den Zeiten.* It seemed to me
that in this new theological movement it was rightly recognized, as over against the " liberal " theology out of which I
had come, that the Christian faith is not a phenomenon of the
history of religion, that it does not rest on a " religious *a
priori* " (Troeltsch), and that therefore theology does not have
to look upon it as a phenomenon of religious or cultural
history. It seemed to me that, as over against such a view, the
new theology had correctly seen that Christian faith is the
answer to the word of the transcendent God that encounters
man and that theology has to deal with this word and the
man who has been encountered by it. This judgment, however,
has never led me to a simple condemnation of " liberal "

theology; on the contrary, I have endeavoured throughout my entire work to carry further the tradition of historical-critical research as it was practised by the " liberal " theology and to make our more recent theological knowledge fruitful for it.

In doing so, the work of existential philosophy, which I came to know through my discussion with Martin Heidegger, has become of decisive significance for me. I found in it the conceptuality in which it is possible to speak adequately of human existence and therefore also of the existence of the believer. However, in my efforts to make philosophy fruitful for theology, I have more and more come into opposition to Karl Barth. Nevertheless, I remain grateful to him for the decisive things I have learned from him! and I am convinced that a final clarification of our relationship (toward which Heinrich Ott has made a beautiful beginning in his book, *Geschichte und Heilsgeschichte in der Theologie Rudolf Bultmanns* [1955]) has not as yet been reached. On the other hand, the community in theological intentions between Gogarten and myself has become more and more apparent.

Finally, I must mention that my work during the Hitler régime was fructified by the struggle of the church. I have belonged to the Confessing Church since its founding in 1934, and, with my friend Von Soden, have endeavoured to see that in it also free scientific work retained its proper place in face of reactionary tendencies.

IS EXEGESIS WITHOUT
PRESUPPOSITIONS POSSIBLE?*

The question whether exegesis without presuppositions is possible must be answered affirmatively if "without presuppositions" means "without presupposing the results of the exegesis." In this sense, exegesis without presuppositions is not only possible but demanded. In another sense, however, *no* exegesis is without presuppositions, inasmuch as the exegete is not a *tabula rasa,* but on the contrary, approaches the text with specific questions or with a specific way of raising questions and thus has a certain idea of the subject matter with which the text is concerned.[1]

I

1. The demand that exegesis must be without presuppositions, in the sense that it must not presuppose its results (we can also say that it must be without prejudice), may be clarified only briefly. This demand means, first of all, the rejection of allegorical interpretation.[2] When Philo finds the Stoic idea of the apathetic wise man in the prescription of the law that the sacrificial animal must be without blemish (*Spec. Neg.* I, 260), then it is clear that he does not hear what the text actually says, but only lets it say what he already knows. And the same thing is true of Paul's exegesis of Deut. 25:4 as a prescription that the preachers of the gospel are to be supported by the congregations (I Cor. 9:9) and of the interpretation in the Letter of Barnabas (9:7 f.) of the 318

* "*Ist voraussetzungslose Exegese möglich?*" Theologische Zeitschrift, xiii (1957), 409-17.

servants of Abraham (Gen. 14:14) as a prophecy of the cross of Christ.

2. However, even where allegorical interpretation is renounced, exegesis is frequently guided by prejudices.[3] This is so, for example, when it is presupposed that the evangelists Matthew and John were Jesus' personal disciples and that therefore the narratives and sayings of Jesus that they hand down must be historically true reports. In this case, it must be affirmed, for instance, that the cleansing of the temple, which in Matthew is placed during Jesus' last days just before his passion, but in John stands at the beginning of his ministry, took place twice. The question of an unprejudiced exegesis becomes especially urgent when the problem of Jesus' messianic consciousness is concerned. May exegesis of the gospels be guided by the dogmatic presupposition that Jesus was the Messiah and was conscious of being so? Or must it rather leave this question open? The answer should be clear. Any such messianic consciousness would be a historical fact and could only be exhibited as such by historical research. Were the latter able to make it probable that Jesus knew himself to be the Messiah, this result would have only relative certainty; for historical research can never endow it with absolute validity. All knowledge of a historical kind is subject to discussion, and therefore, the question as to whether Jesus knew himself as Messiah remains open. Every exegesis that is guided by dogmatic prejudices does not hear what the text says, but only lets the latter say what it wants to hear.

II

1. The question of exegesis without presuppositions in the sense of unprejudiced exegesis must be distinguished from this same question in the other sense in which it can be raised. And in this second sense, we must say that *there cannot be any*

such thing as presuppositionless exegesis. That there is no such exegesis in fact, because every exegete is determined by his own individuality, in the sense of his special biases and habits, his gifts and his weaknesses, has no significance in principle. For in this sense of the word, it is precisely his " individuality " that the exegete ought to eliminate by educating himself to the kind of hearing that is interested in nothing other than the subject matter of which the text speaks. However, the one presupposition that cannot be dismissed is *the historical* method of interrogating the text. Indeed, exegesis as the interpretation of historical texts is a part of the science of history.

It belongs to the historical method, of course, that a text is interpreted in accordance with the rules of grammar and of the meaning of words. And closely connected with this, historical exegesis also has to inquire about the individual style of the text. The sayings of Jesus in the synoptics, for example, have a different style from the Johannine ones. But with this there is also given another problem with which exegesis is required to deal. Paying attention to the meaning of words, to grammar, and to style soon leads to the observation that every text speaks in the language of its time and of its historical setting. This the exegete must know; therefore, he must know the historical conditions of the language of the period out of which the text that he is to interpret has arisen. This means that for an understanding of the language of the New Testament the acute question is, " Where and to what extent is its Greek determined by the Semitic use of language?" Out of this question grows the demand to study apocalypticism, the rabbinic literature, and the Qumran texts, as well as the history of Hellenistic religion.

Examples at this point are hardly necessary, and I cite only one. The New Testament word πνεῦμα is translated in German as " *Geist.*" Thus it is understandable that the exegesis of the nineteenth century (e.g., in the Tübingen school) interpreted the New Testament on the basis of the idealism that goes back to ancient Greece, until Hermann Gunkel pointed out in 1888 that the New Testament πνεῦμα meant something entirely different—namely, God's miraculous power and manner of action.[4]

The historical method includes the presupposition that history is a unity in the sense of a closed continuum of effects in which individual events are connected by the succession of cause and effect. This does not mean that the process of history is determined by the casual law and that there are no free decisions of men whose actions determine the course of historical happenings. But even a free decision does not happen without a cause, without a motive; and the task of the historian is to come to know the motives of actions. All decisions and all deeds have their causes and consequences; and the historical method presupposes that it is possible in principle to exhibit these and their connection and thus to understand the whole historical process as a closed unity.

This closedness means that the continuum of historical happenings cannot be rent by the interference of supernatural, transcendent powers and that therefore there is no "miracle" in this sense of the word. Such a miracle would be an event whose cause did not lie within history. While, for example, the Old Testament narrative speaks of an interference by God in history, historical science cannot demonstrate such an act of God, but merely perceives that there are those who believe in it. To be sure, as historical science, it may not assert that such a faith is an illusion and that God has not acted in history. But it itself as science cannot perceive such an act and reckon on the basis of it; it can only leave every man free to determine whether he wants to see an act of God in a historical event that it itself understands in terms of that event's immanent historical causes.

It is in accordance with such a method as this that the science of history goes to work on all historical documents. And there cannot be any exceptions in the case of biblical texts if the latter are at all to be understood historically. Nor can one object that the biblical writings do not intend to be historical documents, but rather affirmations of faith and proclamation. For however certain this may be, if they are ever to be understood as such, they must first of all be interpreted historically, inasmuch as they speak in a strange language in concepts of a faraway time, of a world-picture that is alien to us. Put quite simply, they must be *translated,* and translation is the task of historical science.

2. If we speak of translation, however, then the hermeneutical problem at once presents itself.[5] To translate means to make understandable, and this in turn presupposes an understanding. The understanding of history as a continuum of effects presupposes an understanding of the efficient forces that connect the individual historical phenomena. Such forces are economic needs, social exigencies, the political struggle for power, human passions, ideas, and ideals. In the assessment of such factors historians differ, and in every effort to achieve a unified point of view the individual historian is guided by some specific way of raising questions, some specific perspective.

This does not mean a falsification of the historical picture, provided that the perspective that is presupposed is not a prejudice, but a way of raising questions, and that the historian is self-conscious about the fact that his way of asking questions is one-sided and only comes at the phenomenon or the text from the standpoint of a particular perspective. The historical picture is falsified only when a specific way of raising questions is put forward as the only one—when, for example, all history is reduced to economic history. Historical phenomena are many-sided. Events like the Reformation can be observed from the standpoint of church history as well as political history, of economic history as well as the history of philosophy. Mysticism can be viewed from the standpoint of its significance for the history of art, etc. However, some specific way of raising questions is always presupposed if history is at all to be understood.

But even more, the forces that are effective in connecting phenomena are understandable only if the phenomena themselves that are thereby connected are also understood! This means that an understanding of the subject matter itself belongs to historical understanding. For can one understand political history without having a concept of the state and of justice, which by their very nature are not historical products but ideas? Can one understand economic history without having a concept of what economy and society in general mean? Can one understand the history of religion and philosophy without knowing what religion and philosophy are? One cannot understand Luther's posting of the ninety-five theses, for instance, without understanding the actual meaning of protest against the Catholicism of his time. One cannot understand the Communist Manifesto of 1848 without understanding the principles of capitalism and socialism. One cannot understand the decisions of persons who act in history if one does not understand man and his possibilities for action. In short, historical understanding presupposes an understanding of the subject matter of history itself and of the men who act in history.

This is also to say, however, that historical understanding always presupposes a relation of the interpreter to the subject matter that is (directly or indirectly) expressed in the texts. This relation is grounded in the actual life-context in which the interpreter stands. Only he who lives in a state and in a society can understand the political and social phenomena of the past and their history, just as only he who has a relation to music can understand a text that deals with music, etc.

Therefore, a specific understanding of the subject matter of the text, on the basis of a " life-relation " to it, is always presupposed by exegesis; and insofar as this is so no exegesis is without presuppositions. I speak of this understanding as a " preunderstanding." It as little involves prejudices as does the choice of a perspective. For the historical picture is falsified only when the exegete takes his preunderstanding as a definitive understanding. The "life-relation" is a genuine one, however, only when it is vital, i.e., when the subject matter with which the text is concerned also concerns us and is a problem for us. If we approach history alive with our own problems, then it really begins to speak to us. Through discussion the past becomes alive, and in learning to know history we learn to know our own present; historical knowledge is at the same time knowledge of ourselves. To understand history is possible only for one who does not stand over against it as a neutral, nonparticipating spectator, but himself stands in history and shares in responsibility for it. We speak of this encounter with history that grows out of one's own historicity as the *existentiell* encounter. The historian participates in it with his whole existence.

This *existentiell* relation to history is the fundamental presupposition for understanding history.[6] This does not mean that the understanding of history is a "subjective" one in the sense that it depends on the individual pleasure of the historian and thereby loses all objective significance. On the contrary, it means that history precisely in its objective content can only be understood by a subject who is *existentiell* moved and alive. It means that, for historical understanding, the schema of subject and object that has validity for natural science is invalid.[7]

Now what has just been said includes an important insight —namely, that historical knowledge is never a closed or definitive knowledge—any more than is the preunderstanding with which the historian approaches historical phenomena. For if the phenomena of history are not facts that can be neutrally observed, but rather open themselves in their meaning only to one who approaches them alive with questions, then they are always only understandable now in that they actually speak in the present situation. Indeed, the questioning itself grows out of the historical situation, out of the claim of the now, out of the problem that is given in the now. For this reason, historical research is never closed, but rather must always be carried further. Naturally, there are certain items of historical knowledge that can be regarded as definitively known—namely, such items as concern only dates that can be fixed chronologically and locally, as, for example, the assassination of Cæsar or Luther's posting of the ninety-five theses. But what these events that can thus be dated *mean* as historical events cannot be definitively fixed. Hence one must say that a historical event is always first knowable for what it is—precisely as a historical event—in the future. And therefore one can also say that the future of a historical event belongs to that event.

Naturally, items of historical knowledge can be passed on, not as definitively known, but in such a way as to clarify and expand the following generation's preunderstanding. But even so, they are subject to the criticism of that generation. Can we today surmise the meaning of the two world wars? No! for it holds good that what a historical event means always first becomes clear in the future. It can definitively disclose itself only when history has come to an end.

III

What are the consequences of this analysis for exegesis of the biblical writings? They may be formulated in the following theses :

1. The exegesis of the biblical writings, like every other interpretation of a text, must be unprejudiced.

2. However, the exegesis is not without presuppositions, because as historical interpretation it presupposes the method of historical-critical research.

3. Furthermore, there is presupposed a " life-relation " of the exegete to the subject matter with which the Bible is concerned and, together with this relation, a preunderstanding.

4. This understanding is not a closed one, but rather is open, so that there can be an *existentiell* encounter with the text and an *existentiell* decision.

5. The understanding of the text is never a definitive one, but rather remains open because the meaning of the Scriptures discloses itself anew in every future.

In the light of what has already been said, nothing further is required in the way of comment on the first and second theses.

As regards the third thesis, however, we may note that the preunderstanding has its basis in the question concerning God that is alive in human life. Thus it does not mean that the exegete must know everything possible about God, but rather that he is moved by the *existentiell* question for God— regardless of the form that this question actually takes in his consciousness (say, for example, as the question concerning "salvation," or escape from death, or certainty in the face of a constantly shifting destiny, or truth in the midst of a world that is a riddle to him).

With regard to the fourth thesis, we may note that the *existentiell* encounter with the text can lead to a yes as well as to a no, to confessing faith as well as to express unfaith, because in the text the exegete encounters a claim, i.e., is there offered a self-understanding that he can accept (permit to be given to him) or reject, and therefore is faced with the demand for decision. Even in the case of a no, however, the understanding is a legitimate one, i.e., is a genuine answer to the question of the text, which is not to be refuted by argument because it is an *existentiell* decision.

So far as the fifth thesis is concerned, we note simply that because the text speaks to existence it is never understood in a definitive way. The *existentiell* decision out of which the interpretation emerges cannot be passed on, but must always be realized anew. This does not mean, of course, that there cannot be continuity in the exegesis of Scripture. It goes without saying that the results of methodical historical-critical esearch can be passed on, even if they can only be taken ver by constant critical testing. But even with respect to the xegesis that is based *existentiell* there is also continuity, nsofar as it provides guidance for the next generation—as has een done, for example, by Luther's understanding of the auline doctrine of justification by faith alone. Just as this nderstanding must constantly be achieved anew in the discussion with Catholic exegesis, so every genuine exegesis that ffers itself as a guide is at the same time a question that must lways be answered anew and independently. Since the xegete exists historically and must hear the word of Scripture s spoken in his special historical situation, he will always nderstand the old word anew. Always anew it will tell him vho he, man, is and who God is, and he will always have to xpress this word in a new conceptuality. Thus it is true also f Scripture that it only is what it is with its history and its uture.

NOTES

INTRODUCTION

[1] Cf. Karl Barth, *Rudolf Bultmann: Ein Versuch, ihn zu verstehen* (2nd ed., 1953), pp. 41 ff.

[2] Markus Barth, "Die Methode von Bultmanns 'Theologie des Neuen Testaments,'" *Theologische Zeitschrift*, xi (1955), 1.

[3] Ibid.

[4] This is true not only of G. W. Davis's *Existentialism and Theology* (1957), which makes use only of works available in English, but even of John Macquarrie's excellent "comparison of Bultmann and Heidegger," *An Existentialist Theology* (1955). And the same is also true of Ian Henderson, *Myth in the New Testament* (1952); G. V. Jones, *Christology and Myth in the New Testament* (1956); and B. H. Throckmorton, *The New Testament and Mythology* (1959). The one exception is H. P. Owen, *Revelation and Existence* (1957), though even here the use of earlier works is quite limited.

[5] Op. cit., pp. 235 and 243.

[6] For a more detailed discussion of the relationship between "demythologization" and "dialectical theology," see my article, "The Debate on 'Demythologizing,'" *The Journal of Bible and Religion*, xxvii (1959), 17-27.

[7] Macquarrie, op. cit., p. 179; cf. also pp. 23 and 80.

[8] Ibid. Cf. the similar views of Henderson, op. cit., p. 49, and Jones, op. cit., pp. 122 and 163. Cf. also the entry "Bultmann, Rudolf," in *The Oxford Dictionary of the Christian Church*, ed. by F. L. Cross (2nd imp., 1958), pp. 206 f.

[9] Cf. espec. the important concluding pages (211-19) of *Jesus and the Word* (1934); 2nd ed. (1958). Cf. also *Theology of the New Testament*, i (1951), 43 ff.

[10] Cf., e.g., *Glauben und Verstehen*, i (1933; 2nd ed., 1954), 265 f.: "Whether Jesus knew himself to be Messiah or not is indifferent. It would only mean that he had become conscious of the decisive character of his work in terms of a contemporary Jewish idea. To be sure, his summons to decision does imply a christology, although not in the sense of metaphysical speculation about a heavenly being or a character sketch of his personality as having a messianic self-consciousness. Rather it is a christology that is proclamation or personal address. Therefore, if the early community designates Jesus as 'the Messiah,' it but expresses in its own way that it has understood him. . . . The proclaimer has to become the one proclaimed because the decisive thing about his proclamation is its 'that,' i.e., its happening here and now as an event, its being spoken in commission, its character

as personal address—in short, Jesus' person, though not his personality."

11 This is not to say, of course, that he has also affirmed a continuity in the *forms of expression* in which the historical Jesus and
the subsequent Christian community articulated their essentially common self-understanding. On the contrary, as the careful historian he is,
he has tried to give full weight to what seem to him to be important
differences in such forms of expression.

12 Cf. James M. Robinson, *The New Quest of the Historical Jesus*
(1959).

13 This question is even raised, though no doubt unintentionally,
by Robinson himself when he speaks of " an undercurrent in Bultmann's writings which already moves in [the] direction [of the new
quest]" (ibid., p. 19 and espec. the long footnote). The question must
be pressed whether what Robinson speaks of here as an " undercurrent " is not really the " main stream " of the " classical Bult-
mannian position."

14 " *Das Problem einer theologischen Exegese des Neuen Testaments,*" *Zwischen den Zeiten,* iii (1925), 340.

15 *Der Römerbrief* (2nd ed., 1922), p. xii (Eng. trans. by Edwyn
C. Hoskyns in *The Epistle to the Romans* [1933], p. 10).

16 Cf. Heinrich Ott, *Geschichte und Heilsgeschichte in der Theologie Rudolf Bultmanns* (1955).

17 Cf. *Kerygma und Mythos,* ii (1952), 196 f. (Eng. trans. by R. H.
Fuller in *Kerygma and Myth* [1953], pp. 196 f.); cf. also the parallel
passages in *Jesus Christ and Mythology,* pp. 68 f.

18 Cf. " Humanism and Christianity," *The Journal of Religion,*
xxxii (1952), 77-86.

19 Cf. *Glauben und Verstehen,* ii (1952), 243 f. (Eng. trans. by
J. C. G. Greig in *Essays, Philosophical and Theological* [1955], pp.
270 f.).

20 *Glauben und Verstehen,* ii, 146 (Eng. trans. pp. 165 f.).

21 Cf. *Jesus Christ and Mythology,* pp. 62 f.

22 Macquarrie, for example, ignores the point completely; and the
same is true of Jones.

23 Cf. *Kerygma und Mythos,* ii, 207 f. (Eng. trans. pp. 210 f.). Cf.
also *Jesus Christ and Mythology,* pp. 83 ff.

24 In his remarks below " on behalf of Christian freedom," Bultmann points out that " ' pure doctrine ' is an ' eschatological ' thing "
and infers that *all* theology is nothing other than a " contribution
to the discussion." Cf. also *Theology of the New Testament,* ii
(1955), 237-41.

25 These are Bultmann's exact words in *Kerygma und Mythos,* ii,
184. Cf. also *Kerygma und Mythos,* i (2nd ed., 1951), 22 f., espec. n.
2 (Eng. trans. by R. H. Fuller in *Kerygma and Myth* [1953], pp.
10 f.).

26 Cf. Kendrick Grobel, "Bultmann's Problem of New Testament 'Mythology,'" *Journal of Biblical Literature* lxx (1951), 99 f.

27 *Jesus Christ and Mythology*, p. 55 and *Kerygma und Mythos*, i, 124 (Eng. trans. p. 104).

28 Cf., e.g., *The Oxford Dictionary of the Christian Church*, p. 206.

29 Cf., e.g., "The Christian Hope and the Problem of Demythologizing," *The Expository Times*, lxv (1954), 228-30; 276-8.

30 Cf. espec. "Theology for Freedom and Responsibility," *The Christian Century*, lxxv (1958), 967-9.

31 Cf. *Kerygma und Mythos*, i, 44-8 (Eng. trans., pp. 38-43).

32 Cf. *Jesus Christ and Mythology*, pp. 68 and 78.

33 Cf. espec. *Kerygma und Mythos*, i, 31-40 (Eng. trans., pp. 22-33). The issue here is not whether God's act and man's authentic response only take place as "event" (for that *is* clearly implied by the basic dialectic), but whether it is only through Jesus Christ that this decisive event of divine-human encounter can be actualized.

34 Cf. the more extended argument in my article, "Bultmann's Project of Demythologization and the Problem of Theology and Philosophy," *The Journal of Religion*, xxxvii (1957), 156-73.

35 Cf. the article referred to *supra* in n. 6.

36 Cf. the way Bultmann himself criticizes Paul's statements regarding the salvation-occurrence in the light of Paul's own "real intention" (*Theology of the New Testament*, i, 300 ff.).

THE NEW APPROACH TO THE SYNOPTIC SYSTEM

1 I may, however, at this point call the attention of those who are interested in the subject to additional literature in which the problems of *Formgeschichte* are discussed. Important contributions are: M. Dibelius, *Formgeschichte des Evangeliums* (1919), and K. L. Schmidt's *Die Stellung der Evangelien in der allgemeinen Literaturgeschichte* (in the second volume of the *Eucharisterion*, memorial volume in honour of H. Gunkel [1923]). These books make positive contributions toward the solution of the problems of *Formgeschichte*. E. Fascher's book, *Die formgeschichtliche Methode* (1924), is an investigation that makes adverse criticisms of *Formgeschichte*.

In addition there are numerous studies of special problems. Material for the investigation of the miracle stories is found in O. Weinreich's *Antike Heilungswunder* (1909), and P. Fiebig's *Jüdische Wundergeschichten des neutestamentlichen Zeitalters* (1911). The transmission of the miracle stories is investigated in a book by the Norwegian scholar A. Fridrichsen, *Le Problème du Miracle dans le Christianisme primitif* (1925). Important studies of the *apophthegmata* are M. Albertz's *Die synoptischen Streitgespräche* (1921), and P. Fiebig's *Der Erzählungsstil der Evangelien* (1925). Rabbinic material to be compared with the utterances of Jesus was collected by P. Fiebig in three volumes, namely, *Altjüdische Gleichnisse* (1904), *Die Gleichnissreden Jesu* (1912), and *Jesu Bergpredigt* (1924). *Formgeschichtliche* investigations of the passion and resurrection of Jesus have been made by G. Bertram, *Die Leidengeschichte Jesu und der Christuskult* (1922), and L. Brun, *Die Auferstehung Christi in der urchristlichen Ueberlieferung* (1925).

FAITH AS VENTURE

[1] [Martin Rade (1857-1940).]
[2] Cf. *Die Christliche Welt,* xlii (1928), 545 f.

THE CONCEPT OF REVELATION IN THE NEW TESTAMENT

[1] Cf. Emil Brunner, *Der Mittler* (1927), pp. 3 f. [Eng. trans. by Olive Wyon in *The Mediator* (1948), pp. 21 f.] Since Brunner neglects to clarify the question by reflecting on the concept of revelation that guides it, he does not succeed in making the differentiations of the religious concept of revelation radically transparent. Edward Thurneysen, *Zwischen den Zeiten,* vi (1928), 453 f., intimates such differentiations without going into them. Max Weiner, *" Zur Geschichte des Offenbarungsbegriffs "* (*Judaica,* Festschrift for Hermann Cohen's seventieth birthday [1912]), p. 1, characteristically grasps only one side of the matter when he defines revelation as a " knowledge that does not owe its origin to the ' natural ' powers of the human spirit, which everywhere manifest themselves in the management of life, but rather is looked upon as a knowledge that somehow flows immediately from the source by an inspiration that is derived from God."

[2] Cf. Jacob Burckhardt, *Weltgeschichtliche Betrachtungen* (Kröner edition), p. 58 : " At the peak of culture stands a spiritual miracle: the languages whose origin lies in the soul independently of an individual people and its individual language; otherwise one could never bring a deaf-mute to speak and to understand language."

[3] This in no way prejudices the question whether we can speak of revelation in a positive sense. For the revelation that we always already know could be something merely negative. I could also say that the *question* concerning revelation belongs to our life, were this statement not open to the misunderstanding that this question is possibly idle and fantastic.

[4] Brunner, op. cit., pp. 4 f. [Eng. trans., pp. 22 f.]

[5] It may be quickly shown in individual cases that the verbs that we

translate with " to reveal," like the cognate substantives, do not designate an illuminating instruction, but rather an act of God or an occurrence. To be sure, this occurrence provides the basis for a knowledge that man can make explicit; but such knowledge can also remain concealed. Cf., e.g., for ἀποκαλύπτειν Rom. 1:17 f., 2:5; I Cor. 1:7; Gal. 3:23; and for φανεροῦν Rom. 3:21; II Cor. 4:10 f.

⁶ Cf. my essay, "*Kirche und Lehre im Neuen Testament*," *Zwischen den Zeiten,* vii (1929), 9.43. [This essay is also reprinted as pp. 153-87 of *Glauben und Verstehen,* i (2nd ed.; 1954).]

⁷ It is, of course, completely clear that the New Testament writings often enough speak of the event of revelation in a mythological way and that they frequently fail to bring its character as something present to conceptually clear expression. Thus it sometimes appears to be a temporal event in the past and at other times an event that is temporally future. However, the intention that is most clearly apparent in Paul and John is probably determinative everywhere else: what is to be affirmed is the actual presentness of the salvation-occurrence. And the simplest mythological expression for this is provided by eschatology.

⁸ The salvation-occurrence is also made present in the sacraments, which have their meaning precisely in that through them this occurrence becomes present uniquely to the individual. They therefore stand alongside of the word, even as Paul can also designate the celebration of the Lord's Supper as a proclamation of the gospel (I Cor. 11:26).

⁹ Cf. my essay, "*Die Eschatologie des Johannesevangeliums,*" *Zwischen den Zeiten,* vi (1928), 4-22. [This essay is also reprinted as pp. 134-52 of *Glauben und Verstehen,* i (2nd ed., 1954).]

¹⁰ Ibid., pp. 6-9.

¹¹ "*Et ita Deus per suum exire nos facit ad nos ipsos introire et per sui cognitionem infert nobis et nostri cognitionem.*" Scholia to Rom. 3:5 ed. Ficker, pp. 67, 21-3. Cf. pp. 136, 18; 196, 2 ss; 25 f., 3-5; Glosses, p. 136, 18. Cf. also Karl Barth, *Die Christliche Dogmatik,* i, 398: " To hear God's word does not mean to wander in the remote realms of metaphysics, but rather at long last to come to oneself, to learn to see oneself, to be revealed to oneself as one really is."

¹² Soren Kierkegaard, *Einübung im Christentum* (2nd ed., 1924), pp. 179 ff. [Eng. trans. by Walter Lowrie in *Training in Christianity* (1941), pp. 202 ff.]

¹³ Cf. ibid., pp. 20-6. [Eng. trans., pp. 28-38.]

¹⁴ Cf. W. Gut, *Der Sinn freier Theologie* (1925), pp. 7 f.

THE HISTORICITY OF MAN AND FAITH

[1] Cf. "*Zum theologischen Problem der Existenz: Fragen an Rudolf Bultmann,*" *Zeitschrift für Theologie und Kirche,* N.F., x (1929), 28-57.

[2] Just as little is the "finitude of man" which philosophy speaks about (cf. Martin Heidegger, *Kant und das Problem der Metaphysik* [1929], p. 219 *et passim*.) the finitude with which theology deals.

[3] Cf. Martin Heidegger, "*Vom Wesen des Grundes,*" *Festschrift für Edmund Husserl* (1929), p. 97, where an analogous case is dealt with in this way.

[4] In this connection, Kuhlmann (p. 43) is clearly confused. His statement, "But Heidegger's philosophy is not at all a 'science of being,' but rather inquires about the '*meaning*' of being,' i.e., is concerned from the outset to 'discover' a specific kind of being as the only being, viz., *man,*" contains several errors. In the first place, the antithesis is false; for what is a "science of being" to do, if not to inquire about the "*meaning* of being?" Precisely this is what I also mean in the statement that Kuhlmann cites somewhat earlier in his argument—the statement, namely, that defines philosophy "as the critical science of *being,* i.e., as the science that has to control all of the positive sciences that deal with *particular beings* on the basis of its concept of being" (cf. *Theologische Blätter,* vi [1927], 73). Kuhlmann clearly means that Heidegger's philosophy is not a science of some *particular being*—exactly what I also say. Furthermore, what follows in the statement is also false, for it clearly means, notwithstanding, that Heidegger's philosophy intends to discover some *particular being,* viz., man. In truth, Heidegger's philosophy (whose intention Kuhlmann in general characterizes falsely) does not "discover" man at all, since the latter can at best "discover" himself. Rather, for Heidegger, man is the primary particular being that must be examined if the ontological inquiry concerning (the meaning of) being in general is to be begun in a methodical way (cf. *Sein und Zeit,* i [1927], Secs. 2-5). Therefore, the further statement that Kuhlmann makes is also false: "The positive sciences are 'sciences of being' [No! they are rather sciences of a particular being or a region of particular beings], i.e., their object is always a 'derivation' of the original being, for which philosophy alone and explicitly is competent." What is this statement supposed to say? It is understandable only if one reads "particular being" every time, instead of "being." But then the statement of Heidegger is relevant: "Ontological interpretation in and on the basis of man's transcendence does not mean the ontic derivation of the sum-total of non-human beings from the particular being man" ("*Vom Wesen des*

Grundes," p. 100, n. 1). What is at issue is not at all the "deriva-tion" of a particular being, but rather the "derivation" of the meaning of being in relation to a specific region of particular beings —which meaning is "derived" from the meaning of being in general. If theology as a positive science speaks of a specific kind of par-ticular being, then the meaning of being that it thereby presupposes must likewise be specific, i.e., a "derived" one; and philosophy must be the court that finds with respect to this "derivation," without thereby in the least encroaching upon theology's independence. Just as little would the independence, say, of the science of art be en-croached upon or works of art be designated as creations of philosophy, if philosophy undertook to determine what understand-ing of being guides the science of art, what the mode of being is of works of art, and how this specific meaning of being is "derived" in relation to the meaning of being in general. If all the positive sciences that have a region of particular being for their object are guided by a specific understanding of being (just as man generally is guided by a specific preontological understanding of being) and if it is precisely because this is so that there is the possibility of a philosophical ontology—still it is not the positive sciences, but rather philosophy that makes this understanding of being its theme. If the basic concepts of a positive science have become uncertain and are under discussion, then it can ask philosophy to contribute to their clarification; but the latter presupposes in its investigations the independence of the positive sciences and the particular beings (or regions of being) that are their themes.

⁵ Naturally, philosophizing can be undertaken *existentiell,* but then it is the philosopher who speaks *existentiell,* not "philosophy."

⁶ At least in the Protestant view, according to which man does not receive a supernatural *habitus* through the *caritas infusa.* Nevertheless, I do not intend to reply to the reproach of "catholi-cism" that Grisebach's circle dispenses so liberally. I will remark, however, that the criticism of Barth and Gogarten that has been made by this circle seems to me, in spite of some justified points in matters of detail, to be negative and unfruitful because it does not proceed by recognizing the intentions of those who are criticized.

⁷ Indeed, "the double possibility of existence to exist authentically or inauthentically shifts the 'choice' to the accomplishment of pro-fane existence itself" (Kuhlmann, op. cit., p. 51). Ontologically this is entirely correct; only ontological analysis says nothing about the factual choice that is talked about by faith and, accordingly, by theology.

⁸ This also settles some of the questions raised by Kuhlmann on p. 46. Certainly revelation makes the two possibilities that being in the world has always had pressing possibilities—although this cannot be perceived ontologically. It can be *understood* ontologi-

cally, insofar as it can be shown that these possibilities are actualized by an *event*, in relation to which it is possible to speak of "before" and "after." However, it is a specifically theological judgment (which can indeed be made understandable, but cannot be proven by existential analysis), that "in a new sense," and that means *factually*, the decision is only actualized when this event is the Christian proclamation. The "before" and "after" that are spoken of in relation to this event neither may nor can be further clarified in an ontological sense.

⁹ Cf. Heidegger, *Kant und das Problem der Metaphysik*, pp. 226 f.

¹⁰ At this point, I may say the following with reference to the essay of Karl Löwith ("*Phänomenologische Ontologie und protestantische Theologie*," *Zeitschrift für Theologie und Kirche*, N.F., xi [1930], 365 ff.). Since the progress of philosophical work is by no means dependent only on the energy and discernment of philosophical thinking, but—inasmuch as ontological understanding cannot be neatly cut off from ontic experience—is just as dependent on the philosopher's specific *existentiell* understanding of existence, it could appear that the theology that is to learn from philosophy is at the mercy of the philosopher's specific "ideal for existence." This depends on the significance of the philosopher's "ideal for existence" for his philosophy, i.e., upon whether he expounds a specific "ideal for existence" that has a definite content, or rather concludes from his own knowledge of an "ideal for existence" that it belongs to man *qua* man to be moved by such an ideal. Now it seems to me to be inadmissible to view Heidegger's concept of "authenticity" as the expression of an ideal for existence. For what is characterized by the concept "authenticity"—at least by intention—is the historicity of man, whose being is a possibility of being, a being that can be authentic and inauthentic—whereby "authenticity" can be defined formally as taking place in resolution and whereby it remains completely open what particular thing is resolved upon. Therefore, the historicity of man is not an ideal that emerges out of the real factuality of man's experiences of life, but, since it characterizes man as such, is what first makes possible such experiences as human experiences and thus also the emergence of "ideals for existence." Löwith is completely right, as against Marck, in holding that Heidegger's analyses are sustained from the outset and in all their details by the knowledge of man's historicity. The only question is whether this "presupposition" emerges out of Heidegger's "ideal for existence" or rather is precisely the subject matter itself, the historicity of human existence, that appears in all the phenomena that are subjected to analysis.

¹¹ Kuhlmann demands a more exact specification of the phrase "in a certain sense" in my statement that for the believer the

world " in a certain sense " ends (cf. op. cit., pp. 44 f.). The meaning of the phrase is ontic or *existentiell*. For faith, the " world " (and this theological concept also is possible only on the basis of the ontological or existential concept of the world) has come to an end as a specific " how " of human existence (which can also be understood ontologically in its formal meaning).

12 Kuhlmann, op. cit., p. 49.

13 Ibid., p. 44.

14 If I do not do this, then there is the danger that I will either understand " sin " as a quality of what is at hand, a mysterious pollution in the sphere of the " magical " or (what is generally the rule today, since it is asserted that in Christianity " naturalistic " and " magical " concepts are spiritualized and ethicized) naïvely identify it with guilt.

15 Op. cit., p. 47.

16 This sentence is not directed against Kuhlmann, but W. Koepp, *" Merimna und Agape," Festschrift für Reinhold Seeberg* (1929), pp. 99-130. Koepp grossly misunderstands Heidegger by taking the latter's concept of " care " in the sense of an ontic phenomenon, instead of as an ontological structure of human existence, and then setting it over against Christian love. He would have a case against Heidegger only by showing that love cannot be understood as a phenomenon of human existence on the basis of the " care "-structure; and this can hardly be shown. If he wanted to set a theological concept over against the philosophical concept of care, then it had better have been the concept " joy " ($\chi\alpha\rho\acute{\alpha}$), which can be defined as the Christian modification of care or, better, of anxiety. In " joy " care and anxiety are indeed " overcome," i.e., " annulled and preserved."

17 *Zwischen den Zeiten*, vii (1929), 9.43. [This essay is also reprinted as pp. 153-87 of *Glauben und Verstehen*, i (2nd ed., 1954).]

18 Even a sermon speaks in concepts and, as a rule, is dependent on a theology. It can be dependent on an appropriate or on an inappropriate theology. Therefore, insofar as the sermon itself or even a biblical writing (for the same thing holds good also of it) is subjected to scientific theological interpretation, the latter must proceed critically and, in given cases, must distinguish by critical analysis between appropriate and inappropriate statements. Whether the author of I John, as distinguished from the source that he uses, has falsely understood Christian existence is a discussible question (cf. Kuhlmann, op. cit., p. 54, n. 1). And if one must say he has, still the " holiness " of the word that is being proclaimed is in no way impugned. The inquirer does not dispense the predicates " holy " and " profane," but the predicates " appropriate " or " not

appropriate. The " it is written" that faith refers to does *not* mean,
" it lies before us as a Christian document and is at the disposal
of inquiry."

¹⁹ To put it briefly, it seems to me that a " natural theology"
that does not proceed from faith, but rather intends to establish
(or to undergird) the theology of faith is illegitimate and impossible. On the other hand, a " natural theology" that understakes
from the standpoint of faith to make the " natural" man (or man
prior to faith) understandable—as Paul does in Rom. 1 : 18-3 : 20—
seems to me to be both legitimate and necessary.

²⁰ Heidegger, *Sein und Zeit*, i, 295.

²¹ Kuhlmann, op. cit., pp. 52 f.

²² And in that case, it is, of course, meaningless to speak about
its being " profane," for the titles " profane" and " holy" do not have
any ontological meaning.

²³ Kuhlmann, op. cit., p. 45.

²⁴ Ibid., p. 47.

²⁵ Ibid., p. 53.

²⁶ Cf. the following passages from *Sein und Zeit*, i : " In accordance
with its ontological essence, resolution is the act of an individual
man who is actually and concretely there. The essence of this man
is his existence. Resolution ' exists' only as self-understanding, self-
projecting resolve. . . . Resolve is precisely the projecting and determining of the actual concrete possibility, which discloses this
possibility" (p. 298). " Resolution brings the self precisely into the
state of being concretely concerned with what is at hand and
thrusts it into a relation with other persons that is characterized by
care for them" (ibid). In resolution, " man understands himself with
respect to his possibility of being in such a way that he comes
under the eyes of death, in order thereby completely to take charge
of the particular being that he himself is in all its thrownness. This
taking charge in resolution of one's own actual ' being-there' means
at the same time resolve in the situation" (pp. 382 f.). If existential
analysis does not have to consider upon what specific thing man
actually resolves, still it shows " whence *in general* the possibilities
can be drawn toward which man actually projects himself" (p. 383).
As " thrown," man exists in a world, exists with others, and exists
on the basis of an inheritance over which he takes charge (p. 383).
Therefore, his resolve is determined as much by his being in relation with other persons as by the choice of an inherited, but
nevertheless free possibility. " From the outset, our destinies are
led into relation with others in the same world and into resolving
upon specific possibilities. And the power of destiny is first liberated
in communication and in struggle. The fateful destiny of man in
and with his ' generation' makes up the fully authentic occurrence
of human existence" (pp. 384 f.). " Only a being that by its very

essence is *future* so that it can be free for its death and, being shattered by death, can let itself be thrown back into its actual being-there—only such an *essentially* future being as this can take charge of its own thrownness by itself passing on the inherited possibility and in the moment exist for ' its own time.' Only authentic temporality, which is also finite, makes something like destiny, i.e., authentic historicity, possible " (p. 385).

27 Op. cit., p. 32.

28 Ibid., p. 36.

29 It is completely misleading when Koepp (op. cit., p. 112) speaks of love as the "fundamental mood," at least if the formal meaning of Heidegger's concept of fundamental mood is to be maintained; but only so is a discussion possible.

30 This is the view of the Franciscans or of pietism, where the laying hold of love is thought of as *imitatio*.

31 Only so can it really be made clear what is meant by a life in the forgiveness of sins.

32 Cf. *Sein und Zeit,* i, sec. 46.

33 Heidegger, *Kant und das Problem der Metaphysik,* p. 226, with reference to the relation of the ontological concept of " care " to the ontic phenomenon of care.

34 *Sein und Zeit,* i, 249.

35 This would be properly spoken of as a proposition of " natural theology."

36 All the quotations are from *Sein und Zeit,* i, 242.

37 Ibid., p. 250.

PAUL

1 Cf. G. Kittel, *Rabbinica* (1920); Hans Lietzmann, *Petrus und Paulus in Rom* (2nd ed., 1927).

2 For the chronology of Paul's life, cf. the article, " *Christentum, I, 6, c,*" in *Religion in Geschichte und Gegenwart,* I (2nd ed., 1927), 1535 f.

ROMANS 7 AND THE ANTHROPOLOGY OF PAUL

1 Werner Georg Kümmel, *Römer 7 und die Bekehrung des Paulus* (1929).

2 So Lietzmann and Jülicher. According to the latter, what is involved is the doing of works against which my conscience protests. And Zahn speaks in the same sense of a contradiction between willing and acting; cf. H. Weinel, *Biblische Theologie des Neuen Testaments* (4th ed., 1928), p. 223. Against this, however, Gerhardt

Kuhlmann has already rightly objected; cf. his *Theologia naturalis bei Philon und bei Paulus* (1930), p. 104, n. 1.

3 Adolf Schlatter, *Der Glaube im Neuen Testament* (4th ed., 1927), p. 331.

4 Cf. W. Mundle, "*Das religiöse Problem des 4. Esrabuches*," *Zeitschrift für die Alttestamentliche Wissenschaft*, N.F., vi (1929). 222-49.

5 Rom. 8:27 makes completely clear that the "mind of the Spirit" that fills and determines the one who prays is hidden from man himself and is only understood by God.

6 Vs. 25b can be misleading here. However, if this statement is not, as I am inclined to think, an interpretive gloss, it still must be understood in terms of what precedes it. Cf. Kümmel, op. cit., pp. 67 f.

7 As Kümmel rightly sees, op. cit., pp. 134 ff.

8 Why Kümmel (op. cit., p. 137) disputes that by "mind" it is said that man stands under God's claim I do not understand, since he himself admits that, according to Paul, "mind" should acknowledge the commandments of God. What does that mean but that by "mind" man's possibility of knowing God's claim is designated? If God says, "Thou shouldst!" then that is something different from when, e.g., a forester says of a tree "It should be felled." This latter "should" does not determine the tree's mode of being, although this is exactly what is done in the case of God's "Thou shouldst" in relation to the being of man. Inasmuch as Gerhardt Kuhlmann (op. cit.) divests the concept of sin in Paul of its historical determination, he naturally cannot acknowledge that man as the "inner man" hears the claim of God. But why Kuhlmann thinks that *if this were so,* then the "inner man" would already signify the rightwising of the "natural" man (p. 106, n. 1), I do not understand. For on the contrary, it is precisely in this that the possibility of condemnation, of "death," is based. When the tree is felled, it does not "die."

9 Cf. Kümmel, op. cit., p. 9.

10 Concerning the concept "commandment," cf. Kümmel, op. cit., pp. 55 f.

11 I permit myself at this point to quote from a seminar paper (by Karl Erdmann): "If what one finds expressed in vs. 15b is the dualistic opposition between good intention and evil deed, then it becomes impossible to bring it into understandable relation with vs. 15a. For what would be involved in such a psychic tension would be precisely the highest *consciousness* of the gulf that separates the ideal intention from the deed that has fallen under the power of matter. The cry for deliverance in 7:24, which is understood as an expression of this tension, gives no indication of any illusions about one's situation. Thus to take vs. 15b as the basis for vs. 15a—'I do

not know what I do'—would be completely meaningless; and so for Lietzmann the latter is 'indeed only a rhetorical expression.' The inner connection of the verse only becomes understandable when one views it as the judgment of a Christian concerning his earlier unfaith. In his new knowledge of the sin of chasing after righteousness, he sees that the will in wanting to achieve righteousness brings about precisely what it did not intend—namely, sin, apostasy from God. The inner break that is spoken of in vs. 15 does not lie between man's willing and doing, but in the understanding of himself in relation to God."

12 It should already be clear from what has been said why I must hold Gerhardt Kuhlmann's interpretation of Paul to be false. Since he understands sin for Paul only negatively, in the sense of godlessness, and does not see the positive relation to God that man has precisely as sinner, the law for him is not God's clear and abiding claim, but rather merely a possibility of the sinful man himself—namely, the possibility of the conscience to place itself under the idea of the good. Since, however, he quite rightly sees that the split portrayed in Rom. 7:14 ff. is not that between good intention and evil doing, he is embarrassed to explain what the evil is that is the outcome of doing. It cannot be transgression of the law. Therefore, how can man " experience " the fact " that what he has done in accordance with his best knowledge and conscience nevertheless is the evil "? One must assume that the evil is " the ' how ' of his action's effect on ' other ' men." " When a man does the best he knows, he must experience in the resistance of the ' neighbour ' that in relation to him, to the ' other,' it is only the evil." He must, when he " does the good with the whole earnestness of his existence," " unavoidably do evil to his neighbour " (op. cit., p. 104, n. 1). In the first place, it is not clear how such a man can grasp the idea of the " neighbour " and how he can come to understand, from the standpoint of his idea of the good, that his action that is directed against the neighbour's resistance is evil. Moreover, it is not said in the text that man *experiences* the fact that what he does is evil. Rather the words " I do not know " (vs. 15) say precisely the opposite. Above all, however, the whole idea is completely un-Pauline and is simply read into Rom. 7.

13 If Adam is actually in Paul's mind in the presentation in vss. 7-13, then he is thinking expressly of the sin of wanting to be like God. Cf., however, Kümmel, op. cit., p. 54.

14 That the concept of authenticity is not read in here, but rather appropriately re-expresses what Paul means is shown, e.g., by Lietzmann's occasional formulation with reference to vs. 9: the " life " of which Paul speaks is life " in the authentic sense of the word." And what is meant when exegetes frequently speak of life in the " pregnant " sense?—what but authenticity of selfhood?

THE TASK OF THEOLOGY IN THE PRESENT SITUATION

[1] F. K. Schumann, *Gegenwartsdämonie und Christusglaube* (1932), p. 26.

JESUS AND PAUL

[1] *Der Mythos des 20. Jahrhunderts* (13th-16th eds., 1933), p. 76.

[2] Ibid., p. 74. According to the note on p. 76, there is not the least compelling reason to assume that Jesus was of Jewish descent.

[3] Ibid., pp. 74 f. Cf. further the quotations from Rosenberg in "*Kirchlichen Anzeiger für die Erzdiözese Köln*," official supplement, December 1934 ("*Der Apostel Paulus und das Urchristentum*," supplement to "*Studien zum Mythos des 20. Jahrhunderts*").

[4] Op. cit., pp. 104, 102, 103.

[5] Cf. *Wer hat das Christentum begrundet, Jesus oder Paulus?* (1907).

[6] Ibid., pp. 95 f.

[7] Op. cit., p. 44 [Eng. trans. by Thomas Bailey Saunders in *What Is Christianity?* (Harper Torchbook edition, 1957), p. 68]

[8] Ibid., p. 42. [Eng. trans., p. 65.]

[9] Ibid., p. 94. [Eng. trans., p. 149.]

[10] For especially characteristic contributions to the earlier discussion, cf. Julius Kaftan, *Jesus und Paulus* (1906) and Adolf Jülicher, *Paulus und Jesus* (1907).

[11] Cf. my sketch of the study of New Testament christology in *Glauben und Verstehen*, i (2nd ed., 1954), pp. 245 ff.

[12] Cf. here and in relation to what follows, my remarks in *Glauben und Verstehen*, i (2nd ed., 1954), pp. 188 ff.

[13] We need not consider here whether Jesus thought that he himself would be this coming Son of Man. Nor need we be concerned that Paul does not use the term "Son of Man"; it is sufficient that he knows the figure.

[14] Op. cit., p. 40. [Eng. trans., p. 62.]

[15] Ibid., p. 39. [Eng. trans., p. 61.]

[16] Cf. Albert Schweitzer, *Die Mystik des Apostels Paulus* (1930), p. 114 [Eng. trans. by William Montgomery as *The Mysticism of Paul the Apostle* (1931), p. 113]: "To establish that Paul relates himself to Jesus independently is misleading if one does not also realize all that he has in common with him. He shares with Jesus the eschatological world-view and expectation, together with all that these imply. The only thing that is different is the time of the world that must always be considered. For both, it is one and the

same range of mountains, but whereas Jesus sees it as lying before him, Paul already stands on it and has its first eminence behind him. . . ."

[17] That Jesus' coming was the turn of the age and that God's judgment has thereby already been carried out is expressed even more sharply by John—who, according to Rosenberg, still breathed an aristocratic air and should have set himself against the bastardizing, Orientalizing, and Judaizing of Christianity. According to John, "whoever believes in him [*sic* Christ] is not condemned, but whoever does not believe in him is condemned already, because he has not believed in the name of the only Son of God. For this is the judgment, that the light has come into the world, and men loved darkness rather than light" (3:18 f.). "Truly, truly, I say to you, he who hears my word and believes him who sent me, has eternal life; he does not come into judgment, but has passed from death to life. Truly, truly, I say to you, the hour is coming and now is, when the dead will hear the voice of the Son of God, and those who hear will live" (5:24 f.). Thus the Christian conviction is that God has acted decisively for the world in Jesus Christ; that through him the world has become new in the sense both of salvation and judgment.

THE SERMON ON THE MOUNT AND THE JUSTICE OF THE STATE

[1] An abundance of statements by Luther which express his understanding of the Sermon on the Mount have been assembled in the valuable little work of H. W. Beyer, *Der Christ und die Bergpredigt nach Luthers Deutung* (1933).

THE MEANING OF THE CHRISTIAN FAITH IN CREATION

[1] Only apparently is there so little said about faith in creation in the New Testament. For such faith does not necessarily express itself in narratives about the past, but can also be expressed in the understanding of the present. For this reason, however, it is also true that criticism of the creation stories is not necessarily criticism of faith in creation.

HISTORY OF SALVATION AND HISTORY

[1] [Eng. trans. by Floyd V. Filson (1950). All page references are to the translation.]

ON BEHALF OF CHRISTIAN FREEDOM

[1] *Junge Kirche, Evangelische Kirchenzeitung.* Edited by Dr. Hermann Ehlert (member of the High Consistory) and Fritz Sohlmann. Göttingen.

[2] *Junge Kirche* imagines that it has to point out to Gross that today "theological discussion is more lively and impassioned than ever" and that it is by no means dominated, "as Gross and his friends perhaps say," by "popes" like Barth, Brunner, and Bultmann "against whom it is impossible to prevail." This is simply comic! It has never occurred to me that Gross could take me for a "pope" who inhibits the freedom of discussion.

MAN BETWEEN THE TIMES ACCORDING TO THE NEW TESTAMENT

[1] Cf. C. H. Dodd, *The Apostolic Preaching* (1936), p. 85: "A particular historical crisis, constituted by the ministry, the death, and the resurrection of Jesus Christ, is interpreted in terms of a mythological concept."

[2] Cf. *Zeitschrift für Theologie und Kirche,* xlviii (1951), 148-72.

[3] For the differences in such admonitions, see Günther Bornkamm, *In Memoriam Ernst Lohmeyer* (1951), pp. 116-26.

[4] This is especially in order with respect to the construction of Martin Werner, *Die Entstehung des Christlichen Dogmas problemgeschichtlich dargestellt* (1941).

[5] The statements in John and the Johannine Epistles that represent the old realistic eschatology are, in my opinion, due to secondary editing.

[6] The question that is so important for Oscar Cullmann (*Christus und die Zeit*), whether time is represented as a cycle or as a straight line, is irrelevant here. Such representation always reckons only with the time *within* which man lives, with *world*-time, instead of inquiring about the temporality of human existence.

[7] Cf. the term "dead works" in Heb. 6:1, 9:14; Herm. Sim. IX, 21:2; cf. also Rev. 3:1. Cf. further, II Clem. 1:6: "Our whole life was nothing other than death." According to Ignatius, the heretics are "tombstones and sepulchres of the dead" (Phila. 6:1) and "bearers of a corpse" (Smyr. 5:2). According to Hermas, the fallenness under death of the previous life is done away with by baptism, "for before a man hears the name of the Son of God, he is dead" (Sim. IX, 16:3); "they go down into the water dead, and come up alive" (16:4).

[8] [Bultmann refers here to a paper by Dodd which is published in the same volume from which the present essay is taken, pp. 9-20.]

IGNATIUS AND PAUL

1 This is the orientation of the sketch of Ignatius' theology which is worked out in Eva Alheit's book, *Paulusverständnis in der alten Kirche* (1937). This sketch is quite unsatisfying because it fails to recognize that many of the agreements between Ignatius and Paul are not due to the influence of Paul, but rather are attributable to their common milieu in the history of religion, as has been shown in a book that the author ignores, namely, Heinrich Schlier's *Religionsgeschichtliche Untersuchungen zu den Ignatiusbriefen* (1929).

2 In doing so, I will make contact several times with the distinguished essay of Théo Preiss, "*La Mystique de l'Imitation et de l'Unité chez Ignace d'Antioche,*" *Revue d'Histoire et de Philosophie religieuses,* xviii (1938), 197-241.

3 Cf. my essay, "Man between the Times according to the New Testament," *supra,* pp. 248-66.

4 This difference has been worked out by Preiss, op. cit.

5 Cf., e.g., I Clem. 59:2; II Clem. 1:6 f.; Herm. Sim. iv, 4; Col. 3:5 ff.; Eph. 2:1 ff.; Titus 3:3 ff.

6 Cf. I Thess. 1:9; Gal. 4:8; I Cor. 6:11; Rom. 6:17 f.

7 For the details I must refer to the concluding chapter of my *Theologie des Neuen Testaments.* [Eng. trans. by Kendrick Grobel in *Theology of the New Testament,* ii (1955).]

8 Paul speaks of the repentance of the Christian only in II Cor. 7:9 f. and perhaps 12:21.

9 Heb. 2:2 f., 10:28 f., 12:25; II Clem. 6:9.

10 I Pet. 2:21 ff., 3:18.

11 Δικαιοσύνη is not found at all as a designation for the substance of salvation. (The word itself only appears in Smyr. 1:1 in the sense of Matt. 3:15). Δίκαιος is very rare; in Mag. 12, with reference to Prov. 18:17, it designates one who acts righteously. The phrase φύσει δικαία occurs in Ign. Eph. 1:1 in a play on words and means something like "through an appropriate dispensation of nature."

12 Ἁμαρτία is found only once in the traditional phrase that Christ has suffered "for our sins" (Smyr. 7:1); and the verb ἁμαρτάνειν likewise is only found one time in the sentence "No man who professes faith sins" (Ign. Eph. 14:2).

13 I do not go into the question whether Ignatius struggles against only one heresy or rather two of them. If the heretical teachers are gnosticizing Jewish-Christians, then the situation is all the more clear.

14 This is correctly pointed out by Johannes Klevinghaus in his presentation of Ignatius' theology in *Die theologische Stellung der*

Apostolischen Väter zur Alttestamentlichen Offenbarung (1948), pp. 78-112.

¹⁵ The gospel is the "perfection of imperishableness" (Phila. 9:2) or the "lesson of imperishableness" (Mag. 6:2). Christ has breathed "imperishableness" on the church (Ign. Eph. 17:1). The prize for the struggle of the Christian is "imperishableness and eternal life" (Pol. 2:3); and Ignatius' drink, the blood of Christ, is "imperishable love" (Ign. Rom. 7:3). The "fruit" that Christians bear as branches of the cross is "imperishable" (Tral. 11:2).

¹⁶ Christian Maurer's *Ignatius von Antiochien und das Johannes-evangelium* (1949) also has not convinced me that Ignatius is dependent upon John. In addition to the differences mentioned above, consider the absence of the concepts "immortality" and "imperishableness" in John. The affinity that exists in the matter of the redeemer-myth is not to be explained as due to Ignatius' dependence upon John, but because both stem from the same milieu in the history of religions. (Cf. the book of Heinrich Schlier that was referred to above.) Ignatius is still more strongly indebted to this milieu than Paul and John are.

¹⁷ Cf. Ign. Eph. 11:2; Ign. Rom. 4:3; also Tral. intro., 2:2; Smyr. 7:1.

¹⁸ Cf. Ign. Eph. 21:2; Mag. 11; Tral. intro., 2:2, Phila. 11:2.

¹⁹ Ign. Eph. 11:1; "last times"; cf. Pol. 3:2; the concepts of judgment, of "the wrath to come" (Ign. Eph. 11:1), and of future retribution (Ign. Eph. 11:1, 16:2; Mag. 5:1; Smyr. 6:1, 9:2).

²⁰ To be sure, Satan is called the "prince of this aeon," but, as is shown by the parallelism of "this aeon" and "world" in Ign. Rom. 6:1, the element of temporality has been supplanted by the element of this-worldliness. Cf. in general the use of "world" as a designation for this world in Mag. 5:2; Ign. Rom. 2:2, 3:2 f., 4:2, 6:2 (where it is parallel with "material things"), 7:1; also 7:3 where instead of "this world" there is "this life."

²¹ Preiss attempts to show that "the pursuit of immortality by imitation is the essential motif both of Ignatius' ideas on martyrdom and his christology" (op. cit., p. 218; cf. espec. pp. 214 f.).

²² For Ignatius the formula ἐν Χριστῷ has the original force that it still has in the deutero-Pauline literature (Col., Eph., rarely in I Pet.), but thereafter loses. Formally, it still occurs frequently in I Clem. and also in Pol. 1:1. It is missing in Jas., Heb., and Barn., in II Pet., II Clem., Did., and Herm. And it occurs in Rev. only in 14:13.

²³ Cf. further Smyr. 13:2; Pol. 1:2, 5:1; Mag. 13;1; Tral. intro., 12:1.

²⁴ Ignatius describes participation in the death of Christ in a number of different expressions (Phila. 3:3, 4:1; Ign. Rom. 6:3, and others) in which participation in the resurrection is naturally im-

plied and often even explicitly stated (Phila. intro., 9 : 2; Tral. intro.; Mag. 11; Smyr. 12 : 2).

25 Mag. 4, 7 : 1; Tral., 2 : 2, 7 : 2; Smyr. 8 : 1 f., 9 : 1; Pol. 5 : 2.

26 Ign. Eph. 8 : 1; Phila. 8 : 2; Ign. Eph. 6 : 2; Tral. 6 : 1.

27 It is characteristic that Ignatius does not speak of baptism, which he only rarely mentions as compared with the Eucharist (Ign. Eph. 18 : 2; Smyr. 8 : 2; Pol. 6 : 2), as the act of forgiving sins of the past. Its effect extends into the future (Pol. 6 : 2 : " let your baptism remain as your arms "). The phrase " forgiveness of sins " (ἄφεσις ἁμαρτιῶν) is not found at all; that the Lord forgives Christians who repent is said in Phila. 8 : 1.

28 Ign. Eph. 1 : 1, 9 : 1, 14 : 1 f., 20 : 1; Mag. 1 : 2, 6 : 1, 13 : 1; Phila. 9 : 2; Smyr. 1 : 1, 6 : 1, 13 : 2; Pol. 6 : 2.

29 Tral. 4 : 2 : " I have need therefore of meekness, by which the prince of this world is destroyed."

30 Cf. also Ign. Rom. 7 : 2; Smyr. 4 : 2.

31 Ign. Eph. 18 : 1; Tral. 4 : 1, 7 : 1; Pol. 4 : 3, 5 : 2.

32 The difference between Ignatius and Paul in this respect has been strikingly pointed out by Preiss in his essay (cf. op. cit.). Although he is certainly correct in asserting that the controlling motif in Ignatius' theology is the longing for immortality, it seems to me to be an exaggeration to say: " He preserves of the thought of Paul only what is necessary in order to assure man his full immortality."

AUTOBIOGRAPHICAL REFLECTIONS

1 [These two essays are reprinted as pp. 1-25 and 114-33 of *Glauben und Verstehen,* i (2nd ed., 1954).]

IS EXEGESIS WITHOUT PRESUPPOSITIONS POSSIBLE?

1 Walter Baumgartner, to whom the following pages are dedicated, has published an essay in the *Schweizerische theologische Umschau,* xi (1941), 17-38, entitled " *Die Auslegung des Alten Testaments im Streit der Gegenwart.*" Inasmuch as I completely agree with what he says there, I hope he will concur if I now attempt to carry the hermeneutical discussion somewhat further.

2 If there is actually an allegory in the text, then, of course, it is to be explained as an allegory. However, such an explanation is not allegorical interpretation; it simply asks for the meaning that is intended by the text.

3 A criticism of such prejudiced exegesis is the chief concern of the essay of W. Baumgartner mentioned above (cf. n. 1).

4 Cf. H. Gunkel, *Die Wirkungen des Heiligen Geist nach der*

populären Anschauung der apostolischen Zeit und der Lehre des Apostel Paulus (1888; 3rd ed., 1909).

[5] Cf. with the following, my essays, "*Das Problem der Hermeneutik,*" *Glauben und Verstehen,* ii (1952), 211-35. [Eng. trans. by J. C. G. Greig in *Essays, Philosophical and Theological* (1955), pp. 234-61], and "*Wissenschaft und Existenz,*" *Ehrfurcht vor dem Leben:* Festschrift for Albert Schweitzer (1954), pp. 30-45; and also *History and Eschatology* (1957), ch. viii.

[6] It goes without saying that the *existentiell* relation to history does not have to be raised to the level of consciousness. By reflection it may only be spoiled.

[7] I do not deal here with certain special questions, such as how an *existentiell* relation to history can already be present in the research of grammar, lexicography, statistics, chronology, and geography or how the historian of mathematics or physics participates *existentiell* in the objects of his research. One thinks of Plato!

BIBLIOGRAPHY

A virtually complete bibliography of Rudolf Bultmann's writings to
1 August, 1954, may be found in *"Veröffentlichungen von Rudolf Bultmann,"*
Theologische Rundschau, xxii (1954), 3-20. This listing, in turn, is based
on two earlier bibliographies, which may also be consulted: *"Bibliographia*
Bultmanniana," Coniectanea Neotestamentica, viii (1944), 23-35 (Uppsala:
Wretmans Boktryckeri A.-B.); and *Festschrift Rudolf Bultmann zum 65.*
Geburtstag (Stuttgart: W. Kohlhammer Verlag, 1949), pp. 241-51. The
following list includes (1) the more important writings of Bultmann
published since 1 August, 1954, but still unavailable in English; (2) the
works by him that are available in English; and (3) a representative
selection from among the innumerable discussions of his thought that
have been published in recent years.

I. RECENT WORKS OF RUDOLF BULTMANN UNAVAILABLE IN ENGLISH

"The Interpretation of the Fourth Gospel: A Review of C. H. Dodd's
   The Interpretation of the Fourth Gospel," New Testament Studies, i
   (1954-5), 77-91. (Although the title of this piece is English, the
   review itself is written in German.)
Articles on *"peitho," "penthos,"* and *"pistis," Theologisches Wörterbuch zum*
   Neuen Testament, vi. Edited by Gerhard Friedrich. Stuttgart:
   W. Kohlhammer Verlag, 1954, 1955.
"Wissenschaft und Existenz," Ehrfurcht vor dem Leben: Festschrift zum 80.
   Geburtstag von Albert Schweitzer. Bern: Paul Haupt Verlag, 1955,
   pp. 30-43.
"Zur Johanneischen Tradition," Theologische Literaturzeitung, lxxx (1955),
   521-6.
"Zum Thema: Christentum und Antike," Theologische Rundschau, xxiii (1955),
   207-29.
"In eigener Sache," Theologische Literaturzeitung, lxxxii (1957), 241-50.
"Allgemeine Wahrheiten und Christliche Verkündigung," Zeitschrift für
   Theologie und Kirche, liv (1957), 244-54.
"Das Befremdliche des Christlichen Glaubens," Zeitschrift für Theologie und
   Kirche, lv (1958), 185-200.
"Ein neues Paulus-Verständnis," Theologische Literaturzeitung, lxxxiv (1959),
   481-6.

2. WORKS OF RUDOLF BULTMANN AVAILABLE IN ENGLISH

Jesus and the Word. Translated by L. P. Smith and Erminie Huntress. London: Fontana Books, 1962

"The Study of the Synoptic Gospels," *Form Criticism: A New Method of New Testament Research.* Edited and translated by F. C. Grant. Chicago: Willett, Clark and Co., 1934, pp. 11-75.

"To Love Your Neighbour," *The Scottish Periodical,* i, 1 (Summer, 1947), 42-56.

Theology of the New Testament, i. Translated by Kendrick Grobel. London: SCM Press Ltd., 1952.

Gnosis. Translated by J. R. Coates. Vol. v of *Bible Key Words.* London: Adam and Charles Black, 1952.

"Humanism and Christianity," *The Journal of Religion,* xxxii (1952), 77-86.

"New Testament and Mythology," *Kerygma and Myth.* Edited by H. W. Bartsch and translated by R. H. Fuller. London: SPCK, 1953, pp. 1-44.

"A Reply to the Theses of Julius Schniewind," *Kerygma and Myth,* pp. 102-23.

"Bultmann Replies to His Critics," *Kerygma and Myth,* pp. 191-211.

"The Christian Hope and the Problem of Demythologizing," *The Expository Times,* lxv (1954), 228-30, 276-8.

"History and Eschatology in the New Testament," *New Testament Studies,* i (1954-5), 5-16.

Essays, Philosophical and Theological. Translated by J. C. G. Greig. London: SCM Press Ltd., 1955.

Theology of the New Testament, ii. Translated by Kendrick Grobel. New York: Charles Scribner's Sons, 1955.

"The Transformation of the Idea of the Church in the History of Early Christianity," *Canadian Journal of Theology,* i (1955), 73-81.

Primitive Christianity in Its Contemporary Setting. Translated by R. H. Fuller. London, Fontana Library, 1960.

The Presence of Eternity: History and Eschatology. Edinburgh University Press, 1957.

"Introduction," Adolf Harnack. *What Is Christianity?* Translated by T. B. Saunders. New York: Harper and Brothers, 1957, pp.vii-xviii.

"The Problem of Miracle," *Religion in Life,* xxvii (1957-8), pp. 63-75.

Jesus Christ and Mythology. New York: Charles Scribner's Sons, 1958.

"The Case for Demythologizing: A Reply to Karl Jaspers," *Myth and Christianity: An Inquiry into the Possibility of Religion without Myth.* New York: The Noonday Press, 1958, pp. 57-71.

"Demythologizing the Bible," *Current Religious Thought,* New Series, ii, 1 (First Quarter, 1958), 7-9.

"Theology for Freedom and Responsibility," *The Christian Century,* lxxv (1958), 967-9.

"Preaching: Genuine and Secularized," *Religion and Culture: Essays in Honor of Paul Tillich.* Edited by Walter Leibrecht. New York: Harper and Brothers, 1959, 236-42.

"Milestones in Books, iv," *The Expository Times,* lxx (1959), 125.

This World and Beyond (Marburg Sermons). London: Lutterworth, 1960.

The History of the Synoptic Tradition. Oxford: Blackwell, 1963.

3. REPRESENTATIVE WORKS DEALING WITH RUDOLF BULTMANN'S THEOLOGY

Barth, Karl. *Rudolf Bultmann: Ein Versuch, ihn zu verstehen.* 2nd ed.; Zollikon-Zurich: Evangelischer Verlag, 1953.

———. *Church Dogmatics,* iv/1: *The Docrtine of Reconciliation.* Translated by G. W. Bromiley. Edinburgh: T. and T. Clark, 1936.

Barth, Markus. "Introduction to Demythologizing," *The Journal of Religion,* xxxvii (1957), 145-55.

Bartsch, H. W. (ed.) *Kerygma und Mythos.* 1: *Ein theologisches Gespräch.* 2nd ed.; Hamburg: Herbert Reich-Evangelischer Verlag, 1951. (Partial English translation by R. H. Fuller in *Kerygma and Myth,* pp. 45-101, 124-90.)

———. (ed.) *Kerygma und Mythos,* ii: *Diskussionen und Stimmen des In- und Auslandes.* 1952.

———. (ed.) *Kerygma und Mythos,* iii: *Das Gespräch mit der Philosophie.* 1954.

———. (ed.) *Kerygma und Mythos,* iv: *Die oekumenische Diskussion.* 1955.

———. (ed.) *Kerygma und Mythos,* v: *Die Diskussion innerhalb der Katholischen Theologie.* 1955.

Brunner, Emil. *The Christian Doctrine of Creation and Redemption.* Translated by Olive Wyon. London: Lutterworth Press, 1952.

Buri, Fritz. "Theologie und Philosophie," *Theologische Zeitschrift,* viii (1952), 116-34.

Davis, G. W. *Existentialism and Theology: An Investigation of the Contribution of Rudolf Bultmann to Theological Thought.* New York: Philosophical Library, 1957.

Dinkler, Erich. "Existentialist Interpretation of the New Testament," *The Journal of Religion,* xxxii (1952), 87-96.

Gogarten, Friedrich. *Demythologizing and History.* Translated by N. H. Smith. London: SCM Press Ltd., 1955.

Grobel, Kendrick. "Bultmann's Problem of New Testament 'Mythology'," *Journal of Biblical Literature,* lxx (1951), 99-103.

Henderson, Ian. *Myth in the New Testament.* London: SCM Press Ltd., 1952.

Jaspers, Karl. "The Issues Clarified," *Myth and Christianity: An Inquiry into the Possibility of Religion without Myth.* New York: The Noonday Press, 1958, pp. 72-116.

Johnson, Sherman. "Bultmann and the Mythology of the New Testament," *Anglican Theological Review*, xxxvi (1954), 29-47.

Jones, G. V. *Christology and Myth in the New Testament*. New York: Harper and Brothers, 1956.

Kinder, Ernst. (ed.) *Ein Wort lutherischer Theologie zur Entmythologisierung*. Munich: Evangelischer Pressverband für Bayern, 1952.

Macquarrie, John. *An Existentialist Theology: A Comparison of Heidegger and Bultmann*. London: SCM Press Ltd., 1955.

Malevez, L. *The Christian Message and Myth: The Theology of Rudolf Bultmann*. Translated by Olive Wyon. London: SCM Press Ltd., 1958.

Ogden, Schubert M. "Bultmann's Project of Demythologization and the Problem of Theology and Philosophy," *The Journal of Religion*, xxxvii (1957), 156-73.

———. "The Debate on 'Demythologizing'," *The Journal of Bible and Religion*, xxvii (1959), 17-27.

Ott, Heinrich. *Geschichte und Heilsgeschichte in der Theologie Rudolf Bultmanns*. Tübingen: J. C. B. Mohr, 1955.

Owen, H. P. *Revelation and Existence: A Study in the Theology of Rudolf Bultmann*. Cardiff: University of Wales Press, 1957.

Smith, R. G. *The New Man: Christianity and Man's Coming of Age*. London: SCM Press, 1956.

Thielicke, Helmut. "Reflections on Bultmann's Hermeneutic," *The Expository Times*, lxvii (1956), 154-7, 175-7.

Throckmorton, Burton. *The New Testament and Mythology*. Philadelphia: The Westminster Press, 1959.

Tillich, Paul. "The European Discussion of the Problem of the Demythologization of the New Testament." A lecture delivered at Union Theological Seminary, New York, November 10, 1952. Mimeographed.

Wilder, Amos. "Mythology and the New Testament: A Review of *Kerygma und Mythos*," *Journal of Biblical Literature*, lxix (1950), 113-27.

———. *New Testament Faith for Today*. New York: Harper and Brothers, 1955.

Wingren, Gustaf. *Theology in Conflict*. Translated by Eric H. Wahlstrom. Philadelphia: Muhlenberg Press, 1958.

NAMES AND SUBJECTS

SCRIPTURAL REFERENCES

THE FONTANA LIBRARY

The Christian Society
STEPHEN NEILL
'A fresh study of church history with many interesting and unusual sidelights.'
CHURCH HISTORY

Primitive Christianity
RUDOLF BULTMANN
An examination of early Christianity against the intellectual and religious background of the ancient world.

Ethics
DIETRICH BONHOEFFER
Essays on the theme of Christian citizenship that illuminate Bonhoeffer's concept of a 'religionless Christianity'.

The Christian Sacraments
O. C. QUICK
A discussion of the nature of the Christian sacraments in relation to the life of Christ.

Symbolism and Belief
EDWYN BEVAN
In these Gifford Lectures a famous scholar discusses the truth of the symbols employed in the expression of religious beliefs.

Between Man and Man
MARTIN BUBER
Five studies that go beyond the conventional boundaries of anthropology in an attempt to understand man in his wholeness.

The Mind and Heart of Love
MARTIN C. D'ARCY
'It comes out of the great tradition of Christian humanism, and is inclusive and comprehensive.'
SPECTATOR